AFTER MOCTEZUMA

yehoatl ipan modiiul, y micpeualoquie
tlatilulca.
Auh iniquac omic Axayacatzin i
niman yeoalmotlalia inTiçoçicatzi
intlatocat Tiçoçicatzin macuilxiuitl ye
hoatl quiuaua inteucalli tenochtitlan.
Auh momic Tiçoçicatzin niman oal mo
tlatocatlali y Auitzotzi intlatocat castol
xiuitl, ypan exiuitl: yehoatl quitzonqx
tin quiieco inteucalli tenochtitlan: iehoatl
tlamamal calchali: auh inica tlamama
liuac: yehoantin tziuhcoaca, peualoque:
auh yehoatl quiquetz ynacuecuexatl,
ymcapachiuhque mexica.
Auh momic Auitzotzin niman ic ual
motlali inMotecueumatzin inipan oa
cico castillantlaca españoles: auh in
tlatocat castolxiuitl ipan vnxiuitl
noipan mochiuh inmayanaliztli mo
tenema nextlauililoc.
Auh momic Motecueumatzin niman
oalmotlali inipan tlatoca yutl Cuitlaua
tzin napoaliltuitl intlatocat yeipan in
castillan tlaca.
Auh momic Cuitlauatzin niman oal
motlatocali in Quauhtemoctzin iehoatl
ipan mochiuh yn yanyutl ineuanh
çoçanacochtli Acolhuaca ynicpoliuh
que mexica auh intlatocat Quauhte
moctzin chiquace xiuitl
Auh momic Quauhtemoctzin niman
ic oalmotlatocatlali yn Otelchiuhtzin
yncolhoaca miquito quiuicaca inguz
mani intlatocat can chico xiuitl.
Auh momic Otelchiuhtzin niman
oalmotlali inxochiquentzin exiuitl
intlatocat.
Auh momic xochiquentzin niman oal
motlatocatlali inUanitzin intlatocat ma
cuilxiuitl.
Auh momic inUanitzin niman ic

ticocicatzin
ixiuhtzon
ixiuhyacamiuh
ixiuhtilma
techilnacay
yxpohoiepal

avitzotzin
ixiuhtzon
ixiuhyacamiuh
ixiuhtilma
techilnacayo
yxpohoiepal

moteucomatzin
ixiuhtzon
ixiuhyacamiuh
ixiuhtilma
techilnacaya
yxpohoiepal

Cuitlaoatzin
ixiuhtzon
ixiuhyacamiuh
ixiuhtilma
techilnacaya
yxpohoiepal

quauhtemoctzin
ixiuhtzon
ixiuhyacamiuh
ixiuhtilma
techilnacayo
yxpohoiepal

motelchiuhtzin
governador

xuchiquentzin
governador

vanitzin

The last tlatoque and first governors of Mexico Tenochtitlan, 1481–1541. From Fray Bernardino de Sahagún, *Historia de Nueva España en lengua Mexicana* (1558–1560), fol. 51v. Reproduced with permission, © Reproducción, Real Academia de la Historia.

After Moctezuma
Indigenous Politics and
Self-Government in
Mexico City, 1524–1730

William F. Connell

University of Oklahoma Press : Norman

Library of Congress Cataloging-in-Publication Data

Connell, William F., 1970–
  After Montezuma : indigenous politics and self-government in Mexico City,
1524–1730 / William F. Connell.
       p.   cm.
  Includes bibliographical references and index.
  ISBN 978-0-8061-4175-6 (hardcover : alk. paper)
  1. Aztecs—Mexico—Mexico City—Politics and government—16th century.
  2. Aztecs—Mexico—Mexico City—Politics and government—17th century.
  3. Aztecs—Mexico—Mexico City—Politics and government—18th century.
  4. Aztecs—Mexico—Mexico City—Government relations—History. 5. Mexico
City (Mexico)—Politics and government—16th century. 6. Mexico City
(Mexico)—Politics and government—17th century. 7. Mexico City (Mexico)—
Politics and government—18th century 8. Government, Resistance to—
Mexico—Mexico City—History. 9. Political culture—Mexico—Mexico City—
History. I. Title.
  F1219.76.P75C66 2011
  972'.5302—dc22

                                                              2010038910

The paper in this book meets the guidelines for permanence and durability of
the Committee on Production Guidelines for Book Longevity of the Council on
Library Resources, Inc. ∞

1 2 3 4 5 6 7 8 9 10

For Cindy, Sean, and Chelsea

CONTENTS

Illustrations

FIGURES

MAP

TABLES

Acknowledgments

I began to think about indigenous self-government as a master's student at the University of South Carolina when Michael Scardaville showed me Andrés Lira's work on indigenous communities in Mexico Tenochtitlan and Tlatelolco. I continued to develop the ideas and to think about *cabildos* in Ida Altman's "Atlantic World" seminar at Tulane University in 1998. Although the work has evolved substantially, I first imagined it in graduate school. It is in these acknowledgments that I thank all of those who generously gave of their time, expertise, and resources to guide me and sustain my efforts along the way. Although I have benefited greatly from the insights and assistance of others, any miscues or mistakes that remain in the text are, of course, my own.

Funding for the research came from a variety of sources. As a graduate student, I was supported by a Fulbright García-Robles grant that allowed me to work in Mexico during 2000 and 2001. The Instituto de Investigaciones Dr. José María Luis Mora provided institutional affiliation while I was in Mexico on Fulbright. I was also funded generously by a fellowship from Tulane University, which supported my research in Mexico and Spain. Christopher Newport University provided funding and several course releases in the form of Dean's Office Grants and a Faculty Development Grant, all of which allowed me to conduct research and to write. I also thank my department chairs at Christopher Newport University, Shumet Sishagne and Phillip Hamilton, who supported this project as I transformed it into a book.

I conducted research at various archives in Mexico City, but most important were the Archivo General de la Nación (AGN) and the

Archivo Historico de la Ciudad de México. The professional staffs of each institution facilitated the research immeasurably. I particularly appreciate the help of the director of the Centro de Referencias at the AGN, Roberto Beristein, who shared his knowledge of the AGN collections and those of many other Mexico City archives generously. I also worked in the Fondo Reservado in the Biblioteca Nacional and the Mapoteca Orozco y Berra and thank the staffs of each institution. In Spain, the Archivo de Indias and its staff, despite the renovations that were going on in 2001, were amazingly helpful. I have also taken advantage of numerous libraries in the United States. The staff of the Latin American Library at Tulane University has always been helpful, particularly in the summer of 2005 and subsequently assisting with image permissions. At Tulane, I thank in particular Guillermo Náñez Falcón, Hortensia Calvo, David Dressing, and Sean Knowlton. I have also regularly utilized the collections at the Perkins/Bostock Library at Duke University, the Davis Library at the University of North Carolina at Chapel Hill, and the Swem Library at the College of William and Mary. I also thank the Mariners' Museum and Mariners' Museum Library for their assistance with images, in particular staff members Claudia Jew and Tom Moore.

I have presented at various conferences pieces of early versions of this book, and I thank all of those who attended those sessions for their questions and insights. Specifically, Kenneth Andrien, Barbara Borg, Rosemary Brana-Shute, Kendall Brown, Louise Gammons, Mack James, Lyman Johnson, and Susan Socolow commented on a chapter at the Virginia-Carolinas-Georgia Colonial Seminar in Charleston in 2008. Apart from that conference, during the winter of 2008, Ida Altman and Lyman Johnson generously read various drafts of chapter 1 and the introduction. John F. Schwaller and Susan Ramírez commented on a portion of chapter 1 presented at the Rocky Mountain Council for Latin American Studies meeting in 2004. In addition, subsequent panel presentations were commented on by Dorothy Tanck de Estrada, Susan Schroeder, and Susan Kellogg. I particularly thank Dorothy Tanck de Estrada for her encouragement when this project was at an early stage and for her thoughtful advice. Funding provided by the history departments of Wake Forest University and Christopher Newport

University supported travel to various national and international conferences, where I was able to present parts of this research.

Many scholars have been generous in other ways with their time, expertise, and resources. I thank Tatiana Seijas, SilverMoon, and Jonathan Truitt for sharing copies of their dissertations. Silver also provided a copy of the Codex Valeriano that she personally photographed in Paris. Richard Conway shared a document from his research on Xochimilco. Scholars who enriched my research in the archives are too numerous to recount, but I can single out a few who were particularly supportive. Trey Proctor and Matt O'Hara both generously shared references in the AGN. Others in the archives to whom I owe thanks include James Garza and Christoph Rosenmüller. Eric Van Young, who was in the AGN in 2005, offered encouragement and counseled me to think about political culture in new ways. Bill Beezley has always provided excellent feedback in our conversations over the years. I also thank Linda Arnold, who gave me a copy of the index she made of the AGN's Ramo Civil and graciously shared her considerable knowledge of that archive. Bill Nelson drew the map for the book, and I thank him for his careful attention to detail as he converted my general ideas into the final map. I also thank Jonathan Truitt for help with pinpointing difficult Mexico City locations that have, in the past several hundred years, been absorbed by modern infrastructure.

During the writing of the manuscript I received constant feedback from Susan Schroeder, who read drafts of the chapters and shared her expertise. Although I usually had to steel my nerves when I opened Susan's envelopes, this work is far better constructed, more solidly argued, and more effectively presented because of her careful and thoughtful comments and encouragement. Susan is seemingly indefatigable and was always willing to read chapters as I sent them to her. I am honored to have had the privilege to work with her. Colin MacLachlan, who directed my dissertation at Tulane, gave me license to explore my interests, providing helpful criticism along the way. This work owes a great deal to his sagacious advice.

I thank also the dedicated professionals at the University of Oklahoma Press with whom I have worked. Beginning with my first contacts with Alessandra Jacobi Tamulevich through the marketing and copyediting of the book, the press has provided excellent guidance. I thank also Ashley Eddy, Emily Jerman, and John Thomas at the press with whom I have worked closely throughout the production phase.

I thank my family and also friends in Mexico. Rosa María Vera, in particular, provided a wonderful place to live in the beautiful colonia of Santa María la Ribera—thank you, Rosie, for your hospitality and good cheer. Cindy, Sean, and Chelsea have supported me throughout the research and writing of this book. Cindy provided careful editorial assistance and was always willing to listen as I told stories and worked through problems encountered in my research.

A Note on Language

Many of the titles for offices, place locations, and names in this book are in Nahuatl, the language spoken by most natives who lived in Mexico City and the wider Basin of Mexico during the timeframe of this book. I follow the style, spelling conventions, and grammatical rules of classical Nahuatl, following James Lockhart, *Nahuatl as Written: Lessons in Older Written Nahuatl, with Copious Examples and Texts* (Stanford: Stanford University Press, 2001), and the various works by Chimalpahin edited by Susan Schroeder, James Lockhart, Arthur J. O. Anderson, Doris Namala, and Rafael Tena. For translation of individual terms, I rely on Fray Alonso de Molina, *Vocabulario en lengua castellana y mexicana y mexicana y castellana,* ed. Miguel León-Portilla (México, 1977 [1571]); and Frances Karttunen, *An Analytical Dictionary of Nahuatl* (Norman: University of Oklahoma Press, 1983). Most Nahuatl translations in this book, however, are the work of those who have greater expertise.

I standardize Nahuatl spellings when possible. For example, "Moctezuma," a spelling I use in the title for the sake of recognition, is in the text "Moteucçoma" unless it refers to the noble title or specific individuals obviously outside of the lineage of the tlatoani (native ruler). In the latter cases, names are reproduced as they appear in the documents (e.g., the Spaniard don Fernando Cortés Moctezuma). The spelling "Moteucçoma" conforms to Lockhart, Schroeder, and Namala in their English translation of Chimalpahin. The name appears in Chimalpahin's Nahuatl with an *h* to indicate the glottal stop (Moteuhcçoma), in Spanish texts in various forms (e.g., Mutezuma in

Cortés's letters), and usually in English as Montezuma, Moctezuma, or Moctezoma. When appropriate I give the Nahuatl form of loan words in Spanish. Deeper discussions are found in the endnotes. Nahuatl terms are generally defined only on their first usage but are available in the index for convenient reference.

Spanish words and phrases are generally modernized. I include accents when they are necessary in modern Spanish. Translations from Spanish to English in the text are my own unless otherwise noted. I translate texts to communicate meaning first and when necessary explain in the endnotes that which is omitted in ellipses. When appropriate, I reproduce text from documents in Spanish in the endnotes.

The native peoples about whom this book is written were Nahuas, a large indigenous group (then and now), all of whom spoke the Uto-Aztecan language Nahuatl. Within that group, however, are numerous subgroups. I focus on one principally, the Mexica Tenochca, or just Tenochca. This is the group popularly understood to be the "Aztecs," who lived in the altepetl (ethnic state) of Mexico Tenochtitlan. Other Mexica lived in the Basin of Mexico as well, including the Mexica Tlatelolca, who shared what was then an island in Lake Tetzcoco with the Tenochca. The Mexica were Nahuas, and the Nahuas were of course only one of many groups of indigenous Americans in the Basin and surrounding regions.

After Moctezuma

Mexico City, circa 1628, based on Gómez de Trasmonte's map. Drawn by Bill Nelson, 2010.

Introduction

Continuity and the Emergence of Indigenous Self-Government in Mexico Tenochtitlan

Mexico Tenochtitlan, reconstructed following the Spanish conquest, became over the course of the sixteenth century both an indigenous and a Spanish city. The Códice Osuna, a pictorial document drawn by native scribes in the 1560s, visually demonstrates the beginning of that transformation. It depicts the four *barrios,* or subunits, of the Mexica *altepetl* (ethnic state) of Mexico Tenochtitlan using representations for churches where, in a precontact codex, palace-*tecpan* images would have appeared.[1] Additionally, the codex provides an image of the second viceroy, don Luis de Velasco (r. 1550–64), distributing the staff of royal justice to the newly elected indigenous government.[2] The accompanying bilingual Spanish-Nahuatl alphabetic text explains the duties expected of the indigenous government. The Nahuatl version quotes the viceroy, who made a speech to the newly appointed first indigenous *cabildo* (municipal council) to explain their duties. Velasco stressed that the *alcaldes* (elected officers), "appointed . . . for the first time," should make sure that those over whom they presided followed Christian doctrine. The cabildo, he further emphasized, should follow the dictates of His Majesty, the king, since they now served as agents of the crown. Finally, he instructed them in the paternalistic mission of the crown, advising these functionaries of their responsibility to care for the *macehualtin* (commoners).[3] Velasco explained, in a way absent from the Spanish-language text, that to care for the macehualtin meant to "treat them with esteem," to withhold judgment in deciding

3

Viceroy don Luis de Velasco distributing the staff of authority to the cabildo of Mexico Tenochtitlan. From *Pintura del Gobernador, alcaldes y regidores de México* (1565), fol. 9v. Reproduced with permission, © Biblioteca Nacional de España.

legal disputes until presented with reason, and to make sure that "everyone cultivates [the land and] no one lives in idleness."[4] After this ceremony, indigenous *principales* (noblemen) from Mexico Tenochtitlan assumed their places as leaders of the new Spanish-styled system of city government.[5]

The *parcialidad* (municipal sector) of Mexico Tenochtitlan—subdivided into the four neighborhoods of San Juan Moyotlan, San Pablo Teopan, San Sebastián Atzaqualco, and Santa María la Redonda Cuepopan—became the seat of one indigenous cabildo. Similarly, indigenous nobles in Mexico Tlatelolco to the north formed a second indigenous government to complete the circle around the center of the city, now governed by a Spanish *ayuntamiento* (city council).[6] Following the violence of the Spanish invasion, this political arrangement extended, in name, the authority of Spanish rule by incorporating the institutions of the native peoples. Such arrangements in Mesoamerica served both the preservation of indigenous identity and the expedient collection of tribute by conquistadores, many of whom later became *encomenderos* (individuals who received royal grants to collect native tribute and initially labor) bent on enriching themselves. Conquistadores, encomenderos, and even the viceregal government relied on the aid of native peoples who provided them with labor and tribute but whose institutions served as a legitimizing and stabilizing force. Such an arrangement, within limits, facilitated the survival of indigenous practices.[7]

Spaniards, when they glimpsed Mexico Tenochtitlan and Mexico Tlatelolco from afar for the first time, may have experienced the wonder enunciated by Bernal Díaz del Castillo, who gazed down upon the city and famously observed, "Great towns . . . and buildings rising from the water, all made of stone, seemed like an enchanted vision from the tale of Amadis. Indeed, some of our soldiers asked whether it was not all a dream."[8] The wonder and amazement that Díaz and his fellow Spaniards felt, of course, did not restrain them and their native allies from razing Mexico Tenochtitlan.[9] Once towering and meaningful, the palaces and other structures became quarries for the construction of the new city. The encounter between Spaniards and Nahuas brought together two groups of people who were in some respects remarkably similar.[10] Both understood and promoted notions of social hierarchy based on heredity and identity. Nobles and commoners existed in both societies. In addition, certain other groups—*conversos* (converted Jews) and *moriscos* (converted Muslims) in Iberia; non-Nahua (e.g., Otomi) in central Mexico—sometimes faced discrimination and persecution because of their differences.[11] Both groups professed great piety and relied on millennial visions to justify aggressive foreign policies. Both groups provoked fear in their neighbors. Both peoples congregated in cities and saw them as fundamental units of social organization.[12] Both maintained elaborate and highly ritualistic military ideologies, saw military service as a noble pursuit that brought glory, and placed military men in exalted positions in government.[13] Both peoples also valued religious officials and understood rulership as a religious and a secular pursuit. Both the Mexica Tenochca and the Spaniards rationalized economically motivated conquests under the guise of spreading what they saw as true religion and superior culture.[14]

Some aspects of indigenous society changed dramatically in the first generation after the Spanish invasion.[15] Epidemic disease, the disruption of everyday rituals, the service to conquering Spaniards that native peoples had to perform, and their general suffering must have made it seem as though the world as they knew it was coming to an end.[16] Indigenous rituals that sustained the world and maintained the political and social order were suppressed. Many who survived, however, worked to preserve native languages, traditions, culture, and identity.[17] At the same time, indigenous peoples struggled in the face of ever-increasing demands on their labor and time. As their numbers dwindled during successive epidemics, demands for labor and on resources increased.

Mexico City, a large, diverse, and densely populated place before and after the arrival of Spaniards, provides a complex and sophisticated backdrop for the study of the evolution of political institutions in indigenous society. Through the sixteenth and seventeenth centuries, the steady construction work of both native and other laborers built Mexico City into one of the western world's great urban centers. It remains so today. Many of the problems that plagued its past (overpopulation, pollution, crumbling infrastructure, and the unequal distribution of wealth) continue to characterize it. Throughout its history of nearly seven centuries, it has been a center of industry, religion, economy, and population.[18] As a political center in the midst of a sea of smaller political entities, it had by 1521 expanded its influence well beyond its immediate environs.[19] The native cabildo of Mexico Tenochtitlan continued to exercise influence and authority and to draw labor from the surrounding indigenous communities. Spaniards made their way to Mexico City for the available political and economic opportunities. The city held, for enterprising Spaniards, all of the comforts of Spanish cities. Even though many economic interests for Spaniards lay in the mining regions, agricultural centers, and port cities, Mexico City provided stability and continuity for successful Spaniards whose economic interests often lay elsewhere. The city also housed the Audiencia (high court), the Spanish ayuntamiento, the court of the viceroy, and the seat of the archbishop. Spaniards interested in currying favor, using their courtly skills, and participating in bureaucratic rituals gravitated toward the viceregal capital. The political complexity and economic centrality of Mexico City make it highly suitable for a study that seeks to explain how indigenous institutions and political culture reemerged and evolved during the seventeenth century.

For native peoples, the city had great ritual and political significance. As the precontact locus of power, Mexico Tenochtitlan had dominated the region. In 1325 the Nahuatl-speaking Tenochca founded the city on an island in Lake Tetzcoco.[20] Forming alliances in 1428 with Tetzcoco and Tlacopan, the Tenochca came to conquer and subjugate the entire basin, besting former overlords such as Azcapotzalco. Over the course of nearly two hundred years, the Tenochca, using Mexico Tenochtitlan as their base, slowly established an enormous tributary empire.[21] Despite the Tenochca-dominated triple alliance's expansion, local rulers retained power—providing they remained loyal, paid the tribute owed, and refrained from plotting sedition.[22]

After the destruction of Mexico Tenochtitlan (1519–24), native laborers and Spaniards rebuilt the city. Its principal square, with the cathedral and viceregal palace, replaced the fabulous main ceremonial site. Spaniards built the Spanish city on top of the ruins. The cathedral, adjacent to the pyramid of Huitzilopochtli and Tlaloc (Templo Mayor), which had dominated the precontact city, became a symbol of European power and culture. The ruins of Moteucçoma's palace, rebuilt as the residence of Hernán Cortés (1485–1547), later became the viceregal palace.[23] In reconstructing the city, therefore, Spaniards planned to retain the indigenous use or function of space while adding a structure that looked Spanish. This provides a useful metaphor that helps to explain the development of indigenous government. Indigenous ideas of government were preserved within an imposed Spanish structure.

Between 1523 and 1550, Spanish officials, cooperating with native nobles, created two indigenous cabildos. Thus viceregal officials imposed Hispanic political divisions over existing indigenous structures. Using Castilian nomenclature, Spaniards called the administrative units over which natives ruled *parcialidades*. Though they used a Spanish name to designate political space, the new municipal areas corresponded precisely to the native altepetl of Mexico Tenochtitlan and Mexico Tlatelolco that already existed. Furthermore, these complex altepetl also had internal subdivisions, which Spaniards called *barrios* (wards).[24] Spaniards thus utilized existing corporate spaces and, whether consciously or not, encouraged tradition by "rebranding" entities that already had meaning for the Mexica Tenochca. Within the new spaces, each parcialidad—Mexico Tenochtitlan and Mexico Tlatelolco—elected native *pipiltin* (noblemen) to serve on Spanish-styled cabildos. Mexico City, therefore, maintained its place as a center of indigenous government.[25]

The four Tenochca subdivisions that collectively made up the altepetl of Mexico Tenochtitlan each had an important ceremonial site.[26] The surviving native nobility also built a palace for native government (*tecpan*) in the barrio of San Juan Moyotlan. The tecpan, sometimes literally called in Nahuatl *tecpan comonidad* (community palace) or in Spanish simply *la comunidad* (the community), became the center of the indigenous municipal council in the parcialidad of Mexico Tenochtitlan.[27] In theory, indigenous governments shared power with Spanish elites and maintained authority over the indigenous city. These accommodations, therefore, theoretically created a parallel republic. Importantly, indigenous peoples were brought into viceregal government as part of an evolving strategy of appeasement and accommodation.[28]

The reorganization of the political landscape of the reconstructed Mexico Tenochtitlan followed closely the indigenous footprint of the city but also made important modifications. Three, not two, distinct

 Sanc Sebastian / los quatro barrios de merico / Sanc pablo.

probisor
bachiler
mureru

Comvanceados años. por orden del bachiller
moreno provisor. Por indios. hizieron tres
campanas. pa la yglia de sant pablo & to-
cibdad los quales se pagaron de cierto zepod-
Juº y xxxxx... Çepº entrelos yndios
& traiblan & xxxx & prospexeron en el
virey ni el arçobispo / Sanc Joseph

 fray pº degante.

 Sancta maria

 Sanc Juan

The four barrios of Mexico Tenochtitlan: San Juan (Moyotlan), San Pablo (Teopan), San Sebastián (Atzaqualco), and Santa María la Redonda (Cuepopan). From *Pintura del Gobernador, alcaldes y regidores de México* (1565), fol. 8v. Reproduced with permission, © Biblioteca Nacional de España.

political zones came to make up the city after Spaniards set up permanent residence. The two parcialidades ruled by semiautonomous indigenous governments represented the indigenous peoples of the city. Spaniards also carved out from that territory the *traza* in the center of the city. The traza contained the space for royal, ecclesiastical, and viceregal institutions. Spaniards built large sturdy houses in this space. To occupy what became roughly thirteen square blocks of real estate on an island with limited area, they pushed indigenous spaces to the periphery.[29] Spaniards, almost immediately after they had secured the city, began the construction of the cathedral, municipal council building, and viceregal palace.[30] This organization left the indigenous governments to exercise limited jurisdictional authority over much of the city.

Spanish observers of the development of both a Spanish and indigenous city noticed its striking presence, beauty, and style. Alonso de Zorita made one such comment when he wrote that the "noble city of Mexico [is] well designed and well built, with very long, wide and straight paved streets . . . large strong houses, many churches, monasteries, and hospitals."[31] Zorita, an *oidor* (high court magistrate) at the Audiencia of Mexico from 1555 to 1566, wrote extensively about the city and advocated the protection of natives.[32] Though he argued for the defense of indigenous peoples, his descriptions of the city focus only on the Spanish quarter. Like most Spaniards, Zorita did not even mention the indigenous parcialidades. Had he done so, a far different image may have emerged. The indigenous spaces of the city, when depicted on maps, often appeared temporary, usually without the grid pattern characteristic of the traza.[33] Indigenous barrios reportedly contained humble dwellings that did not inspire comment from writers like Zorita.[34]

Indigenous government in the barrios was constantly evolving in the sixteenth century. The Nahua historian Chimalpahin chronicled the early succession of indigenous leaders in Mexico Tenochtitlan and characterized the 1520s as a period of chaos when false *tlatoque* (indigenous rulers, sing. *tlatoani*; Nahuatl: "he who speaks") who did not come from the royal line came to power to accommodate Spanish interests. From the death of the last tlatoani, Quauhtemoctzin (d. 1525), to 1538 a succession of nondynastic rulers led the indigenous communities. As a potential source of instability and illegitimacy, this arrangement could not have been sustainable for any significant length of time. The first viceroy, don Antonio de Mendoza (r. 1535–50), began the process of restoring legitimacy to indigenous government when he empowered don Diego de Alvarado Huanitzin, a nephew of the late Moteucçoma Xocoyotzin (r. 1502–20) as ruler.[35] This act reestablished the legitimate royal lineage in Tenochtitlan.[36]

Though it is surprising that Chimalpahin, an independent indigenous voice, saw the actions of Viceroy Mendoza (and the institutions of the crown he represented) as a force that restored some legitimacy to indigenous government, his observations help to explain the complexity of postcontact politics and society. Chimalpahin's comments are particularly surprising in light of Mendoza's obvious paternalism toward native peoples and his characterization of them as children.[37] The colonial world was not divided clearly along indigenous and Spanish lines. Both groups had hierarchies and internal divisions. The regularization of indigenous government paralleled the empowerment of royal institutions.[38] Chimalpahin contrasts sharply the two interim rulers, don Andrés de Tapia Motelchiuhtzin (r. 1525–30) and don Pablo Xochiquentzin (r. 1532–36)—both appointed after the death of Quauhtemoctzin—with the appointment of Huanitzin (r. 1538–41).[39] Motelchiuhtzin and Xochiquentzin were not legitimate rulers because they were not descended from the royal line. Huanitzin, on the other hand, had legitimacy because he was directly related to Moteucçoma in a way that signaled to the Tenochca that he had the right to rule. The legitimacy of indigenous government was established nearly simultaneously with the elevation of New Spain to the status of a viceroyalty. Coming on the heels of hopeless infighting between Spaniards—manifested most clearly in the debacle of the first Audiencia—the creation of the viceroyalty was intended to bring stability to the city.[40]

Chimalpahin wrote that Nuño de Guzmán, as a representative of the illegitimate first Audiencia, "appointed don Pablo Xochiquentzin to govern the Tenochca as if he were tlatoani, even though he was not of noble birth and previously had served only as a *calpixqui* [minor official] in Mexico [Tenochtitlan] . . . the two most recent rulers [he and don Andrés Motelchiuhtzin] were *quauhpipiltin* and thus not from the governing families of Tenochtitlan, the *tlazopipiltin* who descended from the recognized nobility."[41] Chimalpahin purposefully contrasts the two groups, the quauhpipiltin and the tlazopipiltin. The term *quauhpipiltin* (eagle noble), as implied in the quotation, suggests that a nonnoble could be elevated to the status of the nobility through service, usually those who distinguished themselves in military service in precontact Mexico Tenochtitlan. The term *tlazopipiltin* (a person of noble birth or legitimate birth) indicates in this usage a legitimate child from the ruling family who apparently possessed the right to succeed.[42] Chimalpahin, by pointing out explicitly that Xochiquentzin was not noble and held only a minor office, suggests the illegitimacy of pretenders who did not descend directly from the royal line.[43] The arrival of Viceroy Mendoza in 1535 provoked Chimalpahin to express the sentiment that justice and legitimacy came with him: with Mendoza came "the improvement of the administration of justice in Mexico . . . and the naming of governors."[44] Mendoza appointed Huanitzin to serve as governor in 1538.

Viceroy Mendoza restored the royal line and provided a foundation for stability that endured, with only minor interruption, until 1565. Chimalpahin also suggests that this order provided stability in indigenous society. For Spaniards, disinterested institutions and the promise of justice accompanied Mendoza's arrival. Legitimate indigenous institutions also potentially had the power to promote stability and order. Mendoza began the process of restoring legitimate indigenous institutions, tainted after the fall of Tenochtitlan through their association with the conquistadores. To restore their legitimacy and respectability, Mendoza returned to authority rulers who descended from the royal line in Tenochtitlan. Some important changes, however, occurred with the new rulers. Mendoza did not appoint a tlatoani but a governor (he did not have the capacity to appoint a tlatoani). These two offices from an indigenous perspective were not the same. Chimalpahin, even in the Nahuatl, written in 1609, uses the loanword *gobernador* specifically, not *tlatoani*, to indicate the distinction.[45] Tlatoque came from a royal line within an altepetl. Indeed, Lockhart asserts that "an altepetl existed where and only where there was a tlatoani."[46] Tlatoque were usually calpolli-based leaders whose authority over the altepetl derived from heading the highest-ranked subdivision of an altepetl. Governors, on the other hand, were not necessarily tied to the structure of altepetl and could therefore come from anywhere, though they generally did not until after 1565.[47] Though, as Lockhart observes, "the governorship permanently took on a great deal of the aura, powers, and characteristics of the preconquest rulership" with such association, the title *tlatoani* ceased to retain its complexity and importance within the postcontact altepetl.[48] Mendoza may have thought he was resurrecting an indigenous office, but in reality he created something new with a Spanish name in the minds of the Nahua.[49] Although new, the gobernador retained ties to legitimate precontact native lineages and thus may have inspired some continuity with traditional forms of governance.

Indigenous self-government, a hybrid system with norms not yet well established or defined by the mid-sixteenth century, should have benefited indigenous peoples living in Mexico City by providing them with continuity to the past and a stake in their own governance. From the very beginning, systematic exploitation by Spaniards had the capacity to undermine attempts to ensure stability. Conquistadores did intend for self-government to encourage harmony and maintain stability, but largely to further their own exploitative ends. The historian Georges Baudot, in his study of postcontact chronicles, notes that "Spanish colonial organization had no intention of eliminating or totally setting aside the native ruling class, the tlatoque and the pipiltin, members of the pre-Hispanic nobility. In a densely populated country . . . the native nobility could serve as an indispensable chain of command, and as ideal intermediary agents to institute methodical exploitation."[50] Baudot uncovers a fundamental reality in the early establishment of order: Spaniards, intent on expanding the authority of the crown, had to rely on indigenous leaders. The extent to which their attempted cooptation served the ends of institutionalizing colonization and ending conflict, however, is somewhat dubious. By building alliances with Spaniards, indigenous leaders may have legitimized the presence of these invaders, but in doing so native leaders also likely had their own purposes and likely hoped to carve out privileged spaces for themselves through such alliance building.

The first attempt to establish a Spanish-styled indigenous government, ostensibly subordinate to Spaniards, came in 1523 as Cortés retreated to Coyoacan, then on the southern shore of Lake Tetzcoco. Before he left the city, he appointed a governing body to organize the reconstruction of Tenochtitlan, which lay in ruin after the siege. In his fourth letter to Carlos I, composed in 1524, Cortés described the growing prosperity of the city under the able hands of rulers he had appointed:

> I charged a captain general [Tlacotzin] whom I had known in the time of Mutezuma with the task of repopulating it [Tenochtitlan]. And so that he should have more authority I gave back to him the title he held when his lord was in power, which was that of *ciguacoatl* [cihuacoatl], which means lieutenant of the king [tlatoani]. I likewise appointed chieftains whom I had known previously to the offices in the government of this city which they had once held.[51]

Cortés carefully selected native peoples who had authority before his arrival. Although his intent was probably to show his ability to command and his skill at delegating authority to his own king, his words betray the degree of his dependence on native rulers. By restoring their offices, he began a process of negotiation with the indigenous nobility and at the same time tried to stifle any potential rebellion on the part of rulers. The tlatoani of Mexico Tenochtitlan, Quauhtemoctzin, retained his title and position but remained in the custody of Cortés. He sent the letter in October, just before he embarked on the expedition to Honduras to capture and punish Cristóbal de Olíd, an undertaking that ultimately afforded Cortés an excuse to execute Quauhtemoctzin.[52] Perhaps, with the act of murdering the last tlatoani, Cortés hoped to make the rulers he entrusted subsequently dependent on him. By appointing them to their positions, Cortés may have expected loyalty in return.[53]

According to Chimalpahin, the cihuacoatl mentioned by Cortés, don Juan Velásquez Tlacotzin, dressed as a Spaniard, carried a steel sword and dagger, and rode a white horse, all privileges granted to Nahua lords who had been particularly helpful. Chimalpahin included his Christian name, indicating that he had been baptized. Tlacotzin, though a "lieutenant" in the hierarchy of Mexico Tenochtitlan, came to his position because he seems to have understood that he stood to gain status by working with Spaniards. Native peoples with leadership credentials in indigenous society could maintain or enhance their positions provided they also served the interests of Spaniards. Quauhtemoctzin suffered unjust execution at the hands of Cortés in February 1525, perhaps conveniently bringing to an end the last legitimate authority of the tlatoque just as he was establishing nondynastic positions.

Granting recognition and title to indigenous nobles also implied that Cortés or other ruling Spaniards could take the bestowed authority away. The rapid succession from Tlacotzin to don Andrés de Tapia Motelchiuhtzin, which happened in the space of less than one year, might seem to suggest that Cortés could easily manipulate tlatoque once they were appointed. Yet Chimalpahin makes clear that Tlacotzin, after his appointment, died during the journey back to Mexico Tenochtitlan in Nochiztlan Quatzontlan.[54] Using such interim rulers, who served while the political process of tlatoani selection took place, had precedent before contact. Cortés selected Motelchiuhtzin to replace Moteucçoma's cihuacoatl from several potential candidates, picking him over others, also in Cortés's custody, who had ties to the royal line, including Huanitzin.[55] Cortés perhaps hoped to use the less legitimate among those he had captured as a means of maintaining control. Motelchiuhtzin came to power in 1525 and kept his position through the establishment of the first Audiencia. He was a commoner (*macehualli*) from the barrio of San Pablo Teopan who distinguished himself as a "great captain of war" and thus served as an "eagle-ruler" (*quauhtlatoani*, interim ruler; pl. *quauhtlatoque*).[56] When Cortés returned to Spain in 1528, Motelchiuhtzin remained in office. Presumably he would have continued to serve were he not killed by an arrow in 1530 after defeating the Teocolhuacan peoples in battle.[57] Thus, even though it may have been advantageous for new Spanish rulers to remove the quauhtlatoani and replace him with an indigenous leader loyal to them, the interim governor retained his office regardless of which Spaniards had authority in Mexico Tenochtitlan.

To the Nahua of Tenochtitlan, interim rulers often held office during times of transition. Quauhtlatoque and cihuacoatl seem to have served to ensure order while political transitions took place unexpectedly, such as when a tlatoani suddenly died.[58] In the 1520s, nondynastic interim rulers followed Tenochca tradition in which such rulers "fill[ed]-in when the normal dynastic succession [wa]s interrupted, either by disputes and the lack of an heir after the tlatoani's death, or when the tlatoani [wa]s in exile."[59] Such continuity with the past likely bred stability in indigenous communities. Cortés benefited by using this tradition, as he notes regularly in his letters. He suggests, however, that cooptation of native nobles who possessed offices and titles facilitated pacification and cooperation among the citizens of Mexico Tenochtitlan and thus helped to expand the authority of the Spaniards.[60] Cortés, perhaps overstating his control to his audience, Carlos I, needed such alliances. They served him far better than his earlier tactics of kidnapping and murder, which both Quauhtemoctzin and Moteucçoma suffered during and after the initial military phase of the invasion.[61] Cortés was aware of his early dependence on indigenous authority, even if he overstated his capacity to control the indigenous peoples: "And to this *ciguacoatl* and the other I gave such lands and people as were necessary for their sustenance, although not as much as they had owned before, nor enough to make them dangerous at any time."[62] Cortés indicated in correspondence to the crown that only by including native rulers with some legitimacy in the eyes of the Tenochca could stability and order return, yet he also acknowledged the possible danger posed by independent rulers. This paradox under-scored the need to supervise and carefully choose specific rulers in the immediate term after the destruction of the city, but it may also explain his reluctance to appoint those associated with the royal lineage.

Though Cortés may have wished to assert authority over native rulers, replacing them with loyal native nobles whom he could appoint, indigenous groups understood and interpreted the political changes of the 1520s as well. Empowering loyal, indigenous rulers with dubious claims to legitimacy and the blessing of certain conquistador factions had the potential to create instability. Quauhtlatoque and cihuacoatl, although part of the mechanisms of indigenous succession before the Spanish invasion, kept order only because they were temporary. Thus, indigenous peoples must have understood and anticipated that their presence represented only the promise that interim rulers would step aside when the tlatoani had been chosen by proper internal native customs. But the introduction of Spaniards into the selection process eroded the very mechanisms for choosing a tlatoani. Spaniards—Cortés and other Spanish groups such as the partisans of Diego Velázquez— would need to have a voice in the selection of any new indigenous ruler, which ultimately confounded the process from the perspective of native Tenochca.

Viceroy Mendoza seems to have made a conscious decision to settle the issue by restoring some semblance of precontact succession practices. He probably sought to preserve the veneer of legitimacy by placing native rulers with legitimate right to the position of tlatoani in a new Spanish-named office. With such a move, perhaps he hoped to restore legitimacy to indigenous government in Mexico Tenochtitlan using the actual royal line. Rebranded with Spanish nomenclature, indigenous institutions theoretically fell under the authority of the viceroy. Mendoza also appointed or officially named the indigenous governor, as Cortés and Nuño de Guzmán had named interim rulers. Such an early step enhanced royal institutions at the expense of the conquistadores and their heirs but also, and more important, regularized the administration of indigenous communities. It also promoted the possibility of justice, removing the arbitrary power of conquerors and replacing it with the rules and fledgling institutions of the crown.

The indigenous city of Mexico Tenochtitlan, because of careful organization, closely resembled in political and spatial sense the city that existed before the Spaniards arrived. Spaniards demonstrated either naïveté or expedience by adapting their word *parcialidad*, sometimes shortened to *parte*, as a means to understand the complex indigenous ethnic state, the altepetl. Native texts, however, continued to use the word *altepetl*, which signified both the physical space of a community and the community of people who occupied that space. Though similar at the surface level to the duality of the Spanish word *pueblo*—which can refer to both a place and a people—*altepetl* suggests the more complicated idea of the ethnic state, a local and autonomous or semiautonomous entity.[63] Spanish terminology recognized that altepetl had subdivisions but in simplified form, using their term *barrio* (neighborhood, ward, or urban subdivision) as an equivalent to the calpolli or *tlaxilacalli*—"semi-independent subgroups of the altepetl."[64] *Barrio* over time came to refer also to the subdivisions of the altepetl in some Spanish-language documentation, as in "the native peoples of the parcialidad of San Juan of this City and its four barrios."[65]

The implication of the word *parcialidad*, a Spanish term denoting a "union of independent entities confederated for some specific end," suggests an attempt, not unlike others in the early sixteenth century, to find linguistic equivalents in Spanish for indigenous concepts. Lockhart discusses the term *tlayacatl*, "complex constituent altepetl," as the nearest Nahuatl equivalent to the idea of the parcialidad. Speaking of Amecameca and Xochimilco exclusively, he writes: "The historian Chimalpahin . . . introduces the useful word tlayacatl for constituent altepetl of a tightly knit composite state. . . . when the Spaniards became aware of these sovereign units within larger states, they were often to call them parcialidades or partes."[66] The tlayacatl seems to mirror the composition of the altepetl itself.[67] Spaniards, who likely did not understand the complexity of indigenous social organization, settled on the concept of the parcialidad because it worked well enough for their purposes. Importantly, native peoples continued to use their own terminology.[68] By implication, native peoples also understood that their own precontact political organization persisted.

Politically speaking, Mexico City was a complicated collection of overlapping and competing jurisdictions. As an urban center, it was divided politically into three municipal zones governed by three different municipal councils—one Spanish and two indigenous.[69] The Audiencia exercised jurisdictional rights to hear legal disputes in the city and five leagues beyond its limits. It also served as an appellate court and viceregal council (*real acuerdo*).[70] Indigenous governments exercised some jurisdictional authority over areas not controlled by the Spanish cabildo, including judicial authority of first instance, tribute collection, and the maintenance of civic infrastructure such as roads and drainage canals.[71] The Spanish ayuntamiento regulated the Spanish part of the city by exercising its authority over matters of justice, regulation of markets (including butcher shops and bakeries), and maintenance of public infrastructure (canals, aqueducts, fountains, bridges, road paving, and other mundane municipal duties).[72]

Indigenous communities in New Spain institutionalized elections in cabildos during the early sixteenth century. In Mexico Tenochtitlan, indigenous *principales* (*pipiltin*, hereditary nobles) elected governors and the cabildos who served under them. Initially governors served for life and the alcaldes and *regidores* (elected officials who staffed the cabildo) rotated their positions following legal restrictions that prohibited reelection.[73] Gradually, governors lost their ability to hold office for multiple terms. By the late sixteenth century the natives and viceregal institutions had standardized the process. Every year beginning in the fall, the viceroy appointed an election supervisor, setting in motion the process that eventually culminated in the election ceremony that usually took place on 1 January (but could vary from late December to February). Election probably legitimized rulers in the parcialidades. As the system of succession adapted to prevailing conditions and matured by the 1560s, indigenous governments began to rely increasingly on elections to determine a principal ruler. Elections allowed natives to move away from the hereditary line of governors, the last of whom to serve, don Luis de Santa María Nanacacipactzin, died in office in 1565.[74] Native elections did not become venal. The crown sold offices on the Spanish ayuntamiento to members of elite families to generate income.[75] The indigenous barrios, however, developed a system of elections that had precedent in precontact Mexico Tenochtitlan. Spaniards saw only the need to find responsible and legitimate rulers who could collect tribute and mediate disputes over "lands, jurisdictions, and succession" within native society.[76] Indigenous communities regularized the process of selection in the late sixteenth century.[77]

Precontact systems of selection can provide explanations for the politics of indigenous elections. Before the arrival of Spaniards, periods of succession had the potential to create insecurity and instability. Tenochca society sometimes experienced succession contests after the death of a tlatoani. Unlike those in other altepetl, the Tenochca chose for their tlatoque the best candidate from among a small group of legitimate candidates. In practice, it appears that fraternal succession came before filial, and thus the "Mexica inheritance typically passed from brother to brother before descending to the eldest son of the eldest brother."[78] Such a succession system had the potential to create instability. Lockhart observes that, in precontact native society, "the losing candidates for the throne had represented a formidable problem. A bloodbath during or immediately after a succession was not uncommon. Surviving unsuccessful candidates often lived in exile in neighboring altepetl, hatching plots against the incumbent."[79]

When male children, all sons of tlatoque, competed for power, a system of negotiation among a small group of close advisors to the former tlatoani helped smooth the succession process by limiting the number of candidates. In addition, the Tenochca tended to limit over time the number of advisors who chose the tlatoani. The anthropologist Frances Berdan, discussing altepetl politics from 1428 to 1519, concludes that "the number of persons allowed to participate in selecting the ruler narrowed considerably during 90 years of imperial growth."[80] Thus, when leaders of the four subdivisions of the altepetl of Mexico Tenochtitlan arrived to elect a tlatoani, voting was often nearly unanimous. Such a result came only because most of the political maneuvering took place well before an election. Real politics existed in Tenochtitlan before 1519. Violence apparently was sometimes a legitimate means of political discourse, but only a last resort after many others had failed. The contests for authority that occasioned such disruption followed unsuccessful bids to build coalitions and garner support from important electors.[81] Thus, to avoid bloodshed and disorder, the precontact Tenochca engaged in coalition building, an inherently political process, which they brought with them into the formation of the native cabildo in Mexico Tenochtitlan.

Avoiding conflict and maintaining stability, however, required more than legitimacy and continuity in the highest office. Indigenous leaders faced severe economic hardship because of pressures placed on them by encomenderos and other Spaniards. Demographic pressures, which limited native rulers' ability to collect tribute, also made governing difficult. Oidor don Alonso de Zorita argued in 1553 that both Spaniards and native leaders made heavy demands on commoners. Excessive demands by Spaniards, he argued, placed pressure on indigenous officials, who then expanded their demands on their subjects. Zorita wrote that indigenous nobles collected an illegal fee "for presents to be given to Spanish officials, and still other [fees] to defray their expenses . . . for lawyers, attorneys, solicitors, and interpreters, so that all year long they levy assessments on the poor macehuales who toil to provide what they [indigenous leaders] demand. . . . their assessments go on endlessly and thus the toil for the common people ever increases."[82] Zorita's comments reveal the intense economic pressures placed on both indigenous leaders and their subjects, magnified no doubt by epidemic diseases that reduced the tribute-paying population.[83] Economic pressure put on the indigenous nobility by

Spaniards for more and excessive tribute forced these governments to pass along the burden to their subjects.[84]

Indigenous government, though designed to establish continuity through the preservation of indigenous autonomy, still created conflict among individuals and groups in Mexico City. Within the parcialidades, political disputes erupted over the equitable distribution of scarce resources, working conditions, and the constitution of the local government. Infighting among the hereditary nobles also existed, despite attempts to share authority. Inequality, violence, and injustice clearly had the potential to generate unrest. Indeed, indigenous governors and other cabildo leaders saw their access to wealth largely stripped away in the sixteenth century by Spaniards intent on appropriating those resources for themselves.[85]

This book is divided into five chapters that trace the growing politicization of the parcialidades. Chapter 1 outlines the initial political conflicts of the late sixteenth century in which the electoral system emerged. It also chronicles the demise of the legitimate royal line of Mexico Tenochtitlan. The second chapter discusses the transition of the office of governor from the royal lineage of Mexico Tenochtitlan to individuals chosen by election, notably focusing on the election and career of don Antonio Valeriano. Chapter 3 postulates that the tribute crises following the 1624 uprising and the flooding of 1629 allowed the viceregal government to involve itself more directly in the political affairs of Mexico Tenochtitlan. Chapter 4 develops further the politicization of the cabildo and demonstrates how natives used the new willingness of the viceregal government to remove elected officials to oppose Spanish attempts to take positions of authority in native government. In so doing, native leaders also helped to define who had the right to serve as governor. The final chapter explores the fully politicized indigenous cabildo as it emerged in the late seventeenth and early eighteenth centuries. Together these chapters suggest a multigenerational effort by native peoples in Mexico Tenochtitlan to preserve indigenous control over their own governance within a viceregal system that actively supported them in their efforts.

CHAPTER 1

UNDERMINING CONSENSUS
THE ORIGINS OF POLITICAL CULTURE IN THE INDIGENOUS GOVERNMENT, 1536–1572

On 2 March 1564, craftsmen of the parcialidad of Mexico Tenochtitlan initiated a civil lawsuit through the Spanish Audiencia that brought the judicial apparatus of the viceregal government directly into the political affairs of the indigenous government. During the course of the consequent investigation, which examined the function and process of indigenous government, indigenous leaders were forced to explain and defend their positions as rulers serving on Spanish-styled indigenous cabildos. By drawing in the Audiencia, this case began a process that altered fundamentally the relationship between viceregal institutions and the indigenous cabildo of Mexico Tenochtitlan.

Three natives initiated the change by presenting the first petition and motions. Juan Daniel, a baker (*panadero*), Pedro Macías, a tailor (*sastre*), and Mateo Suárez, a reed carrier (*zacatero*), represented both artisans and manual laborers.[1] In the name of the native peoples of Mexico Tenochtitlan, the three solicited the assistance of the viceregal legal system to help them stop the abuse they allegedly suffered at the hands of their Spanish-styled indigenous government.[2] Importantly, the suit began with a direct challenge against the indigenous cabildo, alleging that, among other things, the principales, alcaldes, regidores, and gobernador had committed a series of impeachable offenses. As the case moved forward, however, it provoked the Audiencia to inquire into earlier complaints raised by the native peoples of Mexico Tenochtitlan. The initial petitions filed in 1564 touched off a lawsuit that looked backward to explore complaints since 1555. Diverse witnesses testified to issues ranging from idolatry to illegal use of *repartimiento* (drafted, rotational tribute labor) workers for personal service.

When examined closely, the evidence suggests that the litigants sought to create political change by discrediting the indigenous nobles who controlled the cabildo and represented a cohesive political bloc. Those who controlled the cabildo also had influence over the election of future leaders and, when the aging governor died in office, the authority to choose his successor. In addition, indigenous governments controlled patronage in the barrios of Mexico Tenochtitlan, the collection of tribute, and organization of labor drafts.[3] If indeed this was a political challenge, those behind this lawsuit indicated that they sought not to reform the system but rather to control the cabildo for their own purposes.

The 1564 lawsuit, unlike previous efforts, successfully engaged the Audiencia to respond. Earlier attempts had failed, probably because the Audiencia was reluctant to interfere in the jurisdiction of the indigenous government. Success in this instance touched off a serious inquiry led by the high court, which sought to determine whether the allegations made by the craftsmen had any basis and also to follow further complaints filed in the past that the viceregal courts had previously ignored. Implicitly this suit looked into the operation of Spanish-styled indigenous government in Mexico City. This lawsuit put great pressure on the sitting indigenous leaders, forcing the governor and cabildo members to prove that they represented good government. The suit also shows how indigenous groups experimented to determine how to challenge their government at the Audiencia, and once engaged how those groups learned to manipulate the court for political gain.

The cabildo of Mexico Tenochtitlan was a hybrid Spanish-indigenous institution made up of offices with Spanish titles held by elected indigenous nobles. The judge-governor led the cabildo, serving as its chief executive. Elected officers included regidores and alcaldes. The officials carried the staff of royal justice and had administrative and judicial duties.[4] Governors, like the tlatoque of precontact Mexico Tenochtitlan, served in the highest office, but the similarities appear to end there.[5] The Mexica Tenochca likely saw continuity with their past, when their governors were chosen from the proper royal lineage—the same lineage from which the precontact tlatoque were chosen. Spaniards

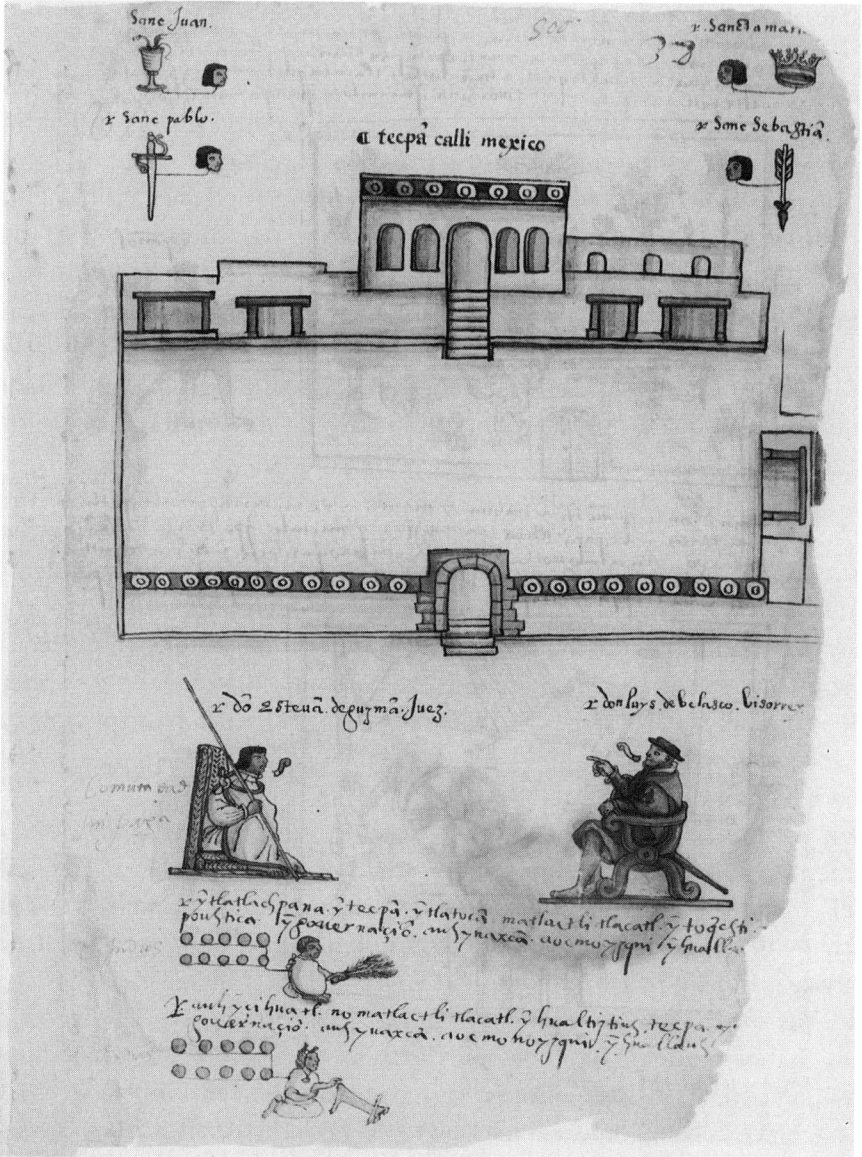

Tecpan cabildo, Mexico Tenochtitlan. From the *Pintura del Gobernador, alcaldes y regidores de México* (1565), fol. 38r. Reproduced with permission, © Biblioteca Nacional de España.

had their own model for the judge-governor and probably hoped that the restoration of the royal lineage would bring about order. Viceregal architects of the native cabildo, however, seem to have had in mind the *corregidor,* a more limited position than the tlatoani, when they imagined the judge-governor. Indeed, judge-governors were like corregidores in that they presided over town government but also had administrative duties apart from the cabildo. Corregidores were also intermediaries within the viceregal government, and outside of Mexico Tenochtitlan Spanish corregidores performed tasks similar to those of the judge-governors. They worked with native leaders to deliver tribute to the crown and took on the same personal financial responsibility for delivering it as the judge-governors in Mexico Tenochtitlan.[6] Governors also seem to have had great influence over the composition of the cabildo. Even though cabildo members were elected, the well-documented rotation system suggests that the governor, through patronage networks, could effectively select cabildo officers.

The purpose of the 1564 lawsuit was to engage the Audiencia in a struggle between competing indigenous groups, something the court seems to have been reluctant to do in the past.[7] The lawsuit identified specifically, though not directly by name, the judge-governor, alcaldes, regidores, and principales as objects of litigation. By choosing to accuse a specific group of leaders who monopolized the government, the plaintiffs targeted a cohesive political network. The conflict involved only native peoples and, despite the charges, related to exclusively internal issues. The Tenochca who engaged the Audiencia in 1564 succeeded where others had failed because they raised issues that seemed relevant, and sufficiently shocking, to merit the attention of the high court. The charges were different than earlier ones in that they addressed issues beyond the local concerns of indigenous government. Their outlandish nature, as it turned out, made them easy to dismiss on close inspection by the court, but it suggests that the point of filing the charges was to get the court's attention. Altogether, the features of the suit indicate that the plaintiffs purposefully and systematically— over the course of nearly a decade, though trial and error—worked to find ways to involve Spanish courts in the internal disputes of indigenous government, ultimately to resolve a political conflict.[8]

The political nature of the engagement, in which indigenous groups outside of the political process sought to challenge the sitting government, made it necessary to frame the complaints in a way that brought the Audiencia into the dispute yet made accusations exclusively against indigenous leaders—a more difficult challenge than it may seem on the surface. Forcing the Audiencia to intervene had to be done without making this case a protest against the viceregal government, even though the root cause of the problem may have been Spanish demands for indigenous tribute and labor. Suggestive of the sophistication of the plaintiffs, the allegations did not target the viceroy, encomenderos, or Spanish officials. Indigenous litigants may have won concessions through a civil suit against Spaniards. The political aims of the plaintiffs, however, required that they focus their attention on those who controlled the political cabildo.[9]

THE COMPLAINT

The three native people who filed the first petition to appear in the nearly 200-folio case file made a series of important allegations against the indigenous government. Some charges seem to have suggested that the cabildo violated indigenous customary practices. Others alleged that the cabildo's practices did not conform to Spanish law. Aided by legal professionals including Agustin Pinto, a *procurador* (legal counsel), and Diego Barrio de Vallejo, an *escribano* (legal scribe), the plaintiffs presented a sophisticated and compelling case illustrating that they understood what constituted good governance in both the Hispanic and indigenous worlds. In the end, their efforts had the potential to force the viceroy to remove the indigenous government.

The *interrogatorio* (legal questionnaire) included nineteen separate allegations against the government officers of the parcialidad of Mexico Tenochtitlan. The charges alleged that the cabildo members could not write or read—both requirements for holding office. It further noted that cabildo members lacked the proper character to hold office, stating that when holding public audiences they treated the people with rudeness and generally set a bad example. Legal disputes brought before the cabildo, they alleged, were heard only when litigants could pay, and judgments went only to those whose resources lasted longest.[10] Indigenous officials allegedly accepted bribes of money and wine.[11] They also used their positions of authority to consort with the women of the community in *temascales* (steambath houses; Nahuatl: *temazcalli*), where they set a bad example.[12] The principales, regidores, and alcaldes, supposedly respectable men, sheltered "thieves and miscreants" for their own benefit and allowed illegal taverns to operate, accepting gifts from the tavern owners and "criminals" instead of bringing them to justice.[13]

The alleged abuses also involved religious practices. The petitioners claimed that indigenous leaders tolerated idolatry, covered up evidence of ritual sacrifices by labeling them "natural deaths," and attempted to reintroduce ceremonial burial practices for the wealthy dead.[14] Ostensibly the latter enabled them to extort fees from wealthy residents who may also have demanded such services to conform with Nahua cultural practice.[15] In addition, the charges alleged that cabildo members took advantage of their position to exact gifts and favors and visited the families of the recently dead "to eat and drink as was customary [*uso y costumbre*] in the last century [i.e., before the Spaniards arrived]."[16]

The petitions charged that officials of the cabildo abused their positions as able stewards of the public trust. They made indigenous peoples from Mexico Tenochtitlan serve in the houses of Spaniards and work in the employ of enterprising Spaniards without pay. Out of sheer greed, the indigenous government allegedly raided the community treasury (*caja de comunidad*), using its resources for their personal expenses rather than for the benefit of the community.[17] The plaintiffs alleged that the cabildo regularly held secret meetings, presumably with residents of the city under the cover of darkness in the early hours after midnight (*madrugada*), where they conducted secret business and collected illegal fees in cash, cacao, and firewood. The charges, a catalog of abuses that questioned the integrity of indigenous officials, if proved should have provoked a serious response.[18] Furthermore, the allegations emanated from a group (the macehualtin) who apparently had no voice in the political world of Mexico and whom the paternalistic crown saw the need to protect.

To support their allegations, five witnesses testified in the interrogatorio. Each witness required the services of interpreter Juan Grande.

Only one witness who testified on behalf of the plaintiffs identified himself as a noble (*principal*), don Francisco Jiménez, a resident of the city from the barrio of San Sebastián. The others who testified offered little in the way of descriptive information beyond their need for a translator. Alonso de San Francisco, who testified first, was fifty-five years old. None of the others gave their ages or provided any other general descriptions in regard to occupation or status. None signed his name; only the escribano and interpreter signed the testimony. The testimony took place over several months, beginning in March 1564 and ending on 10 July 1564. As expected, the witnesses generally supported the allegations made by the craftsmen.[19]

The indigenous petitioners found in the Spanish judicial bureaucracy an eager audience, ready to hear their grievances.[20] On the basis of the testimony by witnesses who supported the charges, the high court oidor, in this case don Pedro de Villalobos, issued an order that threatened the arrest of the entire cabildo on the basis that they "appeared guilty."[21] The order—directed at the sitting governor, don Luis de Santa María, two alcaldes, and twelve regidores—made clear that the allegations against the cabildo had substance. It also demonstrated Spanish legal paternalism in Mexico City. The indigenous craftsmen who filed the suit must have taken this as an encouraging sign that they had made their case well. They provided compelling evidence that indigenous leaders had abused their authority. The high court order also suggests that Spanish courts sought to defend the rights of those generally perceived as weak. Courts struggled to live up to this standard. Latching onto a case like this gave the Audiencia an opportunity to establish its legitimacy further.[22]

Indigenous leaders under threat of arrest found motivation to respond with vigor. This threat gave Spanish institutions leverage to intervene in the affairs of indigenous government. The high court used this case as an opportunity to limit the authority of indigenous rulers over their subjects. Though driven by indigenous litigation, such an intervention suggests an erosion of indigenous autonomy that continued through the seventeenth century. It led to the promotion of Spanish institutions, which gained legitimacy through their ability to dispense justice.[23] Over the next 150 years, the court continued to take such opportunities to define its authority over indigenous governments.

THE CABILDO RESPONDS

The leaders of Mexico Tenochtitlan responded through a Spanish procurador from the Audiencia, Juan Caro. In their defense, Caro wrote an extensive petition that attacked the list of charges individually, focusing first on the character of the plaintiffs. He followed this with a detailed interrogatorio designed to provide sworn evidence to support the argument contained in his petition. Caro argued that the plaintiffs bore personal grudges against the cabildo. Lacking honor, they sought to involve the courts in private matters. No substance or legitimacy underlay their complaints. He attempted to expose flaws in the character of his accusers, stating, "Those who presented the said charges, made them to satisfy their individual *passions and ambitions*, like vile common people . . . of poor customs, [who] are seditious and look to create scandal: [they are] womanizers and drunks who have been punished many times by justices [my clients] for their abominable crimes."[24] Caro attempted to reduce the plaintiff's claims to vendetta. The common people of Mexico Tenochtitlan had suffered no abuse. The plaintiffs had brought charges in the name of the macehualtin to gain sympathy for their real purpose—to settle personal scores with the loyal and honorable members of the indigenous cabildo. The cabildo, according to Caro, acted only to execute the duties that the crown had empowered it to perform. The discontent came from men of low character, whom the indigenous cabildo had nobly tried to control and punish.

In this opening petition Caro also acknowledged subtly the political nature of the challenge. Without providing specific details, he suggested that the plaintiffs had certain individual "passions and ambitions" that motivated them disingenuously to press their claims in the name of the common people. He also implied that the plaintiffs presented their cause as derivative of the people to gain political advantage over his clients. The presence of one principal among the witnesses, though not mentioned specifically by Caro, may have also led him to conclude that a larger political agenda lay behind this suit. Evidently with a purpose in mind, Caro contrasted his clients' noble credentials and right to rule with those of the plaintiffs. He emphasized, promoting their status and credentials, that his clients were "and had always been from the nobility" and thus had the right to hold "offices of the republic."[25] Caro thus suggested implicitly that the accusers did not have such credentials. In a carefully constructed legal document the procurador mentioned only details germane to the case. If Caro did not believe the plaintiffs sought ultimately the offices on the cabildo, it seems unlikely that he would have expended such great effort to point out that they had no right to occupy those offices.

Caro cleverly framed his responses to gain advantage with the Audiencia. To Caro, and likely to those whom he represented, this case was not a vote of no-confidence from the subjects of Mexico Tenochtitlan but instead treason against the king by a small group of rabble-rousers. The court should, he argued, dismiss out of hand the complaints of the plaintiffs and "punish them for rebellion and sedition." This small group who accused the "said governor and alcaldes bore false witness and made false accusations with no regard for the law but with malice founded on wickedness [*mal celo*]." Those who accused the virtuous indigenous government did so out of a desire to provoke "conflict and scandal," and in the guise of asking for justice the macehualtin accusers in reality sought only "injustice for reasons of malice."[26] Caro knew that Spaniards in positions of authority revered stability but also feared and anticipated indigenous rebellion. He sculpted his arguments so that the courts would perceive his clients as forces of justice and stability. Any effort to aid the seemingly aggrieved parties, the plaintiffs, would put royal institutions in consort with common rebels.[27] Caro's clever argument countered the plaintiff's appeal for paternalism with an argument designed to compel viceregal officials to follow the royal mandate to preserve order and good government.

Caro did not specifically deny all the charges leveled against his clients; some he acknowledged, adding explanations in exoneration. To the claims that the indigenous rulers could not read or write, he argued that despite this flaw they were still capable administrators, and no different from many illiterate or semiliterate Spanish officials. Many of them could write their names quite well and demonstrated their ability in the documents by signing with a flourishing rubric.[28] He answered the charge that the cabildo members bathed in public baths with women of the community, incredulously claiming that they bathed only for reasons of health, "without giving offense, with decency and honesty and without generating scandal or bad example."[29] In other instances Caro denied the charges flatly, characterizing them as egregious. The cabildo did not, he stated, confiscate property illegally for the private benefit of its members.[30] Caro also denied the allegation that the indigenous cabildo extorted money from citizens during ceremonial occasions such as weddings and funerals. When officials of the cabildo attended such events, Caro argued, they did so only "to give honor to the citizens." At such events, he continued, the said members of the cabildo did not eat or drink.[31] Caro attempted to persuade the court that a dishonorable cast of scoundrels tried to smear his honorable clients, who had done nothing inappropriate. Furthermore, the cabildo acted for the benefit of members of the community in the interest of performing ceremonial duties that citizens expected.

The interrogatorio that followed this petition provided a series of questions posed to witnesses selected by the cabildo. Its purpose was to provide evidence in the form of sworn testimony to support the arguments offered by Caro. As expected, the witnesses backed the claims without revision.[32] They also portrayed the plaintiffs as men of low character bent on revenge. Caro crafted questions to answer the specific charges brought against the cabildo, but he also tried to reduce the complaints made by the plaintiffs to self-interested slander designed to empower and enrich individual opportunists at the expense of the indigenous authorities.

Caro chose witnesses that made it more difficult for the plaintiffs to claim that their complaints originated with the common people. The nine witnesses represented a broad spectrum of the population. Three—don Antonio de Santiago, Juan de San Miguel, and Graviel Bonifacio—described themselves as principales. The remaining six— Miguel Melchior, Martín de la Cruz, Cristóbal Tlacuxialcalt, Gaspar de Aquino, Juan Daniel (likely not the same one mentioned above as a plaintiff), and Miguel de Santiago—came from seemingly more humble backgrounds.[33] The second group of witnesses did not volunteer their occupations or provide direct statements that might clarify their social and economic status. Significantly, the second, seemingly more quotidian group of six testified on the same day, several days after the first three principales. Only one of the six nonnoble witnesses, Miguel Melchior, could sign his name.[34] Their ages, the only concrete details provided about their identities, may have been relevant to their selection. Aged forty-two to sixty-two, even the youngest of this group had lived longer than most in sixteenth-century Mexico City.[35] The older witnesses did not have noble credentials, but likely they had special knowledge of past events, including an understanding of precontact indigenous government. It is also possible they had special status in the community because of their age.[36] The non-principales who could not sign have left little obvious evidence about their status.[37] Perhaps the diversity of this group, and its apparent commoner roots, represented a strategy on the part of the cabildo: although the plaintiffs claimed to represent the macehualtin, not everyone of this status agreed with the charges. The cabildo offered six witnesses whose apparent plebeian roots allowed them to testify credibly that they had experienced only "good government" from the cabildo. They also knew and had seen directly or had heard that the plaintiffs were "rowdy upstarts who looked to create scandal."[38]

REMEMBERING REBELLION IN MEXICO TENOCHTITLAN

The cabildo responded thoroughly, in part provoked by the threat of arrest. They sought to clarify in unambiguous terms that they had done nothing illegal and that those who accused them lacked character and status. They purposefully alleged that their accusers, by bringing the charges, sought to inspire rebellion. Raising the specter of rebellion may have been a ploy by the cabildo to curry the favor of the Spanish courts by playing on the fears of native rebellion. Casting the complaints as an attempted rebellion may have served to cast the plaintiffs further as accusers who sought to create a disruption to the peace. Only scoundrels bent on causing disorder would stoke the flames of rebellion.[39] Invoking rebellion also suggests that the cabildo may have realized that Spanish courts would respond to their case once they had planted the seed.[40] Yet rebellion resonated in important and similar ways in the political traditions of both Spaniards and Nahua.

Factions within both European and indigenous government traditions sometimes used rebellion to resolve serious political disputes. The

Trastamara dynasty came to power when Enrique II (r. 1369–79) seized the Castilian throne in the fourteenth century. Though he is remembered as a regicide who started a civil war in Castile, his descendants ruled until 1700.[41] Isabel I (r. 1474–1504), who descended from Enrique II, along with her husband Fernando, from Aragón (r. 1479–1516), established their authority through rebellion and civil war in the fifteenth century, relying on the backing of the Mendoza clan for political support to defeat Isabel's half brother, Enrique IV (r. 1454–74).[42] A political challenge that also presented the possibility of a military uprising would not have been unusual or unexpected for Iberians.

Political actors in Mexico Tenochtitlan also had profound experience with rebellion as a challenge to the authority of the tlatoque before 1519. Rebellion or the threat of disorder was an element of political discourse for the Mexica Tenochca.[43] In the context of precontact Mexico Tenochtitlan, rebellion sometimes accompanied periods of uncertain succession. Itzcoatzin (r. 1426–40) became the tlatoani of Tenochtitlan after the death of Chimalpopoca (r. 1415–26). As the uncle of the former tlatoani, Itzcoatzin was not the next in line for succession; an uncle should not have succeeded his nephew. The unusual and untimely death of Chimalpopoca, which happened during a moment in which the Tepanecs threatened Tenochtitlan and other altepetl in the Basin, created a political crisis for the Tenochca. Playing this situation well, Tenochca leaders used the disorder to ally with Tlacopan and Tetzcoco to form the triple alliance against Azcapotzalco, the Tepanec imperial capital and dominant imperial group in the early fifteenth century.[44]

The complex details of political intrigue have caused some confusion in interpretation among the many sources that consider these events.[45] According to Rounds, Chimalpahin wrote that Itzcoatzin and Moteucçoma Ilhuicamina (r. 1440–68) conspired to kill Chimalpopoca and to install themselves as tlatoque. They were quite successful in this account largely because they blamed the murder on Maxtlatzin, the tlatoani of Azcapotzalco, and subsequently used this alleged treachery to wage war on their neighbors. Other accounts, including the most recent work on Chimalpahin, however, offer a more plausible version that Chimalpopoca was murdered by agents of the Tepanec empire, which fostered the alliance between Mexico Tenochtitlan and Tetzcoco, whose leaders had also suffered under the Tepanecs.[46]

Tenochca politics in the fifteenth and sixteenth centuries occasionally generated violence internally and externally. The most dangerous moments for internal political disputes, however, came when tlatoani succession was unclear. Such uncertainty had the potential to create regional warfare not unlike the political struggles in Iberia. Internal struggles also created conflict by encouraging even those with distant claims to rulership to vie for the highest office. The Tenochca, because of the structure of their complex altepetl, chose the best candidate from among a small group who had the right to rule. Brothers of the tlatoani generally succeeded before the next generation of sons. But the Tenochca needed a ruler who had the necessary political and military skill to survive in the sometimes hostile Basin, so they chose the most capable candidate from among a group of contenders within a very specific royal line. With each passing ruler, this system created the possibility of disorder as the number of legitimate candidates multiplied. Though the system theoretically was designed to create stability through the selection of the best candidate, passed-over candidates sometimes disagreed with the wisdom of electors. Defeated candidates sometimes rebelled, resulting in bloody internal power struggles.[47]

In suggesting that the plaintiffs had no legal right to occupy positions on the cabildo, Caro seems to make the argument implicitly that the plaintiffs sued to win control of the cabildo. If this is so, his assertions may indicate that he suspected a political rebellion rather than a violent uprising. Because of their political traditions, both the Mexica Tenochca and the Iberians might have understood the challenge presented by the plaintiffs as a political one. In both traditions danger accompanied political succession at the highest level and, in 1564, Governor Santa María was nearing the end of his life. For the heirs of the Tenochca, the memory of disruptive political succession likely remained fresh or survived in their historical memory. Witnesses brought by Caro, many of whom knew firsthand about the political world of Mexico Tenochtitlan, understood the challenge by the plaintiffs. Rebellion on the part of the plaintiffs, though it also motivated the viceregal government to respond, had meaning in the indigenous world and represented a legitimate means to challenge the political authority of the ruler.[48]

The political culture of Mexico Tenochtitlan had apparently lost its violent edge by the middle of the sixteenth century, but problems of political succession continued to characterize early transitions between governors.[49] The endurance of precontact ideas of political succession influenced how native peoples moved to manipulate the transitions between rulers. Indigenous leaders throughout the sixteenth century drew on precontact indigenous political traditions. Many had direct memory of precontact political succession or had learned how to be political from mentors who had lived before the Spanish invasion. Succession for the heirs of the Tenochca first set into motion the process of coalition building. Electors in precontact Mexico Tenochtitlan weighed politically their decisions to support specific candidates. They formed coalitions to support an heir to the highest office well in advance of the death of the tlatoani. Resonances of this practice survived into the colonial period.

By 1564, when the initial petition began the case that opens this chapter, or perhaps even earlier, many knew that the electors of Mexico Tenochtitlan would have difficulty choosing a successor to don Luis de Santa María.[50] Indeed, the electors apparently failed to choose a successor from within the royal lineage. Chimalpahin recognized the problem nearly half a century later: "It was 45 years ago in the year 8 house, 1565, that the lord don Luis de Santa María Nacacipactzin, ruler in Tenochtitlan, passed away . . . and with him it came to an end that descendants of the Mexica and Tenochca rulers should rule in Tenochtitlan any more; at that time their governing as rulers was cut off forever."[51] Though it is unclear what mechanism brought to an end the royal lineage in Mexico Tenochtitlan, the political maneuvering manifest in the civil suit of 1564 may reflect a group of political actors preparing for the coming succession crisis. Many electors who had direct knowledge of the political system of independent Mexico Tenochtitlan probably fell back on traditional political culture in the absence of a clear method outlined by the rules governing succession in the Spanish-styled cabildo.[52] Principales who participated in the lawsuit against the sitting cabildo could thus have gained political advantage by challenging the cohort of principales and officeholders who had the capacity to choose the next governor.

The appointment of don Francisco Jiménez as interim ruler in Tenochtitlan ended the legal challenges brought by the macehualtin of Mexico Tenochtitlan.[53] He apparently took this office because the electors of Mexico Tenochtitlan found no viable successor for Santa María within the royal line. Appointed as a judge only, Jiménez seemed to occupy the position provisionally like the quauhtlatoque (see introduction) had done.[54] An outsider from Tecamachalco (near Puebla de los Angeles), Jiménez filled the office of governor for five years between 1568 and 1573, without apparently holding the title of judge-governor.[55] This followed a three-year period of uncertainty when no governor sat in Mexico Tenochtitlan. Mexico City, more broadly, was in a kind of political transition in the 1560s, and political challenges also appeared among Spaniards. Chimalpahin reported that officials foiled an uprising attempted by Alonso de Avila and Gil González de Alvarado and noted their executions in 1566. Nineteen others were imprisoned and two additional participants were beheaded in 1568 in connection with this uprising.[56] In the midst of such turmoil, Mexico Tenochtitlan could find no suitable ruler, and eight years passed between the death of Santa María and the seating of the next regular governor, who stayed in office for nearly the remainder of his life, don Antonio Valeriano (the elder, r. 1573–99).[57]

The interim governorship served the Mexica Tenochca well and replicated another political tradition that has its origins in Mexico Tenochtitlan. The eight-year interregnum, however, was the longest since the conquest era and much longer than the previous hiatus in which don Esteban de Guzmán (r. 1554–57) held the office of de facto governor. Spanish law, though it encouraged litigation through royal institutions to mitigate violence during succession, did not dictate to the Tenochca how to choose successors but rather left such matters to local custom and tradition.[58] Indigenous leaders behind the 1564 lawsuit who had at stake their political futures sought to control the process by engaging the Spanish courts. Such courts had the ability to award them advantages in the face of the looming uncertainty promised by the coming succession crisis. In the immediate term, however, neither the plaintiffs nor the defendants seemed to emerge with a clear advantage from this initial exchange.

A NEW BEGINNING

Despite its apparent ineffectiveness—the initial phase of the lawsuit stalled after Caro's response—other litigants engaged the Audiencia anew in a long-standing conflict between the citizens of Mexico Tenochtitlan and the current ruling cadre who controlled the cabildo. Apart from frightening the cabildo and governor through threatened imprisonment and forcing their legal counsel to produce a long defense of its actions, the initial phase of the lawsuit seems to have had little real effect. It did, however, engage the high court in the indigenous dispute. In the long term, it also made relevant a whole series of petitions previously filed against the cabildo and ignored. The Audiencia, after reviewing the 1564 complaint, considered the earlier petitions. Though the cabildo's response suggested that an isolated group of disgruntled subjects who lacked character brought the charges for personal reasons, the subsequent litigants revealed to the Audiencia a far larger problem. After 1564 the Audiencia received petitions that asked the courts to consider broader and more substantive issues that it had ignored for more than a decade.

In 1565, Toribio Lucas, Miguel García, Martín Vázquez, and Domingo Hernández, all literate native peoples from the barrio of San Pablo in the parcialidad of Mexico Tenochtitlan, offered a more elaborate series of charges that alleged systematic abuse endured by the community since the regency of judge don Esteban de Guzmán.[59] In their petition they stated, "The governors of Mexico Tenochtitlan . . . and the holders of the offices of alcalde and *mayordomo* whose charge it has been to administer justice and to govern us . . . have assessed many and excessive tributes well above the standard level/rate [*tazación*] we are obligated."[60] The charges against the cabildo in this new petition resonate only tangentially with those of 1564. In addition to the claim that the cabildo charged excessive tribute, the plaintiffs alleged that for more than a decade it had not paid suppliers properly for procuring materials used in construction projects. A complicated issue lay at the center of the dispute. The plaintiffs, supported by reason and the law, argued that the cabildo had to pay repartimiento workers for the cost of construction materials they brought into the city in addition to their daily wage. Substantial supporting documentation in the form of *memorias*, annual written accounts listing the value and volume of the materials brought into the city for the years 1554–65, accompanied the new petitions. The memorias appear to list obligations for which the cabildo had not compensated the workers.[61] Native witnesses testified to support the memorias, adding detail and sworn support to the written allegations.

The cabildo should have had the funds to pay for the work. In practice, the community treasury (*caja de comunidad*) should have set aside funds collected from tribute payments to pay repartimiento workers for their labor and materials. Because the plaintiffs' testimonies and memorias suggested otherwise, the charges indicate that the cabildo had taken the community funds designated to pay for public work. The plaintiffs supported the serious allegation of corruption with solid evidence in the form of petitions, legal complaints, and testimony in a way that forced the Audiencia to act.

Administrative malfeasance of such a high order coupled with exacting and meticulous evidence properly sworn and ratified meant that the indigenous cabildo had to counter the allegations with an equally strong response. The cabildo did this first by producing evidence that seemed to confirm the allegations made by the plaintiffs. The cabildo produced two judgments, one from 1556 and a second from 1557, in which the oidores of the Audiencia asked judge don Esteban de Guzmán as well as indigenous governor don Cristóbal de Guzmán (r. 1557–62) to pay repartimiento workers properly for their service.[62] The judgments seem to make credible the complaints by the repartimiento laborers and also provide an instance where the Audiencia had forced the indigenous cabildo to pay significant sums to native workers for their labor. The cabildo, however, used the judgments to show that they had complied with the orders of the Audiencia, thus undermining the complaints of the plaintiffs. As to the remaining charges, the judgments provided few answers and the native workers continued to press their case.

For nearly a decade after the 1557 judgment, the cabildo and Audiencia had ignored the complaints of repartimiento workers. Between 1558 and 1565 the repartimiento workers filed numerous petitions but received no reply or acknowledgment from the various cabildos.

The Audiencia likewise did nothing to force the cabildo to respond. The palpable frustration from repartimiento laborers must have grown as their cabildo continued to demand labor and by their estimation refused to pay them even the cut-rate compensation owed repartimiento workers.[63] Given the lack of response, the petitioners apparently experimented with numerous rhetorical strategies designed to engage the Audiencia and cabildo. In an important petition in 1561, they complained: "We, the native peoples of the four barrios of Mexico, say that we have been abused and mistreated many times by the said governor, regidores, and alcaldes who ask of us tributes that we have already paid and other such abuses as we have repeatedly argued in many petitions to Your Excellency before our oidor, but they have not given us what we justly ask for."[64]

By 1561, litigants showed that they had made their case many times and complained legitimately that their government abused them. All of this continued with no response, despite repeated efforts. Subsequently petitioners asked for more extreme measures to have their complaints heard fairly. They made the case explicitly, apparently because the Audiencia refused to respond, that the viceregal institution did not have the capacity to provide a fair and impartial judgment. Seeming to goad the Audiencia into action, the plaintiffs asked for an external review of the evidence they had presented. They alleged that only collusion between the high court and the cabildo could have defeated their just arguments. The petition offered a potential solution to resolve the apparent conflict of interest by asking that the Audiencia appoint two judges, "one from the outside [*fuera de aquí*] and the other a native [*natural*] in order that justice might be served and that nothing [was] suborned or perjured."[65] Even a brazen allegation of malfeasance presented in 1561, however, produced no response from the cabildo. The Audiencia similarly made no effort to provide an external judicial review. No indigenous justices gave their opinions on the merits of the petitioners' claims, and no outside justice from another court read their petitions.

Trial and experimentation did, however, eventually pay off for those who sought to engage the attention of the Audiencia. Even though for seven years repartimiento workers repeatedly made accusations using a variety of tactics, the petitions did nothing to engage the viceregal courts. The petition and interrogatorio from 1564, which alleged idolatry, ritual activity, abuse of authority, and various other forms of misconduct, finally forced the Audiencia and cabildo to respond. The renewed engagement reopened the older disputes. Clearly the indigenous peoples of Mexico Tenochtitlan had learned strategies to engage the courts. Such education in the short term let their grievances be heard. The long-term implications, however, suggest that they learned how to integrate themselves into the political affairs of their town.

THE POLITICAL CABILDO

Challenges to the cabildo and governor, despite the seeming inattention paid to them, had the potential to undermine the patronage system that concentrated authority in the hands of the judge-governor. Politically, a governor ruled indefinitely, augmented by a cabildo largely composed of his clients legitimized through an electoral process. While the royal line persisted, governors drew their legitimacy from precontact tradition. Governors and other powerful indigenous agents helped to elect cabildos of their choosing. Elected annually, the cabildos consisted of fourteen officers.[66] Frequent elections and restrictions on immediate reelection meant that during a ten-year period a large group of individuals should have served on the cabildo. Yet, through a system of rotation, important and powerful cabildo officers regularly cycled through different offices and thus maintained their presence in the body in a predictable and regular system, despite the restrictions imposed by Spanish law.[67]

Governors probably used the rotation system to distribute patronage to supporters. The leaders of Mexico Tenochtitlan faced a major problem adapting to the new Spanish-styled indigenous government introduced in the early sixteenth century. The parcialidad consisted of four large subdivisions whose leaders all expected representation on the cabildo in the most important position, alcalde. The Spanish system of town government, however, provided for only two alcalde positions. To accommodate indigenous practice, indigenous leaders utilized a rotation system that ensured that each of the four subdivisions within the altepetl held the position of alcalde in alternate years.

The cabildos, made up of indigenous nobles, ruled Mexico Tenochtitlan as one stable homogenous group that endured for long stretches of time. Though Gibson argues persuasively that the practice of rotation served to minimize conflict by allowing for representation as alcalde from each of the four subdivisions, stability in the office of governor (whose occupant ruled until death and who served unaffected by the annual elections directly) made it possible to manipulate the small electorate and enabled a small group of indigenous nobles to control the rotation.[68] The cabildo rotation cycles show that the very same members elected between 1555 and 1564, the decade at the center of the political dispute under discussion, remained in some indigenous office for the entire period, even though a new cabildo was elected each year. The ability to represent specific factions and constituencies on the cabildo in a regular rotation pattern also indicates that someone had the ability to control elections. The two-year rotational cycles studied by Gibson allowed San Pablo and San Juan Moyotlan to hold the alcalde seats one year and Santa María la Redonda and San Sebastián to hold the offices in the subsequent year.[69] An "annual alternation" thus occurred. Such a systematic redistribution of offices could not happen without manipulation.[70]

Particularly well connected officials occupied many positions while they waited their turn at alcalde. Martín Cano appeared consistently in the documentation generated about the indigenous cabildo of Mexico Tenochtitlan. Cano held the office of alcalde in 1558 and 1562. In 1564 he became a regidor. Though piecing together the careers of individuals can be an uncertain and difficult task, some evidence indicates that he held other minor posts in the community, such as *alguacil* (constable), in the years when he did not hold a seat on the cabildo.[71] In addition, Cano performed tasks for the indigenous government, including serving as a witness for indigenous wills.[72] In other words, even when he did not hold an office, he had some duty that kept him involved in the ordinary workings of the cabildo of Mexico Tenochtitlan. Other indigenous principales practiced career strategies similar to that of Martín Cano. For example, Pedro de la

Cruz Tlapaltecatl, a principal from San Juan Moyotlan, served as alcalde in 1553, 1558, and 1562 and as regidor in 1556.[73]

The office of alcalde provides an interesting demonstration of the manipulated character of cabildo elections, but it appears that individuals who rotated off the cabildo could continue to serve in some less-visible capacity. Later, in the seventeenth century, ex-officials continued to occupy prominent places in indigenous society, using their former service as a means of establishing their credibility. Such figures often appear in legal documents with their title followed by *pasado* ("in the past").[74] It is also worth noting that the Spanish titles that accompanied cabildo offices may have had a different meaning for native officials. Whatever the title, powerful clients of the governor probably continued to exercise authority beyond their offices. Perhaps the elections were to show the Audiencia compliance that masked a different political culture.

The governor likely had the capacity to orchestrate cabildo elections. When legitimate and in office for life, he could also distribute patronage. Accordingly, he held together an elaborate system engineered to guarantee the election of his clients, year in and year out. The highest office must therefore have been a sought-after prize.[75] Apparently no official inquiry ever investigated the process of election manipulation that empowered governors to exercise control over cabildo composition. Expecting one, however, assumes that the Audiencia or those who challenged the cabildo would have found such practices unusual or illicit.[76] Though the absence of such evidence does not indicate that all found the practice acceptable, it would be reasonable to expect the complaint to have been included in the catalog of abuses amassed between 1555 and 1564. Patronage likely explains why indigenous leaders competed forcefully for the governorship.[77] Controlling a political cabildo created opportunity. Those who did challenge the cabildo and its electors did so to wrest control from one political bloc that controlled elections, but doing so makes sense only if they wished to replace them with a different political network. Such an effort constituted a political challenge so that the challengers too could enjoy direct control over the political cabildo through the legal framework of the viceregal government.

Cabildo manipulations appear outside of office rotation. In the 1564 complaint and interrogatorio discussed above, a small group of powerful officials loyal to the sitting governor worked to determine the outcome of the cabildo ahead of the election. Though the craftsmen, making an obviously overstated case in their complaint, do not offer the most objective perspective, their words provide insight into how the process may have worked: "It is customary and usual each year when it is time to elect new alcaldes and regidores and alguaciles for the alcaldes and regidores to choose candidates from among themselves in secret without entering into the cabildo . . . and to conceal their actions."[78] From this allegation, the plaintiffs appear to indicate that secrecy and collusion produced a slate of candidates that the electoral process legitimated. Though it is plausible that the litigants saw only hints of something illicit, they offered testimony from one elector who supported and added detail to the allegation. Don Francisco Jiménez (principal from San Sebastián, not the interim ruler in 1568), who had the right to vote in cabildo elections, said in response to the craftsmen's statement that, beyond the collusion suggested by the question, alcaldes and regidores solicited votes for candidates who had not yet received a nomination before the election took place.[79] Were there no collusion, how could the alcaldes and regidores know who would stand for election, Jiménez argued. Though their investigative reach was limited, the craftsmen who filed the complaint probably witnessed indigenous officials from the barrios making rounds. Jiménez seems to have based his comments on personal experience. Beyond such observations, however, the craftsmen would not have had access to or seen any other aspect of the process. The uncertainty expressed by the allegations suggests that members of the community saw only a very small part of an elaborate, complex, and ultimately secret system for choosing and then electing officials.[80]

To understand the challenge requires the consideration of the plaintiffs' motive and rationale for sculpting the particular suit with the specific arguments. Ultimately, it seems they could have denounced the hybrid system of indigenous self-government as corrupt. They did not, even though such a position may have enhanced their case before the Audiencia. Removing the current officeholders who monopolized the selection process would, however, make it possible for the challengers to win control of the cabildo. Indigenous noblemen who participated in the suit stood to gain considerably should they acquire additional leverage over indigenous elections. Most important, however, to gain authority and position within the political climate of Mexico Tenochtitlan required a preservation of the current order without disruption of anything other than the people who sat on the cabildo and controlled the selection process.

A second and equally important feature of indigenous politics also requires consideration—the tightly controlled succession of the governor, who then had great influence over the election of the cabildo as well. After the death of don Diego de San Francisco Tehuetzquititzin (r. 1541–54), an interruption occurred in the regular succession of governors. Perhaps, though the evidence is fragmentary, the fraternal line ended.[81] Whatever the circumstance that made it difficult to choose a successor, the process took three years. An interim leader, don Esteban de Guzmán from Xochimilco, served as a judge only, meaning that for three years Mexico Tenochtitlan had no governor. This period of uncertainty lasted until 1557 when the viceroy appointed, on the recommendation of indigenous electors, don Cristóbal de Guzmán Cecetzin, the son of former governor don Diego de Alvarado Huanitzin (r. 1538–41).[82] Whatever happened to make it difficult to replace the governor remains uncertain. Chimalpahin provides no clue, reflecting only on the succession and saying nothing of the politics. The Codex Telleriano-Remensis, though chronicling this period, has nothing specific to say about the succession either.[83] Don Cristóbal de Guzmán's claim to the highest office, based on what we know of precontact Tenochca succession patterns, likely resulted from negotiation. Several possibilities might explain the length of the process. It is possible that Cecetzin was the best candidate for governor universally agreed on by all involved but had not yet reached the age of majority. Yet, including the many sons of Huanitzin (of whom, Cecetzin was apparently the oldest), the four male children of Tehuetzquititzin also stood to serve as well.[84] According to Chimalpahin, who did not have much to say specifically about succession, primogeniture did not exist among the Nahua; rather, they chose or elected the best candidate from among a group of contenders. Although he reports the succession of individuals in precontact Mexico Tenochtitlan, Chimalpahin does not comment on the birth order of those who became tlatoque. He does state that in some instances tlatoque actively engaged in campaigns for themselves to seek the office. Thus, we can assume that a selection process existed in the precontact altepetl and that some chose to campaign actively by soliciting the support of electors.[85] The apparently smooth succession likely covered a messy and long process that ultimately resulted in the choice of this particular son of Huanitzin. It also suggests the presence of other contenders with legitimate claims to the governorship.[86]

In filing their lawsuit in 1564, the plaintiffs may therefore have been engaging in an overtly political maneuver designed to remove those who controlled the nomination process. By eliminating contenders, they could win a victory over an entrenched bloc of officials who could not be defeated in an election. The rotation system, proposed by Gibson as limiting conflict, presumably also excluded a large number of eligible native peoples from such offices. To remove a ruling cadre, therefore, native peoples had to discredit those who controlled the cabildo and the elections—ultimately those who secretly chose the candidates and solicited support on their behalf. The pattern seems to resemble the succession strategies that appear in better-documented form in the seventeenth and eighteenth centuries. It also appears to resemble indigenous political practices that persisted from the precontact period, adapted innovatively to fit the colonial context. Native peoples had already begun to develop the political strategies that involved soliciting the aid of Spanish institutions to resolve conflicts among different factions of the indigenous population.[87]

AN EXPANDING COMPLAINT

The original petitions filed by the craftsmen of Mexico Tenochtitlan made serious allegations without any real corroborating evidence beyond the sworn testimony of witnesses. The second phase of the suit had more physical evidence. The allegations that the cabildo did not pay repartimiento laborers generated documentation. In addition, scores of witnesses, the victims of abuse, had real stories to tell in testimony to support the allegations.[88] To counter such evidence, the cabildo also needed to supply physical evidence. They could not deny their role plausibly without firm proof. In unambiguous terms, viceregal orders confirm that the indigenous government had to pay repartimiento laborers a wage for their service and compensate them for their expenses. One order makes clear that repartimiento laborers could not be drafted if they "live[ed] more than ten leagues from the city." Furthermore, because they worked in the service of the king, the laborers "must be paid for their work at a [daily] rate of one real and a half for craftsmen and three quarters of a real for unskilled workers."[89] Together, the documents used to authorize the drafting of workers (*llamamiento*) and the testimony of laborers who had not received payment offer a clear denunciation of wrongdoing on the part of the cabildo.[90]

After the transition of the suit from the initial complaint brought by Macías, Suárez, and Daniel, the issue of overwork and low or no pay became the central complaint. The plaintiffs raised the stakes of this legal battle but in pursuit of the same purpose—to dislodge the sitting government for violating the rights of its subjects. The plaintiffs argued that indigenous leaders had reclaimed their rights to collect tribute as though they were the ancient lords of Mexico Tenochtitlan who reaped the benefit of the surplus labor of conquered peoples of the Basin of Mexico without compensating them for their work or paying for the supplies they brought into town. Specifically, the lawsuit alleged that the indigenous cabildo forced indigenous workers to build public buildings, including the tecpan, and to repair others already built.[91] Indigenous cabildo members also forced the macehualtin to work on the completion of the complex system of water supply and drainage, especially important after the flood of 1555.[92]

The allegations spell out broad, systematic, and widespread abuse that involved native peoples and Spaniards. The abuses look like a kind of organized extortion. Petitions charged that indigenous workers purchased or worked to gather supplies for the labor performed for civic construction. They argued specifically that the alcaldes, regidores, and gobernador of Mexico Tenochtitlan had "forced [them] to pay excessive tribute apart from that which [they] owed, made [them] bring into [Mexico City] lime, sod, stone, adobe, support beams, wood, and other building materials, and to work for them [the indigenous government] without payment."[93] To further support their claims that no payment had taken place, the macehualtin petitioners provided testimony from the workers themselves, who stated succinctly that the indigenous cabildo had failed to pay for their labor or expenses. The laborers' statements provide individual accounts of the alleged misdeeds of the cabildo. One witness, an eighteen-year-old native person, Gabriel Jacobo, stated that "he had heard the allegations and observed that the said governor, alcaldes, regidores, and principales of this city have made the native peoples of the four barrios bring quantities of materials, lime, stone, wood, and other things and it had been done at their expense without paying or reimbursing them."[94] With the direct testimony of workers who participated in the civic construction projects and detailed records of the quantity and value of materials and labor provided, the macehualtin of Mexico Tenochtitlan presented a powerful argument that took aim directly at the indigenous cabildo. Similar testimony exists to document all years from 1555 to 1564.

The macehualtin also claimed that their indigenous government demanded labor and the importation of raw materials for building projects but refused to pay them for either. The sum owed to them exceeded 5,000 pesos.[95] On 23 November 1558, a series of native people testified about the failure of the indigenous government to pay for *zacate* (Nahuatl: *zacatl*, a reed used in construction) they had brought into the city.[96] Miguel Pérez, from San Juan Moyotlan, reported that "those who procure the zacate are Pedro Acuicacatl and Martín Niçenpita and having brought in *cargas* (loads) of the said herb, I have never seen them pay for the said zacate." Pablo Tomás, a forty-one-year-old native person from the barrio of San Pablo, reported that during the time of judge don Esteban de Guzmán he had labored and "all that time he paid us not one single thing, not even a cacao bean [for the zacate]."[97] Twenty witnesses in total related various versions of the statements referenced above to establish that the cabildo had for more than ten years systematically forced zacateros to perform labor and services without paying them in cash, kind, or even cacao.[98]

The complaint includes statements to indicate the debt owed to workers and the community for services they performed for the city as repartimento laborers. The workers indicated that the indigenous government gave repartimiento workers to important Spaniards as well. According to the allegation, "Pedro Yonotl, a native person, served in the house of the Señor viceroy eight days by order of the alcaldes [of Mexico Tenochtitlan] and worked in the house without receiving any payment, and the regidores indicated to the *tepixque* [overseers] to charge the viceroy's financial administrator for the work and daily wage."[99] Other allegations continued this claim, suggesting that officers of the Audiencia and indigenous cabildo members themselves similarly received indigenous workers for personal service. Like their Spanish counterparts, indigenous officials allegedly brought personal servants into their homes to work without compensation. More insidious, the tepixque—minor officials of the indigenous government in charge of tribute collection, sometimes called *merinos* in Spanish-language documents—charged those who received the service a fee to cover the expenses incurred by workers and wages owed them for their work.[100] Spanish law had long before ended all personal service with the New Laws of 1542 and had reissued the same mandate in subsequent decrees. Spaniards and indigenous nobles, however, continued to demand unpaid indigenous servants.[101]

Those who provided testimony to support the allegation of improper labor drafts all came from the four barrios of the parcialidad of Mexico Tenochtitlan and from nonnoble backgrounds. None described himself as elite, principal, or noble. Most, if they chose to remark about their work at all, held low-status, low-skilled jobs or worked as manual laborers. Importantly, however, they all owed repartimiento service, the labor component of tribute. Only certain natives owed such labor—nonnobles age twenty to fifty.[102] Although principales paid tribute, their status exempted them from the labor requirement.[103]

The cabildo responded in late 1565, relying again on arguments that played on Spaniards' stereotypical understanding of indigenous peoples. The natives in this response appear as lazy and devious, lurking, and scheming to rise up in rebellion. This rhetorical strategy and a bulk of expensive and glossy evidence swayed the Audiencia to issue a definitive sentence that effectively ended the case. The cabildo produced two important document sets accompanied by an explanatory petition designed to undermine the credibility of those who testified against the cabildo. After such a long period in which they did not engage the petitions by the repartimiento laborers, the cabildo documents detail specific payments made to the caja de comunidad of Mexico Tenochtitlan to compensate the workers.

The cabildo, governor, and procurador Juan Caro ultimately presented a lengthy petition that broke their long silence. Caro began by denying any wrongdoing, stating that officials had served in their offices "loyally as good Christians and [had] administered justice fearful of God and according to their office and obligations."[104] On the more pertinent accusation of withheld payment for services, he blamed the natives who did not receive their payment. Repartimiento workers, he insisted, instead of bringing materials from areas distant from the city purchased materials readily available in the markets, increasing their cost. The cabildo argued that it should not have to pay for the convenience of contracted repartimiento workers. Furthermore, their allegations blamed natives for being lazy and devious—unwilling to travel into the hinterlands of the city to collect materials and then scheming to force the community to pay extra.[105] In the end, beyond their alleged laziness, the cabildo also accused natives who filed suit against them of rebellion, claiming: "As shown by our account of expenditures . . . the charges and allegations brought by the macehuales and craftsmen, serve only to attack us without foundation as our evidence has demonstrated. [The plaintiffs] show only their ill will and dishonesty [mala intención] by continuing to press on with the case despite their defeat driven by caudillos and principales who pay no tribute but rather attempt to lead the natives of the four barrios in insurrection [alboroto]."[106]

The first supporting document, the residencia (official review) of don Esteban de Guzmán from 1557, shows a payment of more than 1,700 pesos. This document provided a key piece of physical evidence. The cabildo with the aid of an Audiencia scribe produced this document at the end of don Esteban de Guzmán's administration in 1557.[107] Because he served in an interim capacity, he retired from the office. The cabildo, therefore, conducted a residencia to review his record of service.[108] During that hearing, conducted on 3 January 1557 by the indigenous government in Nahuatl, the issue of payment for repartimiento service emerged. The document reports a payment of 1,774 pesos and eight tomines, collected by the indigenous government and paid into the community treasury. The residencia document reports that "Miguel Díaz, regidor and others took the said pesos and put them in the community [*caja de comunidad*] in presence of the governor don Cristóbal de Guzmán and the alcaldes don Luis de Santa María and Tomás de Aquino."[109] The deposit of the pesos occurred under the supervision of future governor (then an alcalde) don Luis de Santa María, alcalde Tomás de Aquino, and Spanish officials. The payment seems to have been a response to an order by Viceroy Velasco to compensate the community for their labor and expenses.[110] The zacateros alleged that officials had not collected the money. They also claimed that the officers of the cabildo had kept the revenue for themselves. The residencia document, which includes a report of the deposit, provided definitive proof from the perspective of the Audiencia that the cabildo faithfully complied with the viceregal order.[111] Don Esteban de Guzmán remained in good standing with the viceregal government after this residencia, it seems, and he was subsequently appointed to serve as governor in Mexico Tlatelolco, 28 October 1560.[112]

The cabildo also produced a lengthy memorial, running twenty-eight folios, that details the expenditures by the cabildo for public works. The entire cabildo and a royal scribe signed this document for authentication.[113] Produced in October 1565, the document counters the charges brought by Toribio Lucas, Miguel García, and the other "officials" (meaning wage earners here, not those who occupy a government office) that they had not been paid. The cabildo also provided copies of the orders issued by Viceroy don Luis de Velasco. To further strengthen their case, they included a lengthy document written in Nahuatl, Spanish, and *pinturas* (indigenous-style illustrations). Separated long ago from the civil suit because of its elegant artistry and novelty, the Códice Osuna (as we now know it) shows graphically in unequivocal terms the materials and costs also provided in the Spanish accounting of expenditures (*memorial de los gastos*). The cabildo continued to claim that they had made all the requisite payments to the indigenous craftsmen and macehualtin who served as repartimeinto laborers. They also showed that the viceroy had ordered all expenditures.[114]

Together, the two documents and petition provided, in language the Audiencia understood, definitive evidence that the cabildo had paid for the labor and materials requested. The signatures and official seals made this evidence virtually unimpeachable; it was witnessed and verified by proper authorities and signed by Spanish and indigenous officials. Such documentation was strong proof that the cabildo had done nothing wrong in the eyes of the Spanish courts. It put the plaintiffs in a difficult position. Their testimony contradicted the physical evidence witnessed and produced collectively by the cabildo and Spanish government. Clearly, the Audiencia believed that the cabildo had produced a better proof than the plaintiffs.

The cabildo also raised the specter of political controversy in the final synopsis of the petition filed by Juan Caro. The cabildo's procurador argued that the craftsmen filed false charges in league with "caudillos and principales" who had a political agenda and filed the suit to advance their political cause.[115] This observation, rather than simply dismissing the charges, reveals that native leaders, principales among them, allegedly instigated the case to achieve a political outcome. In unequivocal terms, the petition reveals that the indigenous leaders on the cabildo understood that the goal of the lawsuit was to create instability and make possible a political uprising. Such an impression, which appears to have guided the response of the cabildo from the very beginning of the suit, suggests deeper political motives of which the cabildo members were fully cognizant.

The Audiencia had seen enough evidence to conclude the case. The signed and sworn statements, the residencia, the orders from Velasco, and a concerted effort on the part of the cabildo prevailed against the sworn testimony of the plaintiffs. The Audiencia dismissed the charges on 1 December 1565. After years of active challenge by the plaintiffs, the suit ended abruptly with a definitive judgment in favor of the cabildo. Though not mentioned in the final summation, don Luis de Santa María had passed away and left the cabildo without a governor. Audiencia justice Villalobos agreed that the cabildo had provided better evidence. On issuing his decision, he minimized any merit from the charges brought by the plaintiffs. In his opinion, he referenced the evidence provided by Spanish escribano Martín Pauper, who oversaw the presentation of the translated residencia, originally presented to justice don Alonso de Zorita, and the memorial de los gastos sworn in the presence of a royal scribe.[116]

Despite the sentence, between May and November 1566, Cristóbal Pérez, a new procurador representing the plaintiffs, issued a new interrogatorio and provided a series of witnesses to testify to its contents. The charges, recycled from the old allegations, tried to demonstrate that despite the cabildo's argument and supporting documents the macehualtin had already proved their claims. They argued that money paid to the community did not wind up in the hands of the laborers. They also stressed that the claims made by the plaintiffs were known by all members of the community (*público y notorio*). The community also knew that in their earlier efforts before the Audiencia they had proved through testimony the charges they levied against the cabildo. Pérez called eight more witnesses, most of whom had special knowledge of government policies and had served the cabildo in the intermediary role of tepixque.[117] Two of the witnesses, Miguel García Chamalara and Pedro Hernández (also a tepixque), identified themselves as principales. The remaining two, a merchant and a tailor, simply had knowledge of the allegations made in the interrogatorio. By using principales and tepixque, Pérez further underscored the political nature of this lawsuit. As intermediary figures, tepixque carried out the work of the government. Tepixque also had firsthand experience taking orders from the cabildo and thus provided especially strong testimony. They also stood to gain should this political challenge succeed, perhaps receiving patronage for their service to the plaintiffs.[118] The tepixque, as a group, seem to occupy a mid-level position (excepting perhaps Hernández) in the service of the government. Their role as tribute collectors served the indigenous principales on the cabildo, and their testimony in support of the civil suit worked against their former patrons.

Caro, still defending the cabildo, responded characteristically by claiming that the witnesses lacked character, caused trouble, drank excessively the "wine of this land" (probably pulque), and had been punished publicly by the cabildo.[119] The Audiencia responded to the renewed challenge with a brief statement by Villalobos, the oidor, who wrote that the cabildo had provided better proof in the residencia and memorial than offered in the new interrogatorio. His decision ended any possibility of challenge to the cabildo, although the last petition filed by plaintiffs is dated 2 July 1568. The challenges continued, therefore, until the moment that Santa María was replaced by don Francisco Jiménez.[120]

At their core, the legal conflicts of the 1550s and 1560s reveal a series of political disputes that percolated below the surface of what appeared to be a dispute mostly about the abuse of repartimiento workers and authority. The architects of the lawsuit and the aggrieved parties of craftsmen and manual laborers succeeded in challenging the ruling cohort of noble natives. They learned how to put the cabildo on the defensive and nearly had them imprisoned—forcing their leaders to produce written documents to defend their actions in court. Principales and minor officials, some of whom could vote in cabildo elections, participated actively in the suit. Thus, the potentially political actors seem to have allied themselves with actors who scholars traditionally have assumed had no place in the political process. Had the noblemen occupied positions on the rotational system of the cabildo, they would have had little complaint or cause to disrupt and undermine the cabildo. They owed no repartimiento labor service. The cabildo, calling its accusers "caudillos and principales" who sought to cause an "alboroto" (uprising/insurrection), also reveal concern about an apparent political challenge.

The challenge also seems to reprise precontact patterns in which rival noblemen sometimes contested the succession of tlatoque. This particular contest came at a trying moment for the cabildo when the legitimate royal line came to an end. It also emerged during a time of great uncertainty about the question of the role of the indigenous government, the longevity of the gubernatorial term, and reconciling the electoral process and terms of service with Spanish law. A challenge by rival factions among the indigenous principales, furthermore, conformed to precontact patterns of succession crises common in the Nahua region.[121]

Even though this political challenge in the 1560s seemed to fail on the surface, the case reveals important early innovations by political challengers that such minority political blocs continued to use into the eighteenth century, refining them to increase their success and in the process fundamentally changing the nature of the governorship. Conflicts existed among the noblemen of Mexico Tenochtitlan, both before and after the arrival of Spaniards. With the authority of the tlatoani in decline as the Spaniards reconstructed Mexico Tenochtitlan and the hinterland, competition for the colonial office of governor continued. After the demise of the legitimate line of tlatoque, Mexico Tenochtitlan faced an uncertain future. How would the new governors establish their right to rule? How would they fend off challengers? What role would the Spanish courts play in the management of succession? Based on the lawsuit of 1564, the answer to these questions seems to have been well resolved. The courts would hear challenges while providing ample leeway for indigenous rulers to govern according to custom and tradition. The courts often supported without serious investigation the claims of the cabildo, suggesting that the Audiencia valued above all else the preservation of order. This, coupled with a strong successor in Mexico Tenochtitlan, don Antonio Valeriano (r. 1573–99), seemed to mitigate political conflict.[122] Though this political challenge did not appear to succeed in unseating the government or reorganizing the patronage networks, native peoples from Mexico Tenochtitlan experimented with the idea of a legal challenge. Future generations resorted to similar strategies to resolve disputes.

CHAPTER 2

INDIGENOUS GOVERNMENT IN
TRANSITION, 1573–1610

"Tui Amantissimus etsi Indignus. Antonius Malerianus"

Judge don Francisco Jiménez vacated his post in Mexico Tenochtitlan in 1573, ceding authority at a time when apparently no viable male heirs of the royal line remained. Taking the office with the full title of judge-governor, don Antonio Valeriano succeeded Jiménez and seemed well positioned to inaugurate a new era.[1] Yet politics persisted in the indigenous community of Mexico Tenochtitlan. Eight years had passed since the death of the last judge-governor, don Luis de Santa María.[2] The long interruption suggests that unspecified problems prevented electors from choosing a successor, though no evidence survives to pin down with certainty their nature. The interruption was unusual in that it lasted longer than previous breaks between judge-governors since the establishment of the institution in the 1530s. No gap of similar duration between judge-governors occurred again through the early eighteenth century.[3] Even though the sources are silent, suggesting little that might provide insight into the problems of succession, several possibilities could explain the hiatus. Electors may not have been able to agree on an acceptable candidate. With the recent political challenges of the 1560s, deep divisions likely persisted among electors. Viceregal officials may have also blocked or stood in the way of choices presented

by the community, though generally the viceregal bureaucracy produced documentation that would verify such intervention.[4] It is
probable, based on the experiences of the 1560s, that political actors
who derived their authority independently from the indigenous
nobility competed with those who usually chose the judge-governor
from among the eligible royal nobles.

The commentary of indigenous annalists, Chimalpahin and to
some extent don Hernando de Alvarado Teçoçomoc, provides some
information about the political issues surrounding succession after
the death of Santa María, though it is frustratingly incomplete. From
their observations and extant archival material, several significant
changes shaped succession patterns in the late sixteenth century. The
royal line did not die out. Rather, heirs to the royal line persisted well
beyond the eighteenth century, limited only somewhat through the
intermarriage of some heirs with Spaniards. After Santa María, rulers
in Mexico Tenochtitlan for decades to come did not descend directly
from the Tenochca royal lineage. Many of the new leaders were not
even born in Mexico Tenochtitlan but came from regional altepetl.
The title held by the ruler of Tenochtitlan, judge-governor, changed
subtly in the late sixteenth century as well. Jiménez's appointment,
probably as only a judge, conformed to an earlier pattern in which
nondynastic foreign rulers did not hold the full office of judge-governor.
His successor Valeriano, however, who also lacked dynastic affiliation
and even noble birth, did hold the title judge-governor. Beyond the
change that made possible nondynastic and non-Tenochca governors,
after Valeriano's retirement from office mestizos apparently entered
indigenous offices more easily. A series of mestizos held the judge-
governorship and some even held the post of alcalde.[5] Such transformations of the political culture of Mexico Tenochtitlan suggest that the
community of electors, the viceregal government, or a combination
of the two made changes that ultimately reduced the influence of the
traditional royal lineage and replaced it with new rulers.

The success and duration in office of Jiménez and Valeriano seem
to have made it possible for the governorship of Mexico Tenochtitlan
to shift gradually away from the Tenochca royal lineage in the late
sixteenth century. Jiménez and Valeriano ably collected tribute during
a series of difficult transitions, which took place when they were in

office. For example, indigenous tribute payers had to make their contributions in cash after 1564.[6] The debilitating epidemics of the 1570s also presented challenges for Valeriano, who had to clarify ownership and establish title to properties in Mexico Tenochtitlan.[7] These changes, beyond the larger transformation to the office of judge-governor, must have seemed slow and hardly perceptible after the death of Santa María in 1565.

In office, Jiménez and Valeriano shared many of the governing characteristics of those who derived their authority from association with the royal lineage. The new leaders remained in office for a generation and apparently served for as long as they chose—Jiménez for five years, Valeriano for twenty-six. Lifelong service in office mimicked the experiences of governors of royal lineage. Additionally, it appears that, like their predecessors from the royal lineage, Jiménez and Valeriano did not have to win annual elections to maintain their position in office. Transformations to the judge-governorship occurred, but the similarity between these new governors and those from the royal lineage must have made any changes largely imperceptible to the Tenochca. Nevertheless, the transition marked a sharp departure from the initial system established by Mendoza in the 1530s that introduced new Spanish nomenclature to native offices. The new alterations within the existing Spanish-styled indigenous government were less profound. Spanish-styled native cabildos, in addition, were all that most residents of Mexico Tenochtitlan had ever experienced by the 1570s. The timing suggests that the transition in native government occurred amid many other changes, including the phasing out of contact-era institutions.[8]

VALERIANO, JIMÉNEZ, AND SPANISH INTERVENTION

There was no shortage of candidates who had legitimate claim to succeed Santa María in 1565, which raises the question of why non-dynastic rulers suddenly took over the office of judge-governor. Ultimately an interim leader, Jiménez—a foreigner and appointed only as a judge according to Chimalpahin—exercised the duties of the governor between 1568 and 1573. Very little evidence survives regarding the tenure of Judge Jiménez apart from a few brief paragraphs in

Chimalpahin. He appears to have filled in well as the leader of Mexico Tenochtitlan, collecting all the tribute owed to the crown by the community in 1572. Such compliance probably indicates the degree to which the Tenochca accepted Jiménez.[9] Valeriano was also an important part of the emerging, long-term trend that brought to office governors who had standing in the community but did not come from the royal lineage of Mexico Tenochtitlan.[10] The transformation, which began with Jiménez, occurred initially without obvious direct meddling by viceregal officials. Though Jiménez and Valeriano were probably well suited for the leadership position, Valeriano also had important connections to the Franciscans, which may have made him a compelling choice from the perspective of the viceregal government. Strong ties to the community of Spaniards, however, may not have translated into popularity among the electors. Support from indigenous electors, therefore, was of paramount importance. Even though the viceregal government may have had an interest in controlling the office of judge-governor in Mexico Tenochtitlan, it had only limited ability to intervene through its capacity to confirm elected officials. The viceregal government could not or chose not to impose candidates it favored.

The viceregal government, however, through its oversight capacity technically had the authority to deny office to elected indigenous officials. It could hold governors accountable to fulfill the duties expected of them and remove officials if necessary. Appointment documents made clear the duties of office and thus served as a kind of contract. The Audiencia could, if it saw evidence to justify such action, legally intervene to remove or replace an indigenous judge-governor. Though endowed with the authority to challenge or declare void an election and to veto the choice made by electors, the viceregal government generally chose not to intervene in the sixteenth century. It had a greater interest in ensuring stability.[11] Natives likely desired that viceregal institutions be impartial, fair, and disinterested. In 1561, as discussed in the first chapter, indigenous litigants reacted with venom when they perceived that the Audiencia had ignored their petitions and demanded that an outside party consider the merits of their case.[12] The conservative judgment rendered by the Audiencia in 1565 that effectively preserved the status quo, however, suggests that the viceregal courts chose not to manipulate indigenous government directly by favoring a political challenge. In addition, the viceregal government had to consider the extent to which it relied on the community of principales to manage tax collection and the maintenance of order in the important city of Mexico Tenochtitlan.

From the perspective of the indigenous intellectual Chimalpahin and likely as well from the viceregal government, a clear distinction existed between rulers whose authority derived from traditional ties to the royal lineage and those who took office through election.[13] Those who, through virtue of their birth, came from the kingly lineage (Nahuatl: *tlatocatlacamecayotl*) of Mexico Tenochtitlan served well the cause of stability and pacification after the initial Spanish invasion in 1519.[14] For Chimalpahin, the royal lineage represented legitimacy as well as continuity with the past. From a viceregal perspective, the royal lineage was a liability for the exact reason that Chimalpahin found it so appealing. Indigenous rulers with independent precontact sources of authority could not, however, be easily removed, changed, or made fully subordinate to Hispanic legal norms for office rotation, residencia, and fiscal accountability. Leaders outside the kingly lineage, on the other hand, had less independence and thus could more easily be held to Spanish norms for officeholding. The Audiencia and viceroy laid out plainly the contractual terms of office for native rulers. The paternalistic litany of responsibilities that accompanied viceroy don Luis de Velasco's speech to the first appointed alcaldes of Mexico Tenochtitlan, discussed in the introduction, still formed the basis of appointment documents. The Audiencia and viceroy, however, could more easily hold elected officials to the terms of this document than those with independent ties to legitimacy from the royal line.[15]

The viceregal government did not rush into making direct and visible interventions to control the succession of judge-governors in Mexico Tenochtitlan. The first regular, firmly documented interventions came in the 1630s. The viceregal government intervened when the city, depopulated because of flooding (1629–36), struggled as the bulk of its labor force migrated to peripheral towns in the Basin of Mexico. Don Cristóbal Pascual was imprisoned for failure to collect tribute and subsequently removed from office and replaced by an appointed native ruler.[16] Despite previous flagrant violations of the appointment contract, the viceroy and Audiencia chose not to intervene in the affairs of indigenous government. Judge-governors, even those with no ties to the royal line, served for life despite legal prohibitions against reelection.[17] The community of electors chose mestizos to serve as judge-governor even though elected offices of the República de Indios could be held only by natives.[18] Despite these irregularities, the Audiencia supervised elections and continued to certify the results. The viceroy or his representative continued to distribute the staff of office to newly elected indigenous leaders, investing in them the authority to act in the name of the crown.[19] Despite the nominal authority and supervisory role given to the viceregal government, it apparently needed a reason and likely also support from factions within the indigenous community to remove a governor.

The importance of the royal lineage because of its precontact legitimacy probably made it difficult for the viceroy to intervene in indigenous affairs. Elected governors, on the other hand, were sworn in and empowered by Spanish officials exclusively, and thus they owed their position and staff of office to the viceregal government. Governors of royal lineage, though technically similarly empowered, had added legitimacy because their right to rule derived from the community independently of viceregal authority. Don Antonio Valeriano could balance the needs of the viceregal government and indigenous electors because he had deep ties to the Spanish and indigenous community of Mexico Tenochtitlan. Born less than a decade after the fall of Tenochtitlan, Valeriano grew up in privileged circumstances.[20] The Franciscans who administered the evangelization of the Nahuas and other groups in the Basin chose him as one of the talented indigenous scholars to attend the progressive Colegio de Santa Cruz in Tlatelolco.[21] At the school, Valeriano worked directly with fray Bernardino de Sahagún and fray Juan de Torquemada.[22] He seems to have chosen to marry an important noblewoman, doña Isabel de Alvarado, for political reasons; she was a woman with direct ties to the royal lineage of Mexico Tenochtitlan. Doña Isabel was the seventh child of don Diego de Alvarado Huanitzin, the first judge-governor of Mexico Tenochtitlan.[23] To marry so well, Valeriano must have had high status within the principal community of Mexico Tenochtitlan.[24] Even though Valeriano could claim high status, Chimalpahin reflected in 1608 that his ascension to the governorship brought to an end an era.[25] What he meant, of course, was that as a by-product of Valeriano's and Jiménez's rise to office the royal lineage lost its hold on the governorship and could never be restored.

Valeriano's assumption of the office of judge-governor represented a political sea change for the community of Mexico Tenochtitlan. Valeriano had no direct connection to the royal line and, according to Chimalpahin, "he was not a nobleman," which would have prohibited him from even voting in native cabildo elections.[26] Chimalpahin knew of don Antonio Valeriano and his grandson of the same name.[27] Yet he also understood the profound significance of the transition that ended the independent legitimacy of office long associated with the heirs of the Tenochca royal lineage.[28]

Chimalpahin did not, however, indicate that the lineage ceased to produce royal heirs. With the death of Santa María, Chimalpahin stated only that "it came to an end that descendants of the Mexica and Tenochca rulers should rule in Tenochtitlan any more," emphasizing only that "their governing as rulers was cut off forever."[29] The term "forever" is an important one because it may imply that the viceregal government or the electors of Mexico Tenochtitlan had made a conscious choice to end the royal lineage's affiliation with the governorship. More likely it reflected the Nahua understanding of lineage which, once removed from its position, could not be restored. Chimalpahin did not know what would happen after 1608 when he made this comment. Indeed, at that moment only three governors, one judge, and one deputy had served since the death of Santa María, hardly constituting an end to the possibility that the royal line would ever return to office.[30] To Chimalpahin, however, the shift seemed to mean that with Valeriano's appointment to the highest office of indigenous government, which bore the title judge-governor, a profound and irreversible change had occurred. Traditional dominance by descendants of the lords of Tenochtitlan ended.[31] Chimalpahin likely assumed that his audience understood Nahua succession and did not need to explain what would have been obvious to them, that the royal lineage could no longer control the governorship. Don Luis de Santa María (r. 1563–65) had a large but indeterminate number of male heirs, his siblings, uncles, nephews, and presumably children, who were part of the kingly lineage of Mexico Tenochtitlan.

THE PERSISTENCE OF THE KINGLY LINEAGE:
THE TLATOCATLACAMECAYOTL

Because there is only limited context, it is difficult to understand exactly what Chimalpahin meant when he emphasized the changes that occurred with the arrival of Jiménez and Valeriano. It could be that he was pointing out that neither was Tenochca. Jiménez came from Teca- machalco and Valeriano from Azcapotzalco. At the same time, neither represented the royal lineage of Tenochtitlan, which also made them different than those who came before. Chimalpahin understood exactly which one of these two conditions mattered more to the Nahua, but the context he has left makes plausible either issue. The terms Chimalpahin used seem to suggest that he was really referring to the royal lineage. When he discussed the appointment of Jiménez and Valeriano, he did not use the term *motlahtocatlalliaya* (was installed in office), though he did use it when he referred to the ascension of judge-governors from the royal lineage.[32] The root term itself, *tlahtocatl*, is related to tlatoani ("he who speaks," from the Nahuatl *tlahtoa*, to speak). The Nahuatl terms for royal (kingly) lineage, tlatocatlacamecayotl, and rulership, tlatocayotl, also derive from the common root present in the word for leader associated with the royal lineage, *tlatoani*. All of this seems to suggest that Chimalpahin, when he chose to use the term motlahtocat- lalliaya, meant rulers associated with the royal lineage.[33]

The royal lineage appears to have had many complex parts. To the Tenochca, only one part of the royal lineage could produce acceptable candidates for the rulership. Tlatoque, before the Spanish invasion, had multiple legitimate wives each of whom bore noble and royal children. It appears, then, that multiple royal lineages existed, but only those children born to the primary royal wife were legitimate contenders to become tlatoani. Moteuccoma Xocoyotzin (r. 1502–20) apparently had more than one hundred wives, but only his primary wife had children who could follow him as rulers. The surviving evi- dence from the era of first contact between Spaniards and natives unfortunately does not appear to reveal which of Moteuccoma's wives was the most important. Circumstantial evidence from the 1520s, however, suggests the significance of royal children of the primary wife. Cortés sought to find and court the daughters of Moteuccoma who had the most potential to bear children who could rule. He courted particularly strongly doña Isabel, whose Nahuatl name was Tecuichpotzin (Lord's Daughter), which suggests the importance of powerful native women who had the capacity to bear dynastic children.[34] Why only one of these lineages seems to have produced heirs to the dynasty remains unclear.[35]

Chimalpahin, with his choice of terms and titles, indicated that Jiménez and Valeriano were different than rulers who had come before. Why did the sudden change happen and under whose direction did it occur? Chimalpahin apparently did not need to provide any explanation because the Nahuas knew what had transpired. Did the electors of Mexico Tenochtitlan turn away from the royal lineage? The conflict among electors in the 1560s or the apparent lack of a viable best choice from the royal lineage (Santa María bore the Nahuatl name "Mushroom Alligator," which is sometimes regarded as derogatory) may have also contributed to an internal choice to find outsider candidates. It is also possible that the viceregal government, through its supervisory capacity, consciously chose to end the association of the royal lineage with the office of judge-governor. Spanish sources do not, however, speak to this issue in any direct way. The absence of such correspondence does not indicate that the viceregal government had no hand in the change, but, as discussed above, viceregal officials seemed reluctant to intervene directly and proactively in the composition of cabildos and with the election and succession of governors. In the end, Chimalpahin's rather cryptic and incomplete commentary that the royal lineage no longer ruled in Mexico Tenochtitlan may be all the extant direct evidence. Yet, to provide further context, it is important to recognize that indigenous heirs to the kingly lineage of Mexico Tenochtitlan abounded after the death of Santa María.

The Moteucçoma branch of the royal family survived well into the twentieth century.[36] Moteucçoma fathered several children. Some accompanied Cortés when he returned to Spain in 1528, including don Martín Cortés Neçahualtecolotzin and don Juan Govamitle.[37] Don Martín returned to New Spain in 1529 after marrying a Spaniard but died shortly thereafter. Don Juan remained in Spain with other principales, including don Hernando de Tapia, the son of the interim ruler of Tenochtitlan, don Andrés de Tapia Motelchiuhtzin.[38] Don

Pedro de Moteucçoma Tlacahuepantzin, who also went to Spain in
1528, survived into the late sixteenth century. As a royal nobleman
(*tlahtocapilli*) he could have contended for the governorship. Don
Pedro, who died on 11 September 1572, outlived don Luis de Santa
María by nearly a decade.[39] By mentioning his passing, Chimalpahin
chronicled the loss of another legitimate contender for the governorship. Unfortunately, his annals do not provide substantive detail
about don Pedro, nor do they explain why Tlacahuepantzin did not
assume the governorship.[40]

Don Pedro's son, Moteucçoma's grandson, don Diego Luis de
Moteucçoma Ihuitltemoctzin, lived into the seventeenth century. He
also held the title of royal nobleman and as such presumably had the
right to hold the office of judge-governor in Mexico Tenochtitlan.[41]
Don Diego Luis lived in Spain, however, and thus probably did not
have an opportunity to develop strong ties to the community of electors in Mexico Tenochtitlan. The political distance probably made it
unlikely that he could cultivate sufficient support to win an election
in any case. The branch of the Moteucçoma family that he represented
also seems to have moved further out of contention for the governorship when he married a Spanish noblewoman, a granddaughter
of the current duke of Alburquerque, doña Francisca de la Cueva.[42]
According to Chimalpahin, don Diego Luis and doña Francisca had
six mestizo children, most of whom remained in Spain with their
mother when their father died in early 1606. Chimalpahin, however,
later wrote that one son of that union, also named don Diego Luis
de Moteucçoma, served as an alcalde in Mexico Tenochtitlan, representing San Sebastián Atzaqualco in 1607.[43] Interestingly, he served
with don Antonio Valeriano, the grandson of the former governor who
represented San Juan Moyotlan on the cabildo in 1607.[44] Chimalpahin,
perhaps to make clear that viable candidates within the royal lineage
existed, commented on the lives of some, noting their affiliation with
the royal line.[45] Chimalpahin also pointed out the slow erosion of the
royal lineage. Even though don Diego Luis de Moteucçoma, a mestizo,
served as an alcalde, he technically could not hold indigenous office.
Since he did become an alcalde on the cabildo, he presumably could
have also served as governor.[46] Several mestizos held the office of

governor in the early seventeenth century, indicating further that he might have been able to press his claim to the office without challenge.

The royal lineage branched outward well beyond the immediate children and grandchildren of Moteucçoma Xocoyotzin. The fraternal lines also produced candidates with the potential to rule in Mexico Tenochtitlan. Indeed, the fraternal line was significantly more germane to succession in Mexico Tenochtitlan because it was more associated with the office of judge-governor. Although no direct evidence bears on the issue, direct descendents of Moteucçoma appear to have been excluded (or to have excluded themselves) from the postcontact office of judge-governor.[47] The royal lineage, nevertheless, survived. Legitimate native royal heirs continued to hold the office of governor through 1565. The first governor don Diego de Alvarado Huanitzin (r. 1538–41) and his successor don Diego de San Francisco Tehuet-zquititzin (r. 1541–54) both fathered male heirs. From the indigenous annalists Chimalpahin and Teçoçomoc, the political careers of some descendants can be partially reconstructed. Some children in the Tenochca line ruled neighboring altepetl in the sixteenth century.[48] Although the details and circumstance of their ascension do not appear in the annals, some must have survived into the 1570s and beyond. Furthermore, these royal heirs likely fathered legitimate children who also extended the royal line—though, even as royal children, they were not necessarily in the correct lineage to succeed Santa María.

Notable among the group of royal heirs who did not hold the office of judge-governor was one of the principal sources for understanding the succession patterns in Mexico Tenochtitlan, don Fernando de Alvarado Teçoçomoc. As a Nahua annalist and the sixth child of don Diego de Alvarado Huanitzin, some biographical details of his life exist.[49] Teçoçomoc was known to Chimalpahin, though the social gulf that separated them and the generational difference likely meant that they did not associate in any meaningful way. Teçoçomoc's *Crónica mexicayotl* (Chronicle of Mexicaness) was edited and incorporated into the writings of Chimalpahin, who saw originals that no longer exist.[50] Teçoçomoc's sister doña Isabel de Alvarado married don Antonio Valeriano, so Valeriano and Teçoçomoc probably knew one another socially and were related through marriage. Lockhart observed that

Teçoçomoc was "an authentic member of the royal dynastic clique of Tenochtitlan." Apparently when a ceremony warranted it, he served as "the public representative of the Mexica and the royal line."[51] Working as a Nahuatl translator (*nahuatlato*) for the Audiencia, he was likely a choice close at hand for such ceremonies. With royal credentials and a dynastic tradition that allowed for fraternal succession, Teçoçomoc was also someone who could have legitimately vied for the office of judge-governor into the seventeenth century. But he did not. Schroeder argues that his office of keeper of records (*tlamachtiani*; Nahuatl: teacher or sage) put him in a position of status and prestige—which also made him an unlikely or even ineligible candidate to rule as governor.[52]

Many in the royal lineage chose to marry into Spanish families, which over time excluded many of their descendants from political positions in Mexico Tenochtitlan. The Moteucçomas were an especially interesting group who, because of their possession of a Spanish noble title, needed to weave their lineage in with other noble families from Iberia to ensure their financial and social well-being.[53] The question remains, however, to what extent the intermarriage with Spaniards alienated those of the royal lineage from the governorship. Though rules were not well enforced at the time, technically to serve in indigenous office a candidate had to be a native. Mestizos held the governorship of Mexico Tenochtitlan on occasion, but in the early seventeenth century they were hardly distinguishable culturally from native rulers. They certainly do not fit the image of mestizos as ladinos (Spanish-speaking and culturally creole).[54] Governor don Gerónimo López (r. 1600–1608), technically a mestizo and the first apparent nonnative to hold the office of judge-governor, was difficult to distinguish culturally from native governors. López, fully literate in Nahuatl, presided over community disputes without difficulty or the need of a translator. He appears to have grown up in an indigenous household, and even though he came from a different altepetl he was culturally like the Tenochca over whom he ruled.[55] Though López followed the mestizo don Juan Martín, the "deputy" (Nahuatl: *theniente*, 1609 loan noun from Spanish *teniente*) of don Antonio Valeriano, Chimalphain claims that Martín never technically served as judge-governor.[56] Though it is not possible to reconstruct the family tree of López, it seems likely that he fit well within the ruling clique of Mexico Tenochtitlan, for he must have received the support of the community of electors. As the governorship moved further away from the royal lineage, political considerations increased in importance and culturally indigenous mestizos had the opportunity to hold the office. On the other hand, as the legal and regulatory apparatus of the viceregal government matured and the political skills of the community increased, mestizos faced possible legal challenges because they were not indigenous (or Tenochca).[57]

The process of *mestizaje*, the blending or mixing of cultures and peoples often described by the antiquated term "race-mixing," was a poorly understood idea in the sixteenth century.[58] The implications when Nahuas married into Spanish families were not well defined in practice or understood by either natives or Spaniards.[59] The practice seemed similar to precontact practices in which dominant altepetl, to further cement ties with conquered peoples, used marriage to unify lineages. By extension, if we accept the premise that the Tenochca thought of the Spaniards much as they thought of the Tlaxcalteca— that is, as a foreign people who competed for dominance in the Basin of Mexico—then by extension marrying into promising Spanish families would have been good strategy that followed native tradition.[60]

From the Spanish perspective, clouded by years of experience with non-Christians in Iberia, such intermarriage created "mestizos" who did not fit into either the native world or the Spanish one. Spaniards also excluded mestizos because many were born illegitimate.[61] Spaniards created the Colegio de San Juan de Letrán in Mexico City in the sixteenth century to educate mestizos exclusively, indicating their perception of this group as different and separate.[62] The very existence of separate institutions for mestizos, natives, and Spaniards demonstrates that viceregal and ecclesiastical authorities understood mestizaje as a problem. Furthermore, *limpieza de sangre* (purity of ancestry) statutes restricted and limited those who descended from New Christians (neophytes to the Christian faith usually defined as those whose families had been Christian for only a few generations) and others from holding high office or attaining high social status. To viceregal and ecclesiastical officials, mestizos, though not descended from New Christians, fit in neither "república."[63] Purity of ancestry rules also provided a precedent for excluding individuals from office and position based on their birth.

As a result, extending such restriction to mestizos could be justified easily by already extant discriminatory practices within Spanish law. Perhaps further indicating the ambiguous though apparently declining position of mestizos, the few students who attended the mestizo colegio found a curriculum that suggested its founders had low expectations of them. Though its professors taught grammar, reading, writing, and Christian doctrine, the curriculum apparently concentrated on more practical skills such as begging for alms and grave digging.[64]

Nevertheless, some mestizos apparently took advantage of the circumstances to gain access to important positions. Many grew up in bilingual households in which both Nahuatl and Spanish were spoken. In the sixteenth century, according to Carrasco, the nahuatlatos for the Audiencia "were either mestizos or Spaniards married to Indian women. In 1578, of six interpreters employed by the Real Audiencia, five were mestizos."[65] Mestizos in the employ of the Audiencia obviously far exceeded the expectations laid out by the curriculum of the Colegio de San Juan de Letrán. The very wealthy (assuming that property contained in a will provides an accurate measure of wealth) and successful native leader Hernando de Tapia served as a nahuatlato for the Audiencia in the sixteenth century.[66] Even the royal Teçoçomoc served as a nahuatlato for the Audiencia. Indeed, in addition to the Spaniards and mestizos who served according to Carrasco in the office of nahuatlato, high-status natives also served.[67]

Hernando de Tapia, although not born into the royal lineage but descended from rulers of Mexico Tenochtitlan, had an outside claim to the office of judge-governor. Tapia's father, don Andrés de Tapia Motelchiuhtzin, served as the interim ruler (quauhtlatoani) (r. 1525–30) before the arrival of Viceroy Mendoza and the establishment of the office of judge-governor. As an heir of an important military officer who served Moteucçoma, Tapia owned significant property in the city. Don Andrés had used his skill as a warrior to elevate himself to the status of eagle noble (*quauhpilli*), so his descendents enjoyed some status beyond their nonnoble birth.[68] Though wealthy and of significant status, Hernando de Tapia did not seem inclined to pursue the governorship. Indeed, he seems to have worked more diligently to cultivate alliances with Spanish families. His father, Motelchiuhtzin, had served the leader of the first Audiencia, Nuño de Guzmán, and his family had apparently done well linking themselves to the conquest generation of Spaniards.[69] Hernando de Tapia also traveled to Spain with Cortés in 1528 and was present at the court of Carlos I (r. 1516–56) while his father ruled in Mexico Tenochtitlan.[70] His extensive last will and testament mentioned the journey to Spain but, more important, it provides an in-depth accounting of his material successes. He cultivated personal connections and business relations with wealthy indigenous principales and Spaniards. Codicils in his will indicate that he lent and borrowed substantial sums of money from other natives and from Spaniards. One such reference notes that he owed a debt of 1,540 pesos to a Damián Martínez. Such a large sum, the equivalent of a lifetime of earnings for many in the city, probably indicates that Tapia had significant property or other collateral.[71] Indeed, Tapia's testament shows that he held extensive landholdings and owned several houses in the city. The urban properties included a house on the central plaza of San Sebastián Atzaqualco that his heirs disputed with the indigenous government of Mexico Tenochtitlan. The disputed property served as the community center and meeting hall.[72]

In his will, Tapia apparently attempted to cultivate further his family's alliances with Spaniards rather than establish political connections within the community of Mexico Tenochtitlan for himself and his descendents. He placed certain restrictions (likely unenforceable) on his daughters: "When they reach the age of marriage it is my will that they marry Spaniards. . . . and I order that they not marry indigenous men [naturales de la tierra]."[73]

Hernando de Tapia, though not of noble descent, saw the benefit of forging alliances with Spanish families. Perhaps his business connections and the service of his father garnered him such success that his vision of the future success of his children lay not with the indigenous community but with Spaniards. Perhaps his claim to rulership had more cachet with Spaniards than with natives. Perhaps, like some of the Moteucçomas, he saw more to be gained through strengthening his connections within the community of Spaniards in Mexico Tenochtitlan and beyond than in trying to cultivate authority within the indigenous community. Whatever his reasoning, Tapia apparently wished that his daughters would marry into Spanish families. Perhaps, because they were apparently not indigenous, he saw benefit in attempting to minimize the indigenous part of their ancestry. As mestizas, Tapia's daughters could, it seems, enhance the position of their heirs through marriage to Spaniards.[74] The wealth they stood to inherit likely made them the objects of many suitors.[75]

Though Chimalpahin and other indigenous chroniclers mention only a few descendants of the Tenochca royal line who survived, surely others lived through the epidemics of the 1570s and continued to produce viable indigenous heirs. The implication is clear, though the impetus and force behind the change less so, that a conscious choice was made to disassociate the royal lineage from the office of judge-governor. Intermarriage of the Nahua nobility with Spaniards, though technically a means to exclude individuals from indigenous office, was not common. Nonnative judge-governors served occasionally in the seventeenth century, many times without obvious contest. Yet the transformation from the royal line to elected judge-governors appears to have begun with Valeriano and to have continued indefinitely for the purpose of removing the heirs of the royal lineage from the powerful political offices of indigenous government. The transition weakened the office of governor over time by further distancing it from the rulers of Mexico Tenochtitlan who may have had traditional legitimacy independent of elected office. Valeriano seems to have facilitated the transition. He served the community for more than two decades as governor. Also working in his favor were his talent and knowledge in Hispanic modes of thought and government.

GOVERNOR DON ANTONIO VALERIANO

The litany of praises that attest to Valeriano's intellect suggest that he was an extraordinary man. He knew Latin fluently and could apparently speak it extemporaneously.[76] He was educated extensively and taught at the Franciscan Colegio de Santa Cruz at Tlatelolco.[77] As a student, he earned distinction and praise from his mentors, Franciscan scholars fray Juan Bautista, fray Bernardino de Sahagún, and fray Juan de Torquemada. Sahagún, whom Valeriano assisted in the production of the Florentine Codex, acknowledged that he was the "best and wisest" of all the natives who attended the colegio.[78] Torquemada, who had learned Nahuatl from Valeriano, praised him in a funeral eulogy as "an excellent talent of whom the king [Philip II] had taken notice and [about whom the king had] written a letter of praise."[79] Chimalpahin admired Valeriano, calling him a scholar and a wise "Latinist."[80] According to Bautista, Valeriano was "a great Latinist who . . . [wrote] with such mastery and elegance that he brought to mind Cicero or Quintilian."[81] Oidor Alonso de Zorita called him an excellent Latinist and referred to him as one of the founders of the Colegio de Santa Cruz.[82] Cervantes de Salazar, who generally had great contempt for indigenous peoples of Mexico, wrote that at the Colegio de Santa Cruz the natives "have a teacher . . . Antonio Valeriano, who is in no respect inferior to our [Spanish] grammarians. He is well trained in the observance of Christian law and is an ardent student of oratory."[83] Such high praise from those who knew and worked closely with him suggests that he possessed extraordinary talent. Few individuals from late sixteenth-century Mexico City could have had the exposure to receive praise from so many different quarters.[84]

Don Antonio Valeriano took office officially in 1573 after the apparent retirement of don Francisco Jiménez.[85] On 4 January 1573, Jiménez left office, and Valeriano replaced him seven days later. The speed of this transition suggests that Valeriano was the presumptive replacement and that Jiménez's departure was planned or expected. Earlier transitions took many months or even years, especially following the death of a judge-governor from the Tenochca royal lineage. It is possible, because cabildo elections usually occurred in January every year, that Valeriano was elected and installed in office subsequently. Obviously groomed for the post for many years and highly capable, he may have been the best choice for the office from the perspective of the native community, the viceregal government, and even the influential Franciscans. Valeriano held the full title of judge-governor, and just like those who came from the royal lineage he served in office for life, apparently without need for reelection. He also chose his successor when he retired unofficially in 1596 as he approached the age of seventy. All of these details suggest that Valeriano was a transitional figure who straddled two important periods in the political history of Mexico Tenochtitlan, the former dominated by the conquest-era heirs of the royal line and the latter by those whose authority was tied to the viceregal bureaucracy.

Valeriano was an important transitional figure culturally as well. As an indigenous intellectual he had deep connections within the Hispanic world, mainly to the Franciscans. He also possessed great political skill. Even Chimalpahin, who rejected the very thing he most stood for, the end of the royal line in Mexico Tenochtitlan, praised Valeriano. As a literate "ethnographer" in the service of fray Bernardino de Sahagún, he had great connections. From the perspective of the viceregal government, Valeriano was probably an appealing choice. Steeped in the evangelical work of the Franciscans, Valeriano could speak and write like the most talented intellectuals in Mexico City, the regular clergy. Educated in a fine religious school, he was culturally in touch with Spanish modes of thought. Indeed, the "colegio imperial" of Santa Cruz in Tlatelolco was conceived as "a seminary of virtue and letters in which the religious brothers of our holy reverend father will teach to the indigenous [principal] children Christian doctrine, politics, and arts presiding in the Castilian and Latin languages so that they [indigenous principales] will serve as secular and ecclesiastical leaders."[86] As an exemplary graduate, Valeriano probably was everything the viceregal government could have desired in a native leader.

Valeriano, in the indigenous community, had the standing of a noble without being tied to the old nobility. Those who found the idea of a transition away from the royal lineage appealing must have seen Valeriano as a fine alternative. Teçoçomoc perhaps articulated resentment toward his lesser-born contemporary when he noted prominently that Valeriano was not of the nobility (*amo pilli*). A potential contender for the office of judge-governor, Teçoçomoc, if he had political ambitions, might have seen in his brother-in-law Valeriano a talented rival, though one without the appropriate qualifications for office.[87] Nevertheless, Valeriano could speak and write in perfect Nahuatl, Spanish, and Latin. He lived, worked, and studied with a select group of privileged natives from all over the region. Many of those who attended the Colegio de Santa Cruz came from the indigenous nobility and royal lineages of altepetl within the Basin.[88]

Further giving him credentials within the indigenous world, Valeriano studied indigenous traditions and customs, helping Spanish intellectuals decipher the complexities of these cultural ways. To do this, he had to gain the trust of indigenous principales who could speak with him about the lives of indigenous peoples before contact. Once they were entrusted, Sahagún charged his assistants to "write down data in its original language and collect from the lips of their elders the moribund ancient knowledge [*sabiduría*]."[89] As an assistant, Valeriano had to read and understand the pictorial and written documents about indigenous history and culture and to help in the production of such works.[90]

To aid a Spaniard such as Sahagún, who dedicated his life to understanding native tradition and language, Valeriano needed to be connected to the complex indigenous world in Mexico City.[91] His life experience must have made him a person who could speak fluently, literally, and figuratively with both natives and Spaniards. As such, he was versed in the ways of Spaniards and indigenous peoples. He was well connected in his home altepetl and also with the Franciscans and eventually the viceregal government. From the perspective of the viceregal government, therefore, he may have provided an opportunity to begin the transition of the Spanish-styled cabildo from a conquest-era institution affiliated with the royal lineage to a colonial institution with elected leaders and increasing dependence on the viceregal government.

Valeriano was remembered as a transitional figure and revered in the seventeenth century (along with other indigenous intellectuals) by those whom Brading has called creole patriots. Don Carlos de Sigüenza y Góngora wrote about him and claimed to have studied manuscripts that he allegedly authored.[92] Largely because of his talent and sixteenth-century fame, some scholars have attempted to credit Valeriano with work he likely had no part in producing. The Nahuatl text that relates the story of Our Lady of Guadalupe, Nican *mopohua* (Here It Is Related), is sometimes attributed to Valeriano. Poole has demonstrated that fundamental errors underlie the assumptions used to tie Valeriano to the text and argues instead that the Nican *mopohua* should properly be attributed to Luis Laso de la Vega, who served as "vicar of the *ermita* de Guadalupe" in the mid-seventeenth century when the Guadalupe story as we now know it reemerged. The Nahuatl text itself, Poole argues, constitutes only one part, "the account of the apparitions" of Guadalupe, within a larger Nahuatl work—the *Huey tlamahuiçoltica.*[93] Furthermore, Karttunen has argued that it defies logic to attribute the idea contained in the text to a student and colleague of Sahagún, who "was near choleric in his denunciation of the association of the Virgin Mary with the place called Tepeyacac," the site where the Virgin of Guadalupe reportedly appeared to Juan Diego.[94]

Valeriano, though talented and invested in both the indigenous and Spanish communities of Mexico City, possibly encountered political problems within indigenous society. Such complications, particularly among the principales, must have been difficult to overcome. He was among the second generation of students of the Franciscans in Tlatelolco. The philosophy for the second cohort, though the constitution of the colegio technically admitted only principales, enabled talented but nonnoble indigenous boys to enter the school. Students chosen by the friars because of their talent rather than their affiliation with important indigenous principal families made up part of the student body.[95] The school also provided scholarships (*becas*) for boys who did not have the resources to attend. The school's constitution suggests that those in need, defined as those from "distant pueblos or in great poverty," received additional funding beyond the beca to cover travel or basic necessities.[96]

Valeriano, though a skilled political figure in Tenochtitlan, had to win the support of the community of electors of Mexico Tenochtitlan. With some grace, he seems to have done well to build support and held the office apparently uncontested from 1573 to 1599, longer than any other postcontact governor. The first major obstacle to Valeriano's acceptance was his foreign birth. Though a Nahua, he came from another altepetl, Azcapotzalco. Valeriano's altepetl of origin also likely presented a problem for Tenochca electors who, in preserving their history, noted their conflict with Azcapotzalco as a seminal event in the rise of the Mexica. Azcapotzaltecas, formerly dominant in the Basin of Mexico, murdered the Tenochca tlatoani Chimalpopoca in 1426.[97] Tenochca electors may have seen the elevation of an Azcapotzalteco within the context of that ancient rivalry.

Valeriano's association with the Colegio de Santa Cruz may have presented a liability, at least among those who had lived during the Spanish invasion. Although he worked alongside indigenous leaders from all over the Basin in a school founded on the premise of producing an indigenous clergy and ruling clique, the students and teachers at the colegio followed a cadre of noble indigenous children who had made enemies within the native nobility.[98] Gibson pointed out that in Tlaxcala in the 1520s the first Franciscans found among the children of the rulers willing students who "learned [Christian doctrine] readily and rapidly." They also internalized, independently of their parents, the "errors" of the old religion. Their newfound faith made these young indigenous nobles willing accomplices to the friars, aiding them in their efforts "to destroy images and to burn temples." In one incident reported in numerous accounts by Franciscans, Tlaxcalan children "stoned to death an indigenous priest dressed as the god Ometochtli, thinking that he was the devil."[99] The zeal with which they allegedly pursued the wishes of the Franciscan missionaries caused great inter-generational discord.[100] Older Nahuas all over central Mexico, apparently with good reason, mistrusted the children who served the first friars, and according to Sahagún the parents eventually punished the children severely when they were returned to their homes.[101] The colegio, following the initial experiment by the Franciscans, seems to have encouraged less radicalism in its students. Valeriano's association with the friars potentially made him an outsider, at least for the older generation of Nahua. Perhaps as the contact-era elders passed away, a new generation saw only his status as a talented indigenous intellectual, which may have made him an appealing candidate for office.

Valeriano clearly possessed a keen intellect and understood how to work his way into positions of high status. Though it is difficult to reconstruct his path to the governorship, several possibilities present themselves. He obviously had a difficult task from the indigenous perspective. Some Tenochca who had lived during the time of the Spanish invasion and subsequent decade probably resisted him because of his association with the friars. His birth in the altepetl of Azcapotzalco and apparent lack of noble birth made him an unlikely choice of Tenochca electors. Yet he was obviously a person whose talent enabled him to succeed. He married well and apparently with political intentions. Doña Isabel de Alvarado, the daughter of don Diego de Alvarado Huanitzin and a noblewoman (*cihuapilli*) of the royal lineage of Mexico Tenochtitlan, gave Valeriano and his children an association with the indigenous nobility.[102] It is also likely that the Franciscans and the viceregal government could have influenced the electors to choose Valeriano, though the mechanism through which they might have extended this influence in the sixteenth century is unclear. Valeriano also seems to have potentially sought an avenue to authority through connection to the royal lineage. Precontact royal lineages, if the chain of male descendants ended, could be reconstituted through the daughters of tlatoque. In such instances the royal lineage could flow through the female line, whose "proper consorts" could bear children who could continue the royal lineage within the altepetl of their affiliation.[103] Though no direct evidence reveals Valeriano's reasoning, by marrying into the royal lineage he may have hoped to elevate the status of his children.[104]

VALERIANO AS A RULER IN OFFICE

Although marrying well may have given Valeriano standing within the altepetl of Mexico Tenochtitlan, other indirect evidence suggests that he was well regarded as a leader. His long uncontested tenure in office provides one clue. Surely the political nature of Tenochca principales presented a great obstacle to Valeriano, whose foreign birth and apparent modest nonnoble social standing presented easy opportunities to litigate. Though the absence of such litigation does not provide sufficient support to conclude that the electors favored or supported Valeriano, it is a curious detail. Valeriano also appears to have possessed remarkable skills when it came to negotiation with the viceregal government. Judge-governors collected tribute and delivered it to royal officials. Valeriano had the capacity to negotiate the level of tazación (amount of tribute owed by the community collectively) during a major epidemic when the population of the city fell sharply. Such skills likely won him support with the indigenous community of Mexico Tenochtitlan and also within the viceregal government.[105] After he could no longer comfortably serve as governor in 1596, Valeriano chose his successor. Don Juan Martín, a mestizo, served as a "deputy" to Valeriano for two years and eight months.[106] Although he was removed from office after Valeriano officially retired in 1599, Martín served thereafter as governor in Mexico Tlatelolco.[107] Such

influence speaks well of Valeriano's standing in the community, particularly among the community of electors. Allegations also exist,
discussed below, that Valeriano won allegiance through the strategic
misuse of his office by allowing native principales and some Spaniards
to profit at the expense of property owners.

Valeriano served during a difficult time in Mexico City. Severe
plagues in the 1570s reduced the population of the city significantly.
The outbreak, identified in the indigenous community as *cocoliztli* (the
Nahuatl term for general sickness), struck the native barrios of Mexico
City and elsewhere in the region from 1576 to 1581.[108] Based on the
symptoms and Nahuatl modifiers Chimalpahin used to describe it, the
disease was probably an outbreak of typhus. The epidemic lasted for
years and caused great suffering and death among the indigenous and
Spanish populations of Mexico Tenochtitlan and beyond, claiming an
unknown number of victims.[109] Anecdotal observations of the time suggest a dire, long-term, and widespread period of suffering that depopulated parts of the city. When he described the illness, Chimalpahin
stated that many thousands perished from "a green fever with heavy
chest congestion (pleurisy) . . . whose symptoms included bleeding
from the mouth and nose; the people begin to die and, as they knew no
remedy, they died by the thousands in all parts of New Spain."[110]

Fray Juan de Torquemada estimated that more than two million
died in 1576 alone and that the toll far exceeded the previous large
epidemic of 1545 by several fold. He explained that "no one was
healthy nor had the strength to treat the dying or to bury them." As
the epidemic extended beyond the capital, he wrote that, "in the
cities and large towns, they dug large ditches and from morning to
night officials [*ministros*] did nothing but collect corpses and throw
them into them [the ditches]."[111] Torquemada and Chimalpahin gen-
eralize the number of dead, but even if their estimates provide an
exaggerated impression of severity they do indicate the devastating
effect on the communities in and beyond Mexico City.

Some archival data provide an objective perspective that reveals the
effect on survivors within the city. The epidemic forced the indigenous
government into action to resolve numerous disputes over property
and inheritance that emerged because of the high death rate. So many

died in Mexico Tenochtitlan that vacant houses soon became a regular feature of the city. Dwellings and sometimes the associated lands (*camellones*) owned by natives in the barrios often lacked a legal title. When the owners and their immediate heirs died suddenly leaving no will or clear path of inheritance, multiple individuals sometimes filed claims of ownership.[112] Members of the indigenous cabildo of Mexico Tenochtitlan, during Valeriano's long tenure, became involved in adjudicating and facilitating a large number of land sales, especially during and after the epidemic. The cabildo worked diligently through the 1580s to title disputed properties in response to litigation. Much of their effort involved simply performing administrative tasks that made the sale and titling of property possible. Presumably many transactions mediated through the cabildo needed no litigation. When litigation did arise the disputes generally ended up in the Audiencia, but often the evidence generated by the native cabildo provided substantive data for the proceedings.[113]

To sell or purchase a property, the buyer and the seller had to be certain that no one held claim to it other than the seller. Such practices, a common feature of real estate transactions, made it possible to avoid or limit litigation but also, when completed, firmly established legal title to property. Indigenous claims to ownership were often based on appeals to prior possession and inheritance supported by the testimony of indigenous witnesses. By the 1570s, some quite elderly witnesses attested to ownership claims for litigants in Spanish courts. Those who had lived (or so they claimed) before the Spanish invasion had apparent knowledge of precontact ownership and sometimes were the exclusive basis of a claim.[114] The native cabildo sat at the center of the titling process. Alcaldes, alguaciles, regidores, and others affiliated with the indigenous government did the initial work to determine ownership in instances of property sales. Presumably the indigenous government had a role in most or even all transactions.[115] The exact documents from the cabildo most often appear as a Nahuatl section within a large case file processed by the Audiencia in Spanish. As a result, it is difficult to determine if the cabildo reflexively titled properties when they were involved in a transaction or if they took action only when multiple claimants vied for a property.

Table 1 Demographics of witnesses in lawsuits over disputed urban properties in Mexico City, 1560–1600

Age Range	Native	Spaniard	Other	Total (%)
20–29	5	3	4	12 (3)
30–39	17	9	1	27 (8)
40–49	28	8	5	41 (13)
50–59	59	6	3	68 (21)
60–69	73	4	3	80 (25)
70–79	33	2	1	36 (11)
80–90	13	0	0	13 (4)
No age given	41	2	0	43 (13)
Total	269 (84%)	34 (11%)	17 (5%)	320 (100%)

Source: Drawn from AGN, Tierras; see also Connell, "Emerging Ladino Spaces," chap. 2.

Note: Percentages in parentheses in "Total" column do not add up to 100 percent because of rounding.

In 1577 a group of indigenous litigants disputed a Spaniard who claimed he had purchased several houses and fields on part of a city block in the neighborhood of Yopico, located at the center of San Juan Moyotlan off of the main plaza near the church and tecpan.[116] Hernán Pérez, the principal Spaniard involved, claimed in a petition that he "had purchased a little house [casilla] from the indigenous governor [don Antonio Valeriano] and the alcaldes of San Juan [Mexico Tenochtitlan] as vacant property [bienes de difuntos]."[117] By bienes de difuntos, Pérez meant that it was a part of the estate of a person who had passed away. Because no legal heir claimed the property, Pérez purchased the house from the indigenous government. He also claimed that he had copies of the sale documents (escriptura de venta), legally executed in Nahuatl and translated into Spanish. The indigenous cabildo's role, it seems, was to adjudicate the probate decisions and clarify that no legal claimants had the right to inherit the property. The cabildo also administered the sale in the name of the estate of the deceased seller.

The act of determining that the property had no claimant was fairly elaborate and began when a purchaser came forward. The indigenous cabildo led by Governor Valeriano and his alcaldes, don Antonio de Mendoza and Francisco Martín, along with the regidor who represented the neighborhood, Pedro Jerónimo, ordered pregonero (public crier)

Diego Atzaxochitl and escribano Lázaro de San Juan to announce the pending sale, in Nahuatl. In the presence of the escribano, Atzaxochitl physically walked the neighborhood, announcing the sale of "several houses that Juan Pérez and Hernán Pérez, his father, Spaniards, bought for seventy pesos that were owned by the late María Xoco in the neighborhood of San Juan Yopico."[118]

Atzaxochitl toured the neighborhood with the scribe. They interviewed tribute collectors (*tepixque*) and recorded their testimony to determine what they knew of the property and the intent of María Xoco. During the three days they made rounds, no one contested the sale. The eight tepixque all stated that it was public knowledge that María Xoco wished to have the houses sold to pay for funeral masses.[119] With signed and sworn documents produced by an escribano and statements from minor indigenous officials witnessed by the pregonero who had also toured the neighborhood making public the pending sale, Valeriano had every reason to be satisfied that his government had done all it could to notify claimants to the property before he ordered its sale.[120]

Less than one month after the completion of the sale, Magdalena Ramírez filed a petition with the Audiencia claiming that, among other things, the alcaldes and governor of Mexico Tenochtitlan had participated in defrauding her and her family of the property. She accused the indigenous cabildo of making false documents and statements (*siniestra falsa relación*) that led to the alienation of the property against the will of its rightful owners.[121] Ramírez, through her attorney Toribio González, also clarified her claim to the property by stating that her late husband Pedro Luis legally possessed the property. He had inherited it from his late first wife Mariana, who had legally inherited it from her parents, Miguel Ocelotl and Ana Tlaco. Mariana and Pedro Luis had a child together, Estevan. Mariana perished during the initial outbreak of cocoliztli, leaving her minor son as the sole claimant to the property, of which he could take possession when he reached the age of majority. As his legal guardian, the argument went, Pedro Luis effectively possessed the property as the caretaker of the estate of his minor son, Estevan. When Estevan died, however, Ramírez argued, Pedro Luis retained de facto possession of the property through his role as guardian. When Pedro Luis died shortly thereafter, Ramírez argued, the property passed to his only surviving minor child, their daughter Juana Xoco.[122] Such a convoluted argument does not follow the normal inheritance patterns in either the Hispanic or indigenous legal traditions.[123] Apparently, though, the clever argument made some sense, particularly in light of the tragic and rapid loss of life during the epidemic. Indeed, Ramírez survived when most of her family did not, further emphasizing the tragic extent of the cocoliztli outbreak.[124]

Hernán Pérez, the purchaser of the property, responded to the petitions filed by Magdalena Ramírez by outlining why he felt entitled to the houses. Initially he argued that the indigenous government had assured him that they had taken all the proper steps to formalize and legitimize the sale. Pérez also claimed innocence, pleading that he had no knowledge of Ramírez's claim before the governor finalized the sale.[125] What suspicion would he have had, since the indigenous leaders had followed all the proper legal formulae established by Spanish law to transfer the property? Ultimately, after a complex story filled with tantalizing details, the court restored possession of the property to Magdalena Ramírez, who was to serve as its administrator until her daughter reached the age of majority.[126]

The question raised by the case: to what extent did the indigenous cabildo attempt to aid Pérez (who appears to have been unaware of any wrongdoing) in acquiring a property that was not vacant? The cabildo went to great effort to clear the title of the lands and houses. They interviewed tepixque, announced the pending sale regularly, and established the intent of the deceased owner. They also worked with Pérez to formalize the sale and presumably gave the proceeds to purchase masses for María Xoco. Ramírez, who had the strongest claim to possession of all who vied for the property, provided a compelling though largely speculative case in her allegation of willful wrongdoing on the part of Valeriano and the cabildo. She won the case for sure, largely thanks to González, her persuasive attorney. In cases tried before the Audiencia previously, González had made arguments based on "complex chain[s] of inheritance" similar to that which gave Ramírez possession.[127] In making this particular case, however, González and Ramírez directly accused the cabildo of fraud. The Audiencia apparently did not take the allegation seriously, perhaps caring only to clarify ownership of the property in dispute. Investigating the internal affairs of the cabildo apparently did not interest the Audiencia but may also indicate the lack of foundation of the allegation.

The unusual claim to possession presented by González, however, may have worked where earlier arguments had failed because of the circumstances of the case. Ramírez was physically present in the community during the time the cabildo allegedly certified that no one claimed to own the house. Indeed, Ramírez and some of her witnesses made it clear that she was living in the very house that the cabildo claimed it had worked diligently to notify the community was about to be sold as the unclaimed part of the estate of María Xoco. It defied logic that the pregonero and escribano thoroughly and diligently made rounds in the neighborhood with Ramírez living then in the very house up for sale. Did the agents of the cabildo not have a duty to check to see if anyone lived in the disputed property? Her presence there called into question the thoroughness of the cabildo's effort to find viable claimants. If the agents of the cabildo had sufficiently cleared the title, then why had Ramírez not heard of the pending sale? She clearly had not. It took nearly a month for her to file a proper complaint contesting the judgment of the cabildo.

Though the allegations raised by Ramírez are suspicious, the cabildo was also quite busy and could have easily overlooked claimants like Ramírez. Valeriano and the cabildo endured a veritable flood of cases in the late 1570s. The epidemic, mentioned regularly in the testimony of those involved in the case, was at its height. Many properties were transferred, and likely it was not always clear which specific properties were being sold. The extent to which the cabildo may have benefited from the sale of lands also seems negligible. The theft of properties— using their positions of authority to validate fraud—likely would have generated an inquiry by the Audiencia. It also would not have produced much revenue. González, as an attorney who regularly worked in indigenous property litigation, would have been in a position to have argued such cases and to have established a pattern of complaints, which he does not appear to have done. He did, as Kellogg's work demonstrates, come up with specific strategies that he adapted for use in multiple cases.[128]

In the end, Valeriano also cooperated with the Audiencia. The case ended with Ramírez in possession of the property after an extensive investigation. She appeared to have the most direct claim but, importantly, neither Pérez nor Valeriano attempted to contest the decision.[129] Valeriano, therefore, apparently oversaw the just outcome of a troubling dispute in which the cabildo assisted in the restoration of the property to a native woman. He also apparently deferred to viceregal institutions, allowing them to investigate and adjudicate the decision.

Other disputes arose out of the epidemics of the 1570s that can add insight into the role of the cabildo and governor in defrauding members of the community. In 1586, the indigenous cabildo took possession of property in one tlaxilacalli of San Pablo by declaring it vacant land (*tierras baldías*). They did this in a ceremony conducted in Nahuatl and recorded by the cabildo escribano, Francisco Xuárez, on 16 December in which the entire cabildo led by don Antonio Valeriano declared that the land had no proper owner.[130] They collectively declared that the lands "pertained to the people of Moyotlan," the principle barrio of Mexico Tenochtitlan, "and also belonged to the four parcialidades and by chance they were returned [*de suerte que estaban repartidas*]."[131] The implication that altepetl lands had been somehow alienated from Moyotlan is clear in the language of the document, hence the need to restore those lands to the community. Miguel de los Angeles, an important alcalde who served multiple (nonconsecutive) terms in office between 1586 and 1596, claimed the property after the cabildo had declared it vacant, promising to cultivate the land that had formerly been left fallow.[132] Furthermore, Governor Valeriano based his original decision in the lawsuit on the testimony of *viejos* (elders) from Mexico Tenochtitlan—Miguel Xacobo, Francisco Jiménez, Martín Xacobo, Tomás Xacobo, Miguel Pablo, and Miguel Hernández—who explained that these lands had always been part of the community and that those who claimed otherwise spoke "falsely" and "without speaking the truth."[133] In addition to the report that declared the land vacant, the cabildo produced a high-quality map painted by a traditional native scribe (*tlacuilo*) that included a detailed description of the property. The cabildo had a clear monopolization over resources and could use images as persuasive tools in argument, as it had in the 1560s when it produced what we now call the Códice Osuna.[134]

There were, however, those who disputed the cabildo's attempt to declare the lands vacant. Francisco Martín and his children claimed the lands were not vacant at all but belonged to him. The indigenous cabildo and its governor, whom Martín named directly in the suit, had taken the land by abusing its authority to declare land vacant. Furthermore, Miguel de los Angeles, a member of that body, had personally benefited from the decision that he helped make. Conflict of interest and lack of recusal on the part of Los Angeles aside, the main accusation levied by Martín claimed that the indigenous government appeared to have taken land from his possession by exploiting its duty to regulate the property in its jurisdiction. In addition, the cabildo appeared to then brazenly distribute "vacant" land to its own members. Francisco Martín, in addressing the cabildo during the suit, actually accused the governor, don Antonio Valeriano, of rewarding his friends through the redistribution of land. Martín alleged that Valeriano literally stole the land and "was an intimate friend and comrade" of Los Angeles, and that their "great friendship" allowed the defendant to possess the land.[135]

Martín appears to have caught the cabildo abusing its authority. The sheepish response by Alonso de Heredia, the attorney for Miguel de los Angeles, suggests his client's indefensible position: "The argument presented [by the plaintiff] . . . to say that the governor is an intimate friend of my client is without foundation because [Governor Valeriano] has equal friendship with all [his subjects] and in regard to the said order he favors none . . . because he is a good Christian."[136] The incredulous assertion that Valeriano's friendship extended equally to all seems to be only a hollow attempt by the defense to find innocence where it did not exist. Though neither Heredia nor the plaintiff's attorney commented further on the alleged collusion, it is exemplary particularly in light of the earlier accusations of improper conduct raised by Magdalena Ramírez. The accusation also brought about a speedy definitive sentence.

Heredia, in defense of Los Angeles, made more substantive though not wholly convincing arguments in which he defended the actions of the governor and cabildo. He argued that the land had been fallow when the cabildo declared it vacant. Since that time, Los Angeles possessed the property. Three years had passed since the original act of possession, and Heredia argued that Los Angeles had committed significant resources to its improvement and had "cultivated and planted it [the land], possessing it physically with the title that the governor and principales provided him with."[137] Even this seemingly firm claim of possession, argued in 1590, reveals only the obvious possession that Los Angeles took formally the three years before. That Los Angeles possessed the land in 1590 was not at issue; rather, Martín claimed that the very process of taking the land had violated his prior possession rights.[138]

On 20 February 1590, the Audiencia ordered don Antonio Valeriano to oversee a ceremony in which a mediated settlement resolved the dispute. Because of the claimed possession, in which he legally, according to Spanish precedent, possessed a titled property, Miguel de los Angeles was allowed to keep the land. The court physically marked off the territory, measuring its boundaries and officially granting title to Los Angeles, as ordered by the Audiencia, which recognized that he had "planted and cultivated" the lands in question. The final sentence also reversed an order given just a month before that gave possession to Martín. Valeriano supervised and officiated over the ceremony that confirmed Los Angeles's possession. Officers of the cabildo, noted principales from the communities of Mexico Tenochtitlan and Mexico Tlatelolco and the judge-governors from both parcialidades (don Juan Martín and don Antonio Valeriano) attended the ceremony.[139] Two translators from the Audiencia attended, aiding the escribano who recorded the official version of the event for the court. The Audiencia, however, also argued that Francisco Martín had lost land to which he likely had a viable claim. To correct the problem, they found additional tierras baldías that fell within the jurisdiction of Mexico Tlatelolco and gave that land to Francisco Martín.[140] The resolution, though probably satisfying only Los Angeles, also afforded Martín, the aggrieved party, some sense of justice. Though the lands to which he had traditionally laid claim no longer belonged to him, he received as compensation lands of apparently equivalent size and value.[141]

Allegations of malfeasance made by Francisco Martín, though they clearly engaged the Audiencia in the case, do not stand up well when considering the resolution. Governor Valeriano cooperated with the Audiencia and encouraged a resolution based on indigenous understanding of land tenure and Spanish legal ideas of prior possession. When the case initially was presented to the cabildo, he acted in the interests of the principal community, declaring the lands vacant and awarding them through an official action to Miguel de los Angeles, who wished to claim and cultivate them. He did this because his investigation ensured that no one claimed the lands at the time. As a political actor on the cabildo, Valeriano responded to an apparent request from the principal community by initiating a legal process that in fact drew out the plaintiff in the suit when it appeared that the lands in question were indeed vacant. Valeriano, it appears, simply responded to the micropatriotism of his constituency, the parcialidad of Mexico Tenochtitlan, when the principales who elected the cabildo annually claimed that the lands in question pertained to the community of Moyotlan.[142] When a legitimate claimant, Francisco Martín, came before the Audiencia to contest the act of possession, Valeriano also cooperated with the Spanish courts to ensure that a fair and just outcome emerged that suited both parties. Even though the resolution took a long time, Valeriano apparently satisfied all involved. The community of principales had the lands restored to a principal of Moyotlan. The Audiencia saw that the legal requirements of possession as defined by Spanish legal culture were met and resolved to clarify who owned the land if a dispute ever arose again. Francisco Martín received lands of equivalent value, which, because he did not continue to dispute the decision, must have satisfied him to some extent. In all, allegations of corruption, though they served well the cause of Martín, seem only to confirm the skill of Valeriano as a politician who sought to balance the needs of all his constituencies.

The cabildo worked to mediate and negotiated responsibly to resolve disputes over land in the barrios. Though it sometimes seemed to interfere in property transactions, the cabildo under Valeriano usually sought to protect and defend the rights of litigants and to establish just outcomes to difficult disputes. Magdalena Ramírez and Francisco Martín both saw the possibility of collusion between the cabildo and purchasers. As these cases played out, however, the Audiencia, governor, and cabildo worked together to resolve the underlying disputes in fair and just ways. There were other cases where allegations of forged documents surfaced but were never fully authenticated.[143] More often, as demonstrated above, the cabildo led by Valeriano repeatedly defended the rights of property owners when they showed a compelling claim to possession.[144] Although the cabildo seemed to aid certain specific constituent groups (in the Martín case, the community elders who wanted lands they claimed restored; in the Ramírez case, Spaniards who wanted land), Valeriano as an actor seems to have relied on the judicial apparatus to work through any complex legal issues that arose among litigants in Mexico Tenochtitlan. He also seems to have stood back and allowed all groups to build support for their cases, following the evidence and due process. Such apparent impartiality must have won him support from ordinary tribute payers and electors who chose and served on the cabildo.

Valeriano was well suited to serve in the role of mediator, as he understood both the traditions and customs of the indigenous society he served and the logic of viceregal courts.[145] Educated in a school run by Franciscans, culturally indigenous, of apparent nonnoble status, and yet the associate of principales from all over the Basin of Mexico, Valeriano could work with any conceivable constituency. Within the Hispanic world he understood the legalistic ways of the viceregal courts. Working with fray Juan de Torquemada, fray Juan Bautista, and fray Bernardino de Sahagún, he cultivated skills needed to tease out the secrets of indigenous elders who had ample reason to mistrust his motives as an ethnographer working with the Franciscans. He must have drawn on his indigenous roots, growing up culturally native in the communities of Mexico Tenochtitlan, Mexico Tlatelolco, and Azcapotzalco. From such experiences he also understood the importance of deferring to the community of elders in Mexico Tenochtitlan and cooperating with powerful principales like Miguel de los Angeles. Straddling both communities allowed him to defer mostly to the legal customs and institutions of the viceregal government, which invariably aided them in their efforts to further their reach into the community of Mexico Tenochtitlan. Decisions therefore tended to preserve native land tenure customs when appropriate or to add legal title to lands when necessitated by dispute. Valeriano was able to make or facilitate judgments that conformed to both customary law and legal tradition. He thus seems to have served all constituencies.

Valeriano also enabled important transformation within the institutional structure of indigenous government in Mexico Tenochtitlan.
He helped move the institutions of the governorship and cabildo out
of the immediate postcontact association with the royal lineage, yet
his reign preserved many elements of the judge-governorship as it
was associated with the ruling Tenochca lineage. He served for life
(or as long as he remained healthy), which apparently conformed to
indigenous custom. Though standard in precontact Mexico Tenochtitlan, life terms in office (excepting the monarch of course) were rare
in Castile, which adapted instead rotational systems for officeholders
(see chapter 1).[146] He apparently did not have to stand for reelection
each year and thus continued the trend that the judge-governor did
not need to rotate in and out of office like other elected officials in the
sixteenth century.[147] Presumably, viceregal officials attempted to ensure
a smooth transition following initial contact by preserving continuity
with the past.[148]

It seems from the evidence available that in the sixteenth century the
corregidor model fits the office of judge-governor, but that gradually
the office changed so that by the mid-seventeenth century (especially
after the 1629 flood) the judge-governor came to resemble other elected
indigenous officials. Rules governing reelection, however, were not
regularly enforced until the early eighteenth century. In chapter 3, I
initiate the discussion of the transformation in the mid-seventeenth
century, during which elections came to be held each year. New advisors
appeared as seventeenth-century governors and cabildos took on additional responsibilities. Important new forces, such as non-Tenochca and
nonnatives living in the barrios, created complexities that did not exist
in sixteenth century Mexico Tenochtitlan. Yet continuities persisted.
Technically, judge-governors could not serve consecutive terms, yet
more often than not they did.[149] In practice the judge-governor, when
associated with the royal line, served for life or until he chose to retire.
After a period of transition and driven by the political needs of the
community itself, the judge-governor eventually was restricted and
bound by written rules that governed elected offices. The changes, as
the following chapters reveal, were largely driven by political actors
within the community of Mexico Tenochtitlan and not by viceregal

officials. Like other changes, the transformation occurred gradually.[150] Valeriano served as long as he chose because those who came before him had served for life. Adhering to tradition established continuity with the past. It took generations and a more complex manner of political culture to make governors rotate and face election annually.

CHAPTER 3

A City Emergent
Viceregal Challenges to
Local Politics, 1629–1654

Mexico City grew substantially in physical size and in population in the seventeenth century. It also became increasingly diverse. Historian Francisco de la Maza has argued that the architectural changes show the transformation physically. He uses two maps (*planos*) of the city, one from 1628 and the other from 1695, to show its growth visually. The first map, by Juan Gómez de Trasmonte, is a well-known and widely reproduced panoramic view looking down on the city from the west. The lake and mountains that surround the city are plain to see, as are details of the urban architecture.[1] The second map depicts the city in 1695. Painted on a wooden screen (*biombo*), it is usually displayed in the museum of Chapultepec Castle in Mexico City.[2] De la Maza wrote, emphasizing particularly the central traza, that "in the painting of 1629 it [Mexico City] appeared to be a place with modest churches and small, one-story houses." The later biombo painting of 1695 reveals a transformation, showing that "several impressive structures dominated the city and the houses were *all* two-story."[3] De la Maza's comments suggest that the city's structures alone reveal the transformations that occurred in the seventeenth century. The city had grown and developed. The physical architecture most impressed de la Maza, and he concluded that it reflected the city's wealth and stature. He reinforced his observations by examining descriptions of the city, contrasting those written at the beginning and end of the century.[4]

Beyond the literary and artistic examples provided by de la Maza, evidence from the late seventeenth-century traza attests to the lavish

90

vertical growth of the city. Citizens, particularly the owners of large buildings, piped water into private courtyards.[5] City officials successfully pushed for and carried out large-scale public works projects, including the erection of bridges over drainage canals. Large companies of workers regularly cleaned the streets at public expense. Workers took on the dangerous and unsanitary work of cleaning the drainage canals that crisscrossed the city. To ensure that the city did not flood, particularly after 1636, workers, mostly natives, removed refuse, which could be anything that happened to fall into the drainage canals.[6] Clogged canals provided a keen source of anxiety for residents, who worried with reason that during seasonal rains flooding would overwhelm the drainage system. Workers also repaired decaying infrastructure, including damaged canals, aqueducts, bridges, and buildings.[7] Street pavers regularly worked to maintain the stone streets and expand the paved parts of the city, often compelling the owners of buildings to pay for repairs and improvements.[8] All of these civic projects suggest that city officials chose to build and expand municipal infrastructure.[9]

Alongside the improvements in urban infrastructure, the city also experienced an equally impressive demographic boom. The expansion of the population made the city more diverse and complex. No longer was it an indigenous city interspersed with transient Spaniards bent on realizing dreams of wealth and then heading home. Rather, a large *criollo* (creole) population existed.[10] Immigrants from Asia and Africa lived alongside those of mixed racial decent. Increasingly, Mexico City became conspicuous for its complexity. As Hoberman observed, "Between 1590 and 1660, the transformation of Mexican society from an Indian to a mixed-blood population continued to progress." To accommodate the rapidly growing population, "hospitals, schools, religious institutions, and public works multiplied."[11] As a result, in the parcialidades, indigenous governments presided over increasingly diverse neighborhoods.[12] Such diversity included the expansion of the indigenous population, including the incorporation and matriculation into the community of significant numbers of natives who spoke languages other than the dominant Nahuatl.

The investment in the infrastructure of the city by private citizens and the government was significant and corroborates much of the anecdotal evidence provided by de la Maza. In short, Mexico City expanded and grew. Its growth probably reflected general prosperity, though a prosperity likely limited to a minority of the population.[13] The emerging merchant community, large viceregal government, and extensive infrastructure affiliated with the seat of the archbishop made the city a vibrant locus of commerce, government, and religion.[14] All of this growth and development occurred in the aftermath of the tumultuous second and third decades of the seventeenth century. The "foiled" Afro-Mexican uprising of 1612, the uprising against the viceroy in 1624, and the 1629 flood—which caused leaders to ponder abandoning the city entirely—preceded the massive growth and expansion of the city.[15] A new city emerged after 1636. The viceregal government, following indigenous leaders, slowly began the process of transforming indigenous institutions to suit the new environment.

For natives in the barrios and the government that presided over them, the increasingly diverse and needy population actually relieved some of the pressure to provide repartimiento labor. Although in the sixteenth century tribute labor drafts provided a constant source of litigation and dissent, the increasing reliance on free-wage labor may have meant that indigenous communities owed less repartimiento service.[16] Urban public works projects relied heavily on free-wage labor even though it cost substantially more. By the end of the seventeenth century, free labor made up a significant portion of the labor force. Though the number of public building projects in the city rose through the seventeenth century, many did not rely on repartimiento labor and those that did drew many workers from outside the city.[17] Repartimiento labor drafts were smaller in physical size than they had been in the past as well. Labor drafts from the 1560s involved thousands of natives; one brought more than 4,500 natives to the city from all over the region. Late seventeenth-century data show that the city used groups of workers that numbered fewer than sixty who rotated weekly. These smaller gangs repaired bridges or cleaned the drainage canals.[18] Free-wage labor likely reduced the burden on indigenous governors, though not substantially in some years.[19]

As opportunistic Spaniards migrated into the barrios, they brought significantly more pressure to bear on the government of Mexico

Tenochtitlan to collect tribute. Though Mexico City resisted the introduction of nonnatives into government posts for most of the early
seventeenth century, it was a difficult struggle. As in other communities
that surrounded the Basin of Mexico, especially in smaller pueblos,
mestizos, Afro-Mexicans, and Spaniards sometimes took posts on the
cabildo; even in Mexico Tenochtitlan and Tlatelolco mestizos occasionally held the office of judge-governor and alcalde.[20] The extension
of Spaniards into the governments of Mexico Tenochtitlan and Mexico
Tlatelolco may have initially resulted from the resistance met by
indigenous tribute collectors when they attempted to collect from
those in the employ of Spaniards. In one instance, in 1635, Spaniards
who employed natives attacked and insulted native tribute collectors.
Perhaps the viceregal government saw use in employing Spaniards to
enhance the legitimacy of tribute collection, particularly for those
natives in the service of Spaniards.[21]

THE FLOOD

From the fall of 1629 until 1634, Mexico City endured a succession of
seasonal deluges that flooded the city, making sections of it uninhabitable.[22] Though the city was not underwater for the entire year, during
the periods of heaviest rain, late spring through September, residents
often had to rely on canoes to move through some areas. During the
dry part of the year, late fall through the spring, the city dried sufficiently to expose some of the roadways. The Marqués de Cerralvo, the
viceroy (r. 1624–35), remarked optimistically in a letter of 2 May 1632,
just before the rainy season, that "the streets are now sufficiently dry to
reveal that the pavement is covered with silt [polvo]." He suggested
that, if the summer rains were weaker than in the past years, the city
could hope to return to normal. The streets, he continued in a hopeful
tone, no longer required canoes for transit but could accommodate those
in "coaches, on horseback, and on foot." He also suggested that the
center of town fared better than the peripheral sections, since during
Semana Santa (Holy Week), which had just passed, the principal streets
had dried enough to permit full processions.[23]

Despite the viceroy's optimism in 1632, the rains returned and so did the floodwaters.[24] Many in the indigenous barrios lost their homes. The barrios, occupying the lowest land in the city, flooded early and remained flooded longer, leaving many destitute. The houses, often not made of stone, literally melted into the floodwaters. All in the city suffered, as suggested by Hoberman in her account of the flooding: "Inside the city, people were stranded in the upper floors of their houses, if they still had houses. The one-storey adobe and cane stalk houses in the indigenous *barrios* were easily brought down, but even the well-built monasteries and family mansions in the Spanish *traza* suffered. Water undermined the foundations, and buildings became uninhabitable either because of interior flooding or the danger of collapse."[25] Up to six feet of water covered sections of the city at the height of the flooding, and despite the highly touted drainage system (*desagüe*) engineered and constructed in the first decade of the century, the water remained for months and years.[26] Such destruction forced many to leave the city rather than endure the hardships that accompanied the flood.[27]

The damage to the city and population loss had ramifications for the collection of tribute. The governor of Mexico Tenochtitlan, don Juan de León, in office when the flood struck, related that many had died in the storm and subsequent inundation and others had lost their homes.[28] Survivors fled to regional cities not affected, such as nearby Coyoacan or Tacubaya, to seek shelter. When the floodwaters did not recede, they remained there because they had nothing to return to in Mexico Tenochtitlan. Once outside the city, migrants often no longer paid tribute. The survivors who fortunately did not lose their homes stayed in the city but still had to pay tribute. The governor, of course, had to make certain that the city raised the amount of tribute it owed. The flooded conditions impelled don Juan de León to plead with the viceregal government to reduce the community's burden. He argued that the community could not possibly pay the required amount for 1629 and 1630. He asked specifically for relief, stating that under present conditions "it is impossible to execute the collection with the few who remain."[29]

Crown attorney (*fiscal*) don Juan González de Peñafiel recommended that the governors of both Mexico Tenochtitlan and Mexico Tlatelolco receive a six-month abeyance. Such a modest reduction must have provided little comfort to the governors. Though the reprieve was granted to preserve the communities and to halt further migrations, with the city's economy devastated and much of its infrastructure destroyed the native population moved to survive, not, as the order assumed, to avoid tribute.[30] A break from tribute could do little to increase collection or encourage those who fled to return.

The flood itself exposed a major problem with tribute collection that facilitated changes in indigenous practices and compelled the viceregal government to pay closer attention to tribute finance. Before the flood, governors were largely left to their own devices and held accountable gently. After the flood, the viceregal government began to make regular interventions to remove debtor governors from office. Judge-governors who could not collect the requisite amount of tribute were forced to use their *fiadores* (financial guarantors) and sometimes to endure prison while their debts were settled. Furthermore, the viceregal government paid increasing attention to setting and upholding standards for financial guarantors, forcing governors to provide detailed statements of their assets.

Slower change also occurred after the flood. Governors had to accommodate additional supervision by viceregal officials. The new office of *alguacil amparador*, a lieutenant of the *amparador de los naturales*, was employed as a liaison who could exercise judicial authority and collect tribute to aid judge-governors. Elections and reelection rules were increasingly enforced by viceregal overseers. The *contador general de los reales tributos y azogues* oversaw tribute collection for all of New Spain and set the amount of tribute owed by each community (tazación). Occasionally, because of the nature of his office, the contador recommended that the viceroy overturn an election on the grounds that the winning candidate did not have sufficient financial backing to serve as governor.[31] After the flood, elections appear to have been held annually for the office of judge-governor. Even though sometimes governors served multiple terms in office after the flood, Mexico Tenochtitlan gradually began to move toward annual governor election, though exceptions exist. Before the flood, it appears that the election of a governor came when the sitting governor chose to leave office or became too ill to serve.[32]

ELECTIONS

Each year, on or around 1 January, electors congregated in the tecpan of Mexico Tenochtitlan to elect a cabildo and sometimes a governor. This act was preceded by the appointment of an oidor to supervise the election. After the completion of the election ceremony, an elaborate confirmation process ended with a new cabildo and sometimes a new governor appointed. The election ceremony evolved during the seventeenth century in ways that first made political maneuvering possible and then more complex as the viceregal government intervened more directly. The Audiencia, over the first half of the century, invested significant resources in supervising and certifying elections. Though it is unclear exactly when these institutions emerged, they appear fully formed in the earliest documents used for this study. The elaborate ceremony served to ensure fairness and provide some oversight of the process but, as an unintended consequence, also provided avenues for appeal.[33]

Multiple observers watched the election ceremony, representing the many interested parties. The Audiencia supplied two nahuatlatos who translated the ceremony for Spanish-speaking officials. Presumably these two translators aided an oidor, also a representative from the Audiencia who attended officially in the place of the viceroy; but others, even non-Nahua indigenous representatives, may have needed the services of a translator. In some ceremonies, an escribano from the Audiencia affiliated with the Juzgado General de los Indios (General Indian Court) also attended.[34] It appears that Audiencia nahuatlatos translated the proceedings orally for the overseer and that native scribes provided a written record of the event. On the basis of some obvious spelling and agreement issues (e.g., don Pascual de *lo* Reyes) in the lists of names, they appear to have been native. Perhaps a native scribe not used to writing in Spanish might make such a mistake. Additionally, some of the same spellings appear common in written Nahuatl, (e.g., don Çebastian de Çuntiago alhuaçil mayor, and the spelling of *paçado* after each of the electors who had formerly served).[35] Indigenous scribes came from each of the four subdivisions of the parcialidad and wrote independent memorias that became public record.[36] The memorias documented the event by registering the name and office currently or formerly held by each elector. By doing this they verified also that each elector was eligible to participate. They also included a tally generated by at least one of the scribes that revealed the number of votes (though the name of the voter was not included in the tally) amassed by each candidate. The scribes and interpreters authenticated the vote tallies and swore to their faithful recording, signing the documents to make them official.[37] The certification indicated that all candidates "were capable, able, and of good character," apparently a requirement for eligibility to hold the office. The contador general also had to ensure that they could secure the necessary financing to hold the governorship.[38] Scribes certified that no one had coerced voters illicitly and that all who participated had the right to cast a vote.[39]

The most complete record of a native election in Mexico Tenochtitlan that I have uncovered took place on 7 January 1674. The document provides in detail a list of all who voted.[40] Elements of the document suggest that derivations of some important indigenous traditions continued. Through the actual votes were secret, the electors were named and listed along with their current or former office. In addition, each of the constituencies represented in the city was listed under a separate heading. Each of the four urban subdivisions of Mexico Tenochtitlan appeared in ranked order: San Juan Moyotlan, San Pablo Teopan, San Sebastián Atzaqualco, and Santa María la Redonda Cuepopan. Other constituencies with representation on the cabildo were also listed, including "the electors of the Chichimecas," who had twelve voters (only three of whom could sign). The complexity had increased since the time when only the four subdivisions of Mexico Tenochtitlan elected or affirmed the election of the chosen governor. Dividing and ranking the subunits according to their position in the city and maintaining traditional subunits suggest the persistence of precontact practices.[41]

Having representatives of each of the four constituent parts of the altepetl gave all who had a stake in the outcome a hand in regulating the election process. Preserving the altepetl divisions, however, was also quite significant. The parishes of the city also constituted a series of divisions in native barrios, and yet politically these divisions apparently had no meaning for native elections.[42] A sufficiently small number of electors made it unlikely, though not impossible, that ineligible voters participated.[43] The mechanism by which scribes determined the eligibility of voters and candidates remains unclear, but absent protest the viceregal government did not generally investigate or verify the sworn statements made by electors.[44]

Within the election system, several avenues for appeal appeared, including exploiting some checks designed to reduce irregularities. In the absence of the royal lineage of Mexico Tenochtitlan, no indigenous family could lay exclusive claim to the governorship. Since the early seventeenth century the office of judge-governor opened up to considerations of politics simply because rival factions unconstrained by ineligibility entered the political arena. By 1659 it appears that anyone who could build a significant support base and convince the tribute collection officials of their capacity to collect the revenue could run for office. Such a scenario demanded oversight. The viceregal government relied on regulation and a thorough vetting of the elected governor's financial backing. Carefully watching elections to make sure that a candidate had the support he purported to command and scrutinizing the financing of tribute by checking fiadores took on increasing importance.[45] Much was at stake in the governorship. The viceregal government had an interest in strict oversight of tribute collection and the preservation of order. Thus, politics and political maneuvering on the part of factions within the cabildo and community of electors served to draw the Audiencia into the process. As a result, the new election system seemed to encourage the viceregal government to intervene in the elections of indigenous cabildos in a way that they had previously eschewed.

In the secret ballot election, the scribes and translators reported their tallies to the officials who had the authority to certify the result.[46] One representative of the indigenous cabildo, usually the current governor, had to endorse the election with his signature. The viceregal bureaucracy also had a representative who certified the election; in Mexico Tenochtitlan it was an oidor who physically attended the ceremony, sitting in the cabildo chamber of the indigenous community.[47] He functioned as a supervisor and also to ensure that those elected were suitable to hold office.[48] The oidor had to "confirm" and certify the elected officials, even stating that "no Spaniard or person prohibited by royal ordinance" voted for the winner.[49] In practice, he also had the authority to make recommendations to the viceroy and Audiencia. In effect, this gave him the authority to recommend that the viceroy veto unsuitable candidates or void an election entirely.

The oidor appointed to supervise indigenous elections generally submitted a petition that certified the election result. Though these documents often use a familiar text that did not vary much from year to year, such language provides clues indicating what the viceregal government expected of a newly elected governor and cabildo. The 1655 appointment of don Diego de la Cruz Villanueva (r. 1653, 1655–57) shows that the viceregal government thought governors should collect tribute, ensure the suppression of idolatry, and behave with proper decorum.[50] Governors should uphold the virtues of "civilized" society. At all times they should be moral, law abiding, and sober.[51] The text of the ceremony of appointment perhaps clarifies the central importance of tribute collection among the various duties a governor had to perform:

> The said oidor has observed the election of don Diego de la Cruz Villa-nueva and has remitted to the viceroy to confirm [the election] and appointment of the said governor of the parcialidad of San Juan [Mexico Tenochtitlan], its four barrios and subject towns. The said don Diego de la Cruz Villanueva should take up the staff of royal justice [vara de real justicia] for the purpose of serving the natives of his barrios and subject towns, in order that he collect [cobrar] royal tribute with punctuality and fidelity without doing harm to the tribute payers, nor charging more than they are required to pay, in the honorable manner of those who came before. The collected tribute is to be deposited in the royal treasury of this court as has been customary in the past.[52]

The section of the appointment document cited above provides only the first part of a longer list of expectations for indigenous governors. It does not mention all duties but instead indicates primarily the expectations of the viceregal government. Although governors performed numerous functions in the context of the communities of Mexico Tenochtitlan, the appointment document spells out first that they should collect tribute and report any abuse or mistreatment to the Audiencia or viceroy. More critical issues like tribute collection appear alongside more perfunctory duties like rooting out idolatry. Even though indigenous officials were warned to avoid moral failings and defend the faith, tribute collection remained the most important function of the governorship from the viceregal perspective.

By laying out expectations and detailing the qualities of a good governor, the appointment document provides a detailed list of ways to challenge the election of a governor. Several issues on which to maneuver politically against a governor exist in the appointment document itself. Those who sought to oppose a governor could focus on his poor treatment or abuse of natives, inability to collect tribute, drunkenness, or liaisons with women (*amancebamientos*). Indeed, many of the complaints against governors that emanated from the community attempted to demonstrate that the governor did not fulfill the terms of the appointment document. Native litigants learned to use these terms to challenge elections. Appointment documents therefore provide exceedingly useful information, and sometimes appended to the file are petitions of complaint against the elected governor. Supervising oidores received such petitions from the contador general, the community, principales, or even groups who supported a particular candidate for office. Also generally recorded were the responses given by the oidor and sometimes the viceroy through his fiscal.

Elected governors, beyond their ability to perform the duties of office, also had to certify after winning enough votes that they had the necessary financial support to serve. The certification process followed all of the political maneuvering that likely brought to the surface any other reasons the Audiencia might dismiss a candidate. Along with sufficient political support, a candidate needed financial backing in the form of financial guarantors (fiadores) who would put up their property (or a portion of it) to guarantee that the governor would deliver all of the tribute owed by the community even if the tribute payers could not. Such a system made the governorship an office restricted to the politically well-connected who had the business and social relationships necessary to put together a substantial financial support package. Finances also became a means to challenge the election of a popular candidate. In addition, the contador could request that the election supervisor reject the election of unsuitable candidates. As elections became increasingly important in the mid-seventeenth century, tribute finance sometimes enabled political actors without the franchise in the indigenous barrios to participate indirectly in elections.[53]

THE GOVERNOR'S FINANCIAL GUARANTORS

To guarantee payment, governors had to secure financial backing from fiadores who collectively underwrote the entire sum of tribute owed by guaranteeing funds using their personal assets as collateral.[54] Regulations regarding the number and financial disclosure of fiadores varied over time. By the late seventeenth century, governors had to provide detailed financial statements. The general trend suggests that in the 1620s simply listing viable financial fiadores and vouching for their character could suffice. Don Antonio Valeriano the younger (r. 1620–24) stated that his two fiadores were Alonso Vásquez, a merchant, and don Juan Bautista Valeriano, a *persona abonada* (trustworthy person), but he did not have to list real estate or even the amount the contador could hold them liable for in the event of a default.[55] By mid-century it was necessary before he assumed office that the governor-elect provide proof that he had sufficient resources to hold the office. In essence, he had to submit a financial statement that listed any property or goods he possessed personally and their value. He also had to include the value of any property offered by fiadores. The contador general supposedly verified these statements, and the governor-elect and his wife (usually) swore to their completeness and accuracy in a formal, witnessed statement. As the century progressed, those who aspired to the governorship needed an extensive and wealthy social network and the ability to distribute patronage to supporters. Initially fiadores were usually natives, other principales within the community who possessed property or had significant wealth.[56] By the 1670s, however, many of the fiadores were Spaniards and mestizos, and only a few natives backed governors financially.[57] Some contadores preferred Spaniards, as suggested by the disqualification of governor-elect don

Juan de Velázquez in 1654. Velázquez claimed that his fiadores were adequate and objected to the imposition of the contador that fiadores "had to be trustworthy (abonados) Spaniards."[58]

Early fiadores, in the 1620s, apparently did not receive much checking by the contador general before their certification. Luis Carrillo y Alarcón, the contador in 1620, stated in the financing document for don Antonio Valeriano the younger that he had read and personally seen that fiadores had been named by the governor-elect. He then obligated them to serve as fiadores for the community and required that they be financially responsible for the total amount of tribute that the community owed according to the records maintained by the office of the contador general (*contaduría*). Yet only two fiadores were responsible for the entire burden should a shortfall occur. With tribute owed by the community in the many thousands of pesos, the two fiadores were possibly extraordinarily generous, and thus willing to mortgage most if not all of their property, fairly confident in the ability of the governor to collect all the tribute owed, or certain that the viceregal government would not hold them to account in the event of a shortfall. The viceroy does not seem to have questioned what the fiadores submitted or to have required any substantial review of their qualifications.[59]

It is unclear when the viceregal government began to check fiadores with care. In 1654 governor-elect Velázquez faced resistance from the contador, and in 1657 governor don Marcos de la Cruz presented a series of fiadores who, when pressed to provide backing, pleaded poverty. In a petition to the Juzgado General, the contador stated that the fiadores for de la Cruz—Diego de Espinoza, Nicolás Valeriano, Nicolás Causino, don Felipe Valeriano, and don Juan de Aguilar— were "poor men without significant wealth or property."[60] Though his petition, given just after the election, brought no immediate response from the overseers, it factored into the dismissal of de la Cruz from office after the first quarter of the year.[61] The viceregal bureaucracy apparently had an increasing interest in the solvency of fiadores in the 1650s not present in the 1620s or apparently before.

Contrasting the process of the 1620s with that of the 1670s reveals a large philosophical transformation. The financial disclosure made by governor-elect don Juan Montaño, prepared on 22 December 1674, illustrates the change. Don Antonio de la Vega y Noroña, then the contador general, oversaw the declaration of Montaño's fiadores. Unlike his predecessor from 1620, contador general Luis Carrillo y Alarcón, de la Vega y Noroña carefully reviewed the assets presented by each fiador. He made certain that Montaño could account for the estimated 12,500 pesos he would have to collect during his one-year term in office. Montaño had difficulty coming up with sufficient backing, though he submitted a detailed accounting of amounts pledged and property that underwrote the commitment by each fiador (see table 2).[62]

Fiadores had to provide significant information to establish their ability to guarantee the debt of the governor by the 1670s. They had to indicate their place of residence. If they lived in the parcialidades they included the ward (tlaxilacalli), or parish, and if they lived in the traza they had to provide the name of their street. Such information probably mattered in one way as a kind of identification, but also likely it provided a location of the property the fiador offered to guarantee the debt. Individuals also had to provide their occupation if it pertained to the debt. Some listed houses and gave no other information about themselves, suggesting that they intended to put up only a portion of that property. If they had a profession, however, many fiadores listed it as well. Presumably master artisans owned their shops and merchants possessed substantial merchandise, both of which could secure a debt.[63] Juan de Rojas, a master goldsmith, likely had available capital in the form of gold bullion in his shop that could serve as collateral. He also listed several slaves who presumably served as additional capital. Andrés de la Maniego listed an hacienda and orchard as collateral. Presumably the proceeds from the agricultural enterprise as well as the capital (buildings, trees, and any equipment) could be assessed for their value. The contador had to inspect the real estate and other property to ensure that the residences were "proper houses made of stone and adobe" and also had to determine their value by assessing how many rooms they contained.[64] Montaño then had to swear a commitment as governor: "Sixteen fiadores . . . would provide secure backing of the tribute that it is my duty to collect guaranteed by goods and real estate, and in my view [it] is sufficient." The oath continued, "They [the fiadores] are obligated with their property [bienes] to pledge financing" in support of the community of Mexico Tenochtitlan.[65] The fiadores promised only 9,000

TABLE 2 Fiadores of don Juan Montaño for 1675

Name	Ethnicity or Racial Designation[a]	Barrio of Residence	Occupation/Collateral[b]	Amount Pledged
First Set of Fiadores				
Diego de Pedrasa	Español	Calle de San Francisco	Master silversmith	500 pesos
Miguel de Piñeda	Español	Calle de San Augustín	Master silversmith	500 pesos
Jerónimo de Cárdenas	Español	Esquina de la Aduana	Owner/trainer of service animals, mule trains	1,000 pesos
Felipe Ponce	Native	Santa Catalina Martyr	Houses as collateral	500 pesos
Francisco de la Cruz	Mestizo	Calle de San Francisco	Master tailor	500 pesos
Juan de Rojas	Español	Barrio de San Juan (Moyotlan)	Master goldsmith/owns slaves	500 pesos
Bartolomé de Piñeda	Mestizo	Calle de Balvaveda	Merchant	1,000 pesos
Don Francisco de Royos	Español	Esquina del Rostro	Houses as collateral	500 pesos
Bernabé Curiel	Español	Salto del Agua	Master printer	500 pesos
Juan Manuel	Español	La Puerta Falsa del Espiritu Santo	Master architect and painter	500 pesos
Tomás de los Reyes	Mestizo	Barrio de Belem	Master gilder	500 pesos
Josef de los Reyes	Native	Callejón de Riofio	Houses as collateral	500 pesos
Don Martín Gonzáles	Native	Barrio de Monserrat	Houses as collateral	500 pesos
Sebastián de la Broa	Español	Calle de San Juan	Master lace weaver	500 pesos
Pedro de la Torre y Mandos	Mestizo	Barrio de Necatitlan	Houses as collateral	500 pesos
Antonio de Alvarado	Español	Calle de Tacuba	Master of painting	500 pesos
Total				9,000 pesos

TABLE 2 Fiadores of don Juan Montaño for 1675 (continued)

Name	Ethnicity or Racial Designation[a]	Barrio of Residence	Occupation/Collateral[b]	Amount Pledged
Second Set of Fiadores				
Juan de Varas	Mestizo	Espaldas de San Juan de Letran	Houses as collateral	500 pesos
Francisco Guerrero	Español	Calle de San Francisco	Master of embroidery	500 pesos
Bernardo Suarez	Español	?	Escribano	500 pesos
Pedro de la Cruz	Native	Barrio de Necaltitlan	Houses as collateral	500 pesos
Cristóbal Vicente de Rivera	Español	?	Procurador	500 pesos
Andrés de la Maniego	Español	Barrio de Monserrate	Hacienda and orchard owner	1,000 pesos
Total				12,500 pesos

SOURCE: AGN, Tributos, v. 10, e. 6.

[a] I am using "native" here, though I would like to use "Nahua" or "Tenochca." The imprecision of the document that uses "indio," however, makes it impossible to determine their ethnicity.

[b] Occupations are translated as follows: *maestro de platero* (master silversmith), *dueño de recua* (owner/trainer of service animals, mule trains), *maestro de sastre* (master tailor), *maestro tirador de oro* (master goldsmith), *mercador* (merchant), *maestro impresor* (master printer), *maestro de arquitectura y de pintor* (master architect and painter), *maestro de guarnición oro* (master gilder), *maestro de pasamanero* (master lace weaver), *maestro de pintor* (master of painting), *maestro de bordadora* (master of embroidery), *dueño de hacienda y huertas en Misquique en Misquique (Mixquic?)* (hacienda and orchard owner).

pesos (see table 2), less than the amount owed. The contador seemed satisfied that the fiadores' pledges would be sufficiently covered by the property listed, but he asked for additional financial support. Montaño had to provide 3,500 pesos in addition to the 9,000 already pledged. He also had to swear that his personal property and that of his wife, doña Josefa de la Trinidad, could be seized in addition to the list of property already established.[66]

The impetus for the additional checks was likely driven by political pressure and financial necessity. The rules did not change and apparently no royal decree or edict issued from the Juzgado General de los Indios altered the regulations for vetting financial guarantors. Rather, challenges from individuals made it necessary to inspect the fiadores. Former governors and brothers don Felipe (r. 1667, 1673) and don Juan de Aguilar (r. 1672, 1674) disputed Montaño's capacity to hold office.[67] Increasing regulation, therefore, was partially driven by internal demand and was also a by-product of election politics, not from a proactive or top-down effort to regulate by the viceregal government. In addition to the internal motivation, the past experiences of former governors who had not met their tribute quotas also apparently increased the need to check fiadores. The likelihood of their use necessitated that their properties be worth at least the amount the fiadores guaranteed and that they be free of other lien. The experience of don Felipe de Aguilar may have prompted the careful attention and forced the Audiencia to inspect carefully the property he advanced to guarantee the tribute. Apparently Aguilar had not delivered all of the required tribute owed by the community the year before, and his fiadores could not cover the deficit. Aguilar had cleverly taken out a loan (*censo*) in the name of the community against the property of a widow, doña María de la Fuente, to cover tribute for the year 1674. Cabildo members elected with Aguilar signed the censo, making them liable along with the judge-governor.[68] The statement reads that the cabildo members, four alcaldes pasados, two regidores pasados, and two alguaciles mayores pasados pledged to pay back (in the event it was necessary) the loan, "the principal of which amounts to 3,000 pesos," taken out "against the substantial houses [*algunas casas altas y bajas*] in front of the chapel of Monserrate" to back the elected governor.[69]

Fiadores, especially those from outside the community, present a series of problems worthy of serious consideration. These financial guarantors obviously took substantial risks to finance a governor, but it is unclear exactly what they expected, if anything, in return for their support. What might have motivated a fiador to choose to assist a governor?[70] Perhaps the financial leverage translated into access to patronage. Certainly the high number of master artisans and merchants may have benefited from a close relationship with the governor and cabildo, which regulated internal markets. A fiador might expect preferential treatment or gain preferential access to community markets.[71] Also unclear is how a governor might compensate a fiador when he had to use one to cover the debts of the community, particularly later in the 1690s when defaults became a regular feature of tribute collection.[72] The Audiencia does not appear to have made a serious inquiry into the financing of governors to make clear how and why fiadores assumed the financial risk.[73] Surely an unwritten contractual relationship between the backers and their candidate existed, but the terms are difficult to establish. Without answering such questions, it is nevertheless possible to speculate that the presence of wealthy Spaniards and mestizos in the financing of indigenous government enabled nonnatives to influence the political affairs of Mexico Tenochtitlan. It also appears that natives resisted using nonnative fiadores. When forced, governors utilized them, but they returned to natives almost exclusively in the late seventeenth and early eighteenth century. A group who could finance a candidate could also choose someone they found sympathetic. Fiadores, however, should not be seen as unusual or even antiquated. They were and continue to be a regular feature in the financial dealings of many in Mexico City.[74]

TRANSFORMATION BY FLOOD

The succession of annual floods that inundated the city (1629–36) inspired changes in the cabildo of Mexico Tenochtitlan by bringing pressure to bear on any occupant of the office of governor. Don Juan de León did not endure long as governor. Don Cristóbal Pascual, elected at the end of 1630, "amidst the fury of the second flood," replaced him.[75] Pascual walked into a nearly impossible task. By no coincidence, his election took place just about the same moment that the six-month hiatus in tribute collection granted by the contador Peñafiel expired. For León, retiring from the governorship likely spared him the indignity suffered by Pascual, who received no relief from the viceroy and Audiencia.[76] By 1634, Governor Pascual faced difficulties collecting tribute and had amassed a large debt. Even though "the good work [*buena mano*] of the governor had resulted in the deposit of more than 9,000 pesos in royal coffers," during his tenure in office he and his entire cabildo, "by order of the contador general de reales tributos," were imprisoned. Pascual claimed he had collected and delivered more tribute than he owed, though this chestnut was hardly substantiated. Using a tactic common to many judge-governors throughout the century, Pascual claimed that the arrears from don Juan de León made it impossible to meet the annual quota. He also argued that the level of tribute owed should have been reduced to reflect the low population and economic hardship residents had endured.[77]

The governor of Mexico Tlatelolco, don Juan Toribio de Alcaraz (r. 1622–42), also had difficulty in the 1630s gathering tribute and repartimiento laborers.[78] He had been imprisoned for failure to collect tribute and released on 19 June 1632.[79] On his release, he ordered the imprisonment of the *mandones* (tribute bosses, sometimes called *tepixque/merinos*) and regidores.[80] Without any other viable option to collect the owed tribute the Audiencia quickly released the tribute collectors (on 17 July), as they had done with the governor, so that together they could gather as much tribute as possible.[81] Apparently the fiadores could not cover the shortfall. Mexico Tlatelolco also had to provide repartimiento laborers for the maintenance of the drainage system. Governor Alcaraz struggled to gather repartimiento workers to clear the *acequias* (drainage canals), a challenge complicated by the difficulty of the work. Apparently the city had not cleaned the acequias for years. The neglect probably amplified the destruction caused by the heavy rains and flooding.[82] Organized labor drafts had been employed at various times since the beginning of the flooding, but the experience of Governor Alcaraz suggests that Tlatelolco also had to cope with depopulation. Although he had 1,400 eligible repartimiento workers on paper, he could not raise fifty-nine laborers twice monthly to staff the necessary cleaning crews in 1634.[83] The Audiencia assisted the governor by granting him permission to compel repartimiento workers from regional towns over which Tlatelolco claimed jurisdiction as a *cabecera* (Ozumbilla, Tolpetlac, Xaloztoc, and Xaloc).[84] Though leaders from these *sujetos* (subject towns) resisted the draft, the regional corregidor in cooperation with the Audiencia and governor compelled the towns to supply the workers.

Between collecting tribute and gathering laborers in a depopulated city, Alcaraz endured difficult challenges that exposed the principal weaknesses of the tribute collection system as it then existed. When crisis struck, no matter what the incentive to governors, they could collect only what the community could pay. When the community came up short, they had to rely on fiadores who legally assumed risk for the governors but whose contributions may not have always sufficed to cover the debt owed.

In Mexico Tenochtitlan, however, don Cristóbal Pascual remained outside the graces of the Audiencia for much of his tenure as governor. Despite his claims to the contrary, Pascual apparently did not perform well as a tribute collector. When examined by the Audiencia, though he claimed to have collected all of the tribute he owed and more, officials alleged that he had only created scandal during his administration. The viceroy, the Marqués de Cerralvo, on the recommendation of his *juez de residencia*, don Pedro de Quiroga y Moya, ordered the arrest of Governor Pascual in 1635 and also "seized his property," all ostensibly "for crimes and abuses committed in the course of the five-year period of his governorship during which he had provided no financial backing [*sin haber dado fianzas*] except for the first year."[85] Though Pascual had failed to collect the full amount of tribute owed by Mexico Tenochtitlan, his gravest failing was his inattention to financial guarantors. He apparently did not provide fiadores annually but rather submitted a list his first year in office only. Not properly updating his fiadores, as required by the treasury (at least according to the contador general de los reales tributos y azogues), forced the hand of the viceregal government. It took five years to remove Pascual from office, and it happened only at the very end of Viceroy Cerralvo's long term in office.[86] When in 1635 Pascual could not collect tribute, no financial guarantors stepped in to cover the debt because technically Pascual had pledged none. Seeming to confirm the allegations of the Audiencia, there is no record, beyond the first year of his term, that Pascual submitted the required list of fiadores. Although no evidence survives to make clear why Pascual offered no fiadores after his first year, several possibilities present themselves. Perhaps because the flood depopulated the city, potential fiadores refused to assume the obvious risk of serving as a guarantor for Pascual or any governor. Perhaps because governors had usually served multiple terms, no bureaucratic mechanism existed to ensure that a multiyear governor continued to provide new fiadores each year.[87] Whatever the reason, the community remained in debt even though Pascual had property taken by the viceregal government.[88]

Led by a new viceroy, the Marqués de Cadereita (r. 1635–40), the Audiencia then stripped from the electors of Mexico Tenochtitlan the right to choose their own governor. Arguing that Pascual had failed miserably and that those who proposed to follow him did not have the capacity to do better, the Audiencia, on the recommendation of the contador general, took action to impose a governor of its choosing. The new viceroy apparently had ideas about the important office of governor.[89] The evidence produced in 1635 seemed also to confirm that, as treasury officials suspected, the tribute arrears occurred during Pascual's administration and not, as Pascual had argued, during the administrations of previous governors. Pascual may have been the first governor of Mexico Tenochtitlan imprisoned for failure to collect tribute. With his arrest and removal from office and refusal to approve a replacement forwarded by the community, the viceregal government manifested authority it had not exercised before. This intervention fundamentally changed the relationship between governors and their communities, strengthening the hand of the viceregal government. The rights had existed before, but prudent viceroys, intent on preserving order and ensuring tribute flows, had resisted interfering. With the additional presence of the viceregal government and its newfound willingness to exercise its mandate, unintended consequences emerged. The viceregal government, by intervening, seems to have created new kinds of political space that indigenous electors, candidates, and even enterprising Spaniards learned how to manipulate.[90]

The viceroy and Audiencia did not find acceptable the proposed candidates for the election of 1636 in Mexico Tenochtitlan. Miguel de la Hara and don Juan Luis had come in first and second place, respectively, in the election. With a single petition, the viceregal government dismissed both candidates. The juez de residencia, basing his comments on the observations of contador general Nicolás Romero de Mello, argued that de la Hara had a reputation for causing disruption in the community. In the petition he stated: "The said natives [of Mexico Tenochtitlan] had an election in the customary manner . . . proposing Miguel de la Hara, a person of importance in their República, who previously the community held in esteem . . . [but who] has become a great hindrance to the peace of the community causing great disruption among the common people during the collection of royal tribute."[91]

Although de la Hara may have seen himself as a viable candidate and the principales who supported him may have thought well of him, according to complaints received by the Audiencia some in the community apparently saw him as a source of disruption. Furthermore, the community of Mexico Tenochtitlan "did not respect or obey" de la Hara, nor did "the tribute collectors" (merinos and regidores) who had served under him because of the treatment they had received.[92] Though Judge Quiroga y Moya did not elaborate on the nature of the community disruptions, surviving evidence suggests that some tribute payers complained to the Juzgado General de los Indios, alleging excessive demands by tribute collectors during the administration of don Cristóbal de Pascual.[93] Perhaps the judge referred to the allegation that tribute payers had been charged excessively, as in the 1633 complaint in which the alcaldes and regidores in all barrios of Mexico Tenochtitlan were reprimanded for forcing individuals to pay more tribute than they owed.[94] Indigenous officials were under extreme pressure, which they had a clear incentive to pass on to their subjects.[95] Though incomplete evidence prevents a full analysis, complaints against the indigenous government probably increased during the flood as tribute payers became scarce and the financial well-being of the city suffered with no significant reduction or postponement of tribute owed by the community after 1630.[96] Perhaps complaints among the commoners of Mexico Tenochtitlan made de la Hara an unsuitable candidate in the eyes of the contador and viceregal government.

The second-place candidate, don Juan Luis, who received a significant portion of the votes cast, was apparently an even worse choice. According to Judge Quiroga y Moya's source he was "a person well known, more for his bad habits than his virtues and from this perspective was not fit for the office of governor nor for any other [office in] the República."[97] Which bad habits and what kind of behavior the document does not reveal, nor do specific allegations appear in the surviving documentation to confirm the accusation made by Quiroga y Moya.

Neither de la Hara nor Luis was given an opportunity to dispute these allegations. The juez de residencia, basing his argument on secondhand observations lacking detail from the contador general, nonetheless made the case that neither candidate who received votes from the electors had the capacity to serve. Based exclusively on the report of the contador general, Judge Quiroga y Moya recommended to the viceroy that neither should be appointed to serve. He pessimistically concluded that Mexico Tenochtitlan could offer no one with the requisite qualities to serve in the office of governor.

After dismissing and disqualifying both aspirants, the viceroy took on the direct role of appointing a new governor. Technically the viceroy appointed all governors after they had been recommended to him by his oidor. The oidor's recommendation, of course, nearly always reflected the choice of the community of electors. Only rarely did the viceroy actually intervene; he usually confirmed the community choice. Even don Juan de León was selected by the electors before the viceroy appointed him on 30 June 1629 to replace his predecessor who failed to complete his term.[98]

The viceregal government effectively served its own interests by allowing community choice. Candidates needed the support of electors who would work with the elected governor to provide assistance in collecting tribute and adjudicating community disputes. The contador and juez de residencia's comments provide insight into this relationship between the community and governor. Miguel de la Hara, once held in esteem by the community, was no longer respected according to the contador. From the perspective of the viceregal government, this made him an ineffective tribute collector and potentially a poor governor. His comments indicate that the community, through noncompliance, could influence the career of a governor by making his

lack of success a barrier to future service. Don Juan Luis's poor reputation also made him an unsuitable candidate from the perspective of
the viceregal government, indicating that such a reputation also
made him a poor tribute collector. Both assertions are based on the
assumption that reputation and popular standing in the community
affected the success of the governor.[99]

In the decades before Viceroy Cadereita rejected the candidacies of
de la Hara and Luis, replacement governors had been appointed
only under certain circumstances. When the royal lineage controlled
the governorship in the sixteenth century, interim rulers put forward
by the community were appointed to serve while the electors sorted
out the choice among candidates of eligible lineage. In the seventeenth
century, after the royal lineage ceased to hold the governorship, the
viceroy appointed interim rulers when illness or sudden death in
office prevented the choice of the community from serving. In 1616,
for example, the viceroy appointed don Francisco Bautista Valeriano
(r. 1616–20) to replace the gravely ill don Juan Pérez de Monterrey (r.
1610–16). The viceroy did not act on his own; rather, the cabildo petitioned the viceroy to appoint Valeriano, who had experience governing
and collecting tribute in a large altepetl—he was then serving as judge-
governor of Iztapalapa. The cabildo surely worried that without an able
hand in the post of governor they might fall behind in the collection
of tribute.[100] Again in 1620, don Juan Valeriano (r. 1620) fell ill in January and was replaced for the year by Jerónimo de León, who had
served as a nahuatlato. The sitting cabildo offered him as a candidate
to serve "in the place of the governor" ("*en lugar de[l] dicho gobernador*").
These specific words are significant because they imply the interim
nature of the appointment: he was not appointed governor but rather
as one who stood in the place of the governor who could not serve.
Furthermore, in these early seventeenth-century cases, the alcaldes
and regidores (e.g., electors) asked the viceroy to appoint a specific
person. In effect, the electors made the decision in an informal election
conducted by native peoples. Although the exact mechanism used in
the selection remains unclear, at minimum the proposed replacement
was selected by the cabildo and may have included other electors and
principales. Indeed, the 1629 replacement document states directly
that "the natives of the parte de San Juan [Mexico Tenochtitlan]"

chose the new replacement. In other words, the language of the document seems to say that all those empowered to speak for the natives of the barrios (all electors) made the choice.[101]

To fill the office of governor in 1636, Viceroy Cadereita chose a candidate from well outside the community. Governors had previously come from outside Mexico Tenochtitlan, but usually from altepetl within the immediate range of the city that had traditionally been affiliated with the precontact Tenochca.[102] In other words, they had been part of the traditional domain of Basin politics dating back to before the Spanish invasion.[103] This innovation on the part of Viceroy Cadereita brought to Mexico Tenochtitlan a governor from Puebla de los Angeles, don Bartolomé Cortés y Mendoza Axayacatzin (r. 1636–37).[104] According to his description in the appointment document, Cortés y Mendoza was particularly well suited to the job of governor because of his "noble blood, and well known habits [*costumbres*] of which the citizens of the city of [Puebla de] los Angeles speak where he is a resident [*vecino*]." Such nobility, though likely simply an excuse to elevate this particular candidate to office, seems to have impressed the viceroy most. He lingered over Cortés y Mendoza's high birth when he sought to justify the appointment of an outsider. Despite this endorsement, Cortés y Mendoza faced enormous challenges, for he had few connections in Mexico Tenochtitlan.

Nobility, it appears, had only minor cachet for those who had their elected choice vetoed. The tribute payers of Mexico Tenochtitlan continued to pay less tribute than they owed during the tenure of Governor Cortés y Mendoza.[105] Perhaps it was his lack of success that made his appointment a rare experiment. After the apparent failure of Cortés y Mendoza, the viceregal government continued to intervene, but within stricter limits. The choices forwarded by the indigenous electors were evaluated more thoroughly, their potential to collect tribute further scrutinized, and the complaints filed by competitors considered more carefully. The viceregal government appears to have relied more heavily on the elected choices of the community as a baseline from which to intervene rather than flatly dismissing indigenous choices. Overall, viceregal administrators turned to regulating elections more carefully rather than intervening directly.

The viceroy, likely inexperienced in the internal affairs of the city, probably embarked on an experiment when he overturned the election of 1636. Clearly no precedent existed to raise to the level of governor of Mexico Tenochtitlan a noble from somewhere as distant as Puebla. Indeed, the nearly two dozen governors who preceded Cortés y Mendoza nearly all had come from Mexico Tenochtitlan or communities immediately within its orbit such as Azcapotzalco, Iztapalapa, or even Xochimilco.[106] The viceroy named the governor in 1636 using the word *experimentaría,* which implies an experimental process. He also asked that the oidor who supervised the election, doctor don Diego de Barrientos, inform those whom the electorate had chosen. Anticipating problems in this appointment, the viceroy also formally stated, "I declare and decree the election null in the said parcialidad [of Mexico Tenochtitlan]." Apparently grasping for augmented authority, the viceroy asserted that nothing infringed on his right to name a governor of his choosing, stating that "no law forbade" his action.[107]

Cortés y Mendoza was unelected, was not supported by local officials, and had been placed in office by the viceroy in lieu of those elected by the community. He assumed the full title of governor yet had not earned this office through community support. He did, however, have advantages his predecessors lacked. By 1636 the floodwaters had receded significantly. According to Hoberman, "Between 1632 and 1634 the city was still flooded, but each successive rainy season was lighter. Losses by evaporation, and a series of earth tremors drew off the water by 1634."[108] Cortés y Mendoza arrived at a time when residents began to return and rebuild. The importance of the precedent, however, cannot be overstated. Viceregal officials later in the century looked back to Cadereita to justify their efforts to overturn elections. In 1654 the contador general stated that "many times in the past viceroys who came before Your Excellency have placed their choice in the office of governor, as in the time of the Marqués de Cadereita who named don Bartolomé Cortés [y Mendoza]."[109]

The viceregal overturn of the election in 1636 promoted significant changes within the indigenous community, opening up new political avenues for aspirants to seek the governorship through challenges of the validity of the elections or the qualifications of the winning candidates. Viceroy Cadereita, perhaps unwittingly, set a precedent that indigenous leaders who sought the governorship could use to remove political rivals. Indigenous leaders who had the financial and social connections to contract fiadores and the political skills to build a coalition (even if not large enough to secure all the votes necessary), thus satisfying the contador general, could use the newly established authority of the viceroy to overturn an election in their favor. In this way, the appointment of Cortés y Mendoza had significance well beyond the immediate election of 1636.

Even after the administration of Cortés y Mendoza, governors continued to struggle to collect tribute and to provide the repartimiento services demanded of them by the viceregal government. Enterprising natives put pressure on the governors by filing complaints when they overstepped their bounds. In 1642, Governor don Martín González (r. 1638–42?) faced a challenge from natives working in one of the urban slaughterhouses (*matadero*).[110] In the name of other native butchers (*carniceros*), Francisco Agustín, Juan Agustín, and Juan Nicolás asked the viceroy to aid them so that they could be exempted from personal service. They argued that they worked constantly in the slaughterhouse and had always been exempted from what they called "personal service" of tribute, by which they meant repartimiento labor. They then indicated that because of the flood and the extra repartimiento service requirements imposed by the viceregal government, the governor and alcaldes tried to force them to abandon the slaughterhouses and join work details to clean the acequias. In addition, the alcaldes asked for money ("*por su defecto les piden dineros*") when they refused to serve.[111] The viceroy, the Conde de Salvatierra, forced Governor González to stop requesting that the exempted natives perform personal service.[112] Of course, this also meant that fewer native laborers could work on the drainage canals.

The flood and subsequent tribute shortfalls enabled the viceregal government to extend in practice its already extant authority. Following mostly the petitions of natives themselves, however, and moving slowly again, the viceregal government placed additional pressure on governors to provide sufficient financial backing and increasingly used its authority to overturn the elections of native governors. Don Juan de Velázquez, elected in 1654, was not allowed to serve because he could not read or write and did not have the financial backing to serve; Viceroy Alburquerque (r. 1652–60) denied his appointment. Following Viceroy Cadereita, however, but modifying the approach, Alburquerque solicited and then took the recommendation of native electors, who forwarded their second choice, don Juan de Aguilar, to serve a one-year term in 1654. Alburquerque's restraint caused him to rule against the recommendation of his contador general. The contador advised the governor to pick a nahuatlato who apparently would do better at finding fiadores. Perhaps Alburquerque thought about the previous experience of Poblano governor Cortés y Mendoza when he sought to empower an alternate choice from within the community rather than follow his contador general's recommendation.[113]

The governorship began to change and open to more politicization, particularly as the viceregal government took a more active part in the confirmation of native elections. The government also seems to have listened and acted on the petitions submitted by native leaders and, as a result, made it increasingly possible for politically savvy natives to use it to realize political ends. The election of 1654 also facilitated the political awakening of nonnative political actors to try to use native elections to serve in the office of governor. Juan López, a Spaniard, ran for governor, though unsuccessfully, because of the new politicization. The Aguilar family (sons, grandsons, and sons-in-law of don Juan de Aguilar), who regularly held the governorship in the late seventeenth century, used the viceregal government effectively to expand their authority.

CHAPTER 4

DIVERSITY AND THE INFILTRATION OF THE CABILDO, 1650–1680

Early on the morning of Saturday, 4 January 1659, native electors gathered in the tecpan in Mexico Tenochtitlan to elect a new governor. Several days before, the viceroy had appointed his most senior Audiencia judge (*oidor más antiguo*), don Andrés Sánchez de Ocampo, to attend the election ceremony along with an escribano from the Audiencia.[1] The indigenous and Spanish officials gathered this way every year to conduct the elaborate public election ceremony. On this January day, however, from a field of five candidates the community made an unusual choice, electing don Francisco Benítez de Inga. Although he claimed he was born into the indigenous nobility and presented himself as a qualified candidate, Benítez technically did not meet all of the legal requirements for office. Two major issues raised questions about his ability to assume the office of governor: he was a foreigner born in the viceroyalty of Peru, and he was allegedly a mestizo. Juan López, the second-place candidate, who stood to inherit the office had the Audiencia disqualified Benítez, also failed to meet the requirements for holding indigenous office. Like Benítez, López was a "foreigner," but in the sense that he was a Spaniard. Don Lorenzo de Santiago, the third-place candidate, though indigenous, was probably not Tenochca but from the altepetl of Mexico Tlatelolco. All of these circumstances raised serious issues about the electoral process and touched off a major conflict over succession.[2]

118

Unusual but certainly not unprecedented, the electoral disputes in 1659 suggest the degree to which indigenous electoral politics had matured and increased in complexity by the mid-seventeenth century.[3] The office of judge-governor, no longer dominated by the royal lineage of Mexico Tenochtitlan, gradually had become subject to annual elections. Rules governing the frequency and cycle of elections and other succession issues seem to have changed gradually.[4] At some point the governorship, an elected office that had become unlike anything in the Hispanic world, changed to conform to local circumstances, perhaps in response to changes within Mexico Tenochtitlan.[5] Additionally, the governorship seemed open to more potential rulers. Apparently anyone who could garner sufficient support and had proper qualifications could run for office.[6] Residence in Mexico Tenochtitlan, a requirement that did not apply to many of the first nonlineage leaders, like don Antonio Valeriano, continued to have little meaning in the seventeenth century. Membership in the royal lineage also had little importance. By the mid-seventeenth century candidates do not seem to have touted their royal birth as a political strategy but attempted rather to entice the political support of current electors. The most important heirs of the royal lineage in Mexico Tenochtitlan, the Moteucçomas, probably excluded themselves consciously from the office of governor. Indeed, many chose to cultivate their connections in Spain.[7] The changing demographics of Mexico Tenochtitlan also made ties to the Tenochca lineage less important for aspiring governors. Foreign Nahuas (not from Tenochtitlan, but other Nahuatl-speaking altepetl) and even the non-Nahua indigenous populations (natives of a different ethnicity, who spoke a different indigenous language) grew in size in the seventeenth century and often matriculated into the tribute rolls. Such groups eventually had their own tribute collectors who reported to the cabildo, giving them some low-level representation.[8] Spaniards and mestizos and even a governor who claimed descent from the Inka ("de Inga") vied for the governorship and received votes, sometimes more than the Tenochca candidates.

The dramatic transformation, quite visible by the late seventeenth century, made the office of governor far more political. Governors were subjected to annual elections and sometimes challenges from powerful rivals. Sitting governors often lost bids for reelection.[9] The viceregal government also placed additional pressure on governors, forcing them to account for the collection of tribute rigorously by imposing stricter regulations. Governors, who technically had always borne personal liability for tribute shortfalls, were now forced to provide detailed accounting of how they would cover uncollected tribute should the need arise. An increasingly important internal force also politicized the office of judge-governor, as electors might skillfully file legal challenges to contest the results of an election. The body of electors also changed in the seventeenth century. Though the data are scarce, by the 1670s the only voters in Mexico Tenochtitlan were apparently former officeholders. Whereas formerly in the sixteenth century all principales possessed franchise rights, by the late seventeenth century noble status no longer guaranteed the right to vote in municipal elections.[10]

NEW KINDS OF CHOICE IN MEXICO TENOCHTITLAN

Because of the safeguards, checks, and reviews, it is unlikely that the electors of Mexico Tenochtitlan did not know in 1659 that don Francisco Benítez de Inga was possibly a mestizo born in Peru or that Juan López was a Spaniard. We must, therefore, assume that electors made a conscious choice to support a non-Nahua. Benítez had lived in the city for thirty years, since he was about fourteen. The "de Inga" in his name further suggested his Peruvian origin, in much the same way Spanish naming patterns could indicate region or city of origin, such as de Córdoba or de Toledo.[11] Juan López too was a familiar person to the electors, cabildo, and community of Mexico Tenochtitlan. He had spent much of his career as an official who represented the interests of the viceregal government. He was physically present in the barrios, particularly when tribute was due.[12] Several major disputes had arisen in quite recent memory that involved López as well, which probably made him somewhat notorious among the common people.

The final candidate who received significant support also did not appear to have the right to hold office. Don Lorenzo de Santiago, though having stated on several occasions that he was technically born in Santa

María Cuepopan, probably did not have to disclose that he was not Tenochca. His father had served for many years as the governor of Mexico Tlatelolco. Questions of origin, race, and ethnicity all ulti- mately emerged from the election as disputed issues among the elec- tors of Mexico Tenochtitlan in a forum mediated by the viceregal government. The political challenges illustrate the role and increasing importance of elections and the skillful way electors and members of the community learned to use legal checks to gain political advantage. Notably absent from the political scene, however, were the descen- dants of the Tenochca royal lineage.

The political maneuvering of 1659 set off a debate within the com- munity of electors that was aired in the Juzgado General de los Indios. Losing candidate don Lorenzo de Santiago, in his petition following the election, raised the issue of who had the right to hold office. Because the viceregal government had been somewhat cavalier in its application of royal law, deferring presumably to local custom and tradition, it took protest from within the community to define the very standards and qualifications necessary to hold the office of governor. The election itself seemed straightforward. Of the 132 recorded votes, don Francisco Benítez received eighty-one, Juan López thirty-six, and don Lorenzo de Santiago twenty-one. The four votes that remained went to Tenochca principal don Juan Lorenzo Súarez, with three, and don Pedro Bernal, the current governor, who received only one vote.[13] Don Lorenzo de Santiago then sued to disqualify Benítez and López, apparently in the hope that he would be allowed to serve.

The community, once don Lorenzo de Santiago made the case, had to determine if mestizos and Spaniards integrated into the commu- nity had the right to serve. Though the viceregal government reduced the complexity of the issue to whether or not the leading candidate was a native, as he claimed, or a mestizo, as was alleged, the implicit argument was whether a foreign-born candidate, even if technically native like Benítez, could serve in important posts such as the office of governor. Indeed, because of the strong stand made by Santiago, the Audiencia forced Benítez to certify his claim that he was a native, suggesting that it cared only to enforce royal law and not local choice. If Benítez could not prove he was a native, they likely would have dis- qualified him. The decision, however, overlooked the issue of ethnicity and suggested that a foreigner from Peru could hold indigenous office in Mexico Tenochtitlan provided he could prove his native noble status to the satisfaction of the community and viceregal institutions who oversaw the election. Would the indigenous community adopt, even for self-serving purposes, the idea that a native from Peru was the same in terms of office as a native from Mexico Tenochtitlan? Don Lorenzo de Santiago effectively asked the viceregal government to settle these questions when he challenged the election of Benítez and López. The viceregal government, it should be noted, would not have questioned Benítez without the petition from don Lorenzo de Santiago. Because of the native impetus—even if resulting in unintended consequences such as all mestizos being barred from service in native offices—the community ultimately shaped the limits on the governorship by asking the viceregal government to enforce certain laws.[14]

Don Lorenzo de Santiago focused his complaint on the allegation that Benítez could not serve because he was a mestizo, and that López had no right to hold the office because he was a Spaniard.[15] He cited viceregal ordinances that prohibited "mestizos, Spaniards, mulattoes and others of mixed heritage [*nación mezclada*]" from holding native offices.[16] As if to affirm the ambiguity of what it meant to be eligible, the complaint also simply stated, following the ordinances, that the successful candidate "had to be a legitimately born native [*indio*] the son of a native man and native woman [*indio y india*] and following this the said candidates Benítez and López were totally ineligible [*totalmente inhábiles*] to receive votes."[17] Santiago avoided the whole question of ethnicity (essentially ignoring the complexity of indigenous identity) and focused exclusively on the Hispanic idea of racial difference.[18] Yet, by the terms stated here, the ordinances not surprisingly say nothing of ethnicity within indigenous society. Thus, it was not that Benítez was a Peruvian cacique but rather that he was allegedly a mestizo. Perhaps he avoided ethnicity, ignoring Benítez's Andean heritage because viceregal law did not make such distinctions, referring to all natives as *indios* regardless of their ethnicity. It is also possible that raising such an issue might have made him, a native who many assumed came from Tlatelolco, ineligible as well.[19] By resorting to the oidores and using Spanish laws and ideas about indigenous identity,

Santiago forced the viceregal courts to enforce written laws that they otherwise seemed poised to ignore.[20]

Viceroy Alburquerque (r. 1652–60) affirmed the choice of the electors in 1659 rather than intervene further. His ministers, however, made an important stand that expanded the developing political frame. Though don Lorenzo de Santiago alleged that Benítez was a mestizo, he had no substantial proof. Viceregal officials in the Juzgado General, however, acknowledged that he had a point when he suggested that mestizos should not hold indigenous office. The court reaffirmed an earlier ordinance that "prohibit[ed] the election of mestizos, Spaniards, and others of mixed heritage" to the office of governor. They apparently listened when don Lorenzo de Santiago somewhat histrionically argued that the legitimacy and health of the office of governor were at stake, and that if a mestizo held the office it would "sicken" a profoundly important institution.[21] Although mestizos had previously held office in Mexico Tenochtitlan, the viceregal government apparently had never sought to intervene proactively. Rather, viceroys waited for the community itself to lead. With the petition by don Lorenzo de Santiago, the viceregal government seems to have followed his suggestion to enforce the ordinances. Such an opportunity to take a stand in effect driven by indigenous complaint facilitated the clarification of the ordinance and its application. The viceregal government did not hand down a decision but simply ruled on a controversial issue when asked by a certain constituency within the community. Indeed, the appointment document that begins the larger case file listed López as a Spaniard, ascribed votes to him, and affirmed that Benítez had won without question—meaning that without protest the viceregal government was prepared to accept a Peruvian and allow votes cast in support of a Spaniard.[22]

The problems, however, presented themselves quickly and showed the difficulty of verifying Benítez's status. To check, the viceregal government would have had to send a representative to Peru to review baptismal records in the parish of his birth thousands of miles away. The impracticality, it seems, called for a creative solution. Oidor Sánchez de Ocampo made an early decision on 23 January 1659 based entirely on the abstract idea that eighty-one legitimate votes were cast to elect don Francisco Benítez de Inga: because Benítez won the most votes, he should be allowed to hold the office; "there [were] no grounds [*no haber lugar*] to contest" the election. Effectively, Sánchez de Ocampo was contending that the most important attribute of a governor was the support of the community of electors. Such an assertion makes sense coming from a representative of the viceregal government because, traditionally, governors with support stood a better chance of collecting all the tribute owed.[23]

The court, however, delayed, waiting for the petition filed several days later on 27 January by Fernando Olivares de Carmona, the procurador representing Benítez. Carmona's statement provided some genealogy and background, stating that Benítez's parents were don Bartolomé Inga from Lima and doña Luisa Ismaquibo from Trujillo. Both were native caciques and had been properly married before don Francisco Benítez was born. Benítez came to New Spain when he was thirteen or fourteen years old in the company of a Spaniard, Captain Alonso Prieto, a resident of the city of Callao (the port city now a part of Lima).[24] These revelations, no doubt provided by Benítez, had yet to be verified, and their obviously self-serving nature made it necessary to check. Despite continued protests from don Lorenzo de Santiago, no record exists to indicate such a verification process took place.[25]

On 4 February 1659, the Duke of Alburquerque affirmed the decision of the court to forward Benítez as governor. In a lengthy appointment document, the oidor made clear the duties of office and appears to have ignored the possibility that Benítez was a mestizo. On the issue of altepetl affiliation, because he had been naturalized over thirty years previously and the electors chose him with a large majority, the court did not seem to take issue with his Peruvian birth.[26] The document simply made it clear that he had to provide the tribute owed by the community delivered in the customary manner and that he had to provide fiadores to cover any shortfalls. He had to provide workers for the ongoing construction project to build the cathedral (a project important to the Duke of Alburquerque) and fulfill all other customary duties of office.[27]

Benítez must have done well as governor from the perspective of both the native community and viceregal government. He was reelected successfully in 1660 and served out that term unopposed. Juan Pérez de Salamanca, the procurador who had represented don Lorenzo de Santiago in 1659, reported his successful reelection on 24 December 1659 in a document that makes no mention of the allegation that Benítez was a mestizo.[28]

The election success of a Peruvian who may have been a mestizo suggests that elections had the effect of opening up access to the governorship, within limits. Benítez's success demonstrates the full realization of an important transformation in the selection of leaders in Mexico Tenochtitlan.[29] Beginning in the sixteenth century with don Francisco Jiménez and don Antonio Valeriano, who led Mexico Tenochtitlan after the royal lineage ceased to be associated with the governorship, the election of 1659 clarified several issues. Altepetl of origin or even ethnicity no longer seems to have had significance as a means to prevent qualified candidates with sufficient support from holding office. The issue of indigenous heritage, however, did matter; the community made it clear that it would not accept mestizos, Spaniards, or anyone of mixed heritage to serve as governor. As a result, from 1659 forward those who sought to challenge the candidacy of elected governors could object by suggesting that a candidate was mestizo, and the courts would investigate. It also settled the apparent challenge from López, who appears to have attempted to work himself into the office of governor over the course of the 1650s by building a coalition of supporters within the community of electors.

The transformations that opened the office of governor to a broader group of indigenous candidates and prohibited mestizos and others apparently derived from the emerging political life within the community of Mexico Tenochtitlan. Even though in 1642 the viceregal government had issued a decree prohibiting nonnatives from holding offices on native cabildos, the election officials allowed both López and Benítez to receive votes and were poised to certify the results until natives forwarded a challenge. The viceregal government appears to have been mostly interested in ensuring that governors could collect tribute, and therefore anyone who could successfully fulfill the primary duty of the governor could hold the office. Natives within Mexico Tenochtitlan, however, had different interests, and as the community changed so too did the characteristics of the individual who held the office of governor. The viceregal government apparently enforced regulations and ordinances only when asked.

Elections, by legitimizing the choice of the community, eased the burden on the viceregal government and reduced the likelihood of conflict and disorder. Viceregal overseers could be fairly well assured that the "best" choice had been put forward and therefore chose to intervene only when petitioned by the community. Authorities only rarely intervened directly to appoint a governor not chosen by the community (1636 and 1649 are two noted examples). In neither case did it work out well. Both viceregal appointments ended up with significant tribute deficits, which may have resulted from the lack of support from the cabildo and community of tribute payers.[30] Elections also enabled representatives of the community to select the "best" candidate, as had been done in the precontact period.

The best, however, meant something quite different in the fifteenth century when a good warrior who had great potential to expand the tributary empire seemed to suit the Tenochca. By the mid-seventeenth century, a good governor was one who could build alliances, find financial backers, and be confirmed by viceregal overseers. Commoners also had some capacity to voice grievances through their right to petition and probably valued governors who did not mistreat them, respected their rights, and protected them from injustice and excessive demands. With an active viceregal government willing to depose governors-elect if persuaded by petition, electors had to take into consideration the potential for challenges from commoners or rival politicians. Thus, governors had to have the ability to create political networks among the community of electors, to find creative ways to collect all tribute, and to do all of this without motivating commoners to petition or giving oppositional political figures the capacity to contest through petition. In other words, governors had to be highly skilled political actors, effectively able to see, understand, and respond to multiple constituencies who often had competing interests.[31]

Elections also seem to have suited well the apparent goals of the viceregal government—by electing candidates who had strong support and could distribute patronage to gain favor and by allowing the pool of talented patrons to expand beyond the Tenochca lineage and the ethnically Tenochca. Yet changes to the qualifications happened within specific limits that the community helped to define. Using appeals to the viceregal government, opposing political factions helped to shape what constituted a viable candidate for governor. The viceregal government limited its involvement and served only to reify the choices of electors. Appeals to the viceregal government took on the character of what we might call a political culture that responded to the needs of electors and even those who lacked the franchise. Legal challenges and complaints filed in viceregal courts became the vehicles through which partisan actors voiced their will. They could reject a candidate on the basis of any number of criteria. Juan López—who may have been a great candidate from the viceregal perspective and even from the perspective of some native electors because he allegedly could gather tribute so well—abused some commoners and was challenged on these grounds. The increased presence of the viceregal government in indigenous elections after 1636 made possible the kind of political maneuvering that could legitimize the introduction of non-Tenochca into the office of governor because elections simply confirmed the choice of the community of electors. Choices came from the popular factions within the indigenous community, likely making them more acceptable than had they been imposed from above.

Elections, however, also contributed to the development of politics within the cabildo, which extended into the eighteenth century. Multiple candidates all working to create viable political support impelled natives in Mexico Tenochtitlan to invent a new kind of system to maneuver for political gain using the oversight apparatus of the viceregal government. Because the viceregal government would intervene, and independent dynastic legitimacy had ended nearly a century earlier, the office could be filled by any proven tribute collector who could cultivate financial supporters and impel his agents to avoid significantly abusing tribute-paying commoners. A philosophical change of this magnitude seems to have provided the political space that made it possible for Juan López to make a case for himself to hold the office of governor. Native choice ultimately defined who could occupy the office of governor. A noninterventionist viceregal government would not enforce written laws without native objection.

POLITICS AND THE ALGUACIL AMPARADOR

The willingness of the viceregal government to intervene in the political affairs of Mexico Tenochtitlan combined with an increasing willingness of the community to file complaints made political development possible. The process of dismissing candidates and annulling elections welcomed into the arena new candidates and magnified the importance of elections. A more open political environment invited those who otherwise might have been excluded to participate.[32] Though the openness lasted only a short time, it implicitly raised serious questions about the nature of the office of governor. Was it possible to elect a Spaniard, particularly if he had demonstrated skills as a tribute collector, to serve as indigenous governor?[33] Individuals, even Spaniards who may have aspired to high office but had little opportunity to take positions of importance in the viceregal government or on local municipal governments, could potentially find opportunities in indigenous communities. Spanish institutions—dominated by those who had the patronage connections or wealth sufficient to purchase positions in a venal system—often did not provide ample space for creoles or those who came from the peninsula.[34] Juan López, a Spaniard who served the Audiencia and governor of Mexico Tenochtitlan in the office of alguacil amparador, used his political clout in an attempt to win indigenous office.

López spent nearly twenty years intermittently serving the viceregal government and indigenous governors of Mexico Tenochtitlan. Over that span, he integrated himself into the internal affairs of the community. By the late 1650s he had embarked on a series of attempts to take control that ultimately concluded with his strong bid for office in 1659. Though it was not unprecedented for someone who was not native to run for governor, López's effort was unusual in Mexico City. Spaniards, mestizos, and those not from the community had held positions ostensibly for indigenous peoples, though usually in areas outside of Mexico City. López's actions demonstrate the degree to which he had integrated himself into the political culture of the southern barrios through his job as a tribute collector. To hold office of any kind in Mexico Tenochtitlan, a candidate had to cultivate substantial patronage or serve well a powerful client like a governor or higher-up in the viceregal administration.[35]

The experiences of López provide clues that show how candidates—indigenous, mestizo, or Spaniard—built such networks. They can also help to clarify how an older indigenous political tradition changed in the seventeenth century. Though he received only thirty-six votes, electors who supported López shunned four native candidates (assuming Benítez was native as he alleged), two of whom were Tenochca. Lopez's constant presence in Mexico Tenochtitlan likely made him a recognizable person in the community of electors. Yet he also seems to have actively cultivated support. His candidacy indicates how the community, sometimes even commoners who could not vote, helped to shape who could run and who could serve in indigenous offices. By filing petitions, many complaining of abuse by López, commoners without the vote could influence the shape of native government. These complaints also suggest that López was well known to some in the barrios as a forceful and abusive presence.

Officially, the alguacil amparador served as a liaison between the amparador de los naturales and the governors of Mexico Tenochtitlan and Mexico Tlatelolco. The office existed, it appears, only from 1642 until 1656.[36] The alguacil amparador was a lieutenant of the amparador de los naturales, a Spaniard and viceregal appointee whose jurisdiction covered both Mexico Tenochtitlan and Mexico Tlatelolco. Each parcialidad in Mexico City had at least one alguacil amparador, and it is unclear if they existed in other parts of New Spain. The office served to provide additional oversight to the native government and assistance in the collection of tribute and the maintenance of order, the two principal functions of the native government. The amparador de los naturales supervised the alguaciles amparadores and served as a go-between for the viceregal government and the cabildos of the parcialidades. According to appointment documents, the amparador de los naturales for Mexico City served both parcialidades, had the right to carry a staff of authority (vara de real justicia), and had the duty to ensure that subjects of the crown received the legal protections entitled by the crown.[37]

Governors had some say in the appointment of the alguacil amparador through their capacity to reject choices, to petition for replacements, and to denounce those who violated the terms of their contracts. Though the alguaciles amparadores were appointed by the ampara- dor de los naturales, governors could limit the actions of the alguacil amparador and exercise limited authority over them. The threat of denouncement probably gave the alguacil amparador incentive to build alliances within the cabildo that elected the governor to protect themselves.[38] Some governors rejected alguaciles amparadores and recommended replacements. In 1653, governor don Diego de la Cruz Villanueva asked to have Miguel de la Cruz appointed to the office of alguacil amparador. Just a few months later, the governor requested to have de la Cruz replaced by don Felipe Valeriano. By the timing, it suggests that de la Cruz had done a poor job and was replaced after the first tribute cycle of the year.[39] The governor in the petition asked for the appointment of both alguaciles amparadores, stating that "I propose him for consideration to serve" in the office. It is not clear from the available evidence if governors recommended all alguaciles amparadores to the amparador de los naturales for appointment. It is also not clear that all alguaciles amparadores were Spaniards.[40]

The appointment document indicates the high status of the posi- tion and provides some detail about the expectations of an amparador de los naturales. It singled out two groups in particular whom the amparador was charged to protect: natives and Afro-Mexicans.[41] The amparador also had to supervise the collection of some fees in mar- kets.[42] To exercise these duties at the community level, the amparador employed lieutenants. Juan López and Diego de Carrión served in these posts for Mexico Tenochtitlan and Mexico Tlatelolco in 1649. That year the viceroy appointed don Fernando Cortés Moctezuma to serve as amparador de los naturales.[43] Obviously a man of high status, the amparador bore the honorific title *don* ("lord"). Yet the alguaciles who served under him usually did not, implying a status distinction between these positions.[44] Alguaciles amparadores were probably limited in their upward mobility and were likely not apprenticing to become amparadores de los naturales, a viceregal appointment tied to the larger transatlantic patronage system.[45] Alguaciles were visible officers in the streets of Mexico Tenochtitlan. When natives lodged complaints against the Spanish officials in their neighborhoods, they invariably named the alguacil and not the amparador.[46] No doubt natives saw the alguacil somewhat regularly and probably never saw the amparador.

The office of alguacil amparador began to appear regularly in the documentation of the Juzgado General de los Indios in the 1630s and 1640s.[47] One early example suggests the utility of this office as an intermediary between the Audiencia and the indigenous governments. In a 1640 dispute involving exclusively natives, the Juzgado General asked the alguacil amparador to carry out a viceregal order. The Audiencia ruled in favor of a native litigant in his complaint against members of the indigenous government. The case involved Baltasar Gómez, an indigenous principal (he called himself a cacique) who attempted to establish a fruit import business (*cosecha*). The indigenous government, using its capacity to regulate markets, attempted to deny Gómez access to Mexico City markets. A successful and enterprising native, Gómez had established a business in which he imported fruit from contracted haciendas in Cuernavaca to sell at the indigenous markets of Mexico City.[48] As a native he should have easily gained access to markets controlled by the indigenous government, yet Gómez indicated in his complaint that the native justices of Mexico Tenochtitlan unfairly singled him out to harass.[49] Gómez claimed a kind of unfair discrimination: because he was married to "a Spanish woman with whom he had fathered three children whom he supports [financially] . . . and who wear Spanish-styled clothing," the indigenous government tried to use its authority to deny him opportunity. To correct this grave injustice, Gómez asked the Audiencia to defend his rights (*amparo*) specifically to engage in legal commerce.[50] In this instance the Juzgado General backed Gómez, asking that the alguacil defend him from harassment by the officials on the cabildo.

Recognizing that members of the indigenous government could not impartially enforce an order against themselves, the Audiencia needed an intermediary who could intercede to avoid a conflict of interest. The corregidor was the logical candidate, but he seems to have been passed over. Indeed, as the office of corregidor increased in authority in the city, he did become the viceregal officer to whom this complaint would have gone in the eighteenth century. It also seems likely that, because this was an appeal for assistance, the amparador de los naturales was a logical choice to resolve the internal dispute, and he sent his emissary to enforce the decision of the viceregal government.[51] The alguacil amparador, as a disinterested intermediary, executed the order for the Audiencia, preventing an awkward conflict of interest and at the same time enabling the viceregal bureaucracy to defend the rights of those discriminated against.

The principal function of the alguacil amparador, however, appears to have been helping the governor to collect tribute. After the 1630s, a dismal time marked by tribute shortfalls, governors likely acceded readily to the aid provided by the alguacil amparador. Governors risked their financial security when assuming their office. The alguacil amparador seemed to provide a ready solution to the problem of meeting tribute benchmarks. Although the exact means by which the crown or viceregal government established the office of alguacil amparador remains unclear, it may have been created to solve the problem of the increasing diversity in the barrios, which made it more difficult for indigenous governments to collect tribute from all under their jurisdiction. The alguacil amparador could also take care of duties within the indigenous communities over which the indigenous government and cabildos had no jurisdiction.

Indigenous governments collected and delivered most of the tribute due in Mexico City three times a year—in April, August, and December.[52] A small fraction of tribute payers, however, did not fall under the authority of the indigenous government. The increasingly large community of free Afro-Mexicans owed tribute to the crown.[53] The ordinances that required Afro-Mexicans to pay tribute did not specifically establish who in the elaborate bureaucracy would collect their tribute. Regional variations in the tribute bureaucracy made it necessary for local officials to create ways to collect. In Mexico Tenochtitlan indigenous governors, at least in regard to tribute, acted much like corregidores or alcaldes mayores in the provincial areas of New Spain. Unlike the Spanish regional administrators, however, indigenous governors had no jurisdiction over Afro-Mexicans. As a result, some other agent of the crown had to take over the collection of tribute from them.[54] The growth of the free Afro-Mexican population, which probably overtook in size the enslaved population sometime in the early to mid-seventeenth century, made the number of tribute-paying Afro-Mexicans substantially larger.[55] In communities outside of Mexico

City, free blacks and mulattoes paid tribute to the alcalde mayor or the corregidor. Just as these regional Spanish officials collected tribute from indigenous communities in their jurisdictions, the governors collected and delivered tribute directly.[56] In Mexico City, as usual, the situation seems to have been more complex, with the indigenous governments in Mexico City not reporting to the corregidor.[57]

Collecting tribute in difficult places may have helped to integrate the alguacil amparador into its role as an agent of the indigenous governor for the collection of tribute. In 1649, Juan López received praise from don Fernando Cortés Moctezuma, the amparador de los naturales, for his ability to collect tribute in textile workshops [obrajes] and bakeries [panaderías] without "receiving complaints [vejaciones] from the indigenous governor or from Afro-Mexicans [including mulattoes] [working] in the workshops and bakeries."[58] One of the duties of the alguacil amparador was to conduct inspections (visitas) of the city jails and to look in the panaderías and obrajes for prisoners who owed tribute.[59] Bakeries and workshops employed significant numbers of free-wage laborers, some of whom owed tribute to the crown. The alguacil amparador operated in the service of both the Spanish and indigenous bureaucracies and thus had the authority to enter these businesses in the name of the viceregal government to extract tribute from free blacks and mulattoes. As a representative of the viceregal government, the alguacil amparador may have had additional influence over obraje and panadería owners.[60] Spaniards, who regularly refused to cooperate with indigenous officials, may have been more inclined to work with a Spanish official. The alguacil amparador obviously did well to assist in collecting tribute in areas where indigenous officers were sometimes not welcome. In the appointment document of Miguel de la Cruz, alguacil amparador in 1653, governor don Diego de la Cruz Villanueva stated directly that Cruz should assist the tribute collectors, "as was customary," accompanying them "so that the alcaldes could enter into the houses of Spaniards and others like them [y otras personas así] in this city and its subject towns and places where natives reside [to collect] the tribute they owe."[61] Though the order does not mention obrajes or panaderías specifically, it shows that the alguacil amparador and indigenous tribute collectors worked together to collect native tribute in places where indigenous officials alone had previously encountered problems.

Alguacil amparador Juan López enjoyed a great deal of success collecting tribute, perhaps explaining why his duties over the years seemed to expand. In 1651 the indigenous cabildo of Mexico Tenochtitlan asked that the viceroy intervene to reappoint Juan López instead of Miguel de la Cruz, whose candidacy the amparador de los naturales supported. Though they did not specifically state why they preferred López over Cruz, it is clear from the context that the cabildo had confidence in López's ability to collect tribute. As the appointment document continues, the viceroy explained the expectations of the alguacil amparador as he issued an order to appoint Juan López. López was to "assist the governor and alcaldes and those who aid him, the tequitlatos [*teguitlatos*] and mandones [tribute bosses] of the said barrios, every time that they come together to collect tribute and to make sure that all the natives pay and take part in the service [*repartimiento y real servicio*] they owe [to the community].[62]

According to the appointment document the algaucil amapardor carried the staff of office, which enabled him to exercise authority in the name of the crown. With the staff he could serve warrants and detain suspects.[63] Although it is not clear that all governors and cabildo members wanted the aid of the alguacil amparador, he did have the authority and specific charge to assist the indigenous governor with the collection of tribute. The alguacil amparador had few official duties. According to other appointment documents, he was somewhat like an indigenous alcalde or regidor.[64] He carried the staff of office and served as an advisor (*aconsejado*) to the governor. The appointment documents sometimes mention his role as a tribute collector and other times appear to assume that it would be impossible to assist an indigenous governor without helping out in the collection of tribute. It is also possible that, since alcaldes and regidores were asked to assist in tribute collection in the late 1640s, the alguacil amparador began to help as well.

AN AGENT OF THE CROWN OR THE GOVERNOR?

The alguacil amparador was an agent whose authority derived from the viceregal government, which made less clear the relationship between him and the governor. The viceroy issued the staff carried

TABLE 3   Governors of Mexico Tenochtitlan, 1648–1660

1648–1652	Don Manuel Tapia Moctezuma
1653–1654	Don Diego de la Cruz Villanueva
1654	Don Juan de Aguilar el Viejo
1654	Don Juan de Velazquez (did not serve; disqualified for insufficient financial backing)
1655–1656	Don Diego de la Cruz Villanueva
1657	Don Marcos de la Cruz
1657–1658	Don Pedro Bernal (1657, June)
1659–1660	Don Francisco Benítez Inga

by the alguacil amparador, just as he issued the staff of office for the governor. Because the staff came from the viceroy, not the governor, the alguacil amparador exercised independent authority that did not derive from the governor. At the same time, the governor, it appears, did have some say in the appointment of the alguacil amparador and occasionally requested that the amparador or viceroy remove an objectionable alguacil amparador. Governors, then, had the authority to contest an alguacil amparador, but they had no ability to limit directly or to remove one. Even though they probably were not often denied their requests, governors had to ask to have an alguacil amparador removed or rebuked.

In 1649, amparador de los naturales Moctezuma petitioned the viceroy to stop the indigenous governor and alcaldes from denying the staff of authority to the alguacil amparador. The document does not lay out the reason for the conflict between the alguacil amparador and the native cabildo and governor. It did not need to provide the reason. It had to show only that the governor and alcaldes had denied the alguacil amparador the use of his vara, which it did. In other words, there was no justifiable cause that would allow the governor and alcaldes to remove the vara directly from the alguacil amparador, because natives did not have this authority. Acting viceroy Torres y Rueda (r. 1648–49), the Bishop of Yucatan, reaffirmed that the indigenous government could not, of its own authority, deny the alguacil amparador the use of his vara. The viceroy also threatened any native official denounced for such an action with a 200 peso fine and loss of office.[65]

Governors, though they could not act directly, had some authority over the alguacil amparador. The standards of the office provided the terms on which he could be challenged or limited. Not meeting his expectations gave the governor limited ability to deny him his vara. In addition, for no reason at all, a governor could request the removal of the current alguacil amparador and recommend the appointment of another. The appointment documents mention that the alguacil amparador must avoid causing disturbances or uprisings (alborotos) in the community, providing a savvy governor a means to check and restrict him.[66] The governor, who often heard native complaints, could probably work with and limit the alguacil amparador. All he needed to do was direct native petitioners to the Audiencia, something that must have given the governor some subtle leverage.

In 1654, for example, Juan López was accused of "causing distur-bances" (inquietudes) in a petition submitted by the indigenous govern-ment (in the name of the "commoners and natives"), which led to his reprimand and the restriction of his political activity by the viceroy.[67] So even though the governor could not exercise direct authority over the alguacil amparador, he could file petitions to force others who had such authority to act. Commoners could petition as well, and thus some avenues enabled the community to limit the authority of the alguacil amparador.

Alguaciles amparadores seem to have participated in defining their duties as well. Diego de Carrión, alguacil in Mexico Tlatelolco, on his own volition requested the right to perform duties usually carried out by the indigenous government. In this case, he asked to conduct night rounds (rondas por noche) of the barrios to guard against criminal activity.[68] The court permitted him to make rounds as an intermediary but stipulated that he deposit natives in the jail of the tecpan, in effect turning them over to indigenous judicial officials, and to place non-natives in the jail of the Audiencia for prosecution by the Sala del Crimen.[69] Since at least the 1640s the alguacil amparador had carried the vara de real justicia, but doing rounds in the barrios was some-thing new, further creating jurisdictional ambiguity.

Some clues exist to provide insight over the limits and extent of his authority in practice. Diego de Carrión in the 1640s justified his need to patrol the neighborhoods by claiming in his petitions that "many robberies and other disturbances" threatened the peace.[70] The order that gave him the authority to patrol at night, however, did not limit his jurisdiction. Provided he deposited the accused with the proper court, he could apprehend whomever he saw fit to accuse. By asking the viceregal government for permission to patrol, Carrión implied that indigenous alcaldes and the governor had failed to maintain order and needed assistance. In addition, his petition also suggests that he met resistance from indigenous officials, who interfered with his attempts to patrol the neighborhoods. He also asked for permission from the Juzgado General de los Indios, indicating that he sought authority over natives and the right to act in the place of the alcaldes of the cabildo. The official order issued by the Juzgado General recognized the possibility that indigenous officials might object by stating that "they [the indigenous government] not impede the execution of this order" to allow Carrión to patrol the streets at night.[71] In the interests of preserving order, the Juzgado General conceded authority usually reserved for the indigenous cabildo and governor to a Spaniard. In effect then, the petition process worked both ways, enabling the alguacil amparador to limit the indigenous governor.

Between 1649 and 1659, Mexico Tenochtitlan experienced acute tribute shortfalls that further served to empower the alguacil amparador. The tribute shortfalls also inspired governors to alter the duties of alcaldes and regidores on the cabildo to include the collection of tribute. Though tribute shortfalls were common in seventeenth-century Mexico City and governors (and their financial guarantors) bore responsibility for delivering the correct amount, governors sometimes found innovative ways to collect.[72] With increasing skill, however, political rivals, the contador general, the alguacil amparador, and commoners learned to file complaints against the governor that engaged the viceregal courts. Governors therefore had to exercise caution not to create disturbances or violate any obvious duties of their office. Tribute collection finance problems were profoundly similar to those during the previous chronic shortages after the flood of 1629.[73]

Governor don Manuel de Tapia Moctezuma (r. 1648–52) was appointed to office in 1648 after the death of don Sebastián Cortés Pizarro (r. 1646–48).[74] Because of the urgency of the final push for tribute, Viceroy Torres y Rueda promoted Tapia Moctezuma, his candidate of choice, apparently without consulting the cabildo or the community of electors.[75] Governor for the final quarter of 1648, he continued to serve in 1649. Tapia Moctezuma came up with an innovative way to collect tribute. He called the idea (it was not original to him) an experiment.[76] He included the alcaldes and regidores elected to the cabildo to augment the mandones who already physically collected tribute. Such a move was not just experimental but somewhat controversial. Adding muscle to the tribute collection apparatus in Mexico Tenochtitlan had the potential to create disorder, even though Tapia Moctezuma was required to keep an elaborate record of who had already paid tribute, perhaps to make it less likely that individuals were charged multiple times. Apparently the cabildo alcaldes and regidores aided the efforts of Tapia Moctezuma significantly, and he asked specifically that the viceroy cancel the election of 1649 completely and allow the cabildo members to continue in their current offices, stating, "Those who currently hold the offices [of alcalde and regidor] are people who inspire confidence and who faithfully meet all of the obligations of their office."[77] He then asked the viceroy to allow those who currently held the offices of alcalde and regidor to "continue in their current offices with their current duties to aid in the collection of tribute." The viceroy approved the request and allowed the officials to serve with their new duties as tribute collectors.[78] Such innovation seems to have avoided tribute shortfalls in the immediate term. The movement of alcaldes into the tribute collection business, however, gave the alguacil amparador a chance to work directly alongside electors. No longer did he simply go around with nonvoting mandones.

AN ATTEMPT AT THE GOVERNORSHIP?

Juan López served intermittently in the office of alguacil amparador during the period of extreme tribute shortfalls and actively sought the governorship beginning in 1654. Gibson points out López's effort (without naming him directly), reporting that "a campaign by . . . [a] Spaniard to secure the governorship in [Mexico] Tenochtitlan later in the seventeenth century included entertainments, banquets, gifts, and extravagant election promises."[79] After the death in office of governor don Juan de Aguilar the elder (r. 1654), López began an active campaign, just as Gibson described.[80] In this very document, however, the seeds of dispute emerged quickly. Though López sought to build support for his own candidacy, the very act brought him into conflict with many and began a rigorous debate about the capacity of a Spaniard or someone other than a native to hold the office of governor.

Almost immediately, the community composed a petition to challenge the candidacy of López on the grounds that he was ineligible. "Alguaciles mayores, mandones, principales, commoners, and natives [común y naturales]," the petition began, argued that López had no right to hold indigenous office. He should refrain, the petition continued, from making disturbances in the community by soliciting votes.[81] The petition referenced an ordinance from 23 August 1642 that stated "it is prohibited to occupy or seek said offices [of indigenous government]" those of "other naciones . . . mestizos, Spaniards, or mulattoes." In clear language, the community spelled out the problem that the offices of the cabildo were "restricted exclusively to natives and their children," and that "Spaniards, mestizos and mulattoes could only serve the native community leaders."[82] The petition continued to praise the indigenous governments of the past, arguing that natives better served as leaders of the indigenous community. "There are many qualified caciques and principales, and it is much more convenient and useful for them to govern the natives of the city with the vision to sustain with love and ancient paternalism absent when others have ruled."[83] The viceregal government concurred that even problematic native rulers who sometimes faltered in their efforts or exercised poor judgment in their decisions were vastly superior to Spaniards, mestizos, or mulattoes. Perhaps natives were, as suggested, vested members of the community and therefore more likely to serve selflessly. This idealistic vision of self-government suggests that the potential protective paternalism of a native governor would likely reduce abuses. It would also likely elevate the living conditions of what the petition calls "miserables naturales," impoverished native peoples. The plotting of López, no matter what kind of politicking he chose to perform, could not likely get around written ordinances, especially after the community petitioned to stop him.

In 1657 tribute shortfalls, or at least the alleged certainty of them, enabled López to vie for the governorship again, or failing that to attempt a de facto takeover of the duties. He argued that the current governor, don Marcos de la Cruz (r. 1657–May 1657), elected in January of that year, did not have the capacity to serve. In a series of petitions, beginning on 21 February 1657, López in conjunction with the contador general don Martín de San Martín made his case to take over the collection of tribute and effectively the governorship.[84] The contador general and the alguacil amparador had enormous influence, and there is some indication that they worked together to undermine the authority of Governor Cruz. López and San Martín had raised similar charges against the previous governor, don Diego de la Cruz Villanueva, in 1655, and thus provide some indication that by 1656 he may have also had trouble delivering sufficient tribute.[85] A petition presented by contador general San Martín raised the issue directly, introducing a lengthy and personal petition from Juan López and sounding the alarm: "Your Excellency must find a new way to meet the tribute quotas for this year, which have grown to a sum so large that, when combined with royal service [real servicio] and public works, rises to nearly 12,000 pesos, which, unless Your Excellency does what is asked, it will be impossible to collect."[86]

The specific complaint originated because San Martín saw that the full 12,000 pesos due would not be collected. To solve the problem, the contador general recommended in March that the viceroy remove don Marcos de la Cruz from office and call for new elections.[87] Further, Juan López should take over the tribute collection duties until the community could elect a new governor.[88] Juan López, just as the introduction by the contador general implied, argued that Governor Cruz was utterly inept. He could not even provide the fiadores necessary to assume his risk.[89] Ever the opportunist, López then made the case, stating in the first person, "I need for Your Excellency to order the governor and alcaldes [of Mexico Tenochtitlan] to accompany and aid me in the collection of tribute."[90] López stated that he had forfeited his salary for two and a half years, apparently attempting to demonstrate that he had no personal financial stake or ambition but acted selflessly "without interest, and without salary . . . at risk of [his] finances [hacienda] and health." The contador general, after submitting this petition from López, recommended that "Your Excellency should do what is asked for and contained in the petition."[91]

Asking for such a dramatic role reversal—the assistant to the governor demanding to take the lead in the affairs of indigenous government—suggests López's political aims and ambitions. He stated that he had done well to gather tribute in the past and continued to find support among the merinos who aided him. Though the cabildo and governor responded loyally, stating that they would do what the contador wished, they recognized the political maneuvering López had undertaken and resisted his grab for authority. With the aid of procurador Juan Pérez de Salamanca, Governor Cruz denounced López, stating that under no circumstance could "a Spaniard be governor."[92] Furthermore, the native cabildo and governor exposed the premise under which López apparently operated by directly accusing him of attempting "to establish a position superior in authority to the governor."[93] The governor stated that the duty of an alguacil amparador was to "attend and obey" (*asista y obedezca*). The procurador then launched into a lengthy tirade filled with allegations of malfeasance against López. Indeed, according to the procurador, López had concocted a profitable scheme that had the potential to make him very wealthy at the expense of the native community, native cabildo, and viceregal government. López allegedly arrested natives without authorization from the native governor and then charged the imprisoned natives one peso each, which he "alleged was for tribute." He then kept six reales (of eight in a peso) as a fee.[94] If this allegation was true, he likely could have made significantly more charging fees for delivering tribute than collecting his salary, making somewhat less altruistic sounding the forfeiture of salary he claimed. Furthermore, his scheme effectively took off the rolls many tribute payers. These natives then could not (or did not have to) pay more and thus provided the native treasury only a fraction of the tribute they owed. The remainder went directly to López. Because López was not held personally responsible for tribute shortfalls, no one would confiscate his property or imprison him as they might a delinquent governor. He therefore had no personal financial liability if the full amount of tribute went uncollected. López also likely had an incentive to undermine the native governor. Tribute shortfalls on behalf of a governor made the contador and López more essential to the viceregal authorities. When working together, the contador and alguacil amparador likely had sufficient authority over the tribute collection in the native barrios to undermine a governor like don Marcos de la Cruz. By doing his job poorly, López could effectively weaken the governor.

On 24 March, three weeks after the initial petition by López, oidor don Andrés Sánchez de Ocampo, who usually supervised the elections for Mexico Tenochtitlan in the late 1650s, made his ruling. He based it on the opinion of the fiscal who spoke for the viceroy. In a strongly worded statement, he made clear that López had overstepped his authority when he proposed that the viceroy make him de facto governor. Sánchez de Ocampo also made it clear, just as don Marcos de la Cruz had stated, that the alguacil amparador had to obey the governor. In addition, following the fiscal, he recommended that Viceroy Alburquerque forbid López from attempting to expand his authority. He also recommended that the viceroy strip López of his capacity to petition, imposing on him "perpetual silence." This rebuke, when affirmed by the viceroy, removed López's ability to submit petitions that requested the expansion of his authority by complaining about the governor.[95] It also seems to have profoundly limited López's ability to hold office in the barrios. He did not serve again as alguacil amparador, and after 1656 the office of alguacil amparador apparently disappeared as an office in the viceregal government.

The very day that Viceroy Alburquerque rebuked López, the contador general pressed further against Governor Cruz. In a separate petition to the viceroy, he argued that the governor had not submitted proper fiadores and could not guarantee the tribute for that year.[96] The timing of the petition suggests that it was in response to the oidor's ruling. The contador's petition impelled the court to check to see if Governor Cruz indeed had submitted insufficient or ineligible fiadores. The April investigation led by don Martín de San Martín concluded that four of the six fiadores supplied by Cruz were "poor men without property or other merchandise" to finance the debt they offered to cover. In effect, should the shortfall presaged by the contador come to pass, these fiadores had no ability to rescue the governor financially and effectively were not viable.[97] The contador also claimed that he confronted, on 26 March, the "governor-elect" to notify him of the deficiencies. According to San Martín, Cruz replied that "he had no other fiadores beyond those submitted in his original account [*memoria*]."[98]

The financing problems proposed by the contador did not immediately cause the viceroy to nullify the election. Alburquerque took almost two months, during which time he demanded that Cruz provide the necessary financing. When that did not happen, he called for new elections in late May 1657. Anticipating resistance to his decision, the viceroy ordered: "As quickly as possible the electors should gather in the tecpan at San Juan [Mexico Tenochtitlan] as is customary and with his [don Andrés Sánchez de Ocampo] assistance . . . through an interpreter so that they understand that the said don Marcos de la Cruz, by not complying, had [lost his mandate to rule] by failing to provide trustworthy fiadores . . . without any kind of grievance or violence they must elect a new governor who will comply."[99] Alburquerque must have recognized the gravity of removing a governor, for he made clear the potential for violence and warned against disorder. The time delay, careful investigation, and clear reasons for his dismissal also likely softened the impact of Cruz's removal, even though it came from the advice of the contador and alguacil amparador. Electors and principales amassed in the tecpan were notified in specific terms exactly why the governor was being removed. Alburquerque's order also implies that violence or some kind of complaint was expected from the community, or at least this appears to be what provoked the unusual call for civility.[100]

The electors chose don Pedro Bernal (r. 1657–58) to serve as governor on 28 June 1657, and he served until the very end of 1658.[101] Bernal appears to have embraced the silenced López and praised him for his ability to collect tribute and for his service to the community. He requested that López be reinstated as a tribute collector but not as alguacil amparador. In a petition, Governor Bernal stated that "Juan López is a person who has had for the past two years the responsibility to collect tribute. He has been punctual and as a measure of his intelligence and familiarity with the community has been able to deliver said tribute."[102]

Bernal then asked permission, not to appoint him to the office of alguacil amparador, but simply to have him serve as an assistant in the collection of tribute (cobrador de los reales tributos) so that they would make the annual quota. Contador San Martín, who apparently survived the affair unscathed, added that López's participation was necessary for the community to collect all of the tribute it owed. San

Martín then proceeded to condemn the community itself, stating that Mexico Tenochtitlan was filled with "natives . . . who are very lazy and averse to paying tribute."[103] In such circumstances, a "creative" tribute gatherer was needed. Additionally, the new governor seems to have restored López to a position of comfort within the community after his comeuppance in March.[104]

None of the efforts of López and his allies in the office of the contador general suggest that they did not have a right to complain or to suggest that don Marcos de la Cruz and don Diego de la Cruz Villanueva had been model governors. Rather, both seem to have had difficulties collecting tribute. Their inability may have warranted or at least enabled Spanish officials to rationalize the arguments made by López. Also implicit in the 1650s are the lines of collaboration between this particular alguacil amparador, Juan López, the governor, Pedro Bernal, and the contador general, don Martín de San Martín. The collusion of these three, which of course by 1658 did not include the amparador de los naturales but the contador general and native governor, suggests that cooperation among officials could concentrate authority even among offices that should have checked one another through competing jurisdictions.

ABUSES AND THE ALGUACIL AMPARADOR

Juan López may have been successful because he employed abusive methods. One of the most damning petitions against him came from the cabildo of Mexico Tenochtitlan in 1655. The full cabildo wrote on 14 October 1655 that López had "cheated" natives and other "common people" (*gente plebe*). He forced them to pay more tribute than they owed.[105] To augment the collection of tribute, the alguacil amparador allegedly sought new streams of revenue. Nonnatives and those not naturalized (*avecindado*) living in the parcialidad of Mexico Tenochtitlan but who obviously by their age and apparent indigenous status owed tribute found themselves shaken down by López and those who aided his efforts.[106] The cabildo referred to López and his accomplices derisively, calling them "common thieves." In conjunction they alleged, as discussed above, that he rounded up natives and threw them in the jail of the tecpan, charging a peso and keeping the bulk of it as a fee. López also caused a stir with the *pulqueras,* women who sold pulque out of their homes, and pulquería owners. Many who ran these establishments complained that López and other alguaciles amparadores entered pulquerías to demand tribute payments from natives. The Juzgado General de los Indios resolved that, even if accompanied by indigenous officials (mandones, regidores, or alcaldes), the alguacil amparador could not enter such establishments under the pretext of collecting tribute.[107] López also unfairly charged tribute from "Chinos," those of Asian origin who lived in the city.[108] Although free Asians did owe tribute, like free Afro-Mexicans, apparently López forced to pay even those who presented a *carta de pago* (receipt) that indicated they had already paid. It is also possible that the strong institutions of the viceregal government impelled the cabildo to keep extensive records because of the tactics of López.

Documents related to the appointment to the governorship of don Diego de la Cruz Villanueva from just two years earlier, in 1655, reveal that the contador wanted to ensure that the Audiencia could hold the governor accountable for tribute collection and reinforce the mandate to collect tribute to which he had been charged. After the standard and usual elements of the appointment document, admonishing the governor to treat his subjects well and to defend the faith against idolatry, the supervising oidor, don Antonio Álvarez de Castro, ordered that the governor make sure that he keep a book that recorded the name and amount paid by each tribute payer signed by the governor and the contador general along with the date the tribute had been assessed.[109] He also had to issue to each tribute payer a carta de pago to serve as proof of payment. Additionally, probably because of the low compliance, he had to matriculate into the tribute rolls all residents. These warnings, which came at the behest of Contador San Martín, also reflect the growing concerns with those who might wish to tax multiple times those with the resources to pay—a well-documented complaint regularly offered by the community.[110]

Other petitions made the case more directly and seemed to come from the common people of Mexico Tenochtitlan. Nicolás Lorenzo and Agustín Pérez complained to the Juzgado General, demonstrating the extent to which the community could use the terms of the appointment document to limit the actions of an overzealous alguacil amparador. Their 6 July 1656 petition stated that López had forced them to pay in cash, on the spot, "one peso and four reales [which] caused great suffering and left them impoverished" and "unable to pay [future] tribute." The petitioners also noted that the alguacil amparador did not listen when they insisted that they had already paid their tribute. They alleged further that the alguacil amparador, along with his assistants, had forcibly entered their homes and threatened to "impose punishments" if they refused to pay.[111] Such tactics presumably marred the process of tax farming in New Spain and beyond, but they clearly illustrate disrespect toward indigenous tribute payers and attention given to those few who had resources during lean years. The Juzgado General, however, had already forbidden in unambiguous terms the practice of Spaniards forcibly entering the homes of indigenous residents to collect tribute in 1649. Though it referred specifically to the homes of those who sold pulque and targeted the tribute collectors who sought to force natives who might have attempted to hide from the collectors in these spaces, the order made it clear that the viceregal government would not tolerate aggressive tax collecting.[112] Furthermore, forceful tactics appeared to target those who could pay, sometimes hitting them up more than once to meet the quotas. The alguacil amparador was apparently not reminded to charge natives only once, but governors heard in their appointment document that they should make sure that no one paid two times.[113] Indigenous commoners resisted by asking the viceregal government to restrict the alguacil amparador.

After 1658, López seems to have continued to attract the attention of indigenous allegations. The "Mixtec and Zapotec principales and commoners" who resided in Mexico Tenochtitlan filed a complaint against him on 5 April of that year. Each year it seems the community of Oaxacans living in the parcialidad of Mexico Tenochtitlan gathered to elect an alguacil to represent them and to collect their tribute in the chapel of Our lady of Rosario in the convent of Santo Domingo. López, with disrespect and "ill will," broke up their ceremony to demand tribute payments from all in the chapel. Apparently having such a large gathering made for efficient collection, but according to the allegation López demanded payment even from those who "showed him a carta de pago." Their representative asked that His Excellency "notify under the threat of grave penalties the said Juan López not to disturb the customary practices [they had] established or mistreat the natives whom [he] represent[ed]."[114] The fiscal and oidor both stated unequivocally that López must stop harassing the natives of Oaxaca who lived in the city.

López apparently tried to increase the number of tribute payers in the barrios. To do this, he hoped to make certain that migrants who came to live in the city matriculated into the tribute rolls as naturalized subjects of the indigenous government.[115] By forcing natives to matriculate, he took tribute away from outlying communities and transferred it to the government of Mexico Tenochtitlan. The city absorbed a heavy influx of migrants during the early 1650s. In 1654 the principales and mandones of Mexico Tenochtitlan reported in a petition to the viceroy that they had made resident (avecindado) numerous non-Tenochca groups living in the city, including Tlaxcalteca, Mixtecs, Zapotecs, Tarascans, and even Chichimeca.[116] Environmental factors pushed migrants into the city, as often happened during times of drought or excessive rain. Migrants from the countryside moved to the city when crops failed to take advantage of the largesse of urban charity or to find work.[117]

With so much influence in the parcialidad of Mexico Tenochtitlan and an increasingly important patronage network, Juan López had gone from minor Spanish official and designee to someone with substantial authority.[118] By 1659, when he ran for governor, he had developed such a powerful patronage network that he finished second in the election despite the prohibitions against Spaniards holding the office of governor, the numerous complaints filed against him in the community, and the resistance of electors. Surely all of the campaigning he did—"hosting grand dinner banquets and dances (convites de comidas y bailes)"— helped to build support.[119] Though he failed to win the governorship, he received more votes than three other candidates and lost ultimately only to don Francisco Benítez.

The slow penetration of Juan López and other alguaciles amparadores into the bureaucracy of tribute collection and town government made them powerful political figures in the barrios of Mexico City. They also served the governors in their efforts to increase tribute rolls by entering into Spanish-owned obrajes and panaderías and helping to matriculate non-Tenocha migrants who settled in the city. The ill-defined duties of the alguacil amparador also enabled the expansion of their authority, eventually including a powerful judicial/policing role. Most important, Juan López, because of his success in collecting tribute, seems to have taken on more responsibility in the 1650s. Performing a task on par with governors—managing the tribute collection bureau-cracy—López appears to have seen a viable possibility to advance. His efforts forced the community to engage the viceregal government to restrict the office of governor to natives. Indeed, the only way candidates like López and Benítez could possibly serve as governor was in a situa-tion where real elections had meaning and the capacity to legitimize the candidacy of those whom the ordinances made ineligible. The diversity "on the ballot" in 1659 seems to indicate the erosion of Tenocha micro-patriotism in the barrios of Mexico Tenochtitlan. Many non-Tenochca appear to have garnered support from an ostensibly Tenochca electorate. More important, however, natives sought to place limits on who had the right to hold office, but they did not speak with one voice. Some factions concentrated on keeping mestizos and Spaniards from seeking native offices. Others more vested in micro-patriotism challenged non-Tenochca and fought to remove candidates on the grounds that they were foreign. All of these activities speak to an increasing politicization of the once orderly selection process.[120]

Despite allowing him to arrest and perform night rounds as well as collect tribute and enforce orders of the Audiencia, the viceregal gov-ernment limited the jurisdiction of the alguacil amparador. These rights were not given carte blanche but rather doled out in response to requests and granted only in specific circumstances. When the alguacil amparador overstepped his authority, the Audiencia reprimanded him. When natives complained of abuse, the Audiencia generally intervened on their behalf as the assumed aggrieved party. Through complaint, therefore, natives to a certain extent controlled the reach of Spanish officials in the barrios. Ironically, by asking the Audiencia to mediate the natives also extended the viceregal government's reach further into the barrios.[121]

The process of mediation, however, worked both ways. López and Contador San Martín also petitioned and had political aims to oust Governor don Marcos de la Cruz. Thus, the increasing willingness of the viceregal government to intervene in the affairs of indigenous government opened up the possibilities of politics in unintended ways.

CHAPTER 5

A TECPAN DIVIDED
A MATURE POLITICAL CULTURE, 1660–1730

A group of principales from Mexico Tenochtitlan filed a petition in 1714 to remove the current governor, don Juan de Ribera, from office and to disqualify him from running for reelection. This event was neither revolutionary nor a new strategy, but it was part of an increasingly important political process in Mexico City's indigenous neighborhoods. In this particular petition, a group of indigenous electors, most of them current or former officeholders, appealed directly to the Audiencia so that it might intervene on their behalf. The viceroy had always had the authority to overturn an indigenous election and had exercised his mandate multiple times beginning in the mid-seventeenth century. Viceregal authorities had shown increasing willingness to exercise this prerogative, but within specific limits. The viceroy generally followed the advice of the supervising oidor and his fiscal, who paid much closer attention to the details of the petitions and had the training to provide a sound legal opinion.[1] Native complaints, rather than preemptive action on the part of viceregal officials, usually raised the issues that impelled officials to act. Strategies adopted by native petitioners to contest elections, however, were created by native politicians and evolved over time to adjust to different viceregal attitudes toward native challenges. These processes, which emerged in the sixteenth century when native governments were first established, by the early eighteenth century had matured into a vibrant political culture.

Natives submitted the petition that sought to oust Ribera on 22 December 1714 through the Audiencia procurador, don Nicolás Antonio de Navia. He wrote on behalf of a group of former governors and alcaldes who had served on the cabildo of Mexico Tenochtitlan and asked oidor don Francisco Valenzuela Vanegas to make certain that the election followed all established legal principles. The petition stated directly the specific grounds that put in jeopardy Ribera's candidacy, claiming that he "appeared to be a mestizo." The direct allegation, given without any supporting evidence, was accompanied by a second charge that the "vice of drunkenness" afflicted Ribera. Only the partisan support in the form of their signatures on the petition of former governors and alcaldes corroborated these allegations.[2] Having made these two charges, the petition then politely reminded the oidor that the ordinances barred mestizos from serving in native offices and that a certain level of decorum was expected of all who served in indigenous government.

Importantly, the group simply requested that the oidor follow the ordinances that laid out the terms under which a governor could serve. They identified two obvious ways in which the Audiencia could disqualify Ribera and then virtually quoted the appointment document to make absolutely certain that the oidor made the proper association. Pointing out the potential problem directly was likely a way to ask the oidor to investigate. By doing this in advance of the election, the natives may have also hoped that the oidor would simply bar Ribera from receiving votes by stating that he was not a qualified candidate.[3] The petition showed that the natives who contested Ribera's candidacy knew well the terms of the appointment document and understood how the viceregal government could aid them politically. The oidor, through his capacity to make a recommendation to the viceroy, could effectively be used to remove a candidate.

The petition itself suggests how candidates for the office of indigenous governor might have maneuvered politically to advance their candidacies. These kinds of actions had become ordinary since the mid-seventeenth century. A new development also presented itself in these eighteenth-century disputes; the conscious formation of native coalitions made up of groups of electors allied to elect a particular candidate.[4] Such coalitions used political strategies developed during the seventeenth century to involve the viceregal government in native elections. All who sought the office of governor in the early eighteenth century probably had to build coalitions of support, and often they had to fend off challenges from rival factions well in advance of the election. Even though ordinances forbade open campaigning, to win an election a candidate had to find ways to build support within the community. The allegations mentioned above, brought by a rather small group (nine natives) who claimed to speak for "the rest of the electors," were filed several weeks before the election took place.[5] Electors therefore knew before the election itself that Ribera planned to run and that he stood to win significant support. It is worth noting that, if the challengers truly spoke for the rest of the electors as they alleged, there would have been no need to file the petition, for they would have simply won the election. The very challenge itself, however, from a group of electors who claimed to speak for many more than their small number, suggests that a faction within the cabildo and community of electors opposed the sitting governor and sought leverage to have a popular candidate removed. They also must have realized that the opposition they represented did not have sufficient support to oust Ribera in the election. Knowledge of this nature implies that native politicians surveyed the electorate carefully, formed voting blocs, and elicited support before any of the official mechanisms of election took place. The very nature of these acts is political and reflects the maturity of the system shaped by the indigenous leaders.

The electors who challenged Ribera made their most substantive claim when they stated that they believed he was a mestizo. It would have been difficult to prove in a meaningful way the charge that he drank excessively, though apparently even having such a reputation could bar one from the office. Those who petitioned, however, knew that they could provide real evidence to determine Ribera's ethnicity. It was then only a matter of asking the oidor to enforce the ordinances that prohibited mestizos from holding the office of governor. To do this, the petitioners first provided information—the parish of his birth, Santa Veracruz in Mexico Tenochtitlan.

Though the oidor took no action in 1714 in response to the initial complaint and Ribera successfully won reelection in 1715, the same group challenged his election when he tried to run for a third term in 1716. The challengers from 1714, including the same nine individuals with two more added to the list, actually conducted their own investigation into the Santa Veracruz parish records in 1715. They found, as don Joseph de la Cruz and his supporters suspected, that Ribera "was baptized mestizo."[6] Even with the solid evidence of a baptismal record, however, they continued to make further allegations against Ribera. According to their petition from late 1715, Ribera had committed other offenses. They alleged that he had purchased votes with alcohol and that he worked as a barber, a low-status occupation. The charge that Ribera was a barber may have been calculated to convince Spanish officials that he was not of the nobility. Although some native leaders had low-status occupations, Spaniards sometimes had difficulty reconciling such a profession with nobility.[7] Following the same pattern as in 1714, they pointed out that the ordinances specifically forbade those who served in common professions from holding the office and also prohibited candidates from seeking votes. The complaint, however, remained focused on the issue of Ribera's birth. In his response, the viceroy, following the fiscal, asked that the oidor make sure to investigate the allegations made by the challengers.[8]

Ribera, who had been under political attack for several years by this same group of political opponents, did not win election in 1716, though it is unclear whether he lost or chose not to run because of the political pressure.[9] None of the challengers—don Joseph de la Cruz, don Antonio de Alvarado, or don Roque Eusebio de Lara—took his place immediately. Rather, don Juan Marcelo Audelo, unaffiliated with the petitioners, apparently won the election and served for the entire year. He must have performed well, because he won reelection in 1717.

Thus, the petitioning group's success in apparently ousting Ribera did not extend into an electoral victory for themselves. They failed to take over the office of governor until 1719, when the viceroy appointed don Antonio de Alvarado to serve in an interim capacity. Their leader, don Joseph de la Cruz, followed Alvarado in office, winning election in 1720. Thus, members of this bloc served in consecutive years. Subsequently don Felipe de Jesús, who also was among the group, won election in 1724.[10] Effectively, the challengers of 1714, through persistent efforts, challenged at least one cohort of electors and eventually won control of the cabildo of Mexico Tenochtitlan for several years after 1719.[11]

Within voting blocs, however, discord could emerge. It appears that voting blocs were only as strong as the current object against whom they formed. Once that obstacle collapsed, sometimes the voting bloc did too. The bloc led by don Joseph de la Cruz apparently was strained heavily in 1720.[12] The cabildo and electors voted for don Joseph de la Cruz to serve, but his predecessor and political ally, don Antonio de Alvarado, contested his election. In a petition filed before the cabildo elections, Alvarado, the current governor, alleged that he should continue to serve after his term as interim governor had expired.[13] Even though Cruz won convincingly, with "236 total votes, more than all the others who received votes," Alvarado disputed his claim and asked for a thorough review of Cruz's qualifications. He indicated that Cruz may not have been eligible to hold office.[14] It is possible that Alvarado was referencing the debt amassed from the last time Cruz had served as governor, in 1692. A 1712 complaint against don Joseph de la Cruz, made by electors and principales hostile to his interests, claimed that in addition to his indebtedness he had also caused many disturbances and had harassed the people (*vejaciones y molestias*).[15] Though the oidor in 1712 ignored the petition and allowed don Felipe de Jesús, an ally of Cruz's, to take the governorship, that petition and other allegations against Cruz suggest that among the community of electors at least some understood that Cruz had been a poor governor who had failed to collect tribute and caused disturbances in the community.[16] A native leader with ambition could attempt to exploit such a perception. Perhaps ambition could overwhelm a political coalition. Despite the collapse of the coalition, or at least the betrayal by one of its members, Alvarado, Cruz was allowed to take office in 1720.[17]

THE INVENTION OF POLITICS

The many allegations made by native electors in the second decade of the eighteenth century suggest that endemic corruption plagued the indigenous cabildos of Mexico Tenochtitlan and Mexico Tlatelolco. From a perspective without the context provided by the political activity of the seventeenth century, the disputes look like petty infighting and not election strategies devised to control the native cabildo. Yet until the independence era such political activities were not a regular part of Spanish cabildos in New Spain.[18] Some suspicious practices seem to bear out the conclusion that corruption characterized the electoral process in the native parcialidades of Mexico City. Natives sought reelection, which was a customary practice although it violated written ordinances. Mestizos ran for and even sometimes won important native offices.[19] Candidates allegedly handed out favors and gifts to purchase support and thus actually campaigned to win elections. Viewed within the context of the century and a half of political history analyzed in the previous chapters, the disputes of the late seventeenth and early eighteenth centuries grew directly out of learned experience. They also reflect a new kind of political maneuvering within the indigenous barrios of Mexico City guided by the able hands of seasoned political actors who had learned their skills in the political struggles of the seventeenth century. Political actors also chose to engage and bring into the fray the viceregal government selectively, aware that oidores sometimes complained about "frivolous" challenges.[20] Thus, they created over time a sophisticated and distinct political culture. When faced with an oidor who seemed suspicious, as in the case against Ribera, petitioners provided firm documentary evidence, noting the violated ordinances to fend off any charge that their allegations were merely political and unfounded.[21] Particularly the challenges that emerged after the uprisings of 1692 and 1696 suggest that the competitions for office and control of the cabildo were chosen carefully.[22] They were well researched and supported, and they utilized well the legal culture of the viceregal government to help win elections. These were not the tactics of the corrupt but the conscious strategies of native politicians.

Petitions filed by indigenous electors constitute the most visible form of political negotiation in the barrios. Indigenous politicians understood how to argue for advantage using the tools made available to them by indigenous custom and Spanish law. They learned how to manipulate the language of appointment documents and the election certification process itself. Candidates also learned how to lobby the representatives of the viceroy, appointed supervisory officials, and the contador general to vie for control of the cabildo, even if they did not have sufficient support of the electors. Interpreting the maneuvers made by native politicians as political suggests that a nascent political culture embedded within seemingly pro forma elections emerged in the barrios of Mexico Tenochtitlan. That the viceregal government usually respected local custom and was willing to intervene only when pressed made it increasingly challenging for potential candidates to win appointment successfully. By encouraging political activity, though perhaps unintentionally, the viceregal government, even when it attempted to limit "frivolous" petitioning, largely failed to curtail the efforts of political actors who had learned how to use the viceregal bureaucracy to satisfy their own ambitions.

By the early eighteenth century, both parcialidades of Mexico City were hives of political intrigue. Mexico Tenochtitlan, where many of the developments seem to have originated, spread its political culture—though to less effect in Mexico Tlatelolco, which had been characterized by greater stability in the seventeenth century.[23] Historians have sometimes dismissed indigenous elections (and Spanish politics for that matter) as public ritual that only served to maintain a monolithic group permanently in power.[24] But a careful assessment drawing on the experiences of the seventeenth century suggests that among the electors many divisions existed and that, through the willingness of the viceregal government to hear complaints, even indigenous commoners could participate in limited ways. With close study, it becomes clear that indigenous political actors competed for positions within native government using Spanish written law and the paternalistic mission of viceregal institutions.[25]

During the first quarter of the eighteenth century, at least twenty-five of the fifty elections in the two parcialidades provoked some kind of dispute over succession or the right of an official to hold office. The surge in activity indicates the extent to which natives in both parcialidades used viceregal institutions to realize political ends. Oversight and regulation increased further after the uprising of 8 June 1692.[26] In their search for stability and order, viceregal officials sought to involve themselves even further in the affairs of indigenous politics, making it possible for increased activity.[27] As a result, regulations and ordinances seemed to matter more than they had in the past. By the second decade of the eighteenth century, the viceregal government had even begun to enforce ordinances without the formerly requisite petitioning of groups within the indigenous hierarchy.[28] Election challenges in the parcialidades also appear to have become increasingly formal, with larger named coalitions often replacing the single petitioner who stood for the mass of residents or the electors and principales.[29]

CONSCIOUS POLITICS

Candidates engaged their communities politically. Three to four candidates usually contended for the seat of governor. Exactly how candidates were selected to run remains unclear.[30] As the election approached, however, candidates and their supporters knew who would contend and how much support each might expect before the official voting ceremony took place. In addition, there was an expectation of annual elections for governor. This contrasts with the experience of much of the early seventeenth century, when governors held office for multiple consecutive terms without facing election. Voting blocs used multi-year strategies designed to remove governors from office and replace them with allied candidates, as the cases described at the beginning of this chapter suggest. All of this political maneuvering, however, took place within the context of an increasingly contentious environment in Mexico Tenochtitlan.

The system for choosing candidates and establishing elector credentials made it difficult to attain the governorship, but new candidates ran for election nevertheless. Candidates needed large voting blocs to support them, often composed of former or current officeholders. Though electors themselves apparently had to have held office previously, candidates for native positions did not face such restriction. Candidates could not have been required to have former officeholding experience. Such a scenario would ultimately have made it impossible for the cabildo to replenish the supply of voters as time passed, and very quickly the cabildo would have run out of eligible individuals. Though it is unclear who or even how individuals were nominated to stand for election to the cabildo or to the office of governor, some mechanism existed to welcome new individuals into the pool of candidates and, once they had been elected successfully, onto the voting rolls.

Based on the size of the electorate, the number of former officeholders increased over time, though the pace was quite slow. In 1659, don Francisco Benítez was elected governor with 81 votes in an election in which only 132 votes were cast.[31] Steadily moving up, in 1674, 184 voters cast ballots.[32] In the election of 1717, electors cast 355 votes.[33] By 1720 the vote totals were likely higher still, when don Joseph de la Cruz won 236 votes.[34] The implication is that a growing number of electors participated. The sitting cabildo and pool of former officeholders, therefore, grew significantly between 1659 and 1720. The voter totals alone indicate that the cabildo included those who had not previously served in some capacity, and probably somewhat regularly. It is the only way to explain the increasing number of voters.

Political maneuvering was real, could be quite dirty, and indicates that candidates probably campaigned to win support in Mexico Tenochtitlan in the eighteenth century. In 1716, Juan Bautista, don Felipe de Jesús, Juan García, and Damién Diego promoted Pedro Martínez for governor in the election of 1717.[35] Those who stood up to denounce tactics employed by Martínez's supporters, in a petition filed by Juan Francisco de Córdoba, the procurador who spoke in the name of "the electors and other officials" on the cabildo, alleged in 1716 that they had engaged in activities his clients found questionable. Bautista, Jesús, García, and Diego, they argued, were "suspicious ringleaders" who had riled the community with "drunken disturbances" (*alborotos embriaguez*). Córdoba argued that such activity, presumably designed to aid in the election of their candidate, went beyond the permissible. In the context of the allegations against Ribera discussed earlier, principally that he had purchased votes by providing favors and gifts of alcohol, the procurador probably hoped to extinguish Martínez's candidacy. Although it seems to have been a fairly regular strategy to accuse a candidate of self-promotion, native electors and even community members complained when they perceived that a candidate actively and overtly campaigned. Because we can likely assume, based on the mere existence of the coalitions themselves, that many candidates solicited support from other electors, those who challenged on the grounds of active campaigning probably did so because it was specifically and clearly prohibited by the ordinances. Latching onto a written decree and attempting to prove the violation of that rule gave challengers an advantage simply because the viceregal government could justify its actions or even be compelled to enforce its own laws.[36]

The purpose of the allegation made by Martínez's opponents was to suggest that he and his supporters illicitly courted voters. Córdoba argued that the coalition to elect Martínez supported his candidacy allegedly "to promote their particular interests."[37] Simply courting the voters was not adequate, even if done to advance a particular agenda driven by supporters of a particular candidate, apparently because Córdoba added more substantive allegations. To undermine the candidacy further, Córdoba argued that Martínez lacked the noble credentials necessary to hold the office of governor. He stated that Martínez was only a humble baker. He then pointed out, just as had been done against Ribera in recent memory, that ordinances prohibited from holding office those who held "low-status occupations." Indeed, Córdoba tried to brand Martínez and his supporters as populists who solicited the support of nonnoble natives, fellow panaderos in the community, in order to pressure the electors in some undisclosed fashion. In the end, Córdoba suggested that Martínez's candidacy was supported by those not qualified to participate in the high politics of Mexico Tenochtitlan and furthermore was designed to promote an agenda driven by the bakeries of the city, whatever that might have been.

The supervising oidor, don Francisco de Valenzuela Vanegas, made short work of the petition in a way that indicates the extent to which political maneuvering characterized elections by 1717. He easily denied the petition to disqualify Martínez on the grounds that, because "commoners could not vote in the said election," there was no reason to exclude Martínez because he had made appeals to them.[38] The oidor's response no doubt reflected mostly his naïveté. Valenzuela Vanegas seems not to have understood the complexity of indigenous politics, or perhaps he did not realize that commoner natives had filed petitions in the past alleging abuse and through such petitions had unseated governors. Indigenous politics differed in significant ways from the Spanish cabildos that he probably understood better. As long as Martínez could legally hold office, Valenzuela Vanegas argued, he could receive votes like any other candidate.

Valenzuela Vanegas, as other supervising oidores had done in the past, made an appeal for peace and attempted to restrict those who rose up to challenge Martínez's eligibility. He asked Córdoba and those he spoke for to cease causing disturbances in advance of the election. The disturbances to which he referred were the political maneuvers of sophisticated actors attempting to use the oidor to realize their political ambitions. To counter the attempt, the opposing candidate Martínez and his supporters used the oidor's desire to keep order and maintain stability to restrict the efforts of their political opponents. Asking the oidor to stop Córdoba from filing petitions effectively closed off the viceregal bureaucracy from Martínez's opponents. In the end, the electors chose Martínez in 1717 and the oidor confirmed his election.[39] The challenge indicates one critically important element of the election of 1717 but also suggests that, even though challengers raised valid concerns, the oidor did not seem to pay them much attention.[40]

Spanish officials unwittingly provided opportunities for political maneuvering by indigenous leaders when they engaged and responded to their petitions. Despite the pomp with which natives celebrated annual elections, the process technically served only to nominate the native governor and cabildo.[41] The viceroy, in a very real sense, controlled the certification process, and Spaniards who reviewed elections could intervene. As a result, the electors and indigenous politicians had to learn how to manipulate Spanish officials politically when they presided over election ceremonies and even when they certified fiadores. The evidence is far from complete, but what does survive suggests a vibrant political culture. The records of elections generally appear only when some faction contested the result. Often, the only indication that an election took place was the viceregal appointment of an oidor to supervise the ceremony.[42] When no one objected and the election went smoothly, the Audiencia did not necessarily comment upon or even acknowledge the successful completion of the process or even name the new governor. The oidor simply confirmed the popular result for the viceroy to certify. When challengers arose, however, they literally forced the ceremony into the historical record, preserving the process.

The petitions and complaints reveal the degree to which the natives involved in the election apparently understood the workings of the viceregal government and thus took advantage to win support and to deny their opponents opportunity when possible. Martínez and his supporters knew in advance the terms of the coming election and actively campaigned to support his candidacy. They did this by courting commoners as well as securing the support of electors. Those who opposed Martínez also knew, probably because of the campaigning activity in the barrios, that a significant challenger sought the office of governor and had solicited support from the community. All of the activity took place several months before the election in November 1716.[43]

It is unclear with whom the complaint originated in 1716 because those who authored the petition were not listed—only the procurador. It seems likely that the bloc led by don Joseph de la Cruz, who had previously opposed don Juan de Ribera, were involved. Yet don Felipe de Jesús, usually an ally of Cruz, appeared among the supporters of Martínez, raising some doubt about the Cruz bloc being behind the challenge. Although Jesús had petitioned against Ribera with Cruz in 1715, his presence in support of Martínez suggests that either the Cruz coalition had come apart or that a new coalition had formed in opposition to Martínez. The serving governor in 1716, don Juan Marcelo Audelo, could have authored the petition to fend off a strong challenge from Ribera. Indeed, quashing Martínez's candidacy would have benefited him in the coming election—Audelo did run for reelection. The oidor in 1717, however, having seen similar challenges before, responded with a brief and direct statement that permitted Martínez to run and rebuked the procurador Córdoba and those whom he represented for making a frivolous challenge.[44]

Challenges to candidates or to the campaign practices of those who sought the governorship often preceded the election by several weeks. In the case involving Martínez, the complaint came months before the election. The petitions that sought to disqualify candidates usually appear as correspondence appended to the document that named the oidor who oversaw the election. Often these petitions followed a standard format, and sometimes, as in that filed by procurador Córdoba in the name of some faction within the cabildo, it is unclear exactly who complained. Not surprisingly, the complaints generally followed the ordinances that regulated the office. Don Juan de Ribera, who faced a challenge in 1715, was the victim of such a challenge when his political rivals pointed out that he was a mestizo. Allegations that candidates sought to court voters with illegal gifts or to sway voters (or commoners in the community in which they lived) with a steady supply of alcohol before the election also suggests that candidates actively sought support. Other kinds of attempts to influence or buy votes surfaced, as did allegations that candidates packed the cabildo with ineligible voters. Petitions sought to disqualify candidates on the grounds that they were *foresteros* (foreigners). This seems to have revived the issue of community residence which, in the previous century, had little meaning.[45] After the uprising of 1692, those who had not matriculated or become resident of the city probably became more conscious of the issue, particularly in light of the decrees ordering all natives to return to their barrios of origin or matriculate into the communities in which they currently resided.[46]

Voting blocs clearly formed and coalitions attempted to advance specific candidates, but their exact motivations remain unclear. Perhaps individuals who formed the blocs hoped their candidate would support them with patronage if elected. Electors themselves may also have been influenced by the apparent support of a candidate coming from commoners who lived in their neighborhoods. Something seemed to make it worthwhile for candidates to solicit the support of those who could not vote. Even though oidor Valenzuela Vanegas did not pay much attention to the allegation that Martínez supporters solicited macehualtin in 1716, the presence of several instances of candidates appealing to commoners makes it likely that within the community it was important to have the support of all—not just of electors. Indeed, nonvoting macehualtin, by petitioning the Audiencia to complain of abuse or mistreatment, could influence the success of a candidate who was ultimately judged by the viceregal government. Tribute-paying natives could also make it difficult for a governor who did not have their support. Through a kind of civil disobedience they could refuse to pay their share, making it difficult for the governor and the sitting members of the cabildo to deliver all the tribute the community owed. Whole cabildos were sometimes held in the Audiencia jail if they failed in their efforts to collect tribute. By the eighteenth century, the political frame that defined Mexico Tenochtitlan accommodated many constituencies, and certainly the candidates had to satisfy more than just the electors to serve successfully. Despite the pressures and all of the political maneuvers, in most elections an undisputed leader emerged well in advance of the formal election ceremony.

Indigenous leaders who brought challenges were not always successful, but they certainly understood how to expand what should have been a simple election involving around 350 voters into a contest that sometimes worked to elevate a losing candidate into the governorship. This was the case in 1717 when Valenzuela Vanegas declared don Pedro Martínez the winner of the election even though he received only the second-highest vote total of four candidates.[47] Don Juan Marcelo Audelo, the governor elected in 1716, technically won the election with 230 votes. Martínez came in second with 123 votes, followed by former governors don Roque Eusebio de Lara and don Felipe de Jesús, who received one vote each.[48] It is quite difficult to say for certain, but because don Roque de Lara and don Felipe de Jesús were both members of the coalition led by don Joseph de la Cruz in the petitions filed against Ribera, one would assume that these two candidates would have received more votes, especially from the Cruz coalition. Perhaps, and I suspect this is why the two did not receive more votes, don Joseph de la Cruz supported one of the other two candidates (probably Martínez), who received the lion's share of support. Though Audelo won significantly more support than his closest rival, Martínez reminded the oidor "that even though his opponent had received more votes, the said don Juan Marcelo [Audelo] should not run for reelection [*no deben correr la reelección*]."[49] Based on this single suggestion by Martínez, the oidor declared the candidacy of Marcelo Audelo invalid, making Martínez the winner.

REELECTION IN THE BARRIOS

Even though ordinances forbade reelection for both indigenous and Spanish officials, only occasionally did the viceregal government disqualify a governor seeking a second term.[50] Indeed, in the living memory of all electors and candidates, veritable dynasties existed. Don Roque Eusebio (de Lara) served as governor from 1706 to 1709, and before him don Bernardino Antonio de la Cruz y Guerrero served from 1699 to 1704.[51] The viceregal government was inconsistent in its oversight. As a result, even firm stands on reelection taken during the two elections that followed the uprising of 1692 (in which the viceroy, the Conde de Galve, rejected reelection outright) gave way to the more gentle approach of the viceroy Conde de Moctezuma, who allowed reelection as was previously customary. By 1699, governor don Bernardino Antonio de la Cruz y Guerrero successfully beat out all challengers and seems to have used effective strategies despite mounting opposition. His rule served to welcome back to Mexico Tenochtitlan the era of multiyear terms in office so common in the mid-seventeenth century.[52] Obvious unease settled over the city after the destructive uprising of 1692. More than a dozen natives and others received capital sentences, and major urban buildings including those that housed the ayuntamiento and the Audiencia, the market on the main plaza, and the viceregal palace were destroyed.[53]

Don Joseph de la Cruz, who served as governor of Mexico Tenochtitlan in 1692, was an interesting person in his own right. He came from a humble background and was made a cacique in 1685. The viceregal government came to his aid by "granting him the status of cacique and the right [poder] to vote and to be governor."[54] He was elected and confirmed in 1686 and served again in 1692.[55] When he ran for reelection in 1693, the viceroy, responding to a petition from native electors, denied him the right by pointing out that the ordinances forbade reelection.[56] Don Matías de los Angeles, elected governor in 1693, had also served multiple, though not consecutive, terms as governor, but he died in office. The second-place candidate, don Mateo de Rojas, replaced him on 22 June 1693 and served out the year-long term.[57]

In Mexico Tlatelolco the issue of reelection also emerged strongly. The cabildo in Tlatelolco appears to have regularly conceded to governors the right to hold office for significant periods, as in the case of governor don Lucas de Santiago y Rojas, who ruled intermittently between 1691 and 1720. Challenges like those in Mexico Tenochtitlan emerged in the late seventeenth and early eighteenth centuries, and Santiago and don Gregorio de San Buenaventura appear repeatedly. Sometimes in the documentation, there is indication of lineage connections among various governors who followed in succession. Related governors included don Lorenzo de San Buenaventura, who was followed in office by don

Gregorio de San Buenaventura.[58] Don Lucas de Santaigo y Rojas and the San Buenaventuras alternated in office occasionally and were clearly allied at times. They appear in the same petitions advocating similar causes, further suggesting their connections.[59] Don Lucas de Santiago y Rojas, however, was contested occasionally by those who sought to deny him office on the grounds that he could not serve multiple consecutive terms. In 1719 he had served for at least three consecutive years and was reelected again. A petition filed by the sitting cabildo in support of Santiago y Rojas insisted that a sitting governor could be reelected provided "he won all the votes cast in the election." This innovative approach seemed logical but probably did not derive from any specific ordinance. In effect, the governor, though unable to solicit votes "actively or passively," could serve in consecutive years. To make it more likely that Santiago y Rojas might win every vote, the cabildo also wanted to restrict suffrage to those currently serving. They argued directly and specifically that "only those who currently hold offices should be allowed to vote" and furthermore indicated that the Juzgado General should certify all eligible voters "two or three days prior to the election."[60]

Such restrictions designed to disenfranchise former officeholders likely met resistance and do not appear to have worked. They do, however, suggest that enterprising politicians in Tlatelolco sought to shape the political culture in order to get around the increasing interventions of the viceregal government.[61] The cabildo also apparently tried to control the number of candidates in the election. In 1720, Santiago y Rojas "won" reelection unanimously with 286 votes. Although it appears that no one opposed him and he was proclaimed the winner despite his apparent ineligibility, the story seems suspicious and is likely not credible.[62]

It seems unlikely that Santiago y Rojas could have won over all those who formerly opposed him. In 1714 a brave group of electors that included don Antonio Gregorio, don Bentura de Santiago, Miguel de los Angeles, Juan Gregorio, Matías de Santiago, and Juan Diego petitioned the oidor in charge of the election for 1715, alleging voter intimidation and grave abuses at the hands of sitting governor Santiago y Rojas.[63] They argued that Santiago y Rojas and his supporters subverted the "common will" of the community of electors. Specifically, supporters of the governor had "worked to intimidate [Gregorio] and [his] supporters maliciously."[64] The petition also alleged that the unassuming electors of Tlatelolco were easily cheated and intimidated by the said governor. With their complaint Gregorio and his supporters asked the viceregal government to intervene on their behalf to stop the governor and his supporters from abusing and intimidating electors. In his investigation, oidor don Joseph de Luna was informed by the fiscal that numerous complaints had come from Tlatelolco that appeared to confirm that electors had been intimidated by the governor. The fiscal ordered the governor and his supporters to cease their intimidations in the interest of preserving "peace and order."[65]

In Mexico Tlatelolco, governors were able to get around prohibitions against reelection. Some governors sought to extinguish their opposition through intimidation and tried to restrict suffrage. Governors made strange arguments that they could win reelection provided they won every vote. These legal and political maneuvers allowed don Lucas de Santiago y Rojas and his ally don Gregorio de San Buenaventura (r. 1723–26) to serve in multiple consecutive terms.[66] At the same time, they could not stop the community from voicing its dissent or the viceregal government from intervening.[67]

Don Gregorio de San Buenaventura was challenged in 1724 by a large coalition of native electors who alleged that he could not read or write and that one of his supporters, Juan Diaz, was a well-known pulquero. The charge of illiteracy was serious because ordinances required officeholders to be able to read and write. The second charge implied that San Buenaventura sought to influence voters with pulque and employed a pulquero to this end. More seriously, however, was the charge that San Buenaventura had stuffed the ballot boxes. According to the official election record, 406 electors cast ballots. This was unusual in that only 263 legitimate voters resided in Mexico Tlatelolco in 1724. To make matters even more interesting, don Antonio de Santiago and don Nicolás Antonio de Sandoval each received votes as well, three and 130, respectively. The number of votes suggests one interesting possibility—that San Buenaventura and Sandoval each received 130 votes.[68] It is also possible that San Buenaventura meant to imply that he had won all legitimate votes (406 - 133 = 273, quite close to the number of legitimate voters) and that his competitors had altered the tallies. In any event, all candidates had developed sophisticated ways to complicate the vote tallies for supervising Spanish officials.

The fiscal and oidor dodged all of the complicated issues raised by the mathematics of the election by simply stating that San Buenaventura had won. They concluded pragmatically that because he had served well in the past he would continue to serve the same way in the future. Apparently the spurious nature of some of the other allegations against San Buenaventura worked against those who sought to challenge him. San Buenaventura could clearly write, for he had signed certain documents in this election and in previous ones. They also dismissed the complaint that he had a supporter, who also happened to be an alcalde, who owned a pulquería, stating that the petition provided no evidence that the pulquero had done anything illicit. The fiscal then argued that restrictions should be placed on natives in the form of penalties for making false accusations, ostensibly for political gain, stating that "petitioners must comply with the obligation to file only truthful charges [*relación*] . . . the penalty for violation, a fine of six months of salary of the office." In addition, the five who filed the claim against don Gregorio, for causing what the fiscal regarded as "discord and rebellion," should be made to stop their activities and "in the interest of peace, made to reveal the truth."[69] The viceroy then approved the election of San Buenaventura without further inquiry. No investigation was conducted into the ballot box stuffing after those who brought this news were deemed to be untrustworthy.

In Mexico Tenochtitlan, the questions surrounding reelection, eligibility, and qualifications necessary to run for office were all addressed in 1723 in an unusual petition from the principales and native electors. They made the incredulous case that "it has been customary since time immemorial in this community that the election of alcaldes and governor of the said parcidalidad and other officials of the Republic should be celebrated annually," though annual elections, at least for governor, had been regularized for less than two generations. The petitioners also stated that "all candidates should be natives without any mixture [*sin mescla alguna*] with preference [*preferencia*] for caciques and principales over those that were not. At the same time the proposed [candidates] should not be foreigners [*foráneos extranjeros*].[70] Included as well are more familiar elements—the capacity to read and write and the prohibition of those who had committed serious crimes or had charges pending against them before the Audiencia. As well, only natives who demonstrated polite customs by not drinking to excess could serve as governors. The petitioners then asked specifically that the supervising oidor enforce the law that prohibited reelection, stating that the "current governor hopes to win reelection" and should be prohibited from receiving votes because "it serves the interests of Your Excellency to prohibit his reelection, just as [Your Excellency] requires that the election of the Spanish cabildo conforms to the law [prohibiting reelection] . . . from the *Recopilación de Indias*."[71] The purposes of such actions are quite clear: to limit the size of the candidate pool; to expand the grounds under which the cabildo, electors, or commoners might challenge the election; and to make it hard for powerful governors to serve long terms, which tended to result in discord and abuse.

HISTORICAL BRIDGES

The issue of election challenge was nothing new in the eighteenth century; it derived from practices refined in the seventeenth century. After the election disputes of the 1650s discussed in chapter 4, the heirs of don Juan de Aguilar (r. 1654) made rather aggressive plays for control of the cabildo and the office of governor. In so doing, they helped to develop and refine some of the political space indigenous leaders could use to maneuver for political advantage within the community of Mexico Tenochtitlan. The Aguilar brothers, from one of the more important families in the late seventeenth century, held the governorship for significant time during the seventeenth century and into the eighteenth. The family came into the office first with the appointment of don Juan de Aguilar in 1654. Although he never won an election, held office only once, and served only part of his term (he died in March 1654), Aguilar was able to establish a connection to the office of governor that facilitated the advancement of his heirs. His grandchildren utilized the connection he provided to advance their own political ambitions. Don Felipe and don Juan de Aguilar the younger alternated in the office of governor in 1667, 1672, 1673 and 1674.[72] During years in which they did not serve as governor, the

Aguilar brothers often held the position of cobrador de tributos.[73] In addition, don Bernardino Antonio de la Cruz y Guerrero, related to the Aguilar brothers by marriage, served in 1684, 1687, 1688, and again from 1699 to 1705.[74] For the fifty-year period between 1654 and 1704, this family controlled the governorship for at least thirteen years, or a little over 25 percent of the time. Their influence, however, extended well beyond the governorship. Don Felipe served in various capacities, including helping his brother-in-law don Bernardino collect tribute in 1684. Don Felipe held the same position in 1686 under Governor don Joseph de la Cruz, and also served as alcalde under Governor Cruz in 1692.[75]

The Aguilar brothers are well documented, better than many, because they faced a series of challenges in the late seventeenth century from tribute payers who complained of abuse and mistreatment. First, a civil complaint filed by a group of principales led by don Juan Montaño claimed on 6 January 1674 that neither Aguilar brother had the ability to serve because they were not natives (*puro natural*).[76] The challenges continued the next year in a separate civil suit in which numerous complaints from the community implicated both don Felipe and don Juan de Aguilar, alleging that they had violated the rules of election and harshly abused their subjects.[77] The challenges, though they refer to specific abuses, all related directly to intense political disputes taking place in the community of electors who were attempting to dislodge the Aguilar brothers from monopolizing the office of governor. They also helped to clarify how the viceregal government came to intervene in the affairs of indigenous government regularly.

In 1674, don Juan de Aguilar won the election despite the complaints launched against him by don Juan Montaño. Indeed, the election was filled with all kinds of trickery that helps to explain why Montaño ran but received only two votes. The oidor, don Miguel de Aguero y Acedo, shortly before the election had been notified by Antonio de Olmos Dávila, the receptor of the Audiencia, that Montaño allegedly faced an unnamed criminal charge and was thus ineligible to hold the office of governor. The oidor then stated that he could not receive votes, even though the allegation was unproved and suggested by a political rival. Nevertheless, the oidor succeeded in discouraging electors from casting their votes for Montaño. The unusual order by the oidor was given without investigation and doomed Montaño's chances in the election. The oidor advised the gathering of electors, further influencing the election profoundly when he stated that electors should not vote for don Felipe de Aguilar either. Aguero y Acedo argued that Aguilar could not serve "because he currently held the office of governor [and] the ordinances forbade his reelection."[78] Such direct manipulation of electors possibly indicates the inexperience of the oidor, who seemed intent upon enforcing rules that had been overlooked in the past. His actions influenced the outcome of the election and touched off a civil lawsuit.

Supporters of Montaño complicated matters by suggesting that a conspiracy underlay the allegation that Montaño faced a criminal charge. They argued that don Juan and don Felipe de Aguilar had provided the false account to the oidor that impelled him to tell the gathered electors not to vote for Montaño.[79] Such an accusation seemed quite plausible, creating additional problems for the court, which now had to determine if the Aguilar brothers had tampered with the election for obvious political advantage. The petition was clear enough and alleged that "the sinister relation came about as a result of a meeting in [which] don Juan and don Felipe de Aguilar schemed and directed [sobernado y cocheado] the voters."[80] Yet the allegations do not provide specifics to make clear how the Aguilar brothers manipulated the vote. Did they spread false rumors and in so doing influence the choices of electors? Did they promise favors and rewards?

The evidence from the suit and the petitions does not provide such substantive details, only a promising lead. The mechanism by which the allegations against Montaño made it to the oidor are difficult to piece together, but it may have resulted from the Aguilar brothers' connections on the Audiencia. The brothers apparently had friends working at the Audiencia whom they may have felt they could influence. A subsequent complaint filed in 1675 accused the brothers of collaborating with Audiencia scribe Joseph Romero, who apparently filed a false report that favored don Juan and don Felipe. In 1674 the alleged collusion between the brothers and Romero was not publically known, and no mention was made in the Montaño suit. Such malfeasance sometimes occurred at the Audiencia, and the circumstantial evidence raises some suspicion of collusion in 1674. Native alcaldes don Joseph de la Cruz and don Agustín de Sandoval, according to their sworn testimony, suspected Romero of aiding the Aguilars because he was their intimate friend.[81] An Audiencia scribe, because of his authority to direct petitions through the judicial process, could influence an oidor sufficiently to act against Montaño.[82] As it turned out, Romero was also the Audiencia scribe present at the election of 1674 in which Montaño was disqualified by oidor Sánchez de Ocampo.[83] He was therefore in a position to influence the oidor. The documents do not indicate that he provided the report to the oidor from the Audiencia that led to the dismissal of Montaño, but they certainly raise suspicion.

The electors who filed the petition denouncing the Aguilar brothers reveal through their actions several processes at work in the elections. They indicated that, despite its prohibition, coalition building and politicking were both normal aspects of elections in Mexico Tenochtitlan. It was alleged that the Aguilar brothers courted electors, invited them into their home, and asked them to vote a certain way, steering their support away from Montaño. The impressive list of Montaño supporters—past governors, former and current alcaldes and regidores, and other principales in Mexico Tenochtitlan (forty-three signers in total)—also suggests that an alternate coalition had formed and worked to elect Montaño. In addition to the coalitions, well-articulated planning framed within the context of viceregal legal culture was exercised by both sides.[84] The Aguilar brothers and their supporters claimed that Montaño could not serve because the alleged criminal charge against him disqualified him according to official procedure. Montaño and his coalition alleged that the Aguilar brothers could not serve because they were mestizos and had made dishonest claims against Montaño.[85]

The Aguilar brothers had probably learned their tactics through earlier experiences with political challengers. Indeed, filing unfounded or unsupported accusations for political gain was not a particularly unusual occurrence in cabildo elections between the 1650s and 1670s.[86] In January 1672, don Juan de Aguilar defeated former governor don Francisco Benítez de Inga. Benítez, however, did not take defeat lightly and challenged Aguilar's right to take office by suing to have him disqualified. Raising the allegation that would resurface later against Aguilar, Benítez argued that Aguilar could not hold indigenous office because he was a mestizo.[87] Benítez also claimed, without providing any substantive evidence or explanation, that Aguilar could not serve

because he had charges "pending against him in the Sala del Crimen."
As with the allegation that Aguilar was a mestizo, Benítez did not
elaborate the nature of the charges. By questioning Aguilar's right to
hold office, however, Benítez and the group of electors who stood
with him attempted to dislodge Aguilar from contention in order to
forward the former governor's candidacy. In 1674, Aguilar adapted
the script used by Benítez to win advantage against his most capable
rival Montaño.[88]

Although Aguilar was allowed to take the office of governor in
1672 and 1674, he had to fight the challenges of those who opposed
him politically.[89] Resisting such challenges probably gave him a wide
range of tools to win and keep political office. It also made him a formidable candidate who seems to have learned how to contest those
who challenged him. He and his brother had also taken certain tools
away from active oidores who might remove them on the grounds
that prohibited reelection by alternating terms of office. Conscious
rotation probably indicates that they actively strategized to hold the
office for significant time. Suppression of strong candidates suggests
that they consciously chose to maneuver politically, especially when
presented with formidable opposition. There is also evidence that the
Aguilar brothers met with electors and identified early potential
challengers well in advance of the election itself. Such tactics resonate
with earlier patterns identified in the sixteenth century. Apparently the
office of governor continued to have great appeal and thus brought
out great rivalries among the contenders. Contests for its control were
fought bitterly but legally through the Audiencia.

In 1675, don Felipe de Aguilar stood to win the governorship, but
his candidacy and eligibility were challenged by a large group of
principales and electors, some of whom currently sat on the cabildo.
They forwarded complaints from the commoners of the barrios who
alleged that the brothers had abused them in order to collect tribute.
These principales argued that the brothers should not serve in any
capacity to collect tribute in the barrios.

The testimony against the Aguilar brothers in 1675 resonates well
with the allegations made by the cabildo in 1674. Joseph Hernández,
a thirty-four-year-old indigenous shoemaker and native of the tlaxilacalli of Tequicaltitlan, complained that it was well known that don

Felipe and don Juan de Aguilar "mistreated and disrespected natives with actions and words . . . forcing some to pay twice." He also complained of *malos tratos* (general mistreatment) visited on those who did not pay, though without providing many specifics.[90] According to his testimony, the brothers ignored official documents like the carta de pago when tribute payers presented them.

Though Hernández set the tone of the complaint against the Aguilar brothers, other natives provided additional details. Another native shoemaker, Diego Maldonado, forty-four years old and from the neighborhood of Xihuitongo, complained that in lieu of payment the Aguilar brothers took from tribute payers' houses blankets (*mantas*) from Xolotepec and sold them, ostensibly to cover tribute owed. Maldonado also alleged that don Juan de Aguilar charged women and old men who did not owe tribute.[91] The recently widowed Antonia Verónica expressed her frustration when she recounted that don Juan de Aguilar, "even after they had shown him the carta de pago," proceeded to take things of value to sell for tribute.[92] In addition, the current alcaldes supported by several past alcaldes and regidores complained that the governor had "imprisoned four native women accused of cohabitation [*amancebamientos*] without the authority of any judge." A subsequent inspection conducted by the Audiencia revealed that the allegations made by the alcaldes had no substance.[93]

The Aguilar brothers also allegedly intimidated electors. One alcalde, don Mateo Salvador, claimed that the brothers ordered his arrest in the tecpan on election day. He alleged that they knew he did not support them and, to make it impossible for him to vote, they placed him under arrest. Although removing one elector probably did not in itself alter the outcome of the vote, it certainly created a climate of intimidation. The governor, don Felipe de Aguilar, in front of the assembled electors in the tecpan with his vara in hand, personally "seized Salvador and violently carried him to the jail" that was in the same building.[94] Would other electors fear similar mistreatment at the hands of the Aguilar brothers? It probably served electors well to vote for the brothers, or at least to show their apparent support for them under such conditions. Even when challengers built significant support for an alternative, the Aguilar brothers regularly succeeded in using the courts to get around election challenges, using fear, abuse of authority, and intimidation to sway the electorate. The act of dragging an elector violently out of the tecpan probably made it difficult for electors to make an impartial choice, even if the ballot was officially secret.[95]

Allegations of abuse, voter intimidation, and false imprisonment were serious, so much so that a groundswell rose in the barrios that ultimately ended the Aguilar brothers' control of the cabildo. In 1675 the electors chose don Juan de Montaño, and though the Aguilar brothers disputed his election he was appointed governor and served for one year. More important, however, the cycle of rotation appears to have been rejected. It was clearly a source of abuse for the taxpayers of Mexico Tenochtitlan.[96] Long service in office and control over the institutions of government and elections made possible the Aguilar brothers' ability to carry out grave abuses against their subjects without fear of reprimand or loss of office. In the end it was also possible for a large coalition to form over time to oppose them in the interest of good government. The final judgment in the second lawsuit condemned them with strong language. It found that the prosecution had proved that the brothers charged some natives in the barrios twice. It also indicated that they inappropriately charged women and the elderly. The mistreatment of taxpayers and abuse of authority featured prominently in their denunciation by the court. In the opinion of the fiscal who made the recommendation for sentence, which the viceroy ultimately confirmed on 6 April 1676, the Aguilar brothers had abused the natives of Mexico Tenochtitlan and had abused their offices and thus were forbidden from collecting tribute in any capacity in the barrios. Those on the cabildo brave enough (or politically savvy enough) to stare down the brothers succeeded in ousting them from the governorship. Yet they did this as a community, thus creating a way to upset the political balance likely unanticipated by the Aguilars. The viceregal mandate to protect the victimized played right into the hands of those who challenged the Aguilar brothers.

Don Felipe still figured in politics as late as 1695, but he did not hold the office of governor again. He actively petitioned the viceroy, however, to restore traditional elections after the uprising of 1692 and won the approval of the Conde de Galve to return to the regular cycle after the ordinances.[97] Don Felipe was also an alcalde in 1692.[98] Don Juan continued to have a voice in the affairs of Mexico Tenochtitlan, but usually in an auxiliary role. When his brother-in-law held the office, don Juan was indicted for abusing natives and using harsh methods to collect tribute as cobrador. Though it is not possible to say for certain, don Juan de Aguilar's reputation from the 1670s probably made him an easy target for such allegations.

CONTENTIOUS ELECTIONS

Indigenous elections became more contentious over time. Spanish observers, like Ramírez de Fuenleal in 1533, could once feel confident with the suggestion that native "elections were . . . more orderly than those of Spanish cabildos."[99] During the seventeenth century indigenous groups began to invent new political strategies that took advantage of the viceregal government's insecurities and its need to exercise oversight. The implication was that there was a general opening of the office of governor to new groups who had the connections, wealth, support, and apparent ability to distribute patronage effectively and displace hereditary nobles. The unintended consequences of the fully formed political system were that certain savvy native actors, using the ordinances, appointment documents, and their knowledge of Spanish law, could invent interesting ways to maneuver into positions of importance. Over time, such political maneuvering led to the creation of real political coalitions that negotiated, used leverage, and vied for control of the governorship and cabildo with the aid of Spanish institutions like the Audiencia, the office of the contador general, the supervising oidores, and ultimately the viceroy.

Though clearly from a litigious and political society, Spaniards in New Spain did not seem to have developed in New World cabildos the same kind of sophisticated political culture in the seventeenth century. Venal offices that restricted service on cabildos to the wealthy and well connected helped keep the crown afloat but also created a closed political culture ripe for abuse.[100] Though the indigenous system also restricted those without noble status and native birth, the differences lay in the capacity and willingness of candidates to use the institutions of the viceregal government to oust otherwise successful candidates and to develop strategies to forward favorites. Indigenous candidates were not able to buy political office in Mexico Tenochtitlan. Although elections there empowered only those from a fairly small sliver of native society, the political manipulations within that group appear quite profound and sometimes, when it was politically expedient, worked to advance the causes of the commoners or could be challenged by commoners.[101]

By the turn of the eighteenth century, particularly the first and second decades, the number of electoral disputes and the level of political activity by indigenous officials were particularly pronounced. Between 1712 and 1725, nineteen separate electoral disputes occurred. Only 1713 passed without a political challenge in either Mexico Tenochtitlan or Mexico Tlatelolco. During many of those years, disputes emerged in both parcialidades. The spike in political activity was related to the elevated level of conflict among well-formed coalitions in each parcialidad. The viceregal government began to enforce rules in a more systematic way, particularly after the uprising of 1692. Rules against reelection, once ignored, were reinstated. Annual elections were regularized and often were highly contentious. New regulations and enforcement of extant rules, however, were driven by indigenous leaders or commoners. Native petitions asked the viceregal officers to intervene. Generally, the viceregal government did not proactively seek to regulate native government.

The election immediately following the uprising in 1692 was highly controlled. The new oidor appointed to supervise the election that year, don Juan de Aréchaga y Casas, received a specific order from the viceroy to prohibit don Joseph de la Cruz from seeking reelection because of the prohibitions in the official ordinances. A large contingency within the community spoke out against the prohibition. Included in this group were former governors, don Juan de los Reyes, don Bernardino Antonio de la Cruz y Guerrero, don Juan de Jara, don Gaspar de Santiago, and don Lorenzo de Santiago, as well as a long list of past alcaldes. They argued that it had always been customary for the viceregal government to "allow the election to take place freely, without intervention."[102] In this case, however, the oidor dismissed the petition by the native electors and effectively prohibited the reelection of don Joseph de la Cruz.[103]

Subsequently, the viceregal government began to interfere directly in the way governors collected tribute. In an order that empowered the Spanish contador general, the viceregal government prohibited governors from seeking to collect tribute arrears (*recaudación*). The contador general in such a scenario might take over much of the work of tribute collection. Don Bernabé de Santiago, the governor in 1694, protested that it had always been the right and obligation of governors to collect the tribute and to bear personal responsibility for its delivery. Remember that native governors sometimes were imprisoned for failing to collect tribute owed and sometimes had their property confiscated. Santiago pointed out that limiting the governors from collecting old debt would make it difficult for them to collect tribute and to find fiadores to cover debts. Natives could avoid tribute collectors for the year and thus effectively avoid their liability to the governor. Even though the contador might still come to collect back tribute, commoners might use such tactics to punish governors yet still contribute to their communities.

The ultimately successful attempt to prohibit governors from collecting back tribute had great ramifications because it put additional pressure on sitting governors to collect all they owed within the year it was due.[104] Although the viceregal government likely assumed control of the recaudación to limit abuse of natives by aggressive tribute collectors, governors probably worked harder to collect debt the first time to compensate. Indeed, natives continued to complain of abuse at the hands of governors. The contador general assumed control of the recaudación amid protests from the sitting governor, many cabildo members, and several former governors. Such a change, they argued, "would make us [native governors] servants of the contador general."[105]

The problem of old debt was significant in the late seventeenth century. The viceroy's fiscal, in a stiff rebuke to native governors, argued that they were poor collectors and had amassed significant arrears. Between 1670 and 1682, Mexico Tenochtitlan had failed to collect 4,865 pesos and three tomines. In addition, the fiadores offered by governors did not generally pay what they had pledged, and a series of viceroys, on the order of the king, had forgiven much of the amassed debt.[106] The debts continued. Don Joseph de la Cruz, governor in 1692, collected only 527 pesos, two reales, and three granos of tribute and delivered it only once that year in October. Since the summer of 1692 was defined by the uprising and trials and executions that stretched from June to August, one might expect October to have been the least likely time to deliver tribute. It should also be noted that the environmental changes that destroyed much of the wheat crop and brought poverty to the native communities likely made 1692 an unrepresentative year.[107]

Governors had often been found culpable of many different abuses during their time in office, and some suffered because of their inability to collect the requisite tribute. Most egregious was the case of don Bernardino Antonio de la Cruz y Guerrero, who was perennially accused of abusing his subjects.[108] He was also removed from office in 1688 because he was accused of a criminal offense related to the abuse of natives and theft of tribute from 1687.[109] The debt he amassed totaled 4,700 pesos, and he was still incarcerated in 1697 for debt.[110] Cruz y Guerrero continued to amass debt, but he also seems to have gotten around the post-uprising adherence to rules. He served, as discussed above, from 1699 to 1704 and was even frequently challenged by former governors who had been held to the no-reelection standard enforced by the Conde de Galve.[111]

After his reelection in 1704, Cruz y Guerrero's fortunes changed. The Spanish corregidor had soon placed him in prison for debt, claiming that he had not provided repartimiento labor, its cash equivalent, or sufficient financing (fiadores) to cover the tribute owed for the general maintenance of the city (*obras públicas y buen policía*). A seasoned governor, Cruz y Guerrero ably directed his council to file petitions on his behalf protesting his imprisonment. He ultimately won release but had to rely on the viceroy to grant him clemency. The corregidor, not the most evenhanded observer, in one petition actually expressed his contempt with the vile slur that his "experience has led [him] to believe that natives only care to drink to excess and employ themselves in robberies, assaults, and other public sins." Cruz y Guerrero, remarkably, convinced the viceroy to order the corregidor to stop the harassment.[112]

This battle festered over the summer, with numerous petitions exchanged but to little effect. By December the former governors who opposed Cruz y Guerrero had allied themselves with the Spanish corregidor. Just before the new election cycle, on 15 December 1704, the former governors in consort with nine former alcaldes filed a petition in which they asked that in the coming election the oidor follow all of the rules that govern elections. On 22 December, the corregidor filed a separate petition against the governor, stating that he owed 752 pesos in back tribute for public works. The former governors appear to have known that indebtedness and imprisonment would disqualify Cruz y Guerrero from the governorship. Their petition was filed before that of the corregidor and seemed to anticipate its allegation. The native challengers also benefited from the arrest of their political opponent, who had little time to resolve the issue before the election.[113] After 1704, Cruz y Guerrero faded from the politics of Mexico Tenochtitlan and, although it is unclear who won the election of 1705, don Roque Eusebio de Lara assumed the governorship in 1706. There had clearly been a political sea change. Eusebio de Lara remained in office until 1709.[114] Although he had not taken part in any of the petitions filed against the former governor, he later joined this group of officials after his time in office. Even though he allied himself with governors who vehemently opposed the reelection of Cruz y Guerrero, he had no problem with his own reelection. None of those who challenged his predecessor on no-reelection grounds challenged don Roque Eusebio de Lara. A fundamental contradiction such as this indicates only the conclusion that those who complained about Cruz y Guerrero did so for political reasons. They clearly did not stand on principle.

These cases demonstrate that indigenous political actors used a combination of custom, tradition, and Spanish legal precedent to engage in politics during the annual elections for governor. The evidence suggests that political blocs formed and that candidates knew well in advance of the election ceremony whether they had garnered sufficient support to win. In many instances, particularly after the turn of the eighteenth century, creative indigenous leaders filed political petitions to solicit legal aid to realize political objectives and thus challenged the more popular candidate and broadened the spectrum of political activity to include more than simply the tally of votes. These tactics were nothing new to native politicians. Rather, they had learned to use the Audiencia in unexpected ways. Although elections did not democratize the offices of the native cabildo, they did open up opportunities to new contenders. Provided candidates could finance the tribute collection, win the confidence of the community of electors, and avoid or fend off challenges that emerged from the contador general, a rival political faction, or the commoners themselves, they could serve in native offices. The viceregal government tended to avoid seeking problems actively, thus allowing natives to shape the cabildo and determine who could run for and win an election independently of the ordinances. When petitioned, however, the viceregal government did act against egregious violations and sometimes removed officials in response to the requests of the community.

CONCLUSION

"The Indians, who are more than half of our population, care little for politics. They are accustomed to look to those in authority for leadership instead of thinking for themselves."

Porfirio Díaz, 1908

In this book I argue that native peoples created a new kind of political culture in Mexico Tenochtitlan after the Spanish invaded and displaced traditional precontact structures of authority. Building on their own political traditions, they invented ways to preserve authority using the new political structures of the Spanish-styled cabildo and the legal structures of the Real Audiencia. Over time, native leaders in Mexico Tenochtitlan replaced the Mexica Tenochca royal lineage with leaders elected by popular majority. Annual gatherings of electors enabled political negotiations to take place that helped to establish and determine what constituted eligibility to serve. In this way, natives took an active role in determining their leaders. In addition, native commoners, from the very outset, also participated in shaping the cabildo through their power to petition, filing complaints against leaders they regarded as abusive. The new political culture that emerged in Mexico Tenochtitlan after the Spanish invasion of 1519 evolved through the seventeenth century. Natives carved out political spaces of authority by choosing their own leaders and resisting heartily any effort to intervene by the viceregal government. Natives accepted such interventions only when members of the community directly asked for them.

Although scholars have usually cast the trajectory of native political structures like the cabildo as one on the decline through the colonial period, the vibrancy of the institution at the local level is clear. Lockhart concludes that "it would not be wrong" to suggest that indigenous government "lasted until the time of Mexican Independence" but then argues that such governments changed dramatically beginning in the mid-seventeenth century.[1] Gibson is more pessimistic, concluding that natives lost their autonomy in Mexico Tenochtitlan almost completely by the eighteenth century, including the authority to regulate markets and collect tribute.[2] But he also states that, because of the failure of the rental system, in which individual Spaniards bid for the right to collect native tribute, Bourbon leaders had to restore native governors to their former position and again make them responsible for tribute collection in 1782. The very persistence and endurance of native-controlled institutions resonates with the changes that occurred in the seventeenth century. Indeed, even though native governments changed and at times viceregal officials stripped, challenged, or otherwise attempted to alter their authority, native control ultimately persisted. Unlike the rather linear trajectory of native government surrendering control, natives used the viceregal government to shape their own political institutions. Imposed governments in the seventeenth century, and then apparently later in the eighteenth, failed to collect sufficient tribute, leaving massive arrears, and also failed to govern their communities well. Native communities resisted Spanish attempts to govern them directly.[3]

Recent studies have effectively demonstrated that native cabildos continued to function as viable entities in Mexico City well into the nineteenth century. Lira González has argued that, despite challenges, native governments preserved substantial authority through the independence era.[4] Others have argued that native governments suffered after the adoption of the Spanish Constitution of 1812. By implication, as Rodríguez and others have demonstrated, native communities in Mexico continued to exercise political authority and to participate in political processes beyond independence.[5] The authority imbued in native offices made positions on the cabildo and the governorship desirable.

Politics existed in Mexico Tenochtitlan well before the Spanish invasion. Native political leaders adapted, created, and expanded political strategies throughout the colonial era. The civil lawsuit at the center of chapter 1 appears on the surface to be about exploitation of laborers by the native cabildo, but closer inspection shows it to be filled with political strategizing by natives. Tenochca leaders, fronted by commoners, attempted to force the Audiencia to depose the elected governor and cabildo. By design, this strategy effectively sought to replace a coalition of leaders who rotated in and out of important offices with a competing coalition. Such political disputes represented the attempt by native leaders in the minority to dislodge another coalition.

Such strategies clearly resonate with precontact practices. Natives in Mexico Tenochtitlan traditionally chose the best candidate from among a limited number of eligible candidates from the royal lineage. Political maneuvering, secret dealings, and backroom compromises apparently characterized precontact political succession. The cihuacoatl and others negotiated to bring to office a viable best candidate and then attempted to avoid political violence. In 1564, similar negotiations leading up to the replacement of the governor appear to have begun in the last year of the governorship of don Luis de Santa María Nanacacipactzin. In the lawsuit, tantalizing bits of evidence scattered through the dispute point to its political nature. Native principal and elector don Francisco Jiménez commented on the political activities of native leaders who sought votes in advance of the annual election.

The lawsuit also detailed unintentionally the sophisticated system of office rotation that empowered native coalitions and likely also the governor. The rotation system ensured representation of the four political subdivisions of Mexico Tenochtitlan in alternating years in the position of alcalde. Yet, perhaps most important, the natives did not challenge the system of rotation or election directly; rather, they argued that the Audiencia should only remove those then in control of the cabildo. Furthermore, the coalition that emerged in the 1560s in league with commoners made it difficult for electors to choose a replacement for Governor Santa María when he died in 1565. Using the viceregal Audiencia, the emergent coalition presented a powerful challenge to sitting native government, but not to the institution of the cabildo or its political culture. Thus, natives learned how to engage the Audiencia, which had previously been reluctant to interfere in native internal politics, and to use its capacity to enforce royal law to mediate internal disputes and empower minorities against a powerful ruling coalition.

Although the authority of governors in Mexico Tenochtitlan changed after the Spanish invasion, native leaders developed new strategies to engage in political conflicts within the indigenous world.[6] Unlike the old tlatloque, governors no longer held sway unchecked over the Basin of Mexico and no longer could summon an army to crush enemies or sponsor the conquest of distant altepetl. Governors, however, did control significant rights of patronage. Native rulers cultivated authority by building alliances, bequeathing grants and honors, managing appointments, and mediating disputes within the jurisdiction left to them within the viceregal government. The newly created office of governor was initially occupied by those entitled to inherit the royal lineage and thus was a position of high status.[7] Those who served in elected posts under the governor on the cabildo, although they took Spanish titles such as *alcalde* and *regidor*, also occupied positions of status and honor within native society and served as clients of the governor. Some also maintained their positions in some form even within a system that forbade their reelection, by rotating in and out of office at regular intervals.[8] The officials usually represented a variety of different districts within Tenochtitlan's four urban subdivisions. Maintaining broad representation from all the barrios, rotation and a stable governorship became the means of eliminating conflict in the parcialidad of Mexico Tenochtitlan.[9] The governor, because of his position of authority, ultimately controlled the networks of patronage and thus bred stability when he represented the choice of the community. When he did not, tribute arrears increased and petitions flooded the Audiencia.

Vestiges of the precontact political system endured into the eighteenth century with subtle changes. Indigenous political ideas fit well into the emerging independent system of elections. Initially, a hereditary tlatoani ruled until his death, and his replacement was chosen through an election that involved important members of all constituent parts of the altepetl. Elements of the Spanish system also eventually fit into the election process. Native peoples who served on the cabildo in the offices of alcalde or regidor could not in principle be elected to successive terms. The rotation strategies developed by native peoples suggest that such restrictions on reelection were enforced. Eventually, by the eighteenth century, courts prohibited governors from holding office in consecutive years. Spanish courts, when petitioned, mediated and resolved disputes.[10] Precontact indigenous canvassing before the actual election and other more violent means of expressing opposition against the tlatoani were replaced over the course of the seventeenth century with specific kinds of legal challenges that sought to dislodge governors and the network of supporters who backed them.

Indigenous governments were dynamic institutions, but they cannot be understood outside their context as entities within a political city. The transformation of government into the eighteenth century shows how native communities adapted to challenges by the viceregal government and individuals who sought to wrest control of the cabildo from electors. Even though elements of the royal lineage survived, other leaders were empowered to rule in their place. In 1573, don Antonio Valeriano, a most remarkable candidate, became the first such governor. He was associated with the royal lineage through his marriage and was also deeply associated with the Franciscans. Although removing the royal line may have weakened indigenous government in the short term, the change fostered an increasing reliance on elections in the seventeenth century.

The uprising of 1624 and the 1629 flood disrupted tribute collection, and the arrears amassed during the 1630s effectively gave the viceregal government justification, at a time when it felt the need, to impose its authority to replace indigenous governors with candidates of its own choosing. Natives resisted the usurpation and rejected the imposition of a governor not vetted by the community. They also found ways to respond to enterprising Spaniards who attempted to take over functions of the cabildo (mainly tribute collection and urban policing). In general, native political strategies of the mid-sixteenth century designed to enlist the intervention of the viceregal government contributed to the development, from the 1650s through the 1670s, of a new kind of political culture rooted in the Tenochca past but utilizing the institutions of the Spanish crown for political ends.

The fully politicized indigenous cabildo emerged in the late seventeenth and early eighteenth centuries. The formation of political blocs, consciously constructed by politically ambitious leaders, made it possible for cohorts of native peoples to vie for control of Mexico Tenochtitlan. It was from this tradition that natives effectively created a political system based on native political traditions within a Spanish institutional structure—mediated by a legal culture which, by the mid-seventeenth century, native peoples had helped to create.[11]

By the early eighteenth century, then, indigenous peoples in Mexico Tenochtitlan had adapted political strategies from precontact indigenous traditions and applied them within the cabildo, an Hispanic institution. The indigenous political tradition, in which the highest official came to power through a selection process undertaken by a small group of important leaders, persisted in the colonial period in modified form. The governor, supported by a cadre of leaders, became increasingly politicized as the size of the electorate increased and the Audiencia expanded its role as a mediator of disputes within the indigenous communities. New institutions within the viceroyalty also introduced Spanish legal ideas about good government and added to the politicization of indigenous communities. Tribute finance documents and birth records were regularly employed to challenge the capacity of governors to hold office. Litigants asked courts to determine whether prospective governors could offer sufficient collateral to finance the tribute owed by the community. Indigenous commoners also engaged and participated in the political process despite prohibitions against active campaigning and their inability to vote in cabildo elections. Commoners fronted challenges by indigenous nobles, testified in support of competing political factions, and sometimes participated in elections. Their indirect participation was effectively made important because the viceregal government had, from the sixteenth century, sought to promote good government.

All such engagements of the viceregal legal system, however, brought Spanish institutions further into native affairs. Indigenous governors lost authority. Governors consistently failed to collect sufficient tribute in the seventeenth century, even after the indigenous population began to increase naturally and through immigration. Though Spaniards attempted to use the failings of governors to gain control over tribute collection, holding governors accountable for tribute shortfalls and adding Spanish bureaucrats in the mid-sixteenth century, indigenous governments maintained their control into the eighteenth century and generally resisted the imposition of mid-level Spanish bureaucracies. Several lawsuits in the seventeenth century further disrupted indigenous government and forced indigenous leaders to seek mediation through Spanish courts. The consequences of such reliance on viceregal institutions to settle internal disputes were manifold. Nevertheless, the contests for control of indigenous governments, which began in the sixteenth century and persisted into the eighteenth, created the generative force necessary for the creation of a new kind of political system that was neither wholly indigenous nor Spanish in origin.

Appendix

Rulers of Mexico Tenochtitlan,

1520–1734

1520	Moteucçoma Xocoyotzin[1]
1520	Cuitlahuactzin[2]
1521–1525	Quauhtemoctzin[3]
1525	Juan Velasquez Tlacotzin[4]
1525–1530	Don Andres de Tapia Motelchiuhtzin (Macehualli)[5]
1532–1536	Don Pablo Xochiquentzin[6]

First judge-governors under first Viceroy don Antonio de Mendoza.

1538–1541	Don Diego de Alvarado Huanitzin[7]
1541–1554	Don Diego de San Francisco Tehuetzquititzin[8]
1554–1557	Don Esteban de Guzmán[9] (judge only)
1557–1562	Don Cristóbal de Guzmán Cecetzin[10]
1562–1565	Don Luís de Santa María Nanacacipactzin[11]

End of original descendents of the lords of Tenochtitlan

1568–1573	Don Francisco Jiménez[12] (judge only)
1573–1599	Don Antonio Valeriano el Viejo[13]
1596–1599	Don Juan Martín[14] (deputy only)
1600–1608	Don Gerónimo López[15]
1608–1609	Don Juan Bautista[16]
1610	Francisco Sánchez[17] (presidente)
1610–1616	Don Juan Perez de Monterrey[18]
1616	Don Francisco Bautista Valeriano[19]
1620	Don Juan Valeriano[20]
1620	Jerónimo de León[21] (interim governor)
1620–1624	Don Antonio Valeriano (December 1620)[22]

1625   Don Francisco Tapia y Barrera[23]
1629   Don Juan de León[24]
1630–1636   Don Cristóbal Pascual[25]
1636–1637   Don Bartolomé Cortés y Mendoza Axayacatzin[26]
1638–1639   Don Martín González[27]
1640–1643   Don Martín González[28]
1646–1648   Don Sebastián Cortés Pizarro[29]
1648–1652   Don Manuel Tapia Moctezuma[30]
1653–1654   Don Diego de la Cruz Villanueva[31]
1654   Don Juan de Aguilar el Viejo[32]
1654   Don Juan de Velazquez (did not serve)[33]
1655–1656   Don Diego de la Cruz Villanueva[34]
1657   Don Marcos de la Cruz[35]
1657–1658   Don Pedro Bernal (1657, June)[36]
1659–1660   Don Francisco Benítez de Inga[37]
1662–1666?   Don Lorenzo de Santiago[38]
1667   Don Felipe de Santiago y Aguilar[39]
1672   Don Juan de Aguilar[40]
1673   Don Felipe de Aguilar[41]
1674   Don Juan de Aguilar[42]
1675   Don Juan Montaño[43]
1676   Don Juan Valeriano[44]
1677   Don Gregorio de los Reyes[45]
1678–1679   Don Juan de Jara 1678–1679[46]
1679   Don Lorenzo de Santiago[47]
1680–1681   Don Matias de Jara[48]
1681   Don Juan de Jara[49]
1682   Don Miguel de la Cruz (elected but did not serve)[50]
1682   Don Matias de los Angeles[51]
1683   Don Gregorio de los Reyes[52]
1684   Don Bernardino Antonio de la Cruz y Guerrero[53]
1686   Don Joseph de la Cruz [54]
1687–1688   Don Bernardino Antonio de la Cruz y Guerrero[55]
1688   Matias de los Angeles[56]
1692   Don Joseph de la Cruz[57]
1693   Don Matias de los Angeles (died in office)[58]
1693   Don Mateo de Rojas[59]

1694	Don Bernabé de Santiago[60]
1695	Don Juan de los Reyes[61]
1696	Don Nicolas Ignacio Moctezuma (died in office)[62]
1696	Don Mateo de Rojas (appointed in February)[63]
1697	Don Juan Felix de Aguilar[64]
1699–1704	Don Bernardino Antonio de la Cruz y Guerrero[65]
1706–1709	Don Roque Eusebio de Lara[66]
1712	Don Felipe de Jesús[67]
1714–1715	Don Juan de Ribera[68]
1716	Don Juan Marcelo Audelo[69]
1717	Don Pedro Martínez[70]
1719	Don Antonio de Alvarado[71]
1720	Don Joseph de la Cruz[72]
1724	Don Felipe de Jesús[73]
1731	Don Mateo de Alba[74]
1734	Don Juan de los Reyes[75]

NOTES

ABBREVIATIONS

AGN   Archivo General de la Nación, México, Mexico City
AGI   Archivo de Indias, Sevilla
AHCM   Archivo Historico de la Ciudad de México, Mexico City
BNM-FR Fondo Reservado, Biblioteca Nacional de México, Mexico City
CC   *Codex Chimalpahin*

INTRODUCTION

1. Elizabeth Hill Boone, *Stories in Red and Black: Pictorial Histories of the Aztecs and Mixtecs* (Austin: University of Texas Press, 2000), 31–55. Boone does not study the Codíce Osuna in detail but provides a general discussion of the significance of place signs and their meaning as representative symbols. The best Nahuatl source for terminology, Chimalpahin, does not provide a term other than *barrio* to describe the four parts of the altepetl, or sometimes *huey altepetl* or even *altepetl ciudad* of Mexico Tenochtitlan. Though it is tempting to follow borrowed terms for subunits like *calpolli* or *tlaxilacalli*, Chimalpahin used neither of these terms to describe what the Spaniards referred to as the four barrios of the parcialidad of San Juan Tenochtitlan. In the context he provides, *calpolli* referred to groups of people who were migrating. Schroeder following Reyes García defined this term as a "group of people on the move." *Tlaxilacalli* refers to people more rooted in place but also seems to refer to a more refined unit within the altepetl; see Susan Schroeder, *Chimalpahin and the Kingdoms of Chalco* (Tucson: University of Arizona Press, 1991), 143–157, and Don Domingo de San Antón Muñón Chimalpahin Quauhtlehuanitzin, *Annals of His Time: Don Domingo de San Antón Muñón Chimalpahin Quauhtlehuanitzin*, ed. and trans. James Lockhart, Susan Schroeder, and Doris Namala (Stanford: Stanford University Press, 2006), 18–19.

2. For the dates of rule for Viceroy Velasco, see C. R. Haring, *The Spanish Empire in America* (New York: Oxford University Press, 1947), 116–117.

3. See discussion of the word *macehualli* in James Lockhart, *The Nahuas after the Conquest: A Social and Cultural History of the Indians of Central Mexico, Sixteenth through Eighteenth Centuries* (Stanford: Stanford University Press, 1992), 114–115, and Robert Haskett, *Indigenous Rulers: An Ethnohistory of Town Government in Colonial Cuernavaca* (Albuquerque: University of New Mexico Press, 1991), 30–32. Lockhart argues that in colonial usage *macehualli* meant human being or person, without indicating class or social differentiation. In this particular Spanish-language document it retains its precontact meaning, denoting hierarchy (commoner). The regular Nahuatl plural, *macehualtin*, does not usually appear in Spanish-language documents, which instead use *macehuales* or *maceguales*. For such usage variations, see Archivo General de la Nación (hereafter AGN), Civil, v. 644, e. 1. Haskett adds that he encountered *macehualtin* in association with the title *don* in Cuernavacan voter rolls, something that would have been impossible if only nobles could vote. He suggests that this served to designate these individuals as "vassals of the Spanish king or the Marqués del Valle." On this reading, principales, or at least those with the right to vote, could be designated macehualtin. In Nahuatl, the possessive *macehualtin* therefore meant "someone's subjects." Many thanks to Susan Schroeder for this clarification. For alcalde, see Lockhart, *Nahuas after the Conquest*, 36, 484, n. 81.

4. See also Lockhart, *Nahuas after the Conquest,* 340, fig. 8.3, for the Nahuatl text. The translation and transcription are his, and the full text reads, "You alcaldes who are being appointed now for the first time, greatly see to the Christian doctrine; let everyone know the service of our lord God. And after that see to the service of our ruler His Majesty; what he desires, what by him is needed you are to see to, you are to take good care of. And as to all the commoners, you are to take good care of them, you are to treat them with esteem; no one without reason you are to judge, and you are to take good care that everyone cultivates (the land), no one lives in idleness." Compared to the Spanish-language text, the Nahuatl version is far more elaborate. In Spanish the text reads, "The order given by the viceroy, don Luis de Velasco, entrusts the staffs [of royal justice] to the alcaldes and alguaciles empowering them [to observe and enforce] the [Christian] doctrine, order and good treatment of indigenous peoples." The details given to the indigenous alcaldes are quite important, for they explain what the audience reading these words in Spanish likely already knew. Many versions of the Códice Osuna are available; see Luis Chávez Orozco, *Códice Osuna: Reproducción facsimilar de la obra del mismo título, editada en Madrid, 1878* (México: Ediciones del Instituto Indigenista Interamericano, 1947), 7–8, 198, 257. But perhaps the most accessible is on the Library of Congress website, http://hdl.loc.gov/loc.hisp/espbnms.0041, under the title "Pintura del Gobernador, Alcaldes y Regidores de Mexico" (accessed, 8/10/2007); an excellent facsimile of the codex with an introduction by Vicenta Cortés Alonso can be found in *Pintura del gobernador, alcaldes y regidores de Mexico* (Madrid: Servicio de Publicaciones del Ministerio de Educación y Ciencia, 1973). The codex image from which the passage above is taken (see p. f 9v)

is reproduced in Charles Gibson, *The Aztecs under Spanish Rule: A History of the Indians of the Valley of Mexico, 1519–1810* (Stanford: Stanford University Press, 1964), pl. 7.

5. See Lockhart, *Nahuas after the Conquest*, 28–35, esp. 35; Andrés Lira González, *Comunidades indígenas frente a la Ciudad de México: Tenochtitlan y Tlatelolco, sus Pueblos y Barrios, 1812–1919* (México: El Colegio de México, 1983), 14–20; and Alonso de Zorita, *The Lords of New Spain: The Brief and Summary Relation of the Lords of New Spain*, trans. Benjamin Keen (New Brunswick: Rutgers University Press, 1963), 88–179. For the divisions of the city, see Pedro Carrasco, *The Tenochca Empire of Ancient Mexico: The Triple Alliance of Tenochtitlan, Tetzcoco, and Tlacopan* (Norman: University of Oklahoma Press, 1999), 61–63, 93–95.

6. Mapoteca de Orozco y Berra, varilla 2, numero de control, 871, "Plano de Mexico Tenochtitlan año de 1519, por Leopoldo Batres, 1892." This map shows the connections between the former indigenous altepetl and the newly established barrios. See also Leopoldo Batres, *Cartilla histórica de la Ciudad de México* (México: Gallegos Hnos. Libreros Editores, 1893), 1–14, esp. 4; and Alfonso Caso, *Los barrios antiguos de Tenochtitlan y Tlatelolco* (México: Memorias de la Academia Mexicana de la Historia, 1956), 7–41, for a description and naming of the barrios. Caso notes the significant variation of names; note, for example, p. 18, in which San Pablo is alternatively Teopan, Zoquipan, or Xochimilca. For the term *altepetl*, see Schroeder, *Chimalpahin*, 118–139. For the Spanish cabildo, see Louisa Schell Hoberman, *Mexico's Merchant Elite, 1590–1660* (Durham: Duke University Press, 1991), 150–180; and Ida Altman, *Transatlantic Ties in the Spanish Empire: Brihuega, Spain, and Puebla, Mexico, 1560–1620* (Stanford: Stanford University Press, 2000). See also Lockhart, *Nahuas after the Conquest*, 25, who notes the counterclockwise (if looking from above on a map) orientation of the naming of these zones of the city in indigenous sources. See Hernando de Alvarado Tezozomoc, *Crónica mexicayotl*, ed. Adrián León (México: Universidad Nacional Autónma de México, 1998). For the more authoritative version of Teçoçomoc, see don Domingo Francisco de San Antón Muñón Chimalpahin Quauhtlehuanitzin, *Codex Chimalpahin: Society and Politics in Mexico Tenochtitlan, Tlatelolco, Texcoco, Culhuacan, and Other Nahua Altepetl in Central Mexico: The Nahuatl and Spanish Annals and Accounts Collected and Recorded by don Domingo de San Antón Muñón Chimalpahin Quauhtlehuanitzin*, vol. 1, ed. Arthur J. O. Anderson and Susan Schroeder (Norman: University of Oklahoma Press, 1997) (hereafter, *CC*, vols. 1–2), which is Chimalpahin's edition of Teçoçomoc's writings and as such is closer to the original than the León edition. See also Yanna Yannakakis, *The Art of Being In-Between: Native Intermediaries, Indian Identity, and Local Rule in Colonial Oaxaca* (Durham: Duke University Press, 2008), 57–62, who describes the parcialidad alternately as a political faction (late seventeenth century), a meaning I have not come across in my research.

7. The idea of the survival of indigenous culture and identity has been studied quite well in general; Matthew Restall, *Seven Myths of the Spanish Conquest* (New York: Oxford University Press, 2003), 65–76, esp. 73. Restall argues that "the fifth dimension of the Conquest's incompleteness was the degree to which native

peoples maintained a degree of autonomy within the Spanish Empire. This was in part an autonomy permitted and sanctioned by Spanish officials, and it was nurtured by native leaders through illegal means and legal negotiations. As a general rule, Spaniards did not seek to rule natives directly and take over their lands. Rather they hoped to preserve native communities as self-governing sources of labor and producers of agricultural products." Restall provides a fine synthesis of scholarship for the past thirty years in this area. See also Stephanie Wood, *Transcending Conquest: Nahua Views of Spanish Colonial Mexico* (Norman: University of Oklahoma Press, 2003), 21–22, 148–149; Laura E. Matthew and Michel R. Oudijk, eds., *Indian Conquistadors: Indigenous Allies in the Conquest of Mesoamerica* (Norman: University of Oklahoma Press, 2007). For the ecclesiastical issues raised, see Louise Burkhart, *The Slippery Earth: Nahua Christian Moral Dialogue in Sixteenth-Century Mexico* (Tucson: University of Arizona Press, 1989), 184–193.

8. Bernal Díaz del Castillo, *The Conquest of New Spain*, trans. J. M. Cohen (New York: Penguin, 1963), 214 (translation by the editor). The ellipsis removes "and cues." I have deduced that Díaz in this quotation and in other places in the work uses "cues" to mean temple or pyramid, and sometimes the place where "idols" are found. The word does not exist in Spanish (and is not translated in the edited texts I have examined). Its closet equivalent is *cue*, which means deity in Yucatec Maya (thanks to Susan Schroeder for assistance with *cue*); see Bernal Díaz del Castillo, *Historia de la conquista de Nueva España*, ed. Joaquín Ramírez Cabañas (México: Editorial Porrúa, 1970), 136, 159.

9. Díaz, *Conquest*, 353–391; for other uses of Bernal Díaz in this way, see Eduardo Matos Moctezuma, *The Great Temple of the Aztecs: Treasures of Tenochtitlan*, trans. Dorris Heyden (London: Thames and Hudson, 1988), 147; and Inga Clendinnen, *Aztecs: An Interpretation* (New York: Cambridge University Press, 1991), 17. Note also the commentary of Peter Hulme, "Tales of Distinction: European Ethnography and the Caribbean," in Stewart B. Schwartz, *Implicit Understandings: Observing, Reporting and Reflecting on the Encounters between Europeans and Other Peoples in the Early Modern Era* (New York: Cambridge University Press, 1991), 158–170, esp. 170.

10. The term "Aztec" is inappropriate to describe the Nahuatl-speaking peoples of central New Spain. I use *Nahua* when discussing the broad linguistic group of Nahuatl speakers of which the residents of Mexico Tenochtitlan were part. To describe the people of the city, I use *Tenochca* or *Mexica Tenochca*, which relate exclusively to residents of Mexico Tenochtitlan. In other instances, for modifying purposes I use "indigenous" or "native" to refer to institutions or people. These conventions allow the work to avoid antiquated, imprecise, or just offensive terms like "Aztec" and "Indian," which do not apply to these groups and in the case of the latter has its origin in pejorative colonial terminology. For these usages and further discussion, see Lockhart, *Nahuas after the Conquest*, 1, and Carrasco, *Tenochca*, 2–5.

11. Serge Gruzinski, "La red agujerada: Identidades etnicas y occidentalización en el México Colonial (Siglos XVI–XIX)," *América Indígena* 46, no. 3 (1986), 411–412.

12. Though it is clear that Mexico Tenochtitlan was an urban center before the conquest, it remains unclear if many of the other peoples who lived in the surrounding region also organized themselves in this fashion. See Schroeder, *Chimalpahin*, 209–212, which suggests that in Chalco no recognizable precontact urban center existed. See also Davíd Carrasco, *City of Sacrifice: The Aztec Empire and the Role of Violence in Civilization* (Boston: Beacon Press, 1999), 15–32, 36–40.

13. Ross Hassig, *Aztec Warfare: Imperial Expansion and Political Control* (Norman: University of Oklahoma Press, 1988), 17–47; note especially 28–30, where Hassig argues that the military culture of Nahua society differed from that of Spanish society in that indigenous warriors had to achieve rank, honor, and glory through earned success on the battlefield rather than through heredity. It should also be noted that the invasion of Mesoamerica by Spaniards was not carried out by soldiers or military officers in the traditional sense of the term; see Restall, *Seven Myths*, 28–33. Restall and others point out that the sixteenth century underwent what historians have often called a "military revolution" and a general professionalization of military affairs. Expenditures in Europe for fortifications, fleets, and armies to defend European possessions took up considerable royal resources; see Geoffrey Parker, *The Grand Strategy of Philip II* (New Haven: Yale University Press, 1998), 111–112.

14. Carrasco, *City of Sacrifice*, 52–56; Clendinnen, *Aztecs*, 1–11; Inga Clendinnen, *Ambivalent Conquests: Maya and Spaniard in Yucatan, 1517–1570* (New York: Cambridge University Press, 1987), 127–128; see also Octavio Paz, *The Labyrinth of Solitude*, trans. Lysander Kemp, Yara Milos, and Rachel Phillips Belash (New York: Grove Weidenfeld, 1985), 96–102.

15. Ross Hassig, *Time, History, and Belief in Aztec and Colonial Mexico* (Austin: University of Texas Press, 2001), xii, 137–142.

16. Fernando Cervantes, *The Devil in the New World: The Impact of Diabolism in New Spain* (New Haven: Yale University Press, 1994), 41–51; Paz, *Labyrinth*, 102–104; Clendinnen, *Aztecs*, 236–273.

17. Gibson (in *Aztecs*) and Lockhart (in *Nahuas after the Conquest*) both address questions of indigenous cultural survival after the Spanish invasion of 1519.

18. Juan Antonio Estrada Díaz, *Identidad y reconocimiento del otro en una sociedad mestiza* (México: Universidad Iberoamericana, 1998), 51–62.

19. Carrasco, *Tenochca*, 93–132.

20. Carrasco, *Tenochca*, 24, 29–40; Ubaldo Vargas Martínez, *La ciudad de México, 1325–1960* (México: Departamento del Distrito Federal, 1960), 9–12; William H. Prescott, *History of the Conquest of Mexico with a Preliminary View of the Ancient Mexican Civilization, and the Life of the Conqueror Hernando Cortez*, vol. 1. (Philadelphia: J. B. Lippincott, 1864), 15–22.

21. Hassig, *Time, History, and Belief*, 75–109.

22. Carrasco, *Tenochca*, 33–40.

23. Juan Miralles Osotos, *Hernán Cortés: Inventor de México* (Barcelona: Tusquets Editores, 2001), 494–495; Anthony Pagden, "Introduction" in Hernán Cortés, *Letters*

from Mexico, ed. and trans. Anthony Pagden (New Haven: Yale University Press, 1986), xl–xlv; Alonso de Zorita, *Historia de la Nueva España* (Madrid: Librería General de Victoriano Suárez, 1909), 179–181; Moctezuma, *Great Temple of the Aztecs*, 11, 25, 147–148. For the Tenochca image of the city and the temple as "ritual space" and "sacred space," see Johanna Broda, Davíd Carrasco, and Eduardo Matos Moctezuma, eds., "Introduction," in *The Great Temple of Tenochtitlan: Center and Periphery in the Aztec World* (Berkeley: University of California Press, 1987), 4–5, and in the same volume Broda, "Templo Mayor as Ritual Space," 67–77, 105–108, and Carrasco, "Myth, Cosmic Terror and the Templo Mayor," 130–133.

24. Chimalpahin, *Annals*, 19, where the editors point out that in Chimalpahin's writings on the subject the four principal subdivisions of Mexico Tenochtitlan were referred to by the term *nauhcan*, which they gloss as "in four places." When writing of these urban subdivisions of the altepetl, Chimalpahin sometimes borrowed the Spanish *barrio; see CC* v. 2. Schroeder's attention to Nahuatl usage in Chimalpahin reveals the complexity and variation of similar forms of space within the Nahua region.

25. Schroeder, *Chimalpahin*, 79, 100–102.

26. Schroeder, *Chimalpahin*, xvi–xvii, 32–33; Lockhart, *Nahuas after the Conquest*, 15–30; Batres, *Cartilla histórica*, 12–33. For a larger discussion of space, see Andrés Lira González, "Les divisions de Mexico aux XVIIIe et XIXe siècles: De la ville des deux Républiques à la ville républicaine," in Christian Topalov, ed., *Les divisions de la ville* (Paris: Éditions de la Maison des science de l'homme, 2002), 102–104.

27. For the Nahuatl translation of *tecpan*, see Fray Alonso de Molina, *Vocabulario en lengua castellana y mexicana y mexicana y castellana*, ed. Miguel León-Portilla (México, 1977 [1571]). I also use Frances Karttunen, *An Analytical Dictionary of Nahuatl* (Norman: University of Oklahoma Press, 1983). See also Dorothy Tanck de Estrada, *Atlas ilustrado de los pueblos de indios, Nueva España, 1800* (México: El Colegio de México, 2005), 33–36, 40–42. For the reference to *tecpan comonidad*, see Chimalpahin, *Annals*, 38–39, which the editors translate as "community palace."

28. On the nature of the colonial state, see William Taylor, *Drinking Homicide and Rebellion in Colonial Mexican Villages* (Stanford: Stanford University Press, 1979) 168–169, and his "Between Global Process and Local Knowledge: An Inquiry into Early Latin American Social History, 1500–1900," in Olivier Zunz, ed., *Reliving the Past: The Worlds of Social History* (Chapel Hill: University of North Carolina Press, 1985), 140–166.

29. José Luis de Rojas, *Mexico Tenochtitlan: Economía y sociedad en el siglo XVI* (México: Fondo de Cultura Económica y el Colegío de Michoacán, 1995), 29–45, esp. map 4. See also Ana Rita Valero de García Lascuraín, *La ciudad de Mexico Tenochtitlan: Su primera traza, 1524–1534* (México: Editorial Jus, 1991), 64–92; Emily Umberger, "Art and Imperial Strategy in Tenochtitlan," in Frances F. Berdan, Richard E. Blanton, Elizabeth Hill Boone, Mary G. Hodge, Michael E. Smith, and Emily Umberger, eds., *Aztec Imperial Strategies* (Washington, D.C.: Dumbarton Oaks Research Library and Collection, 1996), 86–87; and Gibson, *Aztecs*, 370.

30. Cortés, *Letters from Mexico*, 263–264.

31. Zorita, *Historia*, 176.

32. Ralph H. Vigil, *Alonso de Zorita: Royal Judge and Christian Humanist, 1512–1585* (Norman: University of Oklahoma Press, 1987), 178–179; AGN, Civil, v. 644, e. 1; Manuel Serrano y Sanz, "Vida y escritos del doctor Alonso de Zorita," in Zorita, *Historia*, lxiv–xciii.

33. Ethel Herrera Morena, *500 planos de la ciudad de México, 1325–1933* (México: Secretaria de Asentamientos Humanos y Obras Publicas, 1982), 22–39; see also Francisco de la Maza, *La Ciudad de México en el siglo xvii* (México: Fondo de Cultura Económica, 1968), images 1–7, 28.

34. Maza, *La ciudad*, 13–14; Miguel León-Portilla and Carmen Agulera, *Mapa de Mexico Tenochtitlan y sus contornos hacia 1550* (México: Elanese Mexicana, 1986), 10, 72–78. By the eighteenth century, Spaniards described the indigenous barrios even more humbly; see Marcela Dávalos, *Basura e ilustración: La limpieza de la Ciudad de México a fines del siglo XVIII* (México: Instituto Nacional de Antropología e Historia, 1997), 28–30, 99–109.

35. *CC*, v. 1, 41, for Huanitzin and his relationship to Moteucçoma; and also Don Domingo de San Antón Muñón Chimalpahin Quauhtlehuanitzin, *Las ocho relaciones y el memorial de Colhuacan*, ed. Rafael Tena (México: CONACULTA, 1998), t. 2, 155 (recto pages in Spanish, verso in Nahuatl).

36. Chimalpahin, *Las ocho relaciones*, 185–201. On the creation of the office of governor, see Charles Gibson, "The Aztec Aristocracy in Colonial Mexico," *Comparative Studies in Society and History* 2, no. 2 (1960), 177–179. For a discussion of Chimalpahin's life, see Schroeder, *Chimalpahin;* Chimalpahin, *Annals*, 3–5; and Susan Schroeder, "The Annals of Chimalpahin," in James Lockhart, Lisa Sousa, and Stephanie Wood, eds., *Sources and Methods for the Study of Postconquest Mesoamerican Ethnohistory, Provisional Version* (Eugene: University of Oregon, Wired Humanities Project, 2007), 1–11, http://whp.uoregon.edu/lockhart/schroeder.pdf (accessed 2/2008). Mendoza, as a viceroy, is generally viewed as a force of stabilization and compromise and worked closely with the early Franciscans; see Georges Baudot, *Utopia and History in Mexico: The First Chronicles of Mexican Civilization, 1520–1569*, trans. Bernard R. Ortiz de Montellano and Thelma Ortiz de Montellano (Boulder: University of Colorado Press, 1995), 111; and Hoberman, *Mexico's Merchant Elite*, 10–11. The succession to a nephew conforms to precontact indigenous patterns in Tenochtitlan, as discussed below. For a complete discussion, see J. Rounds, "Dynastic Succession and Centralization of Power in Tenochtitlan," in George A. Collier, Renato Rosaldo, and John D. Wirth, eds., *The Inca and Aztec States, 1400–1800: Anthropology and History* (New York: Academic Press, 1982), 65–73. Lockhart, *Nahuas after the Conquest*, 31–33, considers this period one of transition and points out that as interim, non-tlatoani rulers, the quauhtlatoani were the key to the transition between tlatoque (the last was Quauhtemoctzin) and gobernadores in the 1520s. The political processes that emerged in Mexico Tenochtitlan appear similar to those in other places where a Spanish veneer overlay

indigenous institutions without dramatically changing the internal structure; see Matthew Restall, *The Maya World: Yucatec Culture and Society, 1550–1850* (Stanford: Stanford University Press, 1997), 51–83.

37. Among other places, see *Instrucciones que los virreyes de Nueva España dejaron a sus sucesores. Añádense algunas que los mismos trajeron de la corte y otros documentos semejantes a las instrucciones* (México: Imprenta, 1867), 228–230. Mendoza says patronizingly in these instructions for his successor that he regularly heard complaints from natives and, "even though many times they lie to me, it does not make me angry," explaining that he did not believe they had the capacity to tell the truth. He concluded that "natives must be treated as though they are children" and thus absolved from adult responsibility. With that said, Mendoza supported the Royal College of Santa Cruz in Santiago Tlatelolco, founded to create a native priesthood. See the discussion of the college and its founding in Frances Karttunen, "From Courtyard to the Seat of Government: The Career of Antonio Valeriano, Nahua Colleague of Bernardino de Sahagún," *Amerindia* 19/20 (1995), 113–115; and SilverMoon, "The Imperial College of Tlatelolco and the Emergence of a New Nahua Intellectual Elite in New Spain (1500–1760)" (Ph.D. diss., Duke University, 2007), 43–144.

38. For this transition, see Gibson, *Aztecs,* 58–66. For the definitive study on Chimalpahin and his work, see Schroeder, *Chimalpahin.*

39. See the important discussion of the quauhtlatoque Motelchiuhtzin and Xochiquentzin in Schroeder, *Chimalpahin,* 188–193. Chimalpahin, *Annals,* 133, might tempt us to temper this somewhat; as I discuss below, four of the five rulers of Mexico Tenochtitlan were in Cortés's custody in 1524, including those who had ties to the royal line and others who were Moteucçoma's advisors, such as Tlacotzin the cihuacoatl. Lockhart, *Nahuas after the Conquest,* 34, tab. 2.1, provides the dates of rule for Motelchiuhtzin and Xochiquentzin; see also *CC,* v. 1, 39–41.

40. Eloise Quiñones Keber, ed., *Codex Telleriano-Remensis: Ritual, Divination, and History in a Pictorial Aztec Manuscript* (Austin: University of Texas Press, 1995), fol. 44, see also the commentary by the editors, 233–234. See also, for the political controversy, Baudot, *Utopia and History,* 28–29, 260–276. Note that the legitimacy brought through institutionalization should not mask that these early governments were quite corrupt; see Charles Gibson, *Tlaxcala in the Sixteenth Century* (Stanford: Stanford University Press, 1967 [1952]), 120–121.

41. Chimalpahin, *Las ocho relaciones,* t. 2, 187. Tena chose the Spanish phrase *se enseñoreó* (verb is *enseñorear*), which I have glossed as "appointed" but more literally might be translated as "to make a lord (*señor*) of him."

42. Schroeder, *Chimalpahin,* 188–193. Chimalpahin, *Las ocho relaciones,* t. 2, 187. For additional commentary, see Camilla Townsend, "Sex, Servitude, and Politics among Pre-Conquest Nahuas," *The Americas* 62, no. 3, (2006), 366.

43. Karttunen, *Analytical Dictionary,* 306, defines *tlazopipiltin* (see the entry for *tlazohpilli*) as someone of legitimate noble birth ("hijo o hija legítimos un principal"). *Quauhpipiltin* follows Lockhart, *Nahuas after the Conquest,* 33, who defines

cuauhtlatoani (*quauhtlatoani*) as a tlatoani not born into the position but who elevated his status through service in battle; literally *quauhtaltoani* means eagle ruler. Christopher P. Garraty, "Ceramic Indices of Aztec Eliteness," *Ancient Mesoamerica* 11, no. 2 (2000), 324, provides a direct definition of quauhpipiltin as "commoners who attained political positions through achievement in battle."

44. Chimalpahin, *Las ocho relaciones*, t. 2, 193.

45. Schroeder, *Chimalpahin*, 162–164, suggests that tlatoque had the power to exercise *tlatocayotl*, which she translates as rulership, or in the Spanish of Molina *señorio* or *reino*. The tlatoani, Schroeder demonstrates, was "dynastic and associated with one specific altepetl." When comparing the tlatoque to governors, she makes the case that the governorship was not something tied to the dynasty. Furthermore, when Chimalpahin uses the terms "governor" and *tlatoani* together, he is suggesting only that the governor came from a legitimate royal line of the altepetl he ruled over as governor, and thus it becomes an important contextual modifier; see 186–188.

46. Lockhart, *Nahuas after the Conquest*, 18. Schroeder adds some complexity to this idea by suggesting that usually altepetl had such dynastic kings; see her *Chimalpahin*, 42; and Rebecca Horn, *Postconquest Coyoacan: Nahua-Spanish Relations in Central Mexico, 1519–1650* (Stanford: Stanford University Press, 1997), 45.

47. Lockhart, *Nahuas after the Conquest*, 18, 33–34, and tab. 2.1. Lockhart uses both *tlatoani* and *gobernador* to denote the dynastic rulers restored by Mendoza. He also shows that rulership (tlatocayotl) varied in different altepetl and was sufficiently flexible to withstand challenge and dynastic changes. See also the relevant discussions in Restall, *Maya World*, 62–63, and Schroeder, *Chimalpahin*, 186–193.

48. Lockhart, *Nahuas after the Conquest*, 31, 109, 132–138; in some usages, by the late seventeenth century, *tlatoani* meant generally "prominent person" or pilli. See also Schroeder, *Chimalpahin*, 187–189, in which she suggests that prominent Spaniards were also referred to as *tlatoque*, including the viceroy and archbishop, leading to a general erosion of the original meaning of the term as Nahuatl transitioned over time.

49. Chimalpahin, *Las ocho relaciones*, t. 2, 193, 196, 197. Lockhart, *Nahuas after the Conquest*, 31.

50. Baudot, *Utopia and History*, 45.

51. Cortés, *Letters from Mexico*, 321, 506, n. 51. See also Baudot, *Utopia and History*, 45, who also discusses the importance of the revival of the cihuacoatl, literally "woman serpent." According to Pagden, who cites the *Codex Aubin* in *Letters* (506, n. 51), the cihuacoatl was named Tlacotzin. See also Chimalpahin, *Las ocho relaciones*, t. 2, 169; and *CC*, v. 2, 43–47, 53–59 (Chimalpahin notes that Tlacotzin was the last cihuacoatl on 57). I am relying on the definition and spelling provided in Karttunen, *Analytical Dictionary*, 34. Karttunen's definition suggests that this office had nearly equal power to the tlatoani: "cuyo poder igualaba casi siempre el del soberano, por cuya razón ha sido equiparado a un virrey o lugarteniente." See also Rudolf A. M. Zantwijk, *The Aztec Arrangement: The Social History of Pre-Spanish Mexico* (Norman:

University of Oklahoma Press, 1985), 98, who defines *cihuacoatl* as "female companion or highest administrator." Rounds continues this argument by suggesting that the cihuacoatl was an important transitional figure during dynastic succession crises who would serve as tlatoani after the death of the ruler. He also suggests this office may have its origins in the "patron goddess of Culhuacan . . . and probably her chief priest"; see his "Dynastic Succession," 65, 79–83; see also Frances Berdan, *The Aztecs of Central Mexico: An Imperial Society* (New York: Holt Rinehart and Winston, 1982), 100–103.

52. On Cortés and his intent in the fourth letter, see J. H. Elliott, "Cortés, Velázquez and Charles V," in Cortés, *Letters from Mexico*, xxix–xxxiv.

53. Restall, *Seven Myths*, 149. For the significance of Quauhtemoctzin, especially in the modern imagination, see Paz, *Labyrinth*, 83–84; Lyman Johnson, "Digging up Cuauhtémoc," in Lyman Johnson, ed., *Body Politics: Death, Dismemberment, and Memory in Latin America* (Albuquerque: University of New Mexico Press, 2004), 207–244; and Claudio Lomnitz, *Deep Mexico, Silent Mexico: An Anthropology of Nationalism* (Minneapolis: University of Minnesota Press, 2001), xiii, 233–239.

54. Chimalpahin, *Annals*, 135.

55. See Chimalpahin, *Annals*, 133, which shows that in 1524 the "rulers in Mexico, Quauhtemoctzin, Motelchiuhtzin, Tlacotzin the cihuacoatl, Oquiztzin, and Huanitzin, were taken to Coyoacan, where they lay imprisoned in irons." Of these, Quauhtemoctzin was the tlatoani, Tlacotzin and Motelchiuhtzin became interim rulers, Huanitzin became the first appointed governor, and Oquiztzin was Huanitzin's brother and grandson of Axayacatzin (r. 1469–81). For Oquiztzin, see Tezozomoc, *Cronica Mexicayotl*, 164; for the more authoritative text of Teçoçomoc's writings, see *CC*, v. 1, 101–103; and Chimalpahin, *Las ocho relaciones*, t. 1, 415, and t. 2, 113. According to Rafaél Tena's work on Chimalpahin, Huanitzin was the nephew of Moteucçoma and son of Moteucçoma Xocoyotzin's brother "Tezozomoctli"; see t. 2, 155.

56. Chimalpahin, *Las ocho relaciones*, t. 2, 187, 221; Schroeder, *Chimalpahin*, 75, 188–193; Lockhart, *Nahuas after the Conquest*, 33; and Gibson, "Aztec Aristocracy," 171–172. For general discussions of the macehualtin, see Alfredo López Austin, *The Human Body and Ideology: Concepts of the Ancient Nahuas*, trans. Thelma Ortiz de Montellano and Bernard Ortiz de Montellano (Salt Lake City: University of Utah Press, 1988), 385–396; and Haskett, *Indigenous Rulers*, 30–31.

57. See Elliott, "Cortés, Velázquez and Charles V," xxxvi, for the details of Cortés's return to Spain in March 1528. For Motelchiuhtzin's term in office, see Lockhart, *Nahuas after the Conquest*, 34, tab. 2.1. On the death of Motelchiuhtzin, see Chimalpahin, *Annals*, 135.

58. Schroeder, *Chimalpahin*, 190–191; Rounds, "Dynastic Succession," 73–77, 85, n. 8, and Lockhart, *Nahuas after the Conquest*, 33.

59. Schroeder, *Chimalpahin*, 191.

60. Lockhart, *Nahuas after the Conquest*, 30–31.

61. Abducting rulers as a conquest strategy is discussed in Restall, *Seven Myths*, 25–26; see also Camilla Townsend, "Burying the White Gods: New Perspectives on the Conquest of Mexico," *American Historical Review* 108, no. 3 (2003), 659–687.

62. Cortés, *Letters*, 321, emphasis on *ciguacoatl* in the original.

63. Lockhart, *Nahuas after the Conquest*, 14–28; Schroeder, *Chimalpahin*, 118–139; S. L. Cline, *Colonial Culhuacan, 1580–1600: A Social History of an Aztec Town* (Albuquerque: University of New Mexico Press, 1986), 36; Carrasco, *Tenochca*, 16–19.

64. Schroeder, *Chimalpahin*, 144–157, in which she shows that *calpolli* was rarely used by Chimalpahin. Schroeder adds that *tlaxilacalli* seems to have been a colonial term, noting only two instances where Chimalpahin used *tlaxilacalli* to describe something precontact. Lockhart, *Nahuas after the Conquest*, 57, discusses the important relationship between *tlaxilacalli* and *barrio* in which the latter eventually became a loanword in Nahuatl, though both remain in usage "through the eighteenth century." See also his more general discussion of *tlaxilacalli*, a word that appears more regularly than *calpolli* in Nahuatl texts (apparently the opposite for Spanish-language ones and thus its usage in Gibson and others). *Tlaxilacalli*, like *altepetl*, referred to both the people and the place but is generally translated as "barrio" or "neighborhood," see 16–18, 479, n. 10, for the etymology. To discuss the Tenochca altepetl of Mexico Tenochtitlan and its four barrios, I generally avoid the term "barrio" and instead use "subunit" or "subdivision."

65. The organization of Mexico Tenochtitlan indicates that *tlaxilacalli* probably referred to subunits within each of the four affiliated subdivisions of Mexico Tenochtitlan (Moyotlan, Teopan, Atzaqualco, and Cuepopan). See the discussion in Caso, *Barrios*, 10–34, and the map in Rojas, *Mexico Tenochtitlan*, 36–39. In both sources the various barrios of Mexico Tenochtitlan (by this they mean tlaxilacalli) are identified according to their function (e.g., Tepetitlan, "hilly place"; Tzapotlan, "place of zapotes"). See AGN, Bienes Nacionales, v. 1072, e. 16, n. 15, fol. 1–1v, where a woman testified in 1577 before the ecclesiastical courts of Mexico City that she was "from the 'barrio' of Tomatlan." In Nahuatl, though we do not have the untranslated speech, she probably used the term *tlaxilacalli* to refer to Tomatlan. In the Spanish translation, with characteristic imprecision, this term appears as *barrio*. Tomatlan was therefore a barrio within a barrio in Spanish usage (the barrio of Atzaqualco). San Sebastián Atzaqualco, a constituent part of the altepetl in indigenous understanding, is, in Spanish, one of the four barrios of San Juan Tenochtitlan. In Nahuatl, however, Tomatlan is a tlaxilacalli within San Sebastián Atzaqualco, which is a constituent part of the larger altepetl of Mexico Tenochtitlan. For the Spanish usage, see AGN, Indios, v. 21, e. 146, f. 133: "los indios de la parcialidad de San Juan de esta ciudad y sus cuatro barrios," which translates "the native peoples of the parcialidad of San Juan [Mexico Tenochtitlan] of this city and its four barrios." Further clarification comes from the usage in AGN, Tierras, v. 866, e. 1, fol. 7–7v (1604), which reads in Nahuatl, "in tlaxilacalli San

Juan Huehuecalco," or "the tlaxilacalli San Juan Huehuecalco," which was a sub-ward of Moyotlan (its northern- and westernmost section) much like Tomatlan in relation to San Sebastián Atzaqualco and Mexico Tenochtitlan; see note 24 above.

66. See Lockhart, *Nahuas after the Conquest*, 21, for the quotation; see also his broader discussion of tlayacatl, 28–29, 36–37. For additional information on this structure, see Schroeder, *Chimalpahin*, 131–136.

67. Gibson, *Aztecs*, 33–38; Lockhart, *Nahuas after the Conquest*, 18–21. For more on the tlayacatl, see Schroeder, *Chimalpahin*, 131–136.

68. Real Academia Española, *Diccionario de la Lengua Española* (Madrid: Real Academia Española, 1992), s.v. "Parcialidad," in its third definition notes the political meaning: "the individual sections in which they divided or that divide up primitive peoples/towns" (translation mine). For linguistic equivalencies, see James Lockhart, "Sightings: Initial Nahua Reactions to Spanish Culture," in Schwartz, *Implicit Understandings*, 219, 224–229; and Lockhart, *Nahuas after the Conquest*, 483 n. 62.

69. Helen Nader, *Liberty in Absolutist Spain: The Habsburg Sale of Towns, 1516–1700* (Baltimore: Johns Hopkins University Press, 1990), 3–5, 122–124.

70. Alejandro Cañeque, *The King's Living Image: The Culture and Politics of Viceregal Power in Colonial Mexico* (New York: Routledge, 2004), 55–57; and Hoberman, *Mexico's Merchant Elite*, 149–182.

71. José Luis Alanis Boyso, *Elecciones de república para los pueblos del corregimiento de Toluca, 1729–1811* (México: Biblioteca enciclopedica del estado de México, 1978), 19–21. Gibson, *Aztecs*, 371, provides a rudimentary explanation of the role of the cabildo and its duties; see a more complete discussion below. See also Haskett, *Indigenous Rulers*, chap. 3, esp. 85; AGN, Obras Públicas, v. 27, e. 1; AGN, Indios, v. 6, pt. 1, e. 146; and Chimalpahin, *Annals*, 29. See also Luis Chávez Orozco, *Las instituciones democráticas de los indígenas Mexicanos en la época colonial* (México: Ediciones del Instituto Indigenista Interamericano, 1943), 11–12.

72. For the ayuntamiento, see the fine discussion in Haring, *Spanish Empire*, 147–165, which, though dated, provides useful information on the function of this body. For market regulation, a useful discussion is found in Archivo General de Indias, Sevilla (hereafter, AGI), Escribanía de Cámara, l. 178a, e. 9, which demonstrates how the ayuntamiento regulated the butcher shops of the city, even those in the indigenous barrios.

73. Charles Gibson, "Rotation of Alcaldes in the Indian Cabildo of Mexico City," *Hispanic American Historical Review* 33, no. 2 (1953), 214–222. Gibson, *Tlaxcala*, 105–106, shows the variability in this arrangement that must have had something to do with local conditions. In Tlaxcala the governorship was elected every second year (with notable interruptions), but with the possibility of immediate reelection. Lockhart continues this discussion, adding that after 1545 tlatoque from the four altepetl of Tlaxcala held permanent seats on the cabildo but could not serve as governor; see his *Nahuas and Spaniards: Postconquest Central Mexican History and Philology* (Stanford: Stanford University Press, 1991), 30. See also Lockhart, *Nahuas after the Conquest*, 36–40. Lockhart, discussing Mexico Tenochtitlan,

distinguishes the indigenous understanding of cabildo offices and argues that over time the distinction between them diminished. No precontact equivalent existed for the regidor, though the office of alcalde seems to correspond to the head of the calpolli (*teuctlatoani*) within an altepetl, an assertion that seems to support Gibson's rotation argument (suggesting that the ostensible reason for rotation had to do with calpolli representation observed in Tlaxcala by Gibson's analysis). In some rare instances, Nahuatl documents actually use teuctlatoani in conjunction with alcalde, which implies continuity. As Lockhart also observed, Nahuatl texts differ in their usage of this term, which sometimes means "judge" (one of the functions of an alcalde). Some Nahuatl texts even call Spaniards who served on the Audiencia *teuctlatoani.*

74. Schroeder, *Chimalpahin,* 186–187, discusses Chimalpahin's emphasis on the end of the legitimate royal line in Mexico Tenochtitlan.

75. Hoberman, *Mexico's Merchant Elite,* 156–160; Linda Curcio-Nagy, *The Great Festivals of Colonial Mexico City: Performing Power and Identity* (Albuquerque: University of New Mexico Press, 2004), 38–39; and Haring, *Spanish Empire,* 154–156. Haring argues, following Lucas Alamán, that the ayuntamiento of Mexico City was dominated by "hereditary regidores, men whose ancestors had possessed the office for generations."

76. Lockhart, *Nahuas after the Conquest,* 33–35. Land disputes in late sixteenth-century Mexico City increased largely because of the high mortality rate among indigenous property owners. Many of these disputes nevertheless ended up in Spanish courts, but indigenous authorities were relied on heavily to mediate; see Susan Kellogg, *Law and the Transformation of Aztec Culture* (Norman: University of Oklahoma Press, 1995).

77. Gibson, *Tlaxcala,* 103–104. Gibson, reading viceregal instructions and various commentaries by Vasco de Puga and Alonso de Zorita, argues that "Indians were to be admitted a few at a time to membership in the Mexico City cabildo, where they were to mix with Spanish regidores. The king encouraged Indians to serve as alguaciles in Mexico City and in the towns." I have seen no documentary evidence to support the assertions by Vasco de Puga and Zorita but note only that perhaps it was the intention of the colonial government to sponsor an internship program of sorts to inculcate the process of Hispanic government to indigenous peoples. It seems likely, however, that for Spanish purposes indigenous governors and their cabildos understood better than their Spanish counterparts how to administer indigenous affairs. According to Lockhart, this was probably the whole reason for setting up indigenous government in the first place; see *Nahuas after the Conquest,* 26–27, 30–31. Such events were happening in many places in the Basin of Mexico; see William T. Sanders and Barbara J. Price, "The Native Aristocracy and the Evolution of the Latifundio in the Teotihuacan Valley, 1521–1917," *Ethnohistory* 50, no. 1 (2003), 77–81.

78. Berdan, *Aztecs,* 100, and see also the discussion in Rounds, "Dynastic Succession," 73–77. Problems exist, however, in trying to reconstruct how the Tenochca

chose successors as uncovered in Schroeder's analysis. She argues that in Nahuatl the best source for succession in Tenochtitlan is Chimalpahin, but he is vague on details that would provide insight into such questions. He also fails to indicate birth order when sons succeeded their father, so we cannot determine if primogeniture was a value in Tenochca society. Words to designate older and younger siblings could also be used to describe cousins; see Schroeder, *Chimalpahin*, 174–180. See also Horn, *Postconquest Coyoacan*, 45, on the issue of primogeniture and succession.

79. Lockhart, *Nahuas after the Conquest*, 32.

80. Berdan, *Aztecs*, 100.

81. Rounds, "Dynastic Succession," 73–77; Lockhart, *Nahuas after the Conquest*, 33–35, 483 n. 68; see also Camilla Townsend, *Malintzin's Choices: An Indian Woman in the Conquest of Mexico* (Albuquerque: University of New Mexico Press, 2006), 130–131.

82. Alonso de Zorita, "On the Exploitation of the Indians," in *New Iberian World: A Documentary History of the Discovery and Settlement of Latin America to the Early Seventeenth Century*, ed. John H. Parry and Robert G. Keith (New York: Times Books, 1984), 438 (translation by the editors). See also Lockhart, *Nahuas after the Conquest*, 101, 112, 508 n. 84; Lockhart points out that Zorita must be read with care since he was not a disinterested party in the affairs of indigenous peoples.

83. Gibson, *Aztecs*, app. 4, 448–451, on the prevalence of epidemic disease.

84. Serge Gruzinski, *La colonización de lo imaginario: Sociedades indígenas y occidentalización en el México español. Siglos XVI–XVIII* (México: Fondo de Cultura Económica, 1988), 143–148; Gibson, *Aztecs*, 167–176. Zorita involved himself directly and personally in the business of indigenous government and watched the political system emerge in the barrios during this crucial time; see Vigil, *Alonso de Zorita*, 277–294. Vigil provides an overly celebratory portrayal of the justice but does point out that he spent considerable time working on indigenous issues. See also the *Códice Osuna: Pintura del gobernador*, fols. 2, 16 vto., for some of the interaction that Zorita had with the cabildo of Mexico Tenochtitlan; AGN, Civil, v. 644, e. 1, f. 82; Lockhart, *Nahuas after the Conquest*, 101, 112, 508 n. 84.

85. Carrasco, *Tenochca*, 95.

CHAPTER 1

1. Craftsmen, particularly *zapateros* (shoemakers) and *sastres* (tailors), were particularly *ladino* (hybrid, indigenous racially but adapting Spanish culture), having taken Spanish surnames and professions. These trade groups have also been identified as being particularly important much later, during the uprising of 1692, when they made up the majority of those apprehended after this uprising. See the important new study by Natalia Silva Prada, *La política de una rebelión: Los indígenas frente al tumulto de 1692 en la Ciudad de México* (México: El Colegio de México, 2007), 251–258. Carrasco, *Tenochca Empire*, 95, suggests that most residents

of the city were craftsmen, which may provide insight into why craftsmen figure so heavily in the first denunciation.

2. See AGN, Indios, v. 5, e. 595, fol. 233v. Zacate, a lake reed, was used as an additive to pulque and was prohibited along with all other additives to pulque during the colonial period. Native peoples also used the reed interchangeably with straw in pottery production, but likely in this case it was used as a building material. For its prohibition, see AGN, Indios, v. 6, p. 1, e. 1241 bis, fol. 345; and Gibson, *Aztecs*, 316, 354. In the case in Indios v. 6, p. 1, from the year 1595, the court apparently regarded zacate as a *yerba* (herb) exclusively. In 1564 the Audiencia treated zacate only as a building material; see also Taylor, *Drinking*, 36, 189 nn. 44, 45; AGN, Civil, v. 644, e. 1, fol. 3v.

3. See the discussion in the introduction regarding *barrio, altepetl, tlaxilacalli, calpolli,* and *tlayacatl,* which clarifies the usage of the terms. I generally follow the documentary language to decide which of the urban/spatial terms best fits the context.

4. Alanis Boyso, *Elecciones de república,* 18–21; Haskett, *Indigenous Rulers,* 95–123. The two sources provide insight into the role and functions of the cabildo and the officers who served on that body.

5. Lockhart, *Nahuas after the Conquest,* 18, 32–34.

6. The most recent and thorough discussion of the corregidor (he uses the term regionally appropriate for Oaxaca, *alcalde mayor*) is Jeremy Baskes, *Indians, Merchants, and Markets: A Reinterpretation of the Repartimiento and Spanish-Indian Economic Relations in Colonial Oaxaca, 1750–1821* (Stanford: Stanford University Press, 2000), 34–36. For the more traditional idea of the corregidor and his duties, see Haring, *Spanish Empire,* 129–132; for Haring's idea that "principales or chiefs" worked with corregidores to distribute native labor and collect tribute, 58–59. Baskes and Lockhart both seem to agree that from an institutional perspective the office of governor was analogous to that of the corregidor; see Lockhart, *Nahuas after the Conquest,* 33. An order from 1613 issued by Philip III suggests further the linkage between corregidores or alcaldes mayores and governors; see *Recopilación de leyes de los reynos de las indias, mandadas imprimir y publicar por la majestad Católica del rey don Carlos II, Nuestro Señor,* 3 tomos (Madrid: Gráficas Ultra, 1943), libro 4, título 9, ley 10, "Que Ningún gobernador Pueda Pedir, ni Solicitar votos, y al regularlos se hallen dos regidores." See also the discussion of financial guarantors in chapter 3 of this volume.

7. *Gibson, Aztecs,* 32–74, 81–82, 368–369. Gibson discusses the moments when the Audiencia ruled on conflicts between indigenous communities from 1530 to 1560. The common feature of the suits is that they involve either (1) directly or indirectly, an encomendero seeking to expand his holdings or enhance his claim to a subject community by promoting it to *cabecera* status (head town with jurisdictional authority over subject towns); or (2) individual indigenous communities using the courts to gain independence from a cabecera on their own within the

jurisdiction of a Spanish corregidor. The suits, in other words, involved parties outside the internal affairs of government. The case here seems to have involved only native peoples and thus needed additional justification to engage the Audiencia. Perhaps, as in the case of other Spanish institutions such as the municipal ayuntamiento, the jurisdictional issue was unclear.

8. AGN, Civil, v. 644, e. 1, fols. 1–3v, which includes the first petition and the subsequent *interrogatorio* (legal questionnaire). In Spanish judicial process, the interrogatorio was produced by the plaintiffs and then affirmed by a group of witnesses. Noble David Cook and Elizabeth Parma Cook argue rightly that the questionnaires, by design, presented "credible but flagrantly biased witnesses" that simply laid out the charges and provided sworn testimony to affirm those charges; see their *Good Faith and Truthful Ignorance: A Case of Transatlantic Bigamy* (Durham: Duke University Press, 1991), 54; for additional detail in the Mexican context, see Kellogg, *Law and the Transformation,* 8–13; and Gibson, *Aztecs,* 54.

9. For examples and a discussion of the political nature of the second Audiencia, see Ethelia Ruiz Medrano, *Reshaping New Spain: Government and Private Interests in the Colonial Bureaucracy, 1531–1550,* trans. Julia Constantino and Pauline Marmasse (Boulder: University of Colorado Press, 2006), 19–25; and the general discussion in *Instrucciones que los virreyes de Nueva España,* 228–230. Indigenous peoples seem to have engaged the courts more regularly; as one principal from "la ciudad de Mexico" noted in an undated letter to Philip II with some regret, they "spend the little [money] that they have" constantly suing other indigenous peoples and Spaniards alike. Though this is obviously an exaggeration in a plea to have tribute levels reduced, it is important that this observer sees excessive litigation as a distinctly new concept, but not absolutely foreign to indigenous understanding. He further suggests that when native peoples were "infidels" they engaged in court battles only irregularly and they were resolved quickly, and likely inexpensively; see "Memorial de las cosas en que los indios principales y naturales de la ciudad de México pedimos y suplicamos a su majestad del rey don Felipe nuestro señor sea servido de mandarnos desagraviar," in Joaquín García Icazbalceta, ed., *Nueva colección de documentos para la historia de México,* t. 4 (Nendeln: Kraus Reprint, 1971 [1886]), 185. I often update the spelling to "Felipe," which in documents from the sixteenth and seventeenth centuries usually appears as "Phelipe."

10. It should be noted that this was not unusual in the Spanish system.

11. This is probably *pulque,* but the document uses the word *vino* without the construction *de la tierra,* which in the mid-sixteenth century was used for pulque. For other references in this case, see AGN, Civil, v. 644, e. 1.

12. For *temazcalli,* see Karttunen, *Analytical Dictionary of Nahuatl,* 222, defined as "sweathouse for bathing." Note that Nahuatl generally did not indicate the plurality of nouns for inanimate things; see James Lockhart, *Nahuatl as Written: Lessons in Older Written Nahuatl, with Copious Examples and Texts* (Stanford: Stanford University Press, 2001), 51. See also Natalia Silva Prada, "El uso de los baños

temascales en la visión de dos médicos novohispanos. Estudio introductorio y transcripción documental de los informes de 1689," *Historia Mexicana* 52, no. 1 (2002), 7–10. Silva Prada uses the Hispanicized word *temascales* or the translation *estufas* when discussing these baths.

13. AGN, Civil, v. 644, e. 1, fol. 2v; the allegation charges that they were "ladrones y personas de mal vivir."

14. AGN, Civil, v. 644, e. 1, fol. 2: "lo séptimo es que los dichos alcaldes e regidores tienen de costumbre en los mitotes [ritual dances/celebrations] que se hacen sacristán e componen de unos trajes y devisas que eran costumbre de ponerse e vestirse aquellos viejos antepasados cuando iban a idolatrar e hacer sacrificio de alguna persona dando la muerte natural y esto no se debe consentir por solo el cargo que tienen." Gibson, "Aztec Nobility," 173–174, discusses the significant discovery of idolatry in the 1530s that involved the tlatonai of Texcoco, who possessed idols of Xipe Totec and Quetzalcoatl and was burned at the stake by Spanish authorities after being denounced by other indigenous nobles. Xipe Totec was important to the Tenochca as well. A temple to this deity was located in Moyotlan; see Carlos Javier González González, "Ubicación e importancia del templo de Xipe Totec en la parcialidad Tenochca de Moyotlan," *Estudios de Cultura Nahuatl* 36 (2005), 47–65. In the Yucatan, Franciscans under Bishop Diego de Landa were beginning to engage in campaigns against idolatry in the 1570s, but according to the most recent scholarship it began in the 1560s and likely was something that Audiencia officials would have been aware of in Mexico City; see John F. Chuchiak, "In Servito Dei: Fray Diego de Landa, the Franciscan Order, and the Return of Extirpation of Idolatry in the Colonial Diocese of Yucatan, 1573–1579," *The Americas* 61, no. 4 (2005), 613–635.

15. The reference to precontact burial must be dubious or a translation problem, because the Nahua traditionally cremated the remains of the dead; see the discussion in López Austin, *Human Body*, 314–331. The petitioners may be referring to the burial of the ashes that remained after cremation, which López Austin concedes was something practiced in the Mexico City region. Based on the observations of Sahagún, Pablo Escalante writes that bodies were burned after being wrapped in paper. This varied depending on the wealth of individuals, but sometimes offerings were made to venerate particularly wealthy or powerful people; see his "Un repertorio de actos rituales de los antiguos Nahuas," *Historia Mexicana* 35, no. 3 (1986), 383–385. López Austin also discusses the importance of ritual offerings to the dead, though often such things were burned to aid in the journey to the world of the dead. Bartolomé de Las Casas also refers to native internment of remains, in *Apologetica historia sumaria*, t. 2, ed. Edmundo O'Gorman (México: Universidad Autónoma Nacional de México, 1967), 458–465. Las Casas suggests that burial ceremonies were public and that shrouds worn by the dead depicted insignia of gods who might judge them (using obviously Christian language). His ideas are important because he implies a public ceremony to which the lawsuit might refer. See also

Stephanie Wood, "Adopted Saints: Christian Images in Nahua Testaments of Late Colonial Toluca," *The Americas* 47, no. 3 (1991), 268–270, though Wood's evidence comes from the Toluca Valley and focuses on a later period (eighteenth century).

16. AGN, Civil, v. 644, e. 1, fol. 2v.

17. Gibson, *Tlaxcala*, 120–121, writes that it was unclear to what extent governors had the right to take tribute directly from the caja for personal use. He cites an example in which don Diego de San Francisco Tehuetzquititzin took 3,000 pesos. Spanish officials commented on this transaction in *Instrucciones que los vireyes de Nueva España dejaron a sus sucesores*, t. 13, fol., 33, as did Chimalpahin, though I am relying on Gibson's citations for this information. The older Rafael García Granados, *Diccionario biográfico de historia antigua de Méjico*, t. 3 (México: Universidad Nacional Autónoma de México, 1995 [1952]), 204–205, makes no mention of the theft, citing Tezozomoc, *Crónica mexicayotl;* Chimalpahin, *Anales de Chimalpahin* (Paris: Maisonneuve et Ch. Leclerc, Editeurs, 1889), 241, 250, 267; and Sahagún, *Historia general de las cosas de la Nueva España*, t. 2 (Mexico, 1938), 282–283. Importantly, neither the *Crónica mexicayotl*, edited by León, nor the *CC*, v. 1, 171–175, makes any mention of the alleged impropriety.

18. AGN, Civil, v. 644, e. 1, fols. 2–3v. Chávez Orosco, *Códice Osuna*, 14–170, provides a partial transcription of this case and correctly links it directly to the Códice Osuna. My investigation and thorough study of this document confirms Chávez Orozco's insight, though, as I argue below, it corresponds specifically to a particular memorial filed by the governor and cabildo. See also "Carta del Licenciado Valderrama al Rey Don Felipe II, sobre asuntos de la gobernación de Nueva-España," in Don Luis Torres de Mendoza et al., eds., *Colección de documentos inéditos relativos al descubrimiento, conquista y organización de las antiguas posesiones Españolas en América y Oceania sacados de los archivos del reino y muy especialmente del de Indias*, t. 4 (Madrid: Frias y Compañía, 1865), 373–377.

19. AGN, Civil, v. 644, e. 1, fols. 3–12. The witnesses were, in order, Alonso de San Francisco, fifty-five years old from the barrio of San Juan Moyotlan; don Francisco Jiménez, from San Sebastián; Juan Sánchez, from the city of Mexico; Martín Guerrero, from the city of Mexico; and Miguel Pablo García, from San Pablo.

20. Kellogg, *Law and the Transformation*, 4, 24–33.

21. AGN, Civil, v. 644, e. 1, fol. 12v. The cabildo members, had they been detained, would have spent the trial in the Audiencia jail or in some kind of alternate custody befitting their status. Prisons were generally holding facilities for suspects during trial. The convicted generally did not receive a term of prison as part of their sentence; see Gabriel Haslip-Viera, *Crime and Punishment in Late Colonial Mexico City, 1692–1810* (Albuquerque: University of New Mexico Press, 1999), 95–96; Woodrow Borah, *Justice by Insurance: The General Indian Court of Colonial Mexico and the Legal Aides of the Half-Real* (Berkeley: University of California Press, 1983), 49–51, 232–234; Colin M. MacLachlan, *Criminal Justice in Eighteenth Century Mexico: A Study of the Real Tribunal de la Acordada* (Berkeley: University of

California Press, 1974), 72–76; and Michael Scardaville, "Crime and the Urban Poor: Mexico City in the Late Colonial Period" (Ph.D. diss., University of Florida, 1977), 275–277.

22. The notion of minimizing inequalities among unequal parties in conflict is well articulated in William B. Taylor, *Magistrates of the Sacred: Priests and Parishioners in Eighteenth-Century Mexico* (Stanford: Stanford University Press, 1997), 5–7, 13, 542 n. 7. For a thorough study of legal paternalism, see Borah, *Justice by Insurance*, 144–148; and Andrés Lira González, *El amparo colonial y el juicio de amparo México: Antecedentes novohispanos del juicio de amparo* (México: Fondo de Cultura Económica, 1971), 7, 16–36, 127–136.

23. Kellogg, *Law and the Transformation*, xxvii–xxix, lays out her principal argument, that Spanish institutions helped to transform the Mexica Tenochca by replacing traditional forms of justice indigenous to native culture. See also Brian Owensby, *Empire of Law and Indian Justice in Colonial Mexico* (Stanford: Stanford University Press, 2008), 18–48; and Owensby, "How Juan and Leonor Won Their Freedom: Litigation and Liberty in Seventeenth-Century Mexico," *Hispanic American Historical Review* 85, no. 1 (2005), 63–71.

24. AGN, Civil, v. 644, e. 1, fol. 15–15v; in the original Spanish, the emphasized phrase reads "por sus pasiones particulares y ambiciones."

25. AGN, Civil, v. 644, e. 1, fol. 17v; specifically, the document uses the construction "nobles desde siempre," literally, though awkwardly, "nobles from always."

26. AGN, Civil, v. 644, e. 1, fols. 15–17v.

27. It is important to note that, in the end, courts made their decisions on the basis of sound argument and the law and did not favor one side over the other. Royal justice, however, was paternalistic and tried to equalize inequalities among contending parties when they came into conflict. Both the cabildo and the plaintiffs seemed aware of this paternalism and offered arguments to position themselves to benefit from it.

28. AGN, Civil, v. 644, e. 1, fol. 173v. In this document, the governor, two alcaldes, twelve regidores, and some who had served in the past sign, for a total of eighteen signatures. As discussed below, many of the same people had served repeatedly on the cabildo in various positions during the entire time of the trial.

29. AGN, Civil, v. 644, e. 1, fol. 20; for more on the temascales, see Silva Prada, "El uso de los baños," 10–13.

30. See AGN, Civil, v. 644, e. 1, for the denial. For a related example in which it seems the cabildo did confiscate property for its private benefit, see the 1578 case, AGN, Tierras, v. 39, pt. 1, e. 2.

31. AGN, Civil, v. 644, e. 1, fol. 19v.

32. Haring, *Spanish Empire*, 141–142, remarks on the problem of contrasting interrogatorios, though he is speaking of residencia hearings. Both sides can see the same problem and testify under oath with absolute certainty to incompatible versions of the same events. It is clear that witnesses were chosen for the interrogatorios for their

sympathy with one side of the case. See also Owensby, *Empire of Law,* 173–179, which is relevant here in terms of legal procedure, even though he is discussing criminal rather than civil litigation.

33. AGN, Civil, v. 644, e. 1, fol. 35; the surname of the sixth witness, Talcuxialcalt, is likely misspelled in the document, though I am presenting it as written.

34. AGN, Civil, v. 644, e. 1, fols. 31v–33v. Though apparently not born into nobility, his literacy indicates that Melchior had attained a level of education that exceeded that of the great majority of the population. Biblioteca Nacional de México, Fondo Reservado (hereafter BNM-FR), ms. 1037, fols. 68v–70v; Fr. Juan Bautista, *Advertencias. Para los confessores de los naturales. Compuestas por el padre Ioan Baptista, de la orden del seraphico padre Sanct Fancisco, lector de Theologia, y guardian del convento de Sanctiago Tlatilulco: de la provincia de la Santo Evangelio* (México, 1600); Ileana Schmidt-Díaz de León, "El colegio seminario de Indios de San Gregorio y el desarrollo de la indianidad en el valle de México, 1586–1856" (Ph.D. diss., Tulane University, 2001); Susan Schroeder, "Jesuits, Nahuas, and the Good Death Society in Mexico City, 1710–1767," *Hispanic American Historical Review* 80, no. 1 (2001), 51–54; Pilar Gonzalbo, *Educación y colonización en la Nueva España, 1521–1821* (México: Universidad Pedagógica Nacional, 2001); Charles E. Dibble, "Sahagún's Historía," in Arthur J. O. Anderson and Charles E. Dibble, eds., *Florentine Codex: General History of the Things of New Spain* (Santa Fe and Salt Lake City: School of American Research and University of Utah Press, 1950–), 9; Emilio H. Quesada A., "Instituciones educativas novohispanas," in Isabel Tovar de Arechederra and Magdalena Mas, comps., *La muy noble y leal ciudad de México* (México: Universidad Iberoamericana, 1994), 130–132; Josefina Muriel, *La sociedad novohispana y sus colegios de niñas* (México: Universidad Nacional Autónoma de México, 1995), 28–36; and Robert Ricard, *The Spiritual Conquest of Mexico: An Essay on the Apostolate and the Evangelizing Methods of the Mendicant Orders in New Spain, 1523–1572,* trans. Leslie Byrd Simpson (Berkeley: University of California Press, 1966), 217–235. Indigenous elites had been chosen to receive education, first at the Franciscan Imperial College of Santa Cruz, founded in the 1530s in the northern parcialidad of Mexico Tlatelolco; for the most recent and in-depth study, see SilverMoon, "Imperial College." Later the Jesuit College of San Gregorio in the center of Mexico City would continue to educate native boys.

35. William F. Connell, "Emerging Ladino Spaces in the Parcialidades of Mexico City: Race, Identity and Indian Self-Government, 1564–1700" (Ph.D. diss., Tulane University, 2003), 70–73, esp. tab. 2.1.

36. Lockhart, *Nahuas after the Conquest,* 88–90, 138–139; Haskett, *Indigenous Rulers,* 30.

37. AGN, Civil, v. 644, e. 1, fols. 23–41v.

38. AGN, Civil, v. 644, e. 1, fols., 19, 32. This is mostly based on question two from the nineteen-question interrogatorio. Similar examples could be brought out with the other charges but would be redundant.

39. Rebellion was also a lingering concern of Spaniards, who worried about sedition constantly. Gerónimo López, a Mexico City region encomendero, wrote to

the king in 1545 to express his feeling that the potential for indigenous rebellion existed and would increase over time. Rumors of potential rebellion concerned many Spaniards, who wrote of their experiences in sixteenth-century Mexico City. The motif appeared in the 1599 account of Gonzalo Gómez de Cervantes, a Spanish alcalde in Mexico City. Gómez de Cervantes made a similar argument to that of López, claiming that native peoples allied themselves with lower-class groups in New Spain and with them existed as enemies who lived among loyal Spaniards waiting only for their moment to strike. Caro's speculations about indigenous rebellion germinating in the barrios of Mexico City likely struck the Audiencia ministers as credible; see Gerónimo López, "1545 Gerónimo López to the King on Native Policy," in Parry and Keith, *New Iberian World*, 447; Gonzalo Gómez de Cervantes, *La vida económica y social de Nueva España al finalizar del siglo XVI* (México: José Porrúa y Hijos, 1944 [1599]), 96–109; and J. I. Israel, *Race, Class and Politics in Colonial Mexico, 1610–1670* (New York: Oxford University Press, 1975), 33. Hoberman, *Mexico's Merchant Elite*, 155, is more skeptical about Gómez de Cervantes's credibility than Israel. See Lockhart, *Nahuas after the Conquest*, 441; and Schroeder, "Jesuits, Nahuas," 72–76, in which she argues that great divisions had always existed between noble native peoples and macehualtin; see also Baudot, *Utopia and History*, 44–49.

40. Restall, *Seven Myths*, 65–76. His commentary on what he calls the "Myth of Completion" was created when Spaniards stopped calling native people who continued to fight the wars of conquest combatants and began to call them rebels, thus making them implicitly subjects of the crown who rebelled against recognized authority. It seems, linguistically, that the indigenous government has cast the actions of political opponents in the same terms. See also Owensby, *Empire of Law*, 250–294.

41. Helen Nader, *The Mendoza Family in the Spanish Renaissance, 1350–1550* (New Brunswick: Rutgers University Press, 1979), 38–49; Nader, *Liberty in Absolutist Spain*, 77–79; and Joaquín Gimeno Casalduero, *La Imagen del monarca en la Castilla del siglo XVI. Pedro el cruel, Enrique II y Juan I* (Madrid: Revista de Occidente, 1972). In Nader's more recent work, *Liberty*, she discusses a method used by Enrique II to consolidate his political control—distributing pieces of the royal domain to win loyalty, particularly among the nobility.

42. Nader, *Liberty*, 81–83; Nader, *Mendoza Family*, 104–122; Bethany Aram, *Juana the Mad: Sovereignty and Dynasty in Renaissance Europe* (Baltimore: Johns Hopkins University Press, 2005), 17–20, 91–110; Peggy Liss, *Isabel the Queen: Life and Times* (Philadelphia: University of Pennsylvania Press, 2004), 54, 70–81; and Marvin Lunenfeld, *Keepers of the City: The Corregidores of Isabella I of Castile (1474–1504)* (Cambridge: Cambridge University Press, 1987), 3, 18–34.

43. The *Tenochca*, those from Tenochtitlan, is preferable here to the *Mexica* or *Nahua*. I am referring to the specific Nahua and Mexica who lived in the city of Mexico Tenochtitlan; see Carrasco, *Tenochca*, 2–5.

44. Carrasco, *Tenochca*, 8–9, 41–45.

45. Some Nahua sources and the subsequent interpretations by modern scholars provide contradictory accounts. Some of the inconsistency can be explained by the understanding that the Nahua sometimes manipulated their history to give themselves increased legitimacy. On the use of history and myth-making, see Gibson, *Aztecs*, 19–20; and Carrasco, *City of Sacrifice*, 59–60. For peri-odization of Mexico Tenochtitlan, see Berdan, *Aztecs*, 7–11. An in-depth analysis and description of Nahuatl annals or histories that also informed this discussion is Lockhart, *Nahuas after the Conquest*, 376–392. Lockhart is principally concerned with written annals composed in the postcontact period (Chimalpahin, Zapata y Mendoza, and Teçoçomoc) and notes the paucity of precontact sources that have survived. He does note that Chimalpahin indicates in his work that he based his descriptions of precontact events on pictorial sources. For an excellent discussion of the often contradictory primary accounts, see Susan Gillespie, *The Aztec Kings: The Construction of Rulership in Mexica History* (Tucson: University of Arizona Press, 1989), 10–18.

46. Carrasco, *Tenochca*, 42–44. Nezahualcoyotzin, like Itzcoatzin, replaced a tla-toani who the Tepanecs had allegedly killed. See also Chimalpahin, *Annals*, 129. Chimalpahin, according to the most recent work on his writings, states in reference to this event that "lord Chimalpopoca, who was ruler in Tenochtitlan, passed away, having ruled for twelve years; the Tepaneca came and killed him." Other sources say only that Chimalpopoca died in 1426 and do not provide further clarification; Rounds, "Dynastic Succession," 69–70. The version of Chimalpahin's writings referenced by Rounds is the 1889 *Anales Mexicanos*. The works of Chimalpahin have become in the years since Rounds wrote his article increasingly accessible. Carrasco, *Tenochca*, 41–49, and most other sources follow accounts of Chimalpahin on this event unavailable in 1980. In their edition of Chimalpahin, *Annals*, 129, Lockhart, Schroeder, and Namala contradict the account by Rounds, placing blame for the killing of Chimalpopoca on the Tepaneca; see also *CC* v. 1, 41 (Spanish summary), 129–133 (detailed account in Nahuatl); and Quiñones Keber, *Codex Telleriano-Remensis*, fols. 30v–33r, and commentary on 214–218, esp. 216.

47. Lockhart, *Nahuas after the Conquest*, 32–33; Rounds, "Dynastic Succession," 76–77. Rounds argues that a "Council of Four" that included the cihuacoatl, the "four closest advisors to the tlatoani," chose the successor who was then confirmed by other electors—a tightly controlled system of succession that guaranteed an experienced choice would emerge from the electoral process. This is confirmed by López Austin, *Human Body*, 398. It is also important to remember, as I discuss below, that a tlatoani often had many wives, though only the principal wife could bear future tlatoque. See Camilla Townsend, "Sex, Servitude and Politics," 369 n. 64, for discussion of primary wives and succession. According to Townsend the primary wife of the tlatoani became the legitimate heir. The position was not necessarily set in stone but could change with changing political allegiances. For more on the importance of women in their capacity to carry on the royal lineage, see Susan Schroeder, "First American Valentine: Nahua Courtship and Other

Aspects of Family Structuring in Mesoamerica," *Journal of Family History* 23, no. 4 (1998), 344–346. See also Las Casas, *Apologetica historia,* vol. 2, 406–407.

48. Rounds, "Dynastic Succession," 69–83.

49. Chimalpahin, *Annals,* 137, 136–137 n. 2. In 1541, governor don Diego Tehuetzquititzin, according to Chimalpahin, fought and defeated the Xochipilteca, as his "first notable deed as ruler." He is vague on detail, but the editors suggest this mimicked a precontact process of "winning a battle or taking captives, but also any other ostentatious deed." Was this a governor acting as though he were a tlatoani, proving himself through the suppression of a rebellion? Chimalpahin does not seem to provide sufficient detail to say for certain. Inasmuch as this event happened before Chimalpahin began to write his annals, it is likely based on another written source, as was customary in Nahua annals; see Lockhart, *Nahuas after the Conquest,* 380.

50. Though Santa María had been an alcalde in Mexico Tenochtitlan, he appears to have been regarded with some antipathy by his peers, according to Schroeder, Lockhart, and Namala; see Chimalpahin, *Annals,* 139, n. 2. Santa María became governor on 30 October 1563, more than one year after the death of his predecessor; see Charles E. Dibble, ed., *Codice Aubin* (México: José Porrúa Turanza, 1963), 73–75 (pp. 103–104).

51. Chimalpahin, *Annals,* 139.

52. Lockhart, *Nahuas after the Conquest,* 32; Gibson, *Aztecs,* 175–176.

53. AGN, Civil, v. 644, e. 1, fols. 173–188.

54. Schroeder, *Chimalpahin,* 191; Chimalpahin, *Annals,* 139. Note that Chimalpahin does not use the term *quauhtlatoani* here to describe Jiménez but rather the loanwords *juez gouernador.*

55. There is some uncertainty about the course of events and contradictory information in different sources; see Chimalpahin, *Annals,* 141; Dibble, *Códice Aubin,* 83 (p. 114); and Lockhart, *Nahuas after the Conquest,* 351–352, esp. tab. 8.8. See also the discussion in chapter 2. In addition, there were extended periods in which Jiménez was absent from the city; see *CC,* v. 2, 43. Chimalpahin has conflicting information on his title; in *Annals,* 139, he lists him as a judge-governor, but on 147 he was only a judge. See also Chimalpahin, *Las ocho relaciones,* 235, where he is referred to as a "the first judge of Tenochtitlan" who came at a time when "it began in the great city of Mexico the rule of the judge-governors."

56. Chimalpahin, *Annals,* 139, also reported in Dibble, *Codice Aubin,* 77–80 (pp. 107, 109). Avila and González de Alvarado were Spaniards caught up in a great conspiracy to assert the rights of conquistadores. Gibson notes that it is unusual that Nahua annalists would mention the details of the stories, but perhaps the political conflict in Tenochtitlan inspired a connection; see Gibson, *Aztecs,* 62. See John F. Schwaller, "The Early Life of Luis de Velasco, the Younger: The Future Viceroy as a Boy and Young Man," *Estudios de Historia Novohispana* 29 (2003), 41–44, for a more detailed discussion of the conspiracy.

57. Some evidence shows that in 1572 he was acting governor before he officially took the title of governor; see AGN, Tierras, v. 20, pt. 1, e. 2. In *Annals,* 141,

Chimalpahin reports that Valeriano was related to the tlatoani line by way of marriage, a son-in-law of Huanitzin (1538–41) but from Azcapotzalco. Gibson, *Aztecs*, 169–170, confirms this assertion. See also the discussion in Schroeder, *Chimalpahin*, 180–186, and chapter 2 of this volume.

58. AGN, Civil, v. 644, e.1, fols. 95–108; Chimalpahin, *Annals*, 137. Chimalpahin notes the absence of a governor, recognizing the passing of don Diego de San Francisco Tehuetzquititzin in 1554 and the ascension of don Cristóbal de Guzmán Cecetzin in 1557, but does not mention don Esteban de Guzmán. The Codex Aubin and the annals of Tezozomoc also fail to mention don Esteban de Guzmán, suggesting that he was seen as transitional and temporary; see *CC*, v. 2, 173–175, 177. When discussing the regular succession, Chimalpahin's version of Teçoçomoc does not mention don Esteban de Guzmán, but he notes his presence later when discussing that nonnoble rulers from other altepetl came to rule Tenochtitlan. See also Lockhart, *Nahuas after the Conquest*, 34, tab. 2.1.

59. AGN, Civil, v. 644, e. 1, fol. 44; in a petition filed in 1565, the plaintiffs allege it had been sixteen years of abuse, which would have placed the earliest complaints in the reign of don Diego de San Francisco Tehuetzquititzin. The documentation provided to detail the expenses owed but not paid by the cabildo, however, extend back only to 1555. This likely means that this early petition, which precedes the memorial that provides detailed evidence to support the complaint, may have misstated the time period.

60. AGN, Civil, v. 644, e. 1, fol. 44. The term *mayordomo*, a cognate with the English word "majordomo," literally means "head steward" and was an ill-defined office on the secular cabildo. It is better understood, as Lockhart describes in his work, as an office on the ecclesiastical cabildo; see his *Nahuas after the Conquest*, 42, 223–229. See also Gibson, *Aztecs*, 181–182, 513 n. 99. It is more often associated with someone who serves as an administrator or overseer, as, for example, "doctor Pedro López, mayordomo del hospital de San Lázaro," who in his official capacity asked for permission to allow the poor in his care to beg in front of the church so that they could sustain themselves; AGN, Indios, v. 6, pt. 1, e. 1286, fol. 359. The ellipses in the petition quotation remove date references. The petition was written after 5 April 1565 yet claims that indigenous government began in 1549, sixteen years before (though this is clearly counterfactual). It is unclear what specifically happened sixteen years earlier. The petitioners might mean that alcaldes were first elected then or that the indigenous government began to be abusive then (a plausible conclusion given other circumstantial evidence about 1549). The second ellipsis removes the phrase "from the present since 1555," which is the first year that the evidence that follows the petition included as they show what they and others were required to collect and deliver to the indigenous government in tribute. For the alleged trouble in 1549, see note 17 above, and Gibson, *Tlaxcala*, 120–121.

61. AGN, Civil, v. 644, e. 1, fols. 46–56v. This section is titled "Memoria de las obras que habemos contribuido en las obras de comunidad" ("accounting of the labor and works that we have contributed to the to the community"). Repartimiento

labor derived from a system that already existed in Nahua society called the *coate-quitl* in which tributary natives on a rotational basis provided labor as part of their taxation. The New Laws of 1542 prohibited the use of native labor for personal service, which eventually restricted the use of such labor to public works projects (e.g., street paving and cleaning drainage canals). See, Lockhart, *Nahuas after the Conquest*, 431; and for the New Laws and their reforms relative to repartimiento, see Lesley Byrd Simpson, *The Encomienda in New Spain: The Beginning of Spanish Mexico*, reprint ed. (Berkeley: University of California Press), 123–144.

62. AGN, Civil, v. 644, e. 1, fols. 59, 89. For the dates of rule, see Chimalpahin, *Annals*, 139–141.

63. Sander Spanoghe, "Los salarios dentro del systema del repartimiento forzado en el valle de México, 1549–1632," *Anuario de Esudios Americanos* 54, no. 1 (1997), 43–64.

64. AGN, Civil, v. 644, e. 1, fol. 80–81v.

65. AGN, Civil, v. 644, e. 1, fol. 80–81v.

66. *Gibson, Aztecs*, 167–175; Lockhart, *Nahuas after the Conquest*, 35–40.

67. Gibson, "Rotation of Alcaldes," 217–220.

68. Gibson, "Rotation of Alcaldes," 217–220; see also Haskett, *Indigenous Rulers*, 30. Haskett's work, focused on Cuernavaca, adds to Gibson's discussion by demonstrating that royal law eventually limited the franchise to former officeholders only. If this practice applied in Mexico Tenochtitlan, then one could see how only certain individuals might restrict access to cabildo positions. See also the discussion in Horn, *Postconquest Coyoacan*, 57–58, on office rotation in Coyoacan. Her example suggests also that "a relatively small group of experienced officials" dominated the cabildo. See also Altman, *Transatlantic Ties*, for comments on office rotation in the Spanish cabildo in Puebla.

69. AGN, Civil, v. 644, e. 1, fols. 46–50v; see also Gibson, "Rotation of Alcaldes," 217–223.

70. Gibson, "Rotation of Alcaldes," 220.

71. AGN, Civil, v. 644, e. 1; AGN, Tierras, v. 39, pt. l, e. 2; AGN, Tierras, v. 54, e. 9. Cano served as alguacil on several occasions. Unfortunately, a full list of his appointments does not exist. Additionally, other offices were available for indigenous leaders, like those on the ecclesiastical cabildo and cofradía; such offices cannot be reliably reconstructed either. For examples, see Hasket, *Indigenous Rulers*, chap. 4, for discussion of other indigenous offices (e.g., *fiscal, teopantopile, alcaldes de doctrina*) that fell outside of the secular cabildo. Native principales had many opportunities in the church as well as in secular government; see Jonathan Truitt, "Nahuas and Catholicism in Mexico Tenochtitlan: Religious Faith and Practice and La Capilla de San Josef de los Naturales, 1523–1700" (Ph.D. diss., Tulane University, 2008).

72. AGN, Tierras, v. 56, e. 8.

73. AGN, Civil, v. 644, e. 1; AGN, Tierras, v. 38, e. 2, fol. 34.

74. For examples of this in practice, see AGN, Tierras, v. 2776, e. 17, fol. 18; AGN, Indios, v. 32, e. 79, fols. 83v–84v; AGN, Indios, v. 31, e. 8, fols. 7–8. Lockhart,

Nahuas after the Conquest, 49, raises this issue and adds that the first instance of this usage came in a Nahuatl document from 1654. The earliest for Mexico City that I have come across is a little earlier, in a Nahuatl document dated 1643 that lists witnesses in a land dispute: "Gaspar Gregorio [and] don Juan Luis allds [alcaldes] pas[ad]o[s]"; see AGN, Tierras, v. 3663, e. 4, fol. 65v.

75. Gibson, "Rotation of Alcaldes," 212; see also *Recopilación de leyes,* lib. 4, tit. 9, ley 13. By rotating skillfully, indigenous elites met the no-reelection requirement mandated by Spanish law. Though not written into the Recopilación until 1609, this law prohibited individuals from seeking reelection to the same office. The law singled out alcaldes, who once elected had to wait a minimum of three years before seeking another term. Regidores had to allow two years between terms of office. Governors may have been motivated by the high salary, but it seems that much more was at stake, particularly when considering that those from the royal lineage already possessed great material wealth. Gibson has shown that the governor of Mexico Tenochtitlan earned an annual salary of 400 pesos, which suggests the status of the position; see *Aztecs,* 186, tab. 14. See also the discussion of salaries in Kevin Terraciano, *The Mixtecs of Colonial Oaxaca: Ñudzahui History, Sixteenth through Eighteenth Centuries* (Stanford, Calif.: Stanford University Press, 2001), 185–186, in which he argues that a high salary may have motivated contenders to seek the office. The office remained highly sought after, even when dismal tribute receipts often forced governors into prison for debt (see chapters 3 and 4). Gibson's data derive from circumstances that are not well contextualized and are too few to allow comparisons. He argues that a "rough index of a town's prestige" can be gleaned from the salary of its governor. Under such an assumption, Tlatelolco seems to have lost out significantly; see AGN, Indios, v. 15, e. 134, fols. 197–198 (1649), where the salary for the governor of Mexico Tlatelolco was 100 pesos de oro común (a third of the salary listed by Gibson for 1590 in Tlatelolco) and subject to seizure should he fail to collect tribute sufficiently. A governor's salary was likely set to the expected tribute. In 1659 the governor of Mexico Tenochtitlan's salary was also 100 pesos; see AGN, Indios, v. 23, e. 370, fol. 344.

76. For manipulation and the politics of the Spanish cabildo, see Hoberman, *Mexico's Merchant Elite,* 156–160; and Altman, *Transatlantic Ties.* Gibson observed that, even though some of the 1564 plaintiffs accused the cabildo of illegal election methods, they never condemned the "formal patterned rotational system involving *alcaldes* and their *barrios,*" suggesting that they did not see a problem with the rotation system. The allegations from the suit also indicate that those who raised the complaint against the cabildo acknowledged and accepted the existence of a formal rotational system. Evidence from the lawsuit made it possible for Gibson to reconstruct who occupied the position of alcalde on the cabildos from 1555 to 1565, revealing a profoundly sophisticated political culture that worked to provide representation for each of the four subdivisions of the altepetl. This evidence did not come from petitions designed to expose that system but

from documents produced by the cabildo itself. Cabildo members had nothing to hide; they released information that detailed the system of rotation without comment or any visible attempt to obscure it. Those who sued the cabildo also made no allegation to challenge the legitimacy of this system; they only remarked on its lack of transparency. Though secretive in nature, the practice seems to have been acceptable; see Gibson, "Rotation of Alcaldes," 215–216. See also AGN, Civil, v. 644, e. 1, fols. 145–173v; the document, titled "Memorial de Gastos," was produced by the cabildo to show they had paid repartimiento laborers for service to the cabildo and town.

77. See Christoph Rosenmüller, *Patrons, Partisans, and Palace Intrigues: The Court and Society in Colonial Mexico* (Calgary: University of Calgary Press, 2008), 4–6, for the subtle kinds of patronage that existed in Mexico in the sixteenth and seventeenth centuries, and 53–78 for the capacity of a viceroy to build a patronage network through appointments, although Rosenmüller is referring specifically to the second Viceroy Alburquerque (r. 1702–10).

78. AGN, Civil, v. 644, e. 1, fols. 2v–3 (fourteenth allegation, mislabeled in the document as "treceno" allegation); partially quoted in Gibson, "Rotation of Alcaldes," 215–216.

79. AGN, Civil, v. 644, e. 1, fol. 7–7v.

80. AGN, Civil, v. 644, e. 1. fol. 7–7v, from the testimony of don Francisco Jiménez in which he alleges that before the election the alcaldes and regidores solicited votes for their candidates and thus rigged the election by influencing voters.

81. Chimalpahin, *Las ocho relaciones,* t. 2, 211; this assumes that don Diego de San Francisco Tehuetzquititzin and don Diego de Alvarado Huanitzin were brothers, a conclusion not directly supported by this passage.

82. Chimalpahin, *Las ocho relaciones,* t. 2, 199, 201. No obvious familial relationship existed between don Cristóbal and don Esteban, and don Esteban left office and returned to Xochimilco, obviously still alive.

83. Quiñones Keber, *Codex Telleriano-Remensis,* fols. 48–50, and the commentary by the editors, 239–240; see also the transcriptions, 276–277. The editors lament that in 1555 the "main artist of the manuscript ceased his work on the historical section," which also ended the detailed pictographic evidence. After 1555, only the Spanish text remains. The Codex Telleriano-Remensis says little about political succession, noting the death and replacement of governors sometimes, without commenting upon the circumstances. The editor provides some context but, more important, interprets the pictorial images. These images are limited; for example the codex chronicles the succession that began in 1536 when Xochiquentzin no longer served and then indicates only that Huanitzin took over the rulership. The codex places the event in 1536 and does not mention Huanitzin in 1538 when he became governor; see fols. 44v–45v, and the editorial commentary, 235–237. See also the discussion in Rounds, "Dynastic Succession," 76–77, on the council of four. The succession between don Esteban de Guzmán and don Cristóbal de Guzmán

appears to follow the pattern of early succession in which a nondynastic ruler stands in while the political process of selecting a new ruler takes place. Choosing the line that descended from don Diego de Alvarado Huanitzin seems to have taken considerable negotiation and may be behind the troubling succession in 1564. See Chimalpahin, *Annals,* 137–139, where he establishes that don Cristóbal de Guzmán descended from Huanitzin.

84. Tezozomoc, *Cronica mexicayotl,* paras. 361–364; see also *CC,* v. 1, 99–105.

85. Schroeder, *Chimalpahin,* 174–180.

86. It is possible that don Luis de Santa María competed for succession—both would have had legitimate claim. He served on the cabildo under don Cristóbal de Guzmán. They were not brothers, however. Cecetzin was the son of Huanitzin, whereas Santa María was the son of former tlatoani Ahuitzotzin (r. 1486–1502) and brother of Quauhtemoctzin. See Chimalpahin, *Las ocho relaciones,* 221–223; Chimalpahin, *Annals,* 131, 133; and Rounds, "Dynastic Succession," 68, fig. 3.1.

87. It should be expected that natives would understand Spanish institutions through their own memories and traditions; see Owensby, *Empire of Law,* 40–48, 153, in which he notes how individual native peoples may have adapted and incorporated Spanish legal culture and how words used by the Nahua reflected their legal understanding. For further analysis, see Burkhart, *Slippery Earth,* 28–31, 87–129.

88. AGN, Civil, v. 644, e. 1, fol. 3, allegation 18, raises the issue of common cause, suggesting that the government had abused native peoples for years. Although they made no direct reference to the repartimiento laborers, one of the main groups involved in the second phase of the suit was the zacateros, and a zacatero helped shape the first set of charges.

89. AGN, Civil, v. 644, e. 1, fol. 128, viceregal order signed by Velasco, 17 March 1564.

90. AGN, Civil, v. 644, e. 1, fols. 128–145. Antonio Rumeu de Armas, *Código del trabajo del indigena Americano* (Madrid: Ediciones Cultura Hispánica, 1953), 10–11, 37–46; Silvio Zavala, *La encomienda Indiana,* 2nd ed. (México: Editorial Porrúa, 1973), 414, 420–421, 441–444, 462–465; 490–493; Borah, *Justice by Insurance,* 28–37, 56–58; Lewis Hanke, *The Spanish Struggles for Justice in the Conquest of America* (Boston: Little, Brown, 1965), 90–105. Paying native peoples for repartimiento labor was a rather recent innovation in the 1550s. Before the New Laws of 1542, encomenderos could force native peoples to perform personal service without compensation. The crown and viceregal government of New Spain had even more recently, in 1549, issued an order that required employers to pay for indigenous labor, repartimiento or free-wage. Viceroy Velasco, by 1555, made clear through issued orders that the indigenous government had to pay repartimiento workers.

91. AGN, Civil, v. 644, e. 1, and Schroeder, *Chimalpahin,* 139–143.

92. AGN, Civil, v. 644, e. 1, fol. 138–138v. Gibson, *Aztecs,* 27, 473–474 n. 79, discusses the first flood of the city. This one was smaller than the devastating flood of 1629. Chimalpahin, *Las ocho relaciones,* 209, reported that on 17 September 1555,

"the rains began that flooded us in Mexico. Many houses fell and others had to be abandoned because they were flooded." Indigenous officials oversaw the digging and establishing of drainage canals and made improvements to the aqueduct that supplied the city with water with the hope of mitigating the danger of floods and improving their chances of surviving the next inundation

93. AGN, Civil, v. 644, e. 1, fols. 44–45.

94. AGN, Civil, v. 644, e. 1, fol. 51e, assigned number 173; his statement in Spanish reads, "indio mercader natural e vecino esta ciudad ocho años [edad de] diez y siete años a esta parte poco mas o menos no le tocan los generales y mediante de interprete dijo que: este testigo ha visto los capítulos contenidos que les sabe que ha visto que el dicho gobernador, alcaldes y regidores e principales a esta ciudad han hecho traer a los indios de los cuatro barrios de mi parte grande cantidad de materiales cal, piedra, madera e otras cosas que lo han tenido a su costa y sin que por ello las pagasen nada e que se remite o los que se capítulos e cuenta que de lo dicho."

95. AGN, Civil, v. 644, e. 1, for the total debt allegedly owed to the community.

96. *Zacatl* or *zacate* is sometimes glossed as "grass" or "hay" in English, though this translation makes it difficult to understand why the reed would have a construction use and was purportedly used as an additive in pulque; see Karttunen, *Analytical Dictionary*, 345.

97. AGN, Civil, v. 644, e. 1, fols. 61v–62. Cacao beans, the very same from which chocolate is made, were used as a form of currency in native society. Natives continued to use cacao into the late sixteenth century; see Lockhart, *Nahuas after the Conquest*, 177–179.

98. In the standard payment system, teams of workers and those in charge of ferrying the materials to the city usually bore the expense of labor and materials until the end of a work week. At that time the workers visited a paymaster (*contador*) of the treasury for their wages and reimbursement of expenses. The documents spell out in detail the exact accounting of all wages and expenses, just as one might expect in a modern account of government spending. Though tributary workers received a lower wage—generally two-thirds of the amount free-wage laborers received—all expected payment in cash. For the systematic process of payment and common schedules, see AGN, Civil, v. 644, e. 1, fols. 43–58; for later examples of these types of pay arrangements, see Archivo Historico de la Ciudad de México (hereafter AHCM), Empedrados, v. 880, e. 13, fol. 6; AHCM, Obras Públicas en General, v. 1509A, e. 1, fols. 1–5. The latter are examples from the late seventeenth century but better show the manner in which indigenous workers received wages.

99. AGN, Civil, v. 644, e. 1, fol. 107v: "Yten se les pone y cargo por los susodichos alcaldes que Pedro Yonotl Indio servió en casa del señor visorrey ocho dias por mandado de los alcaldes en el servicio de el y no le dieron ni pagaron cosa alguna y los dichos regidores indicaron a los tepixques a cobrar del mayordomo del dicho señor visorrey el trabajo y jornal."

100. AGN, Civil, v. 644, e. 1. For additional information on the tepixque, see Gibson, *Aztecs*, 206–207; Lockhart, *Nahuas after the Conquest*, 43–44.

101. See Zavala, *La encomienda*, 1, ch. 2. See also Simpson, *Encomienda in New Spain*, 109–110; Hanke, *Spanish Struggles*, 86–91; and José Miranda, *El tributo indígena en la Nueva España durante el siglo xvi* (México: El Colegio de México, 1952), 99–106.

102. Robert Haskett, "'Our Suffering with the Taxco Tribute': Involuntary Mine Labor and Indigenous Society in Central New Spain," *Hispanic American Historical Review* 71, no. 3 (1992), 456–459.

103. Lockhart, *Nahuas after the Conquest*, 96–107. No principal had personal experience serving as such a laborer to recount. The testimony that accompanies the allegations is divided up into a series of documents presented by different groups of workers. One set presents the arguments made by those who brought zacate into the city as part of their repartimiento service. AGN, Civil, v. 644, e. 1, fol. np (this is a libretto, for lack of a better term, that is included in the case file but has a different numbering system; appears after 79v). The zacateros provided an unusual, elaborate, and lengthy interrogatorio. In this questionnaire, unlike others found in the documentation, each witness made a statement following a posed question. Rather than identify each individual by name in each case, all witnesses were identified by a number. Only eight statements appear in the trial brief, numbered 176 to 183. Though possible, it seems unlikely that the total number of witnesses reached or exceeded 183. Each number corresponds to one witness and seems to have been an innovation in taking witness statements. Some witnesses provided only brief affirmations of the question. In response to the fourth question, which asked him if he performed labor for which he was not paid, witness 178, Miguel Garcia Chimalaca, stated, "The statements made in the question are true regarding the said payments." Others gave detailed statements that extended and elaborated, going beyond the scope of the question. Like the interrogatorios discussed above, all witnesses verified the allegations made in the questions. The ambiguous and highly unusual numbering system may imply that others not included also testified. Nothing beyond pure speculation exists to support such a claim. Eight statements make for unnecessary redundancy; 180 or so would have been torturous and possibly damaging to a case. Spanish legal rules limited the number of witnesses a litigant could present to thirty. For more on the legal rules of testimony, see Kellogg, *Law and the Transformation*, 33–35; and Borah, *Justice by Insurance*, 54.

104. AGN, Civil, v. 644, e. 1, fol. 121.

105. AGN, Civil, v. 644, e. 1, fol. 121v.

106. AGN, Civil, v. 644, e. 1, fol. 126v.

107. AGN, Civil, v. 644, e. 1, fols. 121–127, 145–173, 190–191. The case includes petitions between the sections from both sides of the suit. This is a large suit, and it involves a series of drawn-out and elaborate allegations and responses. The interrogatorio from the craftsmen appears on 176–184 and was designed to state

definitively the important allegations made earlier in the suit and to refine their message. This is in part a response to the evidence provided by the cabildo.

108. Haring, *Spanish Empire*, 138–143, provides a helpful definition of the residencia and a discussion of its usefulness in promoting good government. He also sees the potential manipulation of the hearing by enemies of an official, which could be particularly damaging due to the public nature of the inquiry. Haring does not comment on indigenous residencias.

109. AGN, Civil, v. 644, e. 1, fol. 190. The original Nahuatl version, which does not include the sworn statement from Miguel Díaz, appears on fol. 191, the entire residencia on fols. 189v–191, the Nahuatl original in the last folio.

110. AGN, Civil, v. 644, e. 1, fols. 59, 89.

111. On the issue of proof, see Owensby, *Empire of Law*, 176–210.

112. Dibble, *Codice Aubin*, 72–73 (p. 101). Dibble's translation into Spanish suggests that he was appointed *señor*. The Nahuatl gloss uses the phrase *motlatocatlallito tlatilolco*, which implies that he took the governorship or "was installed as ruler," using a specific form of the verb *tlahtocatlalia*. Other uses of *motlatocatlallito* appear in alphabetic texts; see Tezozomoc, *Cronica Mexicayotl*, 103 (para. 175). The root word variant form *tlatocatlalli* refers to the lands pertaining to the tlatoani or the tecpan, as discussed in Lockhart, *Nahuas after the Conquest*, 156. For a broader discussion of the term in reference to the governorship, see Chimalpahin, *Annals*, 138 n. 1; see also *CC*, v. 1, 118–119, for an example, see the 1391 assent to authority of Huitzilihuitl.

113. AGN, Civil, v. 644, e. 1, fols. 121–124, for the petition, and 145–173v for the memorial.

114. AGN, Civil, v. 644, e. 1, fols. 145–173v; see also the Codíce Osuna.

115. AGN, Civil, v. 644, e. 1, fol. 126v.

116. AGN, Civil, v. 644, e. 1, fols. 189–189v.

117. AGN, Civil, v. 644, e. 1, fols. 175–184v. See also AGN, Indios, v. 5, e. 295, fol. 148v, for *mandón* and *tepixque* used interchangeably. *Tepixque* later becomes *merino*, which was a minor post affiliated with the altepetl or calpolli; see Lockhart, *Nahuas after the Conquest*, 610; and Gibson, *Aztecs*, 605. According to Lockhart and Gibson, the Nahuatl word from which this derives is *tepixqui*, meaning literally "he who guards or keeps the people." For the tepixqui or merinos' role in tribute collection, see Gibson, *Aztecs*, 206–207; and Teresa Rojas Rabiela, "La ogranización del trabajo para las obras públicas: El coatequitl y las cuadrillas de trabajadores," in Elsa Cecilia Frost, Michael C. Meyer, and Josefina Zoraída Vázquez, eds., *El trabajo y los trabajadores en la historia de México* (México: El Colegio de México y University of Arizona Press, 1979), 53–60.

118. Christina M. Elson and R. Alan Covey, eds., *Intermediate Elites in Pre-Columbian States and Empires* (Tucson: University of Arizona Press, 2006), 4–6. Frances Berdan has written about intermediary elites in this same volume and suggests that, despite the complexities of Mexica politics before and after the

conquest, tlatoque had to rely on the assistance of networks of nobles inside and outside the altepetl to forge consensus, a far more useful tool than the military one many commentators use to explain political action in the Nahua world. This reliance facilitated the empowerment of people within Tenochtitlan who supported the tlatoque. Without that support, Berdan observed, the intermediaries could bring down a ruler. Berdan's insights also suggest that first the Spanish conquest and then the arrival of Spanish institutions provided further opportunities for inter-mediaries to advance their political position; see her contribution to the above cited volume titled, "The Role of Provincial Elites in the Aztec Empire," 154–165.

119. AGN, Civil, v. 644, e. 1, fol. 187.

120. AGN, Civil, v. 644, e. 1, fol. 192v. The petition dated July 1568 is found on an unnumbered folio between fols. 173 and 174 in the case file. See also Chimalpahin, *Annals*, 139, who notes that in 1568 Viceroy don Gaspar de Peralta left office and was replaced by don Martín Enríquez.

121. Schroeder, *Chimalpahin*, 75–79, 162–188. Chalco and Tetzcoco had unusual succession patterns as well.

122. See also the discussion of Valeriano in SilverMoon, "Imperial College of Tlatelolco," 43–144; and *Gibson, Aztecs*, 169–170. Valeriano worked with the Franciscan scholars frey Bernardino de Sahagún and Juan de Torquemada. He also married well, choosing one of former governor and descendent of the royal line Huanitzin's daughters (doña Isabel), according to Teçoçomoc, which likely gave his heirs political advantage; see Tezozomoc, *Cronica mexicayotl*, para. 356. Don Antonio Valeriano the younger was governor (r. 1620–24) and was the grandson of don Antonio Valeriano, governor from 1573 to 1599. See AGN, Indios, v. 9, e. 272, fol. 132v; and AGN, Archivo Historico de Hacienda, v. 1418, e. 28, fols. 400–403. In 1634 a former governor mentioned him; see AGN, Tierras, v. 1720, e. 7, fol. 54, and also noted that he was named governor in December 1620.

CHAPTER 2

Epigraph. The quotation translates as "your most loving, but unworthy, Antonio Valeriano" and comes from a letter he wrote to fray Juan Bautista, a Franciscan with whom Valeriano had a deep and enduring friendship. Bautista authored the *Sermonario en lengua mexicana.* See Ricard, *Spiritual Conquest of Mexico*, 223.

1. A significant literature exists for the study of Valeriano, but unfortunately it is dominated by the discussion of his alleged authorship of the Nican Mopohua, the Nahuatl chronicle of the Guadalupe story. See the abbreviated commentary on Valeriano and Our Lady of Guadalupe below. Valeriano is discussed in a variety of secondary works: Gibson, *Aztecs*, 169–170, 175–176, 382; Lockhart, *Nahuas after the Conquest*, 34 (tab. 2.1), 351–352; Stafford Poole, *Our Lady of Guadalupe: The Origins and Sources of a Mexican National Symbol, 1531–1797* (Tucson: University of Arizona Press, 1995), 83–84, 156–170; Ricard, *Spiritual Conquest*, 41–44, 222–224; Karttunen, "From Courtyard to the Seat of Government," 113–120; Karttunen, "Cuicapixqueh:

Antonio Valeriano, Juan Bautista de Pomar, and Nahuatl Poetry," *Latin American Literatures Journal* 11, no. 1 (1995), 4–20; Schroeder, "Jesuits, Nahuas, 52–53; Miguel León-Portilla, *Bernardino de Sahagún: Pionero de la antropología* (México: Universidad Nacional Autónoma de México, 1999), 93–94, 121–124; and extensively in Silver-Moon, "Imperial College," 153–184.

The primary material is extensive: Sahagún, *Florentine Codex* 12, eds. and trans. Arthur J. O. Anderson and Charles E. Dibble; Chimalpahin, *Las ocho relaciones;* Chimalpahin, *Annals;* Tezozomoc, *Crónica mexicayotl;* Francisco Cervantes de Salazar, *México en 1554: Tres diálogos latinos que Francisco Cervantes de Salazar escribió e imprimió en México en dicho año,* ed. and trans. J. García Icazbalceta (México: Andrade y Morales, 1875); and Fray Juan Bautista, *Serminario en Lengua Mexicana* (México: Casa de Diego López Davalos, 1606), cited in Karttunen, "Cuicapixqueh." There are additional primary materials, including those in edited collections: "Códice de Tlatelolco," in Joaquín García Icazbalceta, ed., *Nueva colección de documentos para la historia de México,* t. 5 (Nendeln: Kraus Reprint, 1971 [1886]), 241–271, and in the same collection, "Carta para S. M., en nombre del provincial y definidores en favor de la escuela de san Francisco de México y del colegio de Tlatelulco," t. 4, 176–181.

2. Chimalpahin, *Annals,* 147, emphasizes that Jiménez was only a judge, though he claims on 139 that he held the title of judge-governor. See the discussion in chapter 1 (p. 36) that Jiménez is better understood as an interim ruler (quauhtlatoani). See also *CC,* v. 1, 42–43, and Tezozomoc, *Crónica mexicayotl,* 175–176, para. 370, where Teçoçomoc calls Jiménez a judge-governor but, to further complicate matters, compares his ascension to this high office with that of Esteban de Guzmán, who took the title of judge because he was from Xochimilco and not Tenochca. *CC,* v. 1, clarifies the discussion with a more informed and detailed transcription based on Chimalpahin's work on the Teçoçomoc text. It is possible that the conflation of terms may come from Chimalpahin's use of Teçoçomoc's work. See also Chimalpahin, *Las ocho relaciones,* t. 2, 235, for additional detail from the Rafael Tena edition.

3. See the appendix, which lists the governors and their terms in office.

4. Where such evidence might be in the AGN or AGI, however, is unclear. Generally such materials are found in Ramo de Indios, the summaries from the Juzgado General de los Indios (General Indian Court), which had yet to be created in 1568 (see chapter 3).

5. Chimalpahin discusses the mestizos integrated into royal lineages at some length; see *Las ocho relaciones,* t. 2, 229–233. I follow Anderson and Schroeder, who write "Teçoçomoc," which conforms to the way his name is written in Nahuatl texts, rather than the modern orthography "Tezozomoc." For further discussion, see Lockhart, *Nahuas after the Conquest,* 591, n. 43.

6. See Chimalpahin, *Las ocho relaciones,* t. 2, 219–221, for the transition to cash tribute that followed the *visita* (general inspection) of don Jerónimo de Valderrama. See also Tulane University, Latin American Library, France V. Scholes Collection,

"Libro de papeles que se han hallado en el oficio de la secretaría del consejo real de las indias tocantes a tasaciones de tributos de provincias y pueblos y otras materias" [AGI, Audiencia de México, l. 256], fols. 64–80. For the significance of in-cash tribute payment, see Susan Ramírez, *The World Upside Down: Cross Cultural Contact and Conflict in Sixteenth-Century Peru* (Stanford: Stanford University Press, 1996).

7. Kellogg, *Law and the Transformation*, xxxix–36. Kellogg provides a path-breaking analysis of native interactions with the legal system but does not focus on the transfer of property within the context of indigenous government. See the discussion below for specific examples. For the epidemics of the 1570s, see Gibson, *Aztecs*, app. 4.

8. The timeframe for the change in governorship in San Juan Tenochtitlan generally parallels the shift outlined by Lockhart's "stage 2" (ca. 1545–50 to ca. 1645–50), "during which Spanish elements came to pervade every aspect of Nahua life, but with limitations, often as discrete additions within a relatively unchanged indigenous framework"; *Nahuas after the Conquest*, 429–436. A complex literature discusses the issues raised here from a variety of perspectives. The classic work for indigenous institutions is Gibson, *Aztecs*, which makes this case for the transition between encomienda and corregimiento, stressing a good deal of continuity in the process. For the important work that suggests limitations on the encomendero community and eventual replacement by those whose influence derived from their wealth in Lambayeque, Peru, see Susan Ramírez, *Provincial Patriarchs: Land Tenure and the Economics of Power in Colonial Peru* (Albuquerque: University of New Mexico Press, 1986). See also Altman, *Transatlantic Ties*, 88–96.

9. Chimalpahin, *Annals*, 139; see also Chimalpahin, *Las ocho relaciones*, t. 2, 239, where he relates that under Jiménez, Mexico Tenochtitlan collected all tribute owed to the crown in 1572, the last year of his rule, a sum of 9,577 pesos and four tomines. The relationship between compliance with tribute payment by tributary natives and acceptance of a governor is difficult to judge. As elections became an increasingly regular (usually annual) feature of the political landscape of Mexico Tenochtitlan, it appears that the Tenochca expressed their lack of support or confidence in their leaders by not paying their tribute.

10. Valeriano did marry into the royal lineage, and his children could have reconstituted the royal line (discussed below). See Schroeder, *Chimalpahin*, 183; and Chimalpahin, *Annals*, 193, where Chimalpahin discusses the nobility of don Antonio Valeriano the younger, who, through his mother's lineage, was connected to the ruling dynasty of Tenochtitlan. Valeriano the elder, apart from his marriage, was also allegedly related in some unspecified way to Moteuccoma Xocoyotzin; see Poole, *Our Lady of Guadalupe*, 83–84. Don Antonio Valeriano, the talented scholar with close ties to the Franciscan order, must have seemed exceedingly appealing as a transitional candidate from the viceregal perspective. He apparently had an interest in occupying the now much diminished governorship of Mexico Tenochtitlan. The seat of indigenous government in Tenochtitlan must

have also been especially appealing for an Azcapotzalteco. The early fifteenth-century defeat of the Tepaneca by the Tenochca-led triple alliance began the decline of Azcapotzalco. Surely the memory of this defeat and his close ties to the people who toppled the Tenochca made him an appealing choice; see Carrasco, *Tenochca Empire*, 41–49, 101–103.

11. Potential disorder or the possibility of an uprising led by indigenous principales existed. Spanish-authored tracts attested to the danger posed by indigenous revolution and found resonance in the actions of viceregal officials; see Gómez de Cervántez, *La vida económica*, 99–106. Gómez de Cervántes provides a compelling account that in itself lambasts the changes that took power away from encomenderos. Thus its contents must be read with care and its context in mind. Israel, *Race Class and Politics*, 33, praises it as a "typical seventeenth-century Creole" account and also comments on the credibility of the "indigenous rebellion" to creoles in Mexico, 164. See also Connell, "Emerging Ladino Spaces," 21–24. Spaniards who sought rewards for their merit and service to the crown often exaggerated their role in successfully containing indigenous rebellion by overstating its threat; see Restall, *Seven Myths*, 11–15, 68–75. Rebellion and resistance continued into the late sixteenth century and sometimes beyond.

12. AGN, Civil, v. 644, e. 1, 80–81v.

13. Chimalpahin, *Las ocho relaciones*, 229–235.

14. For a broader discussion of the term *tlatocatlacamecayotl*, see Schroeder, *Chimalpahin*, 176, and chapter 1 of this volume.

15. For the contract given to the alcaldes of Mexico Tenochtitlan, see Lockhart, *Nahuas after the Conquest*, 340, fig. 8.3. On the increasing litigiousness and engagement of indigenous communities, see Francisco Gonzalez-Hermosillo Adams, "Macehuales versus señores naturales. Una mediación franciscana en el cabildo indio de Cholula ante el conflicto por el servicio personal (1553–1594)," in Francisco González-Hermosillo Adams, ed., *Gobierno y economía en los pueblos indios del México colonial* (México: Instituto Nacional de Antorpología e Historia, 2001), 127–129.

16. Pascual was the second governor of Mexico Tenochtitlan during the devastating floods after 1629; see AGN, Indios, v. 12, e. 116, fol. 77; AGN, Archivo Histórico de Hacienda, v. 1430, e. 52; AGN, Reales Cedulas Originales y Dubpicados, D11, e. 393, fol. 298v.

17. Though neither source has much to say about elections and appointments of officials on councils, they provide important details concerning the tension between local urban governments and royal authorities, which is the substance of the conflict here between viceregal officials and indigenous governments over the replacement of officials on the cabildo; see Altman, *Transatlantic Ties*, 90–96. For a discussion of earlier town organization in Castile, see Teofilo F. Ruiz, *Crisis and Continuity: Land and Town in Late Medieval Castile* (Philadelphia: University of Pennsylvania Press, 1994), 187–195.

18. See the appendix and discussion in later chapters of the restrictions on officeholding, including nonnatives, and prohibitions against reelection. The

issue of mestizos in office and reelection became increasingly important. The mestizos elected were don Gerónimo López (r. 1600–1608) and don Juan Bautista (r. 1608–1609). Don Juan Martín (r. 1596–99) served as interim governor in place of Valeriano and later served as governor of Mexico Tlatelolco. Chimalpahin, *Annals,* 143, 147, calls Juan Martín only a deputy and states that he was a mestizo. For López, see AGN, Tierras, v. 165, e. 4 (1600); AGN, Tierras, v. 866, e. 1 (1604); Chimalpahin *Annals,* 145 (noting his death in office after serving ten years, eight months, and twenty-one days); and Lockhart, *Nahuas after the Conquest,* 34, tab. 2.1. For Bautista, see also Chimalpahin *Annals,* 145–147.

19. Accounts of elections do not appear regularly in the documentation until the sixteenth century, when governors appear to have first faced competition for office. The first governor replaced in office by the viceregal government was don Juan Pérez de Monterrey (r. 1610–16), who fell ill in office (1616); see AGN, Indios, v. 7, e. 21, fol. 9–9v. The first documented order for an oidor to attend an election is in AGN, Indios, v. 12, e. 192, fol. 120 (1635), though its language indicates that this was a customary practice. As I discuss in chapter 3, the *oidor mas antiguo,* the more important of the two justices of the Audiencia, supervised the elections of Mexico Tenochtitlan. In smaller pueblos the duty generally went to the regional corregidor; see AGN, Indios, v. 7, e. 9, fols. 3v–4, for the corregidor as supervisor of elections in the pueblo of Tepetlaoxtoc (1615).

20. Valeriano's birth year is not known with certainty, though many have speculated. Poole, *Our Lady of Guadalupe,* 84–86, argues that he was born in the 1530s but concedes that he could have been born as early as 1524, if he was ten or twelve when the Colegio de Santa Cruz de Tlatelolco was founded and was one of its first students in 1536. See also Karttunen, "Cuicapixqueh," 4–5, who suggests around 1531 as a probable birth year. D. A. Brading, *Mexican Phoenix Our Lady of Guadalupe: Image and Tradition across Five Centuries* (New York: Cambridge University Press, 2001), 183–185, suggests around 1530.

21. BNM-FR, ms. 1037, fols. 68v–76v. The school constitution held in the Biblioteca Nacional de México is a copy of the 1537 original made in the eighteenth century.

22. SilverMoon, "Imperial College of Tlatelolco"; León-Portilla, *Bernardino de Sahagún,* 93–94, 121–124; and Karttunen, "Cuicapixqueh," 7–12.

23. Tezozomoc, *Cronica mexicayotl,* para. 356; *CC,* vol. 1, 177; and Chimalpahin, *Annals,* 193, which gives doña Isabel de Alvarado's full name, unlike the other sources. See Chimalpahin, *Annals,* 104–105, for the term *tlahtocapilli* and its usage.

24. Schroeder, *Chimalpahin,* 14.

25. Chimalpahin, *Las ocho relaciones,* t. 2, 235, based on the statement, "With him [Jiménez] began in the great city of Mexico Tenochtitlan the government of judge-governors," by which he means nondynastic and non-Tenochca rulers. In Nahuatl, "yc ye onpeua yn yn juezgovernadortin ye quihualpia huey altepetl ciudad Mexico," and in Tena's Spanish translation, "con él comenzó en la gran

ciudad de México el gobierno de los jueces gobernadores." In the Schroeder, Lockhart, and Namala edition, Chimalpahin, *Annals,* 138–139, it reads, "He [Jiménez] first began it that judge-governors from various other altepetl have come to govern in Tenochtitlan," or in Nahuatl, "yn altepetl ypan ye hualhui yn juezgouernadores. In ye huallapachohua Tenochtitlan." *Huallapachohua* is an interesting combination of two verbs—*hualla* (to come hither) and *pachohua* (to govern)—which implies an outsider coming to rule.

26. Tezozomoc, *Cronica mexicayotl,* para. 356; and Karttunen, "Cuicapixqueh," 4, indicate that Valeriano was not "born into a noble family"; see also *CC,* v. 2, 172, 176–177.

27. Chimalpahin, *Annals,* 107–109.

28. Schroeder, *Chimalpahin,* 14.

29. Chimalpahin, *Annals,* 139.

30. Chimalpahin, *Annals,* 137–139, and for a list of the governors since Santa María see 147. See also Lockhart, *Nahuas after the Conquest,* 34, tab. 2.1.

31. Chimalpahin carefully makes the distinction between tlatoque and governors in a particularly clear way, purposefully not using the root term *tlatoani* to refer to judge-governors. See the discussion in Schroeder, *Chimalpahin,* 162–164; see also the commentary in Chimalpahin, *Annals,* 138–139 n. 1.

32. *CC,* v. 1, 174–175 (for example, though many others appear); and Chimalpahin, *Annals,* 137–139; see also 64–65, in which the variant form *omotlahtocatlallitzino* is used to describe Philip III being "installed as ruler." Chimalpahin uses this term for "installed" even though other words for "crowned" exist in Nahuatl. See Karttunen, *Analytic Dictionary,* 150, 266, 333. The translations are by the editors of each version of Chimalpahin.

33. In the edition and translation by Anderson and Schroeder, *CC,* v. 1, 174–175, the editors seem to suggest the foreignness of the nondynastic rulers, taking the meaning of *tlatocatlalli* to suggest a ruler not associated with the lands of the tecpan or the tlatoani. See the commentary on tlatocatlalli in Lockhart, *Nahuas after the Conquest,* 156, and this volume, chapter 1, note 112. For a subtly different interpretation of Chimalpahin's text, which implies more that Chimalpahin was referring to their lack of association with the royal line than their apparent foreignness, see Chimalpahin *Annals,* 137–139. Schroeder is an editor and translator common to both editions of Chimalpahin, which makes it difficult to relegate the nuance here to editorial choice.

34. Cortés, *Letters,* 139, 479, n. 94. Pagden's notes indicate the extent to which Cortés went to have children with important daughters of Moteucçoma, including doña Ana, who perished during the Noche Triste but allegedly was pregnant by Cortés when she died. Another daughter, doña María, may have been Cortés's child by a daughter of Moteucçoma (Chimalphain calls her doña María Cortés de Moteucçoma), for he left a significant inheritance to her in his will. It is clear from Cortés's behavior and efforts to pair important allies with the daughters

of the royal lineage that these women could provide some political advantage to the invaders. Chimalpahin also discusses the children of Moteucçoma; see *CC*, v. 1, 87–89. On doña Isabel Tecuichpotzin, see Townsend, *Malintzin's Choices*, 95.

35. Schroeder, *Chimalpahin*, 174–180. Thanks to Susan Schroeder for her assistance on royal lineages in Mexico Tenochtitlan. The surviving evidence does not indicate why the Nahua regarded only one of the multiple lineages (descendant from individual wives of Moteucçoma after the Spanish invasion) as significant. What does seem clear, though I do not develop this idea fully, is that the tlatoani was only one significant part of a royal pair who established the royal lineage. Equally important in generating royal children was the primary wife of the tlatoani. Even though all children descended from the tlatoani were part of a royal lineage, only those from the primary wife could rule. See also Schroeder, "First American Valentine," 344–345; and Townsend, *Malintzin's Choices*, 94–96, 164–165, 261–262, n. 29. For a Mayan variant on polygamy, see John F. Chuchiak, "Secrets behind the Screen: *Solicitantes* in the Colonial Diocese of Yucatan and the Yucatec Maya, 1570–1785," in Susan Schroeder and Stafford Poole, eds., *Religion in New Spain* (Albuquerque: University of New Mexico Press, 2007), 87–89.

36. A great deal of work has been done examining the Moteucçoma family, but much of it is incomplete; see Pedro Carrasco, "Indian-Spanish Marriages in the First Century of the Colony," in Susan Schroeder, Stephanie Wood, and Robert Haskett, eds., *Indian Women of Early Mexico* (Norman: University of Oklahoma Press, 1997), 90–91; Howard F. Cline, "Hernando Cortés and the Aztec Indians in Spain," *Quarterly Journal of the Library of Congress* 26 (1969), 84–88; and Schroeder, "Nahuas, Jesuits and the Good Death Society," 52–53. For a book-length genealogical study of the Moteucçoma family, mostly as they descend from doña Isabel Moteucçoma Tecuichpotzin, see Donald E. Chipman, *Moctezuma's Children: Aztec Royalty under Spanish Rule, 1520–1700* (Austin: University of Texas Press, 2005); and Alfonso de Figuero y Melgar (Duke of Tovar), "Los Moctezuma en España y America," *Hidalguía* 20, no. 111 (1972), 217–223. Chipman points out (xiii–xiv) that in the 1930s the post-revolutionary governments ended a subsidy paid to the heirs of Moteucçoma Xocoyotzin.

37. Figuero y Melgar, "Los Moctezuma," 217–229, notes that Moteucçoma had sixteeen children, many of whom died precontact. Figuero y Melgar does not mention don Juan Govamitle, but see Cline, "Hernando Cortés," 85, who apparently found evidence of his existence. My suspicion is that "Govamitle" is not the correct spelling, but without having seen the primary source from which it derives I hesitate to modify it. Tezozomoc, *Crónica mexicayotl*, 228, mentions several of Moteucçoma's children, including Ihutiltemoc, Xocopehualco, Quauhtlecoatzin, Acamapich, and Chimalpopoca, according to Figuero y Melgar, and princesses whose names Teçoçomoc did not know. The most reliable sources are *CC*, v. 1, 87–105, and *CC*, v. 2, 59–119, which include a detailed accounting of the kingly lineages of Mexico Tenochtitlan. The real problem here is that the available evidence does not provide critical details about Moteucçoma's wives and does not

give the necessary detail about the acceptability of their children to rule. See also the important discussion in *CC*, v. 2, 159–165. I take the spelling of don Martín Cortés Neçahualtecolotzin from the Codex Chimalpahin. Chimalpahin's account reveals numerous problems in Cline's work, but this says more about the state of Cline's evidence; we have much better access to sources unavailable to him in 1969. For example, don Marín Cortés Neçahualtecolotzin's demise was malicious and intentional according to Chimalpahin, who relates that "the Mexica just poisoned him on his way back from Spain." Chimalpahin, in contradiction to Figuero y Melgar, lists nineteen children for Moteucçoma. Chimalpahin does not mention any son baptized don Juan and none with a name resembling Govamitle.

38. Cline, "Herando Cortés," 85.

39. Chimalpahin, *Las ocho relaciones*, t. 2, 239; Chimalpahin, *Annals*, 104–105 (Schroeder, Lockhart, and Namala translate the word *tlahtocapilli* as "royal nobleman"); and *CC*, v. 2, 160–161, though in this version the "de Moteucçoma" is omitted.

40. Chimalpahin, *Las ocho relaciones*, t. 2, 239.

41. Chimalpahin, *Annals*, 107.

42. Chipman, *Moctezuma's Children*, 124. The dukes of Alburquerque were heavily associated with New Spain, and two served as viceroys in the seventeenth and eighteenth centuries; see William F. Connell, "A 'Morisco Assassin' in the Cathedral of Mexico City: Due Process and Honor in the Seventeenth Century," *Journal of Colonialism and Colonial History* 11, no. 1 (2010); Virgilio Fernández Bulete, "La desconocida relación de gobierno del Duque de Alburquerque, Virrey de Nueva España," *Anuario de Estudios Americanos* 55, no. 2 (1998), 684–685; and Manuel Romero de Terreros, "El Virrey Duque de Alburquerque y las Bellas Artes," *Anales del Instituto de Investigaciones Estéticas* 19 (1951), 92.

43. See Chimalpahin, *Annals*, 107, for the election to alcalde; and see Chipman, *Moctezuma's Children*, 126, for the death of don Diego Luis de Moteucçoma the elder, whose will was dictated on 31 May 1606 and, according to Chipman, "later died" in Valladolid.

44. Chimalpahin, *Annals*, 107. There is a suggestion in Horn, *Postconquest Coyoacan*, 58–59, based on an observation by Lockhart, *Nahuas after the Conquest*, 37, that Mexico Tenochtitlan had four alcaldes after 1600 and eight after 1610. Lockhart cites Chimalpahin to support the claim, but I have seen no direct evidence to support this assertion. Lockhart does not appear to have been fully certain, suggesting that "it may be that neither of these schemes was carried out with full consistency." It also seems odd that Chimalpahin would mention only two, *Annals*, 107, if there were an additional two in 1607. He may be pointing out only the two that he found relevant to discuss because of their association with the royal line and governorship. The 1604 cabildo is mentioned in AGN, Tierras, v. 866, e. 1, fol. 7–7v, which lists the cabildo (in a Nahuatl document) and yet lists only two alcaldes who, along with governor don Geronimo López, approve the document generated by *pregonero* (town crier, or announcer) Diego Aztaxochitl

and his scribe Juan de Santiago. Even by 1692, when there are much more detailed records of the cabildo (the uprising of that year), there are only two alcaldes listed for Mexico Tenochtitlan; see AGN, Indios, v. 32, e. 37, fols. 39v–41v. Even in the tempting document from 1694, AGN, Indios, v. 32, e. 207, ff. 186–186v, a petition from the whole cabildo and active community of electors, only two of the listed alcaldes bear the designation *actual*. I suspect that the remaining are past alcaldes (*pasado*) and that the active alcaldes bear the modifier *actual* after their titles to indicate current service. Though there are alcaldes with no modifier, the document also lists three individuals with the title *gobernador* with no modifier. No one would conclude based on this information that Mexico Tenochtitlan had three governors in 1694.

It is difficult to resolve with certainty the size and composition of the cabildo because of the nature of the documentation. Disputes involving the cabildo usually happened in only one regional division of the city. A house sale might enlist the service of only a single alcalde who represented that part of the city, as in the 1604 dispute discussed in this chapter; see AGN, Tierras, v. 866, e. 1. Very few disputes covered the whole parcialidad, making it likely that only the relevant officers would appear for any given dispute that involved the cabildo. The 1694 document provides a rare example in which the entire cabildo and government were involved, because the dispute had to do with the payment of back tribute that was creating a burden for current governors and cabildos. The document therefore refers to the "cuatro parcialidades" of Mexico Tenochtitlan, making it likely that in reality only two alcaldes served on the cabildo in 1694. This is not to say, however, that it was impossible for the cabildo to have four alcaldes in 1600 and two in 1694. Indeed, according to Chimalpahin, *Annals,* 67, four alcaldes were elected and installed in 1600: "one was chosen for each of the four parts."

45. Chimalpahin, *Annals,* 105; and *CC,* v. 2, 159–165.

46. For mestizos in office, see AGN, Tierras, v. 165, e. 4, ff. 17–17v (1600); AGN, Tierras, v. 866, e. 1, fols. 2–7v (text in Nahuatl, does not refer to López as a mestizo); and Chimalpahin, *Annals,* 143–145, which does refer to him as a mestizo. It is important to point out that at the time rules prohibiting mestizos were apparently not enforced, or other compelling reasons that are now unclear made mestizos better choices than natives.

47. The principal heirs of Moteucçoma probably did better adjusting their affairs to matters on the peninsula; see the discussion in Chipman, *Moctezuma's Children,* 124–141.

48. Tezozomoc, *Crónica mexicayotl,* 7, and paras. 349–356; see also *CC,* v. 1, 59–66, 98–105, and *CC,* v. 2, 127–129.

49. I briefly discuss annalists in chapter 1, but for a thorough discussion see Lockhart, *Nahuas after the Conquest,* 376–392; and José Rubén Romero Galván, *Los privilegios perdidos: Hernando Alvarado Tezozomoc, su tiempo, su nobleza, y su crónica Mexicana* (México: Universidad Nacional Autónoma de México, 2003), 77–94.

50. *CC*, v. 1, contains the work of Teçoçomoc. The editors identify Teçoçomoc's variant spellings of certain words that serve as a kind of personal signature that allows them to establish definitively that these writings incorporated into the Codex Chimalphain are the only surviving originals. It is also important to note, as Anderson and Schroeder do in the introduction, that Teçoçomoc and Chimalpahin came from distinctly different backgrounds. As a high-born member of the royal lineage, Teçoçomoc was in a different social category than Chimalpahin, who "probably remained peripheral to indigenous high society" throughout his life; see *CC*, v. 1, 4–8. The editors also claim that Teçoçomoc was a mestizo, grouping him with don Fernando de Alva Ixtlilxochitl. In his own writings, Teçoçomoc rejects this attribution, but he had an interest in claiming legitimate descent from the royal lineage and thus may have sanitized some elements of his own past. I thank Susan Schroeder for her assistance with the translation of *mexicayotl*.

51. Lockhart, *Nahuas after the Conquest*, 389.

52. According to Susan Schroeder, "he was the great grandson of Axayacatzin (r. 1469–82) and the grandson of Moteucçoma Xocoyotzin"; "Writing Two Cultures: The Meaning of '*Amotli*' (Book) in Nahua New Spain," in David Cahill and Blanca Tovías, eds., *New World, First Nations: Native Peoples of Mesoamerica and the Andes under Colonial Rule* (Brighton: Sussex University Press, 2006), 19–22 and n. 45. For additional detail on the life of Teçoçomoc, see Romero Galván, *Los privilegios perdidos*, 82–94; though this study does not reveal much in the way of new information, it does indicate that Teçoçomoc was a nahuatlato for the Audiencia, probably born in the late 1530s and died in 1610, making him a close contemporary of don Antonio Valeriano. For further detail on the descendants of Huanitzin, see Tezozomoc, *Crónica mexicayotl*, paras. 349–356; and *CC*, v. 1, 100–105.

53. Chipman, *Moctezuma's Children*, 119–141, makes a compelling case for many of the direct descendants of doña Isabel de Moteucçoma and their quest for nobility on the peninsula.

54. Yannnakakis, *Art*, 11–18, 36–39; Connell, "Emerging Ladino Spaces," chap. 2; and for a synthesis of the scholarship on the issue, Colin M. MacLachlan and Jaime E. Rodríguez O., *The Forging of the Cosmic Race: A Reinterpretation of Colonial Mexico* (Berkeley: University of California Press, 1980), 199–201, 216–217. MacLachlan and Rodríguez O. write that "legitimate children of such unions [native and Spaniard] raised as 'Spaniards' in effect became criollos, while the offspring raised among the natives became Indians."

55. See AGN, Tierras, v. 866, e. 1, fols. 2–7v. The governor, a mestizo, don Geronimo López, presided over a Nahuatl-language dispute over land without the aid of an interpreter, indicating that he could understand the indigenous language of his community. We also know from AGN, Tierras, v. 165, e. 4, fols. 17–17v, that Judge-Governor López knew well the father of the indigenous litigants. The issue here is somewhat muddied as well by the issues raised by Chimalpahin in regard to non-Tenochca rulers in Mexico Tenochtitlan; see particularly, *CC*, v. 1, 174–175. Is

the problem that he was mestizo or that he was not royal, or that he was not from Mexico Tenochtitlan? Chimalpahin clearly knew, but without additional context it is difficult to say for certain.

56. At Chimalpahin, *Annals,* 143, 147, "deputy" is stressed, and 146 shows the Nahuatl usage of *theniente,* which appears to come from *teniente* in Spanish. The translation is by the editors. Juan Martín served, after the death of Valeriano, as governor in Mexico Tlatelolco.

57. The number of variables here is bewildering, but only a few had meaning in Spanish courts. I treat them more fully when I consider actual challenges made later in the seventeenth century that brought the issues to the forefront. For consideration, however, it was possible that from an indigenous perspective altepetl affiliation, ties to the royal lineage, and perhaps even birth order or some kind of internal tlaxilacalli/calpolli designation had meaning. To Spanish law, however, only legitimacy of birth and status as a native (*natural*) had meaning. Thus, political disputes tended to focus exclusively on matters relevant to the legal issues at stake. It is possible, however, as Chimalpahin reminds us, that lineage, altepetl affiliation, and birth order or specific talent had more meaning within the communities themselves.

58. See Carrasco, "Indian-Spanish Marriages," 87, for his recent definition of the term. See also Yannakakis, *Art.*

59. As discussed by Carrasco, "Indian-Spanish Marriages," 100, mestizo nahuatlatos proliferated on the Audiencia, yet at the same time Spanish officials sometimes worried about the implications of mestizaje in seemingly racial terms; see Viceroy Mendoza's comments in "Relación apuntamientos y avisos que por mandado de S. M. di al Señor don Luis de Velasco visorey y gobernador y capitán general desta Nueva España," in *Instrucciones que los virreyes de Nueva España dejaron a sus sucesores. Añadense algunos que los mismos trajeron de la corte y otros documentos semejantes a las instrucciones* (México: Imprenta Imperial, 1867), 227–228, 239–241, where mestizos appear to be a source of trouble in the mid-sixteenth century, both for their potential for sedition and because mestizo children might be abandoned by their parents. Viceroy don Luis de Velasco continues the general reaction to mestizos in 1554 as one of suspicion; see "Cartas del Virrey don Luis de Velasco el viejo," AGI, Audiencia de México, l. 19, n. 13, fol. 3–3v.

60. Carrasco, "Indian-Spanish Marriages," 89–98, 100–103. Unfortunately Carrasco does not deal specifically with the issue of mestizaje and the cultural implications of the marriages he describes. For a discussion of altepetl affiliation and native world view, see Susan Schroeder, "Introduction," in Schroeder, Wood, and Haskett, *Indian Women,* 13–14.

61. A particularly rich document that illustrates the changes in status of ordinary mestizos comes from the Cofradía de Transitos; see AGN, Bienes Nacionales, v. 732, e. 3. This is a criminal lawsuit adjudicated by the ecclesiastical courts in which the cofradía members were attacked by priests who regarded them with suspicion when they came to collect the valuable items they hoped to use to parade

through the streets from the church of Santa Veracruz. The prejudice of the brothers of the capilla of San Juan de Dios at the church seems to have stemmed from their assertion that the cofradía was made up of illegitimate mestizos who were not trustworthy. It also appears here that terms like "transitory," "mestizo," and "orphan" were used interchangeably.

62. On the colegio, see AGI, Audiencia de México, l. 70, r. 2, n. 18, fol. 1–1v, a letter from Archbishop don Pedro Moya de Contereras (r. 1574–91) to the king, 24 April 1579. See also *Recopilación de leyes*, lib. 1, tit. 23, ley 14.

63. The work of María Elena Martínez is strikingly original on the topic of early modern racial identity; see her *Genealogical Fictions: Limpieza de Sangre, Religion, and Gender in Colonial Mexico* (Stanford: Stanford University Press, 2008), 24–60; and "The Black Blood of New Spain: 'Limpieza de Sangre,' Racial Violence, and Gendered Power in Early Colonial Mexico," *William and Mary Quarterly* 61, no. 3 (2004), 480–485. Martínez contends that, unlike the unredeemable Africans, mestizos "could achieve a social and spiritual status equivalent to that of Spaniards," provided Spanish "old Christian" blood predominated. This observation conforms well to the uncertainty of status afforded mestizo governors. See also "Cartas del Virrey don Luis de Velasco el viejo," AGI, Audiencia de México, l. 19, n. 13, fol. 3–3v.

64. Gibson, *Aztecs*, 383. Apparently begging for alms and grave digging were among the more important subjects taught in the school. In a letter from the archbishop of Mexico to Philip II, the more practical skills of begging and digging were emphasized, at least in 1579 when the letter was written; see AGI, Audiencia de México, l. 70, r. 2, n. 18, fol. 1–1v.

65. Carrasco, "Indian-Spanish Marriages," 100.

66. AGN, Tierras, v. 37, e. 2, fols. 69v–85.

67. That both Teçoçomoc and Tapia were probably Nahua seems to contradict the evidence provided by Carrasco that the nahuatlatos were mestizo or Spanish; see "Indian-Spanish Marriages," 100.

68. Cline, "Hernando Cortés," 85; Schroeder, *Chimalpahin*, 82, 160–161, 188–189, in which she argues that eagle nobles did not have the same real status as those born into royal or noble lineages. She confirms Cline's general notion with firmer evidence, pointing out that Chimalpahin qualifies *quauhpilli* ("war leader") with *çan* ("only"). At least from his perspective, rulers and leaders who emerged because of merit did not have the same status as those born to lead.

69. AGN, Tierras, v. 37, e. 2, fol. 79v, where Tapia recounts that his father, don Andrés Tapia, "died in the war for Jalisco in the service of Governor Nuño de Guzmán and [he] my father governed Mexico [Tenochtitlan]." Though he does not use his father's indigenous name, Motelchiuhtzin, in this instance, the case involved a dispute over the possession of a house in San Pablo that was built during the reconstruction of the city by his father and eventually became the tecpan of the neighborhood. Motelchiuhtzin is regularly identified by his indigenous name and mistakenly called "governor" of Tenochtitlan in the document. The document also relates the story of Motelchiuhtzin's presence with Cortés on

their trip to Honduras to subdue Cristóbal de Olíd. For the Olíd mission, see Restall, *Seven Myths*, 149; and Chimalpahin, *Annals*, 133. For further identification, see Kellogg, *Law and the Transformation*, 14; Carrasco, "Indian-Spanish Marriages," 90; and García Granados, *Diccionario biográfico*, 202.

70. See Henry Kamen, *Spain, 1469–1714* (London: Longman, 1991), 62–121, for the dates of his rule. Carlos I is better known in European historiography as Charles V.

71. AGN, Tierras, v. 37. e. 2, fol. 71v. For the value of currency, see Gibson, *Aztecs*, 357–358. Some additional context: the entire yearly tribute collected by the entire parcialidad was 9,577 pesos and four tomines, for the year 1572; see Chimalpahin, *Las ocho relaciones*, 239.

72. AGN, Tierras, v. 37, e. 2, fols. 15, 90v–103v; specifically relevant are the responses to questions, 7, 8, and 10, which suggest that the house was part of the municipal property and a hall for "fiestas y bailes" (parties and dances) and municipal meetings, since it was built by Motelchiuhtzin. The main tecpan of Mexico Tenochtitlan was located on the plaza of the barrio of San Juan Moyotlan on the western side of the city south of the park. For a similar example of the descendants of past rulers continuing to live on community property, see Terraciano, *Mixtecs*, 195–197.

73. AGN, Tierras, v. 37, e. 2, fol. 79v, for the quotation, and for the broader will, fols. 69v–85. See also the brief discussion in Kellogg, *Law and the Transformation*, 14.

74. Carrasco, "Indian-Spanish Marriages," 102–103, explains that property sometimes was at the core of such marriage choices. For a documentary example, though many appear in Tierras, see AGN, Tierras, v. 58, e. 3, fols. 156–159v. The issue of "whitening" or "racial passing" is raised by the statement made here. I make the statement based on the observations of Martínez, "Black Blood," 480–485, who, looking at limpieza de sangre petitions, observed that those who sought access to high positions could diminish their mestizo ancestry through marriage into Spanish families. Obviously this applied only to those who sought high-status positions and thus was limited to a small segment of the population. She argues this point much more completely in *Genealogical Fictions*. For the "limitations" of the racial passing argument that posits that most in Mexico City (and probably also in other parts of Spanish America) did not seek to whiten their heirs through strategic marriages, see R. Douglas Cope, *The Limits of Racial Domination: Plebeian Society in Colonial Mexico City, 1660–1720* (Madison: University of Wisconsin Press, 1994), 49–85, 162–163.

75. Though he called his daughters—Justina, Ynés, and Sebastiana—"naturales de Mexico" and referred to Justina as a native child (*hija india*), and furthermore referred to all three as legitimate, Tapia's wife, Isabel de Cazeraz, was apparently a Spaniard. Kellogg, *Law and the Transformation*, 14, suggests that she was a Spaniard. I found no direct reference in the text of the lawsuit to her as a Spaniard (racial designations in sixteenth-century documents were not required, usual, or regular); see AGN, Tierras, v. 37, e. 2. Carrasco contends that she was Spanish following García

Granados, *Diccionario,* t. 3, 202, which references a document that appears in Icazbalceta, "Visita al Virrey don Antonio de Mendoza," in *Colección* t. 2, 87. The document in Icazbalceta reads only "fué casado con española" ("he was married to a Spanish woman") but does not mention Isabel de Cazeraz directly; see Carrasco, "Indian-Spanish Marriages," 90. See also Cline, "Hernando Cortés," 84–85, and AGN, Tierras, v. 37, e. 2, fol. 73–73v. Cline does not provide much detail and misidentifies Tapia as a principal (noting Chimalpahin's objection that he was not from the royal lineage), probably because the royal decrees on which Cline's article is based (*reales cédulas*) treated him as though he were a noble. Following Chimalpahin, for Nahuas, Spaniards did not have the ability to grant a macehualli the status of a pilli. Though many use the honorific *don* with his name, in his will he is simply referred to as Hernando de Tapia.

76. Note 1, this chapter, provides an elaborate bibliography of works relevant to Valeriano's life and career. They mostly reiterate the precious few bits of biographical data that emerge from printed sources (Torquemada, Sahagún, Teçoçomoc, Chimalpahin, Cervantes de Salazar, and Juan Bautista). See also Poole, *Our Lady of Guadalupe,* 83–86; and Brading, *Mexican Phoenix,* 44, 92–93.

77. BNM-FR, ms. 1037, fols. 69–75v, details the rules and constitution of the colegio. Tuition was free for students who earned a place, and their maintenance was paid by the viceroy. Valeriano should not have been admitted, though, since he did not meet the minimum requirement that he be a principal; macehualtin were excluded from the colegio. Apparently the funding source later was rent from investments; see AGN, Indios, v. 23, e. 178, fols. 168v–169; Gibson, *Aztecs,* 99; Karttunen, "Cuicapixqueh," 6. The most recent and complete institutional history and analysis is to be found in SilverMoon, "Imperial College," 43–144.

78. León-Portilla, *Fray Bernardino de Sahagún,* 123.

79. Fray Juan de Torquemada, *Monarquía indiana,* ed. Andrés González de Barcía Caballido y Zúñiga, facs. ed., t. 3, lib. 15, cap. xliii (México: S. Chávez Hayhoe, 1943–1944), 113–115.

80. Gibson, *Aztecs,* 170.

81. Bautsita, quoted in Karttunen, "Cuicapixqueh," 8, and reproduced in SilverMoon, "Imperial College,"154, from *Serminario en lengua mexicana* (México: Casa de Diego López Dávalos, 1606). According to SilverMoon, who is quoting Gruzinski, fray Juan de Torquemada also made reference to Valeriano's spoken Nahuatl.

82. Zorita, *Historia,* 287.

83. Cervantes de Salazar, quoted in Poole, *Our Lady of Guadalupe,* 84.

84. García Granados, *Diccionario,* t. 3, 223–224.

85. Chimalpahin, *Annals,* 141, reports that he returned to his pueblo after serving five years in office. Some report that Jiménez died in office; see Dibble, *Códice Aubin,* 83 (p. 114); Lockhart, *Nahuas after the Conquest,* 351–352, esp. tab. 8.8; *CC,* v. 2, 41–43 (which reports that he served in office only one year and five months); Tezozomoc, *Crónica mexicayotl,* 175–176, paras. 370, 371; and *CC,* v. 1, 42–43, 78–79. The reason for this discrepancy is not clear.

86. From the preamble of the founding constitution, BNM-FR, ms. 1037, fol. 69. The document uses *cacique* instead of *principal*, but it is a copy made at a time when such a usage would have been common; see Lockhart, *Nahuas after the Conquest*, 133. See also Ricard, *Spiritual Conquest*, 218–223, where he discusses the founding of and purpose of the colegio.

87. *CC*, v. 2, 172, 176, 177; in this instance, Chimalpahin states that he was "only" a scholar, using again the word *çan* to make clear his point. For the Nahuatl usage, see Schroeder, *Chimalpahin*, 160; Gibson, *Aztecs*, 169–170; and Tezozmoc, *Crónica mexicayotl*, 171, para. 356. SilverMoon, "Imperial College,"156–157, points out that Teçoçomoc was not a disinterested observer and is the principal source of the information.

88. BNM-FR, ms. 1037, fol. 70; the rules required only that a student be *indio de legitimo matrimonio* ("native legitimately born") and that they be noble, specifically stating that they "not be masgual" or, in Nahuatl, a macehualli. The idea, well explored elsewhere, was that the colegio would train the native nobility to be priests and leaders of the indigenous community. Enrique Florescano, "Sahagún y el nacimiento de la crónica mestiza," *Relaciones: Estudios de Historia y Sociedad* 23, no. 91 (2002), also comments further on the founding of the colegio, 77–79; and see Ricard, *Spiritual Conquest*, 224–225; and SilverMoon, "Imperial College,"123–127.

89. As Sahagún apparently would have it, these informants were those "indigenous youths already cultivated in the manners of the west," quoted in Florescano, "Sahagún y el nacimiento," 80–81.

90. SilverMoon, "Imperial College," 158–160. The works of Sahagún, the *Primeros memoriales,* ed. and trans. Thelma D. Sullivan (Norman: University of Oklahoma Press, 1997), and the Florentine Codex were probably part of what Valeriano was working on from the 1560s onward; see Karttunen, "Cuicapixqueh," 7–10.

91. Karttunen, "Cuicapixqueh," 5–9

92. D. A. Brading, *The First America: The Spanish Monarchy, Creole Patriots, and the Liberal State 1492–1867* (Cambridge: Cambridge University Press, 1991), 119, 353–354, 385–386; Brading, *Mexican Phoenix,* 117–118, 322–326; Poole, *Our Lady of Guadalupe,* 168–169.

93. Poole, *Our Lady of Guadalupe,* 168–169. Poole takes apart the assertions made for more than three centuries (though with the most confidence in the twentieth) that base the connection to Valeriano on the seemingly clear statement by Sigüenza y Góngora that he believed the original text was in Valeriano's handwriting.

94. Karttunen, "Cuicapixqueh," 11. Karttunen makes the case that the continued close relationship between Valeriano and Sahagún makes it unlikely that he authored the text. For the literature that purports that Valeriano authored the text, see Javier Escalada, S.J., *Guadalupe arte y espelendor* (México: Enciclopedia Guadalupana, 2002), 31–34. Escalada cites Lockhart, who has written that the Nican Mopohua, based on the Nahuatl, "could have been written at any time from 1550 or 1560 forward"; see his *Nahuas after the Conquest,* 250 for the quotation, 245–251 for the broader discussion. Escalada seems to take Lockhart out of

context and to use his assertion that the text could have been written during Valeriano's life to suggest a conclusion that Lockhart does not support in his work. Lockhart does contend that "such fluent and idiomatic Nahuatl" suggests that "Laso de la Vega would have had to possess very unusual language gifts to have written it himself unless he was guided by an already existing model." He suggests a Nahua ghostwriter, not that Laso de la Vega's text was written much earlier. For the definitive study on Guadalupe, see Poole, *Our Lady of Guadalupe*, 156–170, 192–213; Father Poole's work goes over the controversy in length and provides compelling evidence that the Nican Mopohua should be properly attributed to Luis Laso de la Vega. For a complete version of this text, see Stafford Poole C. M., Lisa Sousa, and James Lockhart, eds. and trans., *The Story of Guadalupe: Luis Laso de la Vega's Huei tlamahuiçoltica of 1649* (Stanford: Stanford University Press, 1998), esp. 1, n. 3, and 20–35, in which the editors relate that the information contained in this work supersedes the discussion in *Nahuas after the Conquest* and clarifies the dating of the Nahuatl to later stage II. See, more recently, Brading, *Mexican Phoenix*, 6, 92–93, 117–118, 340–345.

Escalada's case, beyond his questionable use of Lockhart, contends that Valeriano had knowledge and close contact with the Franciscans, giving him the best opportunity to have been the author of the text. He was also intelligent and one who could write perfect Nahuatl. Such an explanation, however, indicates only that Valeriano was one plausible candidate to have produced the text, and it is rather insulting to insinuate that he was the only indigenous person alive in the sixteenth century with such talent. Escalada essentially makes the case that Valeriano was a potential author but provides no direct evidence to show that he was the author.

95. Sahagún is the source for this detail in Karttunen, "Cuicapixqueh," 8; for further discussion, see 5–9. For further detail on the founding, see Gibson, *Aztecs*, 382, and Viceroy Mendoza, "Relación apuntamientos," 227–241, esp. no. 13; see also SilverMoon, "Imperial College," 73, 76–78.

96. BNM-FR, ms. 1037, fols. 70v–71. The limitations of the constitution to explain the actual functioning of the school are understood, but at the same time the document provides the attitude of the Franciscans as they conceived of indigenous education in a formal setting.

97. For Chimalpopoca and the Tepaneca war, see *CC*, v. 1, 40–41 (Spanish); and Chimalpahin, *Las ocho relaciones*, t. 2, 69. On Valeriano and his foreign birth, see esp. *CC*, v. 1, 174–175; and Chimalpahin, *Annals*, 141.

98. BNM-FR, ms. 1037, fol. 69–69v. The use of the ambiguous phrase "para poder ejercer los gobiernos eclesiásticos y seglares" ("to be able to exercise the offices of ecclesiastical and secular government") suggests the purpose of the school as stated in the constitution, which was written during a time of extreme volatility. Within the broader context of the document itself, it probably refers to the expectations of the students. It could be interpreted to refer to bringing the students into accord with Spanish understanding of ecclesiastical and secular government so that

they could be more easily governed by secular and ecclesiastical Spanish authorities. Several important philosophical issues, however, suggest the problem with this interpretation. The notion of indigenous self-government, part of Viceroy Mendoza's vision of governing New Spain discussed in the introduction and chapter 1, in which indigenous governmental traditions were incorporated into Spanish-styled cabildos, suggests a degree of autonomy for these communities as part of the founding vision for establishing order. The small size of the colegio, the envisioned exclusive "cacique" or principal student body, and the very real expectation (at least in 1537) that some of the students would become indigenous clergy seem to suggest that the purpose of the school was in fact to train the students to exercise government functions in the secular and ecclesiastical purview of indigenous society according to European ideology. Note also, for the Tlaxcalan case, Gibson, *Tlacala*, 40, in which he points out that governor Diego de Paredes was educated by Franciscans and lived as a penitent in the monastery in Tlaxcala. Gibson also notes the fluidity in the 1530s between the secular and ecclesiastical offices that served the indigenous community. Gibson, like many scholars influenced by the work of Ricard, overstates the ability of regular clergy to influence their indigenous charges; see Burkhart, *Slippery Earth*, 8–10, 19–25; see also David Charles Wright Carr, *Los Franciscanos y su labor educativa en la Nueva España* (México: Instituto Nacional de Antropología e Historia, 1998), 40–41; and Martin Austin Nesvig, *Ideology and Inquisition: The World of the Censors in Early Mexico* (New Haven, Conn.: Yale University Press, 2009), 93–103, 155.

99. Quotation from Wright Carr, *Los Franciscanos*, 36–37. Wright Carr cites Fray Toribio de Motolinia, *Historia de los indios de la Nueva España*, ed. Edmundo O'Gorman (México: Porrúa, 1979), 19, 127, 174–175, 182; and Sahagún, *General History*, vol. 10, chap. 27. The account is also reproduced in Gibson, *Tlaxcala*, 33–34, and SilverMoon, "Imperial College," 67–68.

100. Burkhart, *Slippery Earth*, 22, observes that "the friars' ethnography was influenced by the goals of missionization. Much was missed or misinterpreted; European cultural categories were imposed haphazardly upon indigenous conceptual schemes. . . . the result is a partially Christianized ethnography, corresponding to the partially Nahuatized Christianity that constituted the other side of the dialogue." The focus of her work is the implications of the differences between what the friars thought natives understood and how the natives likely interpreted the meaning of the images, teachings, and parables. Burkhart and others have also noted that friars tended to overstate their missionary success, thus influencing the important though now read-with-caution work of Robert Ricard, esp. *The Spiritual Conquest of Mexico*. She provides a note of healthy critical perspective on the "successes" of early evangelization efforts. The discord between the generations described here, admittedly, could have resulted from any number of factors including that children felt liberated through the encouragement of the friars. That the friars took the response from native children to mean they developed an intense attachment to Christianity would follow the "mutual misunderstanding"

idea developed by Burkhart. See also the comments in the subsequent note for Karttunen's observations on discipline. See Ricard, *Spiritual Conquest*, 37–38, in which he argues for a judicious assessment (and the avoidance of overgeneralization) of the friars, who sometimes preserved and respected indigenous buildings, manuscripts, and ideas and sometimes sought to destroy such things.

101. Karttunen, "Cuicapixqueh," 5–9; and BNM-FR, ms. 1037, fol. 72–72v. Further complicating matters, the laxity of rules and lack of discipline facilitated trysts among students, who lived in the dormitories, creating scandal. The lack of discipline is quite surprising; as Karttunen observes, students flagellated themselves with the friars. When students broke rules, drank alcohol, or even showed disrespect for the rectors, they were punished corporally. Scandalous behavior and violence apparently forced the Franciscans to end their first informal education program with children of principales and to open the colegio, and it was after such scandals that the Franciscans returned the children to their homes. See Frances F. Berdan and Patricia Rieff Anawalt, eds., *The Codex Mendoza*, vols. 3 and 4 (Berkeley: University of California Press, 1989). The third section of the codex details Nahua practices for raising children in which a heavy regime of corporal discipline included binding, beating, and pricking with maguey thorns adolescent children, who likely would have also been those educated by the Franciscans. SilverMoon, "Imperial College," 53, 90–91, finds evidence of strict discipline and concerns among the friars of sodomy in the main dormitory. Silver-Moon also discusses the punishment of pricking with maguey thorns, but for students who "failed to rise" for midnight prayers. See also Wright Carr, *Los Franciscanos*, 30–34, in which he describes the educational practices of the Tenochca in the precontact era and suggests that, according to the work of Sahagún, the natives also had harsh punishments for those found in a state of inebriation or having sexual encounters in the school. Such information indicates that precontact indigenous students also violated rules and engaged in conduct that the Franciscans found so offensive, according to Karttunen.

102. Gibson, *Aztecs*, 170, who cites Tezozomoc, *Crónica mexcayotl*, 171–175; see also Chimalpahin, *Annals*, 85. See also the important discussion, relating to Oaxaca, in Terraciano, *Mixtecs*, 171–190, in which he makes an effective case that women of the royal lineage in Oaxaca inherited similarly to men in the lineage and ruled jointly or at least "shared" responsibilities of rulership, and that women often continued to rule after the deaths of their husbands. A major change with the arrival of Spanish-styled cabildos was that women could not serve in elected office in the new system to which the Ñudzahui had to adapt.

103. On the possibility of reconstituting the royal lineage, see Schroeder, *Chimalpahin*, 176–187; and Terraciano, *Mixtecs*, 179–182, 186–190.

104. Some of his descendants may have become important figures in the government of Mexico Tenochtitlan. Though I have made no effort to connect the individuals genealogically, the name Valeriano appears regularly throughout the seventeenth century in various positions on the cabildo and in offices affiliated

with the cabildo. It is important to point out, however, that there was likely no chance that Valeriano sought to create or could have created an alternative dynastic lineage even by marrying into the family of Huanitzin.

105. Gibson, *Aztecs*, pl. 8, depicts a single image from the Codex Valeriano that shows the direct intervention by Valeriano to reduce the tribute owed by the community. He wrote a personal note that accompanied the pictorial documents in this image, testifying to the death of tributary Francisco Tzetzel. For the codex itself, see it under the title *Livre des comptes, des tributes, a payer par les indigenes de San Pablo Teocaltitlan á leur gourverneur D. Antonio Valeriano*, 1574. I thank SilverMoon for generously sending me a copy of her scanned images of this document. Additionally see AGN, Indios, v. 3, e. 510, fol. 119, in which the repartimiento judge (*juez repartidor*) was ordered to deliver to Valeriano tributary natives from the pueblo of Totoltepec and others of uncertain origin to serve in Mexico Tenochtitlan in 1591.

For additional information on the deeds of Valeriano, see SilverMoon, "Imperial College," 177–180. She recounts a dramatic defense of community interests by Valeriano by protecting the nuns of Santa Clara that the archbishop had ordered removed. For SilverMoon, this event gave Valeriano standing in his community among native peoples shortly after he took over as judge-governor (the event took place in 1574).

106. Chimalpahin, *Annals*, 41, which suggests that don Juan Martín served on the cabildo as an alcalde representing San Pablo in 1593, indicating that he worked with Valeriano during his term as governor on the cabildo. Chimalpahin uses the honorific title *don* for Juan Martín.

107. Chimalpahin, *Annals*, 59, 143. Don Geronimo López, a mestizo also, replaced Martín in 1600 and died in office in 1608; see Chimalpahin, *Annals*, 145. See also Horn, *Postconquest Coyoacan*, 45. Horn argues that the first postcontact governors ruled for life because they were in effect tlatoque. Mexico Tenochtitlan seems to have evolved differently from Coyoacan on this point, because Horn argues that after the first generation governors stopped serving for life. She suggests this happened after the appointment of Juan de Guzmán in the 1550s, who served, like don Esteban de Guzmán (no relation, Estéban was from Xochimilco) in Mexico Tenochtitlan, as a judge only. For don Esteban de Guzmán, see Chimalpahin, *Las ocho relaciones*, 228; and Lockhart, *Nahuas after the Conquest*, 34. Governorship for life, unlike in Coyoacan, continued well past the first generation and into the seventeenth century in Mexico Tenochtitlan.

108. AGN, Tierras, v. 39, pt. 1, e. 2; see also Gibson, *Aztecs*, 449, where he identifies the disease as the "great cocoliztli."

109. Gibson, *Aztecs*, 449, 485–486; Noble David Cook, *Born to Die: Disease and New World Conquest, 1492–1650* (New York: Cambridge University Press, 1998), 99–102, 120–133, 138; Hanns J. Prem, "Disease Outbreaks in Central Mexico during the Sixteenth Century," in Noble David Cook and W. George Lovell, eds., *The Secret Judgments of God: Native Peoples and Old World Disease in Colonial Spanish America* (Norman: University of Oklahoma Press, 1992), 22–50; see Sahagún, *Florentine*

Codex, pt. 9, bk. 8, 4, for the description of the cocoliztli epidemic as smallpox. Also see the useful discussion in Rodolofo Acuña-Soto, Leticia Calderón Romero, and James H. Maguire, "Large Epidemics of Hemorrhagic Fevers in Mexico, 1545–1815," *American Journal of Tropical Medicine and Hygiene* 62, no. 6 (2000), 734–735. See Chimalpahin, *Annals*, 92–93, 240–241, where the editors translate *cocoliztli* as "illness" and usually see it as a modifier of a specific kind of illness (e.g., *cocoliztli matlaltotonqui*, which is typhus). Chimalpahin also uses *cocoliztica* to mean "epidemic," further underscoring it as a general term for sickness and not a specific illness. See also Torquemada, *Monarquía indiana*, t. 1, lib. 5, cap. 22, 642. Spaniards also perished regularly because of epidemic disease; see Rebecca Earle, "'If You Eat Their Food . . .': Diets and Bodies in Early Colonial Spanish America," *American Historical Review* 115, no. 3 (2010), 688–713, which discusses the recent literature concerning the apparent fragility of European bodies in America.

110. Chimalpahin, *Las ocho relaciones*, t. 2, 244–245. On 244, the Nahuatl uses *cocoliztli* to identify the disease: "cocoliztli . . . yehuatl yn itoca pestilencia" ("cocolistli what is called pestilencia"). Note also the discussion in Chimalpahin, *Annals*, 92, n. 2, which in describing a different passage from Chimalpahin's work finds a similar word for "green fever," transcribed by Tena as *matlaltotonqui*, which the editors explain etymologically: "*totonqui* means hot; *matlal-* refers to a dark color most often indicated as green." So, the works generally agree this is a reference to a green fever literally. In actuality, however, this was probably typhus, a parasitic disease that causes high fever, delirium, and great suffering. Chimalpahin seems to put it well when he states that "because they knew no remedy," typhus also apparently proved fatal.

111. Torquemada, *Monarquía indiana*, t. 1, 642. See also Acuña-Soto, Calderón Romero, and Maguire, "Large Epidemics," 735.

112. See Kellogg, *Law and the Transformation*, 17–20, which is a study of how the viceregal legal system altered traditional native notions of family, community, and land tenure and used the spike in legal suits as its foundation.

113. Any of a sizable number of legal disputes in the AGN within Ramo Tierras provides an example of the transfer of jurisdiction from indigenous to viceregal courts. See, for examples, AGN, Tierras, v. 55, e. 2, fols. 156–164; AGN, Tierras, v. 38, e. 2; and AGN, Tierras, v. 42, e. 5. Kellogg discusses the first and third cases in *Law and the Transformation*, 33 and 23.

114. Kellogg, *Law and the Transformation*, 4–5, 122–137; Connell, "Emerging Ladino Spaces," 70–72, and table 1 in this volume, which shows that 76 percent of witnesses in a sample of twenty-six contested cases (320 total witnesses, 269 of whom were indigenous) who appeared before the Audiencia were over the age of fifty.

115. Most, though not all, of the cases that appear in AGN, Ramo Tierras, involved disputes over possession. I have made no effort to examine the sixteenth-century notarial records, in part because the archive that houses them in Mexico City does not generally make these fragile documents available to researchers. See the discussion as well in Kellogg, *Law and the Transformation*, 39, n. 2.

116. AGN, Tierras, v. 39, pt. 1, e. 2, fols. 32–39: "las dichas casas y camellones que son en esta ciudad en el barrio de San Juan Yopico junto a la iglesia" ("the said houses and fields that are in this city in the neighborhood of San Juan Yopico next to the church"). In the modern city, it is adjacent to the old and now closed tobacco factory on Plaza San Juan near Salto del Agua.

117. AGN, Tierras, v. 39, pt. 1, e. 2, fol. 14–14v. This document is not paginated in sequence according to how it appears in the volume but according to the index; includes fols. 296–373. I use the internal numbering of folios to designate pages.

118. AGN, Tierras, v. 39, pt. 1, e. 2, fol. 15–15v (from which the translation derives); in Nahuatl, 7–8v. I modify two spellings: "Atzasulchitl" is updated to "Atzaxochitl" and "Joco" to "Xoco."

119. AGN, Tierras, v. 39, pt. 1, e. 2, fols. 15v–18.

120. See don Eusebio Bentura Beleña, ed., *Recopilación sumaria de todos los autos acordados de la Real Audiencia y Sala del Crimen de esta Nueva España, y providencias de su superior govierno; de varias reales cédulas y ordenes que después de publicada la Recopilación de Indias han podido recogerse así de las dirigidas á la misma audiencia ó gobierno, como de algunas otras que por sus notables decisiones convendrá no ignorar,* tomo 2 (México: Zúñiga y Oniveros, 1787), Ordenanza 42 and 43, 21–22. These two ordinances regulated the rules governing transference of indigenous property and both are from 1579; see also AGN, Tierras, v. 39, pt. 1, e. 2, fol. 316. The use of a pregonero did not constitute recognition by the governor that a problem existed but was a standard part of any transfer of property under Spanish law, as shown by the ordinance found in Beleña, which states that without a pregonero and all proper formalities the sale could be voided.

121. AGN, Tierras, v. 39, pt. 1, e. 2, fol. 1–1v.

122. AGN, Tierras, v. 39, pt. 1, e. 2, repeatedly underscores the significance of the epidemic, alternately in the case called the pestilence (*pestilencía*) or cocoliztli. All of these individuals, Mariana, María Xoco, Estevan, and finally Pedro Luis, died within a two-year span.

123. Kellogg, *Law and the Transformation,* 16–18.

124. AGN, Tierras, v. 39, pt. 1, e. 2, fols. 26–39v; Kellogg, *Law and the Transformation,* 18–19.

125. AGN, Tierras, v. 39, pt.1, e. 2, fols. 41–48. This argument did not conform to established inheritance patterns in Hispanic jurisprudence. It may have had an indigenous precedent, but precontact inheritance patterns varied greatly by region and therefore could be manipulated easily. By choosing to hear this argument, the court established its willingness to show flexibility by allowing customary practices to outweigh legal precedent. It also demonstrates that the court was willing to support the claim of, or at least to defend the rights of, weaker or oppressed litigants. Clearly Magdalena Ramírez had experienced great tragedy. She lost her husband to cocoliztli and then had her home taken by the indigenous government and sold. Medieval and Habsburg notions of flexibility, if they

ever functioned in Mexico City, should have come into play in this instance. By recognizing that the just resolution to this dispute involved aiding Ramírez, the court seized on the opportunity to show paternalism, protecting the weak even though it defied written law and went against the convention established in probate law. See Lockhart, *Nahuas after the Conquest*, 90–91; and Cline, *Colonial Culhuacan*, 59–66. Cline points out that an individual who owned property could bequeath it to whomever he/she chose in a will. Absent such a document, probate laws established who had legal claim to property. Ramírez had to make this rather bizarre claim to counter probate law. For legal paternalism, see Lira González, *El amparo*, 17–34. On the flexibility of Habsburg government, see John Leddy Phelan, "Authority and Flexibility in the Spanish Imperial Bureaucracy," *Administrative Science Quarterly* 5, no. 1 (1960), 49–60; John Leddy Phelan, *The People and the King: The Comunero Revolt of New Granada, 1791* (Madison: University of Wisconsin Press, 1978), 6–17; Colin M. MacLachlan, *Spain's Empire in the New World: The Role of Ideas in Institutional and Social Change* (Berkeley: University of California Press, 1988), 11–66; Taylor, *Magistrates of the Sacred*, 13.

126. See AGN, Tierras, v. 39, pt. 2, e. 1, fols. 51 (first sentence), 91, 92–98, for the subsequent dispute and confirmation of the definitive sentence giving possession of the property to Ramírez. Kellogg discusses this case in some detail in *Law and the Transformation*, 16–17.

127. Kellogg, *Law and the Transformation*, 15–19.

128. See Kellogg, *Law and the Transformation*, 15–19, in which she goes through several of González's cases and establishes that he used these complicated arguments with mixed success regularly before the Audiencia.

129. AGN, Tierras, v. 39, pt. 2, e. 1, fols. 92–93v; another litigant, Juan de la Cruz, disputed the sentence but received no further consideration from the Audiencia.

130. AGN, Tierras, v. 55, e. 2.

131. AGN, Tierras, v. 55, e. 2, fols. 158 (Nahuatl) and 164 (Spanish translation).

132. AGN, Tierras, v. 55, e. 2, fols. 165v–166. Miguel de los Angeles was also a part of other disputes over lands; see AGN, Tierras, v. 54, e. 5, fols. 214–295; AGN, Tierras, v. 59, e. 3, fols. 124–140; AGN, Tierras, v. 56, e. 3, fol. np.

133. AGN, Tierras, v. 55, e. 2, fols. 166, 167–170 (in Nahuatl, see fols. 158–163v). One limitation of the Nahuatl documentation here is that it provides only the cabildo's side of the case. The first appearance of the plaintiff, Francisco Martín, comes when the Spanish documentation begins. He states in a brief petition, "I, Francisco Martín, *indio* poor and native of this city [of Mexico] present before Your Excellency [*Vuestra Alteza*] a complaint against the governor and Miguel de los Angeles in whose favor he ruled."

134. AGN, Tierras, v. 55, e. 2, fol. 167 (image). On Nahua writing, see Lockhart, *Nahuas after the Conquest*, 326–334; and Kellogg, *Law and the Transformation*, 39, though neither spend significant time discussing the role or function of indigenous maps and drawings in litigation.

135. AGN, Tierras, v. 55, e. 2, fol. 177. The petition uses the words "yntimo amigo y compañero" and later "muncha amistad" to describe the relationship between Valeriano and Los Angeles.

136. AGN, Tierras, v. 55, e. 2, fol. 178–178v. The quote reads in Spanish, "las que tiene y es sin fundamento decir que el dicho gobernador es intimo amigo de mi parte por que con el tiene igual amistad que con todos y en caso que el dicho auto se haberse de confirmas ninguna persona . . . . el dicho don Antonio Valeriano gobernador por ser buen Cristiano [xpiano]."

137. AGN, Tierras, v. 55, e. 2, fol. 178; I adjust the tense for the English translation. In Spanish, it would read "the lands," reflecting the plural "las tierras," whereas English generally suffices with just "the land."

138. See the discussion in Gibson, *Aztecs*, 213, where he remarks, "Collusion between gobernadores and Spanish authorities . . . for the alienation of property are numerous and unmistakable."

139. Remember, of course, that Juan Martín was a close associate of Valeriano and served in his place as his deputy from 1596 to 1599.

140. AGN, Tierras, v. 55, e. 2, fol. 182–182v.

141. The land itself was by a stream and was twenty brazas (1.67 meters, or two varas) by sixty brazas; AGN, Tierras, v. 55, e. 2, fol. 182–182v. For the measurements, see Kellogg, *Law and the Transformation*, 221, 228; and for the measurement equivalencies, see J. Villasana Haggard, *Handbook for Translators of Spanish Historical Documents* (Austin: University of Texas Press, 1941), 72, 84.

142. For the issue of communal land and land that belonged to indigenous social units, see Lockhart, *Nahuas after the Conquest*, 142–149. Lockhart's work suggests that altepetl land and calpolli land were effectively the same thing, in that the calpolli was a subunit of the altepetl.

143. AGN, Tierras, v. 59, e. 3, fols. 132v, 166v–167.

144. There are many examples of the cabildo acting as a mediator. See, for a particularly clear example beyond those discussed in this chapter, the case of Pedro Hernández, whose claim to land and a house in Moyotlan was disputed by two Spaniards. Valeriano and the cabildo aided Hernández in maintaining possession; AGN, Tierras, v. 56, e. 3, fols. 6v–9 (not paginated within the volume).

145. Yannakakis, *Art*, 25–26, 36; see also her "Witnesses, Spatial Practices, and a Land Dispute in Colonial Oaxaca," *The Americas* 65, no. 2 (2008), 162–165; and Connell, "Emerging Ladino Spaces," 121–124.

146. It is difficult to determine if or in what capacity he was "elected," for no records exist to document elections during Valeriano's tenure in office. On Spanish customs, see the discussion in chapter 3, and Altman, *Transatlantic Ties*, 82–85. Altman notes as well that great variability persisted in Castile from the medieval period. See Ruíz, *Crisis and Continuity*, 180–193, where he discusses the issue of variability among towns.

147. Karttunen, "Cuicapixqueh," 10, notes his "ill-health" late in his life; see also Chimalpahin, *Annals*, 59, and n. 5, which refers to the retirement of Valeriano

because he "no longer could hear" (*tlacaqui:* to hear something) but what the editors take to mean that he had become senile. If the viceregal government understood the position of judge-governor as a similar position to the elected offices of alcalde and regidor, then the judge-governor received an exception of some kind. Apparently this exception applied to heirs of the royal line but continued with transitional figures like Jiménez and Valeriano, who seem to have served as long as they wished or were able.

148. Baskes, *Indians, Merchants and Markets,* 31–37; Lockhart, *Nahuas after the Conquest,* 33; Lunenfeld, *Keepers of the City,* 10–23; Nader, *Liberty in Absolutist Spain,* 143–149; and Gibson *Aztecs,* 80–97. These sources all discuss various aspects of the role of the corregidor in Spanish and American towns. If the viceregal government considered the judge-governor as a royal appointee, like a corregidor, then the office would have existed outside of the electoral rules. In that case, the governor-corregidor as we might call him was conceived of as a steward who served at the will of the crown or viceroy.

149. For rulers serving in office for life, see *CC,* v. 1, 231–237, which lists deaths of rulers and their successors. For a discussion of traditional Mexica succession, see Gillespie, *Aztec Kings,* 14–16.

150. For the philosophical rationale behind the glacial pace of change in Habsburg New Spain, see MacLachlan, *Spain's Empire.*

CHAPTER 3

1. Gibson, *Aztecs,* pl. 13 (follows 370), provides a reproduction of the Gómez de Trasmonte map. See Richard Boyer, "La Ciudad de México en 1628: La visión de Juan Gómez de Trasmonte," *Historia Mexicana* 29, no. 3 (1980), 447–471, for a detailed discussion of this map and the city in 1628. Trasmonte's map does tend to embellish certain elements of the city, for example, imposing a tower on the cathedral that did not exist; see Maza, *La ciudad de México,* 15. Apparently the mountains that ring the city provided the perspective or some approximation of it in the seventeenth century not apparent today. The 1554 Latin dialogues of Francisco Cervantes de Salazar provide some context. In one of the dialogues the two fictitious characters, one an experienced resident who is showing a newly arrived person the sites, climb the slopes of a western mountain ridge to look at the city in much the way the Trasmonte map seems to show; see Cervantes de Salazar, *Life in the Imperial and Loyal City of Mexico in New Spain and the Royal and Pontifical University of Mexico as Described in the Dialogues for the Study of the Latin Language Prepared by Francisco Cervantes de Salazar for Use in His Classes and Printed in 1554,* ed. Carlos Eduardo Castañeda, trans. Minnie Lee Barrett Shepard (Westport: Greenwood Press, 1970 [1953]).

2. There are several seventeenth-century biombos, some in Spain, others in Mexico City and beyond. Other than the one in Chapultepec Castle, the Franz Meyer Museum in Mexico City contains a well-known example. For a photographic collection of these documents, see Manuel Ramos Medina, ed., *Historia*

de la Ciudad de México en los fines del siglo (XV–XX) (México: Gropo Carso, 2001), 109–139, which includes biombo images and their physical location.

3. De la Maza, *La ciudad,* 15, emphasis added. In this style of painting, the traza tends to be depicted with greater detail and the indigenous barrios with substantially less.

4. De la Maza, *La ciudad;* Woodrow Borah, *New Spain's Century of Depression* (Berkeley: University of California Press, 1951); see also John Lynch, *Spain under the Habsburgs,* vol. 2, 2nd ed. (New York: Basil Blackwell, 1981). This detail challenges the then popular notion that New Spain had, like Spain in the seventeenth century, endured a severe economic depression following the booming postconquest period. Historians usually point to this period, the mid-seventeenth century, as the birth of creole identity. The architectural and physical structure of the city reflected the strength of the internal economy; see Brading, *First America,* 3–5, 253–361; Jacques Lafaye, *Quetzalcoatl and Guadalupe: The Formation of Mexican National Consciousness, 1531–1813* (Chicago: University of Chicago Press, 1976), 149–176, 301–311; and Poole, *Our Lady of Guadalupe,* 218–225.

5. AHCM, Aguas, v. 319, e. 1, e. 2, e. 3; AHCM, Aguas, v. 58, e. 1.

6. AHCM, Ríos y Acequias, v. 3871, e. 1, fols. 1–16; AHCM, Ríos y Acequias, v. 3871, e. 5; AGN, Obras Publicas, v. 27, e. 1, fols. 2–11v.

7. AHCM, Obras Públicas en General, v. 1509A, e. 1, fols. 1–5; AHCM, Empedrados, v. 880, e. 2, e. 3, e. 4; AHCM, Paseos, v. 3584, e. 1. Some notable exceptions include the water diversion dynamo on a border between Tlatelolco and the traza, over which the Parroquia de Santa Catarina Martir disputed responsibility for repairs for more than a century with various governors of Mexico Tlatelolco; see AGN, Bienes Nacionales, v. 796, e. 12 (1716), and AGN, Indios, v. 6, pt. 2, e. 695, fol. 160 (1592). I thank Matt O'Hara for pointing me to the Bienes Nacionales document.

8. AHCM, Empedrados, v. 880, e. 9, fol. 1; AHCM, Limpieza de Ciudad, v. 3240, e. 1, fol. 4; AHCM, Limpieza de Ciudad, v. 3240, e. 2, fol. 11; see also Esteban Sánchez de Tagle, *Los dueños de la calle: Una historia de la vía pública en la época colonial* (México: Instituto Nacional de Antropología e Historia, 1997). Sánchez de Tagle's work deals with the late eighteenth century, but his points are relevant regarding the issue that Spanish law makes clear that building owners were also quite literally the owners of the streets and therefore responsible for street repair.

9. Cope, *Limits,* 28–29, comments on the poor state of decaying urban infrastructure by the late seventeenth and early eighteenth centuries.

10. Brading, *First America,* 3–5. A creole is generally understood to be a Spaniard born in Spanish America.

11. Hoberman, *Mexico's Merchant Elite,* 7–9. See also Cope, *Limits,* 38–39, 86–105, which adds an important layer of complexity to Hoberman's assertion that after 1660 a "constructive equilibrium [formed] at midcentury, which lasted for the rest of the colony."

12. Cope, *Limits,* 27–39.

13. Irving Leonard, *Baroque Times in Old Mexico: Seventeenth-Century Persons, Places, and Practices* (Ann Arbor: University of Michigan Press, 1959), 40–50. See the comments of Cope, *Limits*, 9–15, 27–33.

14. Hoberman, *Mexico's Merchant Elite*, 13–17, 264–273.

15. On the uprising in 1612, see Martínez, "Black Blood," 481–488, and for primary accounts see Chimalpahin, *Annals*, 212–229; and Luis Querol y Roso, "Negros y mulatos de la Nueva España: Historia de su alzamiento de 1612," *Anales de la Universidad de Valencia* 12, no. 90 (1931–1932), 121–162. For the uprising in 1624, see Israel, *Race, Class and Politics*, 135–175; and Rosa Feijoo, "El tumulto de 1624," *Historia Mexicana* 14, no. 1 (1964), 42–70. On the flood, see Richard Boyer, *La gran inundación: Vida y sociedad en la Ciudad de México (1629–1638)* (México: Secretaria de Educación Pública, 1975); and Louisa S. Hoberman, "City Planning in Spanish Colonial Government: The Response of Mexico City to the Problem of Floods, 1607–1637" (Ph.D. diss., Columbia University, 1972).

16. AGN, Obras Públicas en General, v. 27, e. 1, e. 2; AHCM, Calzadas y Caminos, v. 440, e. 3, fol. 82; AHCM, Puentes, v. 3716, e. 3, fol. 8; AHCM, Rios y Acequias, v. 3871, e. 5, fol. 10; AHCM, Alcaicería, v. 343, e. 1, fols. 1–318; all of these documents show a mix of free-wage and repartimiento labor. The rate of pay for each group makes them easily distinguishable. By the end of the century, as shown in the Alcaicería project (built to replace the burned market stalls destroyed in the fire of 1692), free-wage laborers outnumbered tribute laborers; see Connell, "Because I Was Drunk"; and Silva Prada, *La política*, on the uprising in 1692. In addition, repartimiento workers often came from pueblos outside of Mexico City; see AGN, Bienes Nacionales, v. 230, e. 45, e. 46, e. 47, which show that Mexico Tenochtitlan and Mexico Tlatelolco sent only a fraction of the repartimiento labor to work on the metropolitan cathedral and other public works for Mexico City between 1575 and 1583. See also AGN, General de Parte, v. 1, e. 22, and AGN, Indios, v. 10, e. 144; this final order, from 1629, reduced the number of repartimiento workers owed by Mexico Tenochtitlan and Mexico Tlatelolco significantly from the earlier totals; see also AGN, Indios, v. 12, e. 167. Public works projects became the only legal means to employ repartimiento workers in the seventeenth century. Apparently the courts, following earlier rulings about the use of repartimiento workers for personal service, concluded that the only way to make repartimiento labor truly public work was to restrict it to services done for the entire community—hence all the street paving, acequia cleaning, and maintenance.

17. AGI, Escribanía de Cámara, l. 178a, e. 9; because of the *repartimiento de turnos*, an illegal tax assessed on the city's slaughterhouses (for more than a century from the late sixteenth through the late seventeenth), public works for Mexico City had a large budget. See also AGI, Escribanía de Cámara, l. 172b, e. 4, which suggests further interference in the collection of tribute by the corregidor.

18. AGN, Mercedes, v. 7, e. sn, fol. 141, which describes the labor draft for 1563; for the 1685–99 period, see AHCM, Ríos y Acequias, v. 3871, e. 5, which lists labor drafts for cleaning the drainage canals that employed more than fifty

laborers a week from all over central Mexico; and AHCM, Obras Públicas en General, v. 1509a, e. 4, which is a 1699 document showing a draft of twenty-five laborers to clean and repair the bridges of the city.

19. There are many ways to see the reduction in the indigenous population, and certainly the well-understood demographic collapse in the late sixteenth century that continued through the seventeenth is one way; see Sherburne F. Cook and Woodrow Borah, *Essays in Population History: Mexico and the Caribbean,* vol. 1 (Berkeley: University of California Press, 1970), 73–118, 280–286; and Gibson, *Aztecs,* 136–149, esp. figs 3–6 and tab. 10, which shows a sharp decline from the mid-sixteenth century continuing until about the 1630s, when a moderate recovery began. Mestizaje also reduced the tribute-paying population, as indigenous men and women married or had children with nonnatives; see Connell, "Emerging Ladino Spaces," 151–153; David Cahill, "Colour by Numbers: Racial and Ethnic Categories in the Viceroyalty of Peru, 1532–1824," *Journal of Latin American Studies* 26, no. 3 (1994), 325–346; Patricia Seed, "Social Dimensions of Race: Mexico City, 1753," *Hispanic American Historical Review* 63, no. 4 (1992), 569–606; and Vicenta Cortés Alonso, "La imagen del otro: Indios, blancos y negros en el México del siglo XVI," *Revista de Indias* 51, no. 192 (1991), 285–289.

20. See the chapter 2 discussion and the appendix, which lists mestizo judge-governors; and Lockhart, *Nahuas after the Conquest,* 34, tab 2.1.

21. AGN, Indios, v. 12, e. 215; see also Cope, *Limits,* 92, who refers to this same document to emphasize the idea that patrons had great control over their clients. Gibson, *Aztecs,* 391–392, makes a similar suggestion to what I have proposed, that Spanish officials initially entered into the service of governors to help collect tribute in houses where Spaniards refused to grant collectors access to the natives under their control; see the discussion in chapter 4 of the alguacuil amparador. See AGN, Indios, v. 15, e. 5.

22. Hoberman, "Bureaucracy and Disaster," 212, lists the major floods prior to 1607 (1555, 1580, 1604, and 1607).

23. AGI, Audiencia de México, l. 31, e. 3, fol. 1–1v. The documents generally confirm the timeframe of rains in Mexico City, but anyone who has lived in Mexico City in the spring knows the dramatic transformation from dry to wet that usually happens in late May or early June. For the Marqués de Cerralvo, see Hoberman, *Mexico's Merchant Elite,* 178–179, who suggests that his administration was marred by corruption and inappropriate dealings with merchants.

24. Boyer, *La gran inundación,* 25–33, discusses the damage and extent of the flooding and the cost to the population.

25. Louisa Hoberman, "Bureaucracy and Disaster: Mexico City and Flood of 1629," *Journal of Latin American Studies* 6, no. 2 (1974), 214. The quotation includes the word "abode" instead of "adobe," but the latter makes more sense in context.

26. Hoberman, "Bureaucracy and Disaster," 212–213, indicates that the construction of the drainage system began in 1607 after the flood of that year receded and cost about 15 percent of the "average annual income of the royal treasury of Mexico City" for 1606–10.

27. Boyer, *La gran inundación,* 33–38. Hoberman, "Bureaucracy and Disaster," 215–220. Hoberman makes the case that the response by city bureaucrats saved the city, carrying on its business and offering disaster relief to those who chose to stay.

28. AGN, Indios, v. 10, e. 276, fol. 156v.

29. AGN, Indios, v. 10, e. 275, e. 276, fol. 156–156v.

30. AGN, Indios, v. 10, e. 276, fol. 156v.

31. Many examples exist, but see AGN, Indios, v. 17, e. 56, fols. 77v–82v, for one particularly compelling case from 1654, in which the contador filed a petition arguing that the governor-elect, don Juan de Velasco, did not have enough financial backing to cover the 6,221 pesos and six tomines and replaced him with don Juan de Aguilar.

32. To provide a sense of the inconclusive evidence, the financing documents in Archivo Histórico de Hacienda match up with the election reports in Indios for the 1620s, which seems to suggest that once elected, a candidate served until deposed or until he stepped down or died in office. See the discussion later in the chapter of Judge-Governor don Cristóbal Pascual (r. 1630–36) for further detail.

33. Many of the election documents certify the result only, but through the Juzgado General de los Indios. Appended to such mundane documents are sometimes found petitions that sought to challenge the election of the governor. Often these did not become full-fledged civil lawsuits but rather were heard only in the Juzgado General. See for example, AGN, Indios, v. 24, e. 127, fols. 79v–81v (1666–67), in which don Felipe de Aguilar contested the election of don Juan de Santiago via petition. Such challenges became increasingly prevalent in the late seventeenth century.

34. AGN, Civil, v. 740, e. 10, fols. 20–21v, which is a certification of the election written by Josef Romero, who described himself as "an escribano of the Juzgado General de los Indios de esta Nueva España."

35. AGN, Civil, v. 740, e. 10, fols. 12–13v, which lists the electors from the four subdivisions of the altepetl of Mexico Tenochtitlan; also included is a fifth subdivision that emerged in the seventeenth century, the barrio of Santa Cruz, which was part of Moyotlan, the tlaxilacalli of Tecpancaltitlan.

36. AGN, Indios, v. 23, e. 370, fol. 339v (1659). The text identifies don Juan de Alva and don Gregorio as interpretors (nahuatlatos) of the "lengua mexicana," or Nahuatl, and indicates that an unnamed escribano from each barrio wrote their own account.

37. Few documents for Mexico City that detail elections or the procedure for election survive. There are many disputes, but actual records of the election ceremony itself are extremely rare. For a particularly elaborate one, discussed at length in chapter 4, see AGN, Civil, v. 740, e. 10, fols. 18–19v.

38. AGN, Indios, v. 23, e. 370, fol. 339v, literally, "hábil, capaz . . . de buena vida y costumbres." The election ceremony allowed for commentary on the election, and until 1666 the most common voice seemed to come from the contador, who sometimes recommended that a governor be disqualified because he lacked

NOTES TO PAGES 97–98

the capacity to gather tribute; see AGN, Indios, v. 17, e. 56, fols. 78v–79, where contador general Martín de San Martín disputed the capacity of the governor-elect to finance the tribute collection for the year 1654.

39. Note the resonance with the early charges levied against the cabildo of Mexico Tenochtitlan in 1564 (see chapter 1). This check seems specifically designed to root out any possibility of collusion and vote solicitation, as outlined in the 1564 allegation that the cabildo had cut secret deals with electors in advance of the election; AGN, Civil, v. 644, e. 1, fols. 2v–3.

40 AGN, Civil, v. 740, e. 10, fols. 8v–17.

41. AGN, Civil, v. 740, e. 10; see the discussion in the introduction and chapter 1 about precontact indigenous elections. For the status/hierarchy divisions, see Lockhart, *Nahuas after the Conquest*, 25.

42. Matthew D. O'Hara, "Stone, Mortar, and Memory: Church Construction and Communities in Late Colonial Mexico City," *Hispanic American Historical Review* 86, no. 4 (2006), 650–667; see also his *A Flock Divided: Race, Religion, and Politics in Mexico, 1749–1857* (Durham, N.C.: Duke University Press, 2010). Although O'Hara's work is rooted in the eighteenth century and focused on the institutional issues surrounding secularization, he highlights the central place of parishes and *doctrinas de indios* within native communities of Mexico City. One might expect these to have some place in the political life and political makeup of electors. My evidence, particularly this election record, suggests that political divisions based on precontact structures remained in place and that, at least in 1674, the political landscape superseded the ecclesiastical divisions. I suspect that for elections the political space of the city retained its importance well into the eighteenth century. On doctrinas and parishes, see also Taylor, *Magistrates of the Sacred*, 83–86.

43. But accusations of ineligible voters did appear in the eighteenth century. In the election of 1724 in Mexico Tlatelolco, some four hundred voters allegedly cast ballots though, according to those who disputed the result, the parcialidad had only 263 eligible voters; see AGN, Indios, v. 50, e. 130, fols. 249–250v.

44. The possibility exists, because of the apparent lack of oversight of elector credentials, that ineligible voters were a common feature of cabildo elections. But the native government may have vetted electors as well, and the small size of the group would make an imposter stand out. It is also possible that the culture of honor and ease of exposure kept the ineligible out of the tecpan on election day.

For the culture and workload of scribes, including their honor-bound nature, see Michael Scardaville, "Justice by Paperwork: A Day in the Life of a Court Scribe in Bourbon Mexico City," *Journal of Social History* 36, no. 4, (2003), 979–987. Scardaville's Bourbon scribe likely differs little from the scribes one might encounter in the seventeenth century. Indeed, fundamental to the assumptions of Scardaville's work is the idea that Habsburg paternalism persisted in Bourbon Mexico City despite the emergence of a new set of philosophical assumptions for governing in the eighteenth century; see MacLachlan, *Spain's Empire,* 125–128. For the issue of honor in the viceregal bureaucracy, see also Mark Burkholder,

"Honor and Honors in Colonial Spanish America," in Lyman Johnson and Sonya Lipsett-Rivera, eds., *The Faces of Honor: Sex, Shame, and Violence in Colonial Latin America* (Albuquerque: University of New Mexico Press, 1998).

45. See AGN, Indios, v. 17, e. 56, fols. 77v–82v, for an example of a governor who could not provide convincing fiadores to satisfy the contador general de los tributos.

46. AGN, Indios, v. 23, e. 370, fol. 339v: "as was their [native] custom they cast their votes secretly."

47. Numerous examples in seemingly mundane election reports in AGN, Ramo de Indios, attest to the authority of the oidor as a central figure in the appeals process. When the oidor reported back to the Audiencia, he included such appeals appended to his certification. Sometimes these appeals became the basis of an inquiry. See chapters 4 and 5.

48. AGN, Indios, v. 14, e. 7.

49. AGN, Indios, v. 23, e. 432, fol. 425.

50. For don Diego de la Cruz Villanueva's tenure in office in Mexico Tenochtitlan, see AGN, Indios, v. 17, e. 21 bis, fol. 33v; AGN, Indios, v. 18, e. 58, fols. 48–49v; AGN, Indios, v. 19, e. 37, fol. 18; and AGN, Indios, v. 19, e. 150, fol. 80. See also Silva Prada, *La política,* 405, where she argues that he may have also served as governor in Mexico Tlatelolco in 1669. There is documentary support that he was likely governor in Tlatelolco in 1669 in AGN, Indios, v. 24, e. 266, fol. 169–169v, but, because the 1669 document does not reference his former service as governor in either Tenochtitlan or Tlatelolco, it is possible that these are two different individuals, a possibility Silva Prada does not entertain. Villanueva was removed from office in March 1657 for failure to collect tribute; see chapter 4.

51. AGN, Indios, v. 18, e. 58, fols. 48–49v.

52. AGN, Indios, v. 18, e. 58, fols. 48v–49.

53. AGN, Archivo Histórico de Hacienda, v. 1418, e. 17, fols. 292–301, e. 28, 400–403, which are respectively from Tlaxcala and Mexico Tenochtitlan in 1620. Archivo Histórico de Hacienda was still being cataloged at the time of this writing, and I examined the cataloged volumes for finance documents of governors that run from roughly 1620 to 1645, with many gaps in coverage. This branch of the archive contains many hundreds of linear feet of uncataloged materials, which may yet yield additional gubernatorial financing documents.

54. The practice of using a fiador or guarantor persists in modern Mexico. Renting property often requires a fiador, who can be purchased for a fee. Suffice it to say that they are far more ubiquitous today than they likely were in the seventeenth century. Gibson discusses the role of "financial guarantors" in tribute collection briefly; in *Aztecs,* 392, he is referring to the same documentation (AGN, Tributos, v. 10, e. 6, fols. 86–93) that is the beginning point of this discussion. For the most recent work on the role of financial guarantors, although in a different and later context for New Spain, see Baskes, *Indians, Merchants, and Markets,* 20–24, 31–38. The alcaldes mayores in Oaxaca whom Baskes studies had to account for significantly more than governors in Mexico Tenochtitlan, but they were also

able to do this because the merchants who backed them were, according to his argument, buying a large stake in the Oaxacan cochineal economy.

55. AGN, Archivo Histórico de Hacienda, v. 1418, e. 28, fols. 400–403. Several Valerianos served as governor in the 1610s and 1620s: don Francisco Bautista Valeriano (r. 1616–20), don Juan Valeriano (r. 1620), and don Antonio Valeriano the younger (r. 1620–24).

56. See AGN, Archivo Histórico de Hacienda, v. 1423, e. 31, fols. 387–388, in which don Francisco de Tapia y Barrera proposed five fiadores, all natives, and many from the city. Regional variation is apparent in the documentation. For an exception, see AGN, Archivo Histórico de Hacienda, v. 1422, e. 4, fols. 47–67, which shows that Tlaxcala was an obvious outlier. The governor in 1624 proposed five Spanish fiadores who pledged support of 8,000 pesos collectively, ranging from 500 pesos to 2,500 pesos.

57. AGN, Tributos, v. 10, e. 6, fols. 88–89v. See also Gibson, *Aztecs*, 392, where he discusses this same document, noting the presence of Spaniards and mestizos.

58. AGN, Indios, v. 17, e. 56, fols. 78v–79. Velázquez was elected but denied office on the grounds that he could not read or write and allegedly because he did not have sufficient financial backing. He rejected the contador's insistence that Spaniards had to provide the backing on the grounds that natives had always had the right to choose their guarantors freely.

59. AGN, Archivo Histórico de Hacienda, v. 1418, e. 28, fols. 400–403.

60. AGN, Indios, v. 21, e. 146, fols. 133v–134.

61. Other aspects of this same dispute are discussed in chapter 4, but it is important to note that the contador general asked the viceroy to nullify the election based on the governor's inability to produce fiadores; see AGN, Indios, v. 21, e. 146, fol. 133v.

62. Apparently the increase in the amount of tribute owed grew significantly, from 6,221 pesos and six tomines in 1654 to 12,500 pesos in 1674, roughly a 100 percent increase; see AGN, Indios, v. 17, e. 56, fols. 77v–82v; AGN, Tributos, v. 10, e. 6.

63. AGI, Escribania de Camara, l. 178a, e. 2, provides a case where two illegitimate children sue to inherit the estate of their father, a merchant. They find that most of their father's wealth was tied up in merchandise that had to be constantly sold and replaced and was heavily leveraged.

64. AGN, Tributos, v. 10, e. 6, fols. 92–95v.

65. AGN, Tributos, v. 10, e. 6, fols. 88–91v.

66. The governorship apparently had no limited liability clause to prevent personal assets from being seized. Though it is unclear why doña Josefa de la Trinidad had to pledge her property in a financial statement that gave her husband control, presumably this was dowry property over which her husband had no legal claim. There are other cases in which the royal couple, so to speak, took joint responsibility for tribute collection. In Mexico Tlatelolco in 1622, don Juan Toribio de Alcaraz (also governor in 1634) and his wife, doña Juana de Alcaraz y Alcaçar, took joint responsibility; AGN, Tributos, v. 10, e. 6, fols. 88–97v. See also

Terraciano, *Mixtecs,* 171–180, on the ruling couple in Oaxaca; and AGN, Archivo Histórico de Hacienda, v. 1418, e. 28, fols. 400–403, for the 1620 election of don Antonio Valeriano the younger, who also had to pledge his personal property and that of his wife.

Montaño apparently did not do so well as a governor, at least from the perspective of electors. He received only two votes when he ran for reelection; AGN, Civil, v. 740, e. 10, fols. 16v–17.

67. The family of powerful governors probably best represents for Mexico Tenochtitlan the idea of the "gubernatorial lineage" articulated by Lockhart, *Nahuas after the Conquest,* 130–132. Don Juan de Aguilar (the elder, r. 1654) had as many as three sons who also ruled. Don Felipe de Santiago y Aguilar (r. 1667, 1673, 1675) and don Juan de Aguilar (the younger, r. 1672) definitely served as governor and were his sons; see appendix for details and sources. It is also possible that don Felipe de Aguilar (the younger? r. 1694–95) is part of this lineage, but I cannot establish the direct connection in the same way as with don Felipe and don Juan. See the discussion of the Aguilar family in chapter 5.

68. AGN, Tributos, v. 10, e. 6, fols. 92v–93.

69. AGN, Tributos, v. 10, e. 6, fol. 98–98v.

70. Baskes, *Indians, Merchants, and Markets,* 31–38, argues that merchants took on the financial risk incurred by the alcalde mayor in exchange for access to markets. Baskes was able to document the process with a series of contracts he uncovered for the late eighteenth century between fiadores and alcaldes mayores. Despite the comparison issues—his data come from the late eighteenth century—Baskes's argument helps to explain why a merchant would assume risk for a government official: because as economic actors, merchants sought to purchase access to markets that they could obtain only by financing those agents who were in closest contact with the producers of cochineal. In effect, the government officers, alcaldes mayores, served as commercial agents for the merchants.

71. See the discussion below and AGN, Indios, v. 13, e. 259; AGN, Indios, 13, e. 226. Gibson makes the case that by the end of the sixteenth century indigenous governments no longer controlled the urban markets; see *Aztecs,* 395, 581, n. 148. Gibson did not use the two seventeenth-century documents from Ramo de Indios but bases his assessment on observations of Cervantes de Salazar (1554), Torquemada (1618), Sedano (1880), and Montemayor y Cordova de Cuenca (1677, cited in Bentura Beleña). The manuscript documents in Indios, by no means an exhaustive list, suggest that in the mid-seventeenth century indigenous rulers had some capacity to regulate access to the indigenous markets of the city. That the viceregal government had the ability to mediate disputes notwithstanding, it seems that in the first instance the cabildo had some capacity to grant access to markets. See the discussion of the fruit import business in chapter 4.

By the eighteenth century, there is additional evidence to suggest that the corregidor of the city regulated the indigenous markets, but this was not absolute. In a 1721 petition, market women Polonia Agustina, Ignacia de Jesús, and María de los Santos appealed to the corregidor to help them fend off a challenge from seven other market women who contested their right to sell potatoes in the market of Mexico Tlatelolco. It is unclear from the petition, however, if this was the first avenue of appeal, and the length of time elapsed (the problem began "in the year before" and the petition was filed on 7 November 1721) between event and appeal to the corregidor suggests that it was not; see AHCM, Rastros y Mercados, v. 3728, e. 5, fol. np. The petition here was written to the viceroy, but it was forwarded to the corregidor, who was to take action. Additional work needs to be done to clarify this issue, which lies outside the scope of this study.

72. See chapter 4 or, for one example, AGN, Indios, v. 33, e. 175, fol. 122–122v.

73. It is possible that an inquiry of this kind exists, but I have not uncovered it for the time period. There is a document compiled in the eighteenth century that provides an assessment of tribute finance done in the seventeenth; see AGN, Archivo Histórico de Hacienda, v. 105, e. 1, fols. 1–312.

74. For nineteenth-century examples, see Brian Hamnett, "The Appropriation of Mexican Church Wealth by the Spanish Bourbon Government: The 'Consolidacion de Vales Reales,' 1805–1809," *Journal of Latin American Studies* 1, no. 2 (1969), 85–90. For a general discussion on the potential influence of fiadores, see Brian Hamnett, *Politics and Trade in Southern Mexico: 1750–1821* (Cambridge: Cambridge University Press, 1971); and Jeremy Baskes, "Coerced or Voluntary? The *Repartimiento* and Market Participation of Peasants in Late Colonial Oaxaca," *Journal of Latin American Studies* 28, no. 1 (1996), 3–5, and n. 5; and the larger discussion in Baskes, *Indians, Merchants and Markets*, 31–38.

75. AGN, Indios, v. 12, e. 116, fol. 77–77v. The document was written in 1634 and does not provide a specific date for his assumption of office, stating only that he became judge-governor at the end of the year. The Audiencia announced preparations for the election to be held in Mexico Tenochtitlan on 5 March 1630; see AGN, Indios, v. 10, pt. 2, e. 25, fol. 202v.

76. AGN, Indios, v. 10, pt. 1, e. 276, fol. 156v, which granted the relief on 23 July 1630. The 1634 document that discusses governor Pascual states that "por los fines del año de 1630 . . . fue electo por tal gobernador." Thus, about six months after the order to halt tribute collection the new governor was elected; AGN, Indios, v. 12, e. 116, fol. 77–77v.

77. AGN, Indios, v. 12, e. 116, fol. 77–77v.

78. AGN, Indios, v. 12, e. 110, fols. 73v–74v. Toribio de Alcaraz had been governor of Tlatelolco since 1622; see AGN, Archivo Histórico de Hacienda, v. 1420, l. 1, fols. 1–4v. He was not elected, however, but rather appointed in place of elected governor don Melchor de San Martín, who the viceroy, the Marqués de Gelves (r. 1621–24), had disqualified on the grounds that he was prohibited from holding office because of his status—in other words, he was not a principal. Toribio de Alcaraz served through the flood and was disqualified from serving in 1643 by viceregal decree based on the recommendation of the contador general; see AGN, Archivo Histórico de Hacienda, v. 1437, l. 78.

79. AGN, Indios, v. 10, pt. 3, e. 25, fol. 304v; see also AGN, Indios, v. 10, pt. 3, e. 13, fol. 297v, in which the contador recognizes the problem in May (just after the first round of tribute deposits were due) and offers aid to the governor of Tlatelolco.

80. Gibson, *Aztecs*, 206–207; and Lockhart, *Nahuas after the Conquest*, 43–45. Lockhart comments extensively on the Nahuatl terminology, providing several variants that appear in the Nahuatl documentation such as *teyacanqui, tequitlato*, and *cihuatepixqui*. The subtle distinctions among these offices seem to have been lost on Spaniards.

81. AGN, Indios, v. 10, pt. 3, e. 46, fol. 313v.

82. AGN, Indios, v. 12, e. 110, fols. 73v–74; and AGN, Indios, v. 12, e. 97, fol. 56–56v. For the desagüe project of Huehuetoca, see Boyer, *Gran inundación;* and Hoberman, "Bureaucracy and Disaster," 212–213, in which she remarks that the system was not well maintained and quickly became "blocked and useless."

83. The repartimiento workers were supposed to serve for fifteen days and then return home and another crew would replace them. Fourteen hundred would have been slightly more than 4 percent of the tributary population, the percentage who were supposed to be used to maintain the drainage infrastructure of the city; see AGN, Indios, v. 12, e. 127, fol. 74–74v, where the governor performs this calculation of 4 percent in his petition, and AGN, Indios, v. 12, e. 97, fol. 56–56v. For a discussion of the legal requirements from the Spanish municipal council, see Hoberman, "Bureaucracy and Disaster," 219–220, which she describes as "workers drafted for the non-harvest period (4% of the tributary population)."

84. AGN, Indios, v. 12, e. 110, fol. 74. See also Gibson, *Aztecs*, 440. Gibson shows that Tlatelolco claimed that these towns were subject (*sujeto*) to the cabecera of Tlatelolco—using the terminology found in Spanish-language documents. On the cabecera/sujeto concept of regional governance, see Gibson, *Aztecs*, 33, 440; Gibson's appendix 2 lists the subject towns for Tlatelolco. See also Lockhart, *Nahuas after the Conquest*, 19–20, 52–58, in which he rightly indicates that this was a Spanish concept that did not translate well into native concepts of land tenure (altepetl, tlaxilacalli, calpolli). I follow the language of the document.

85. AGN, Archivo Histórico de Hacienda, v. 1430, l. 52, fol. 733.

86. Though I have not made a systematic effort to follow the governorship and its association with the viceregal court, there is an important patronage connection. For a specific discussion that focuses on the viceregal court, see Rosenmüller, *Patrons, Partisans and Palace Intrigues*, who suggests that indigenous governors were often called to testify in residencia hearings for the outgoing viceroy, which Rosenmüller argues made them essentially clients of the viceroy; and Linda Arnold, *Bureaucracy and Bureaucrats in Mexico City, 1742–1835* (Tucson: University of Arizona Press, 1988). Arnold points out that the official processions that brought new viceroys to New Spain usually stopped in Tlaxcala and Mexico Tenochtitlan to establish relations. For the viceregal shifts, see Israel, *Race, Class and Politics*, 190–195. It is also important to recognize that the Audiencia and viceroy had previously imprisoned Pascual for debt in 1634 but restored him to the governorship

after the initial warning; apparently the viceroy and his ministers did not believe Pascual's claim that he had collected and deposited all the tribute owed by Mexico Tenochtitlan for the years he served as governor; see AGN, Indios, v. 12, e. 116, fol. 74v. This order from 1634 released Pascual from the viceregal jail and allowed him, and his cabildo, to continue their work collecting tribute.

87. I have searched the finance books available for the years 1630–37, examining every legajo, and have found no record of the tribute finance reports for Mexico Tenochtitlan; see AGN, Archivo Histórico de Hacienda, v. 1431, ll. 1–72, fols. 1–274v; and AGN, Archivo Histórico de Hacienda, v. 1432, ll. 1–51, fols. 1–448v. The absence of the report does not indicate absolutely that none was filed or that none existed or that it was particularly unusual to name fiadores only for the first year in office. AGN, Archivo Histórico de Hacienda, v. 1423, e. 31, fols. 387–388, lists fiadores for don Francisco de Tapia y Barrera for the first year he served but not for subsequent years. The Archivo Histórico de Hacienda ledgers are registries designed to put in one central place a record of tribute finance and include important governors like those of Mexico Tenochtitlan, Mexico Tlatelolco, and Tlaxcala, but they also include the tribute financing for alcaldes mayores and corregidores. They provide fine documentation for economic analysis, inasmuch as they indicate tribute levels for all indigenous towns in New Spain. Further confirmation is provided in the finance document records of the subsequent governor, don Bartolomé Cortés de Mendoza Axayacatzin (r. 1636–37), in which the juez de residencia, don Pedro de Quiroga y Moya, indicated directly that Pascual had not submitted fiadores except for the first year he served; see AGN, Archivo Histórico de Hacienda, v. 1430, l. 52, fol. 733.

88. Pascual was released from his imprisonment subsequently by royal order and apparently did not lose all of his property and status; AGN, Archivo Histórico de Hacienda, v. 1430, e. 52; AGN, Reales Cedulas Originales y Dubpicados, D11, e. 393, fol. 298v. For his release in 1636 and his subsequent troubles in 1640 for demanding personal service from Sebastián Ramírez, a seventy-year-old native lame in his left arm (*manco del brazo izquierdo*), see AGN, Indios, v. 12, e. 73, fol. 202.

89. AGN, Archivo Histórico de Hacienda, v. 1430, l. 52, fol. 733–733v. This petition, in the name of the Marqués de Cadereita, provides a damning look at Pascual and those elected to fill his post in 1636. Cadereita aggressively sought to increase the revenue of the city and was sometimes rebuked by the crown; see Hoberman, *Mexico's Merchant Elite*, 123, 200–204. It is plausible that Cadereita had or wanted a say in the establishment of the governorship of Mexico Tenochtitlan. By promoting a candidate and placing him in a native office, the viceroy gained a client. There is later evidence of viceroys working to solicit the native governors as clients. See also the brief discussion in Israel, *Race, Class, and Politics*, 190–195.

90. See AGN, Indios, v. 12, e. 116, fols. 77–78, for Pascual's imprisonment. See AGN, Archivo Histórico de Hacienda, v. 1430, l. 52, fol. 733; and AGN, Reales Cedulas Originales y Duplicados, D11, e. 393, fol. 298v, for his release in 1636. I

am hesitant to say definitively that he was the first based only on the lack of a previous documented example. Further research may provide evidence that I did not uncover. Though I believe my research was comprehensive in all the usual places governors appear, much remains uncataloged in the AGN and AGI. It also seems that the Audiencia might have made more of the arrest had it been the first, though I suspect that governors in the hinterlands of New Spain who presided over smaller pueblos had faced arrest for debt, making it common enough to escape fanfare in 1634. See, for example, AGN, Indios, v. 6, pt. 2, e. 260 (1591), which is from the pueblo of Huaquechula (jurisdiction of Puebla), in which the governor, alcaldes, and principales were imprisoned for "causa del rezago de indios que deben"—unpaid tribute owed by the community. They were immediately released. The cabildo of Mexico Tenochtitlan, as discussed in chapter 1, faced the threat of arrest in 1564; AGN, Civil, v. 644, e. 1.

91. AGN, Archivo Histórico de Hacienda, v. 1430, l. 52, fol. 733.

92. AGN, Archivo Histórico de Hacienda, v. 1430, l. 52, fol. 733–733v. It is unclear from this document in what position de la Hara served to cause such a lack of confidence among the community members.

93. For the important process of native officials as intermediaries who felt pressure from both native communities and viceregal officials, see Yannakakis, *Art*, 47–64.

94. AGN, Indios, v. 10, pt. 3, e. 182, fol. 382 (1633). Ramo de Indios is filled with complaints of abuses allegedly committed by agents of the indigenous government. They extend back before the flood; see AGN, Indios, v. 10, pt. 1, e. 111, fol. 59v (1629), a case in which two native pulque venders complained that the alguaciles scaled the wall of their home regularly to harass them even though they had a license to sell pulque granted by the viceregal government.

95. One of the clearer examples of passing along the pressure to collect tribute came during the flood in Mexico Tlatelolco in the north, when the governor imprisoned the "merinos and regidores" who had failed to collect all of the tribute they were responsible to gather; see AGN, Indios, v. 10, pt. 2, e. 146, fol. 257v.

96. Complaints coming from New Spain in general increased during this period, and probably disproportionately from Mexico City because of the flood and tribute problems; see AGN, Reales Cedulas, v. 1, e. 164, fol. 315, in which the crown suggests in 1636 that the petitions from New Spain had increased significantly in recent years and that local officials needed to defend the rights of local native groups more effectively.

97. AGN, Archivo Histórico de Hacienda, v. 1430, l. 52, fol. 733v.

98. AGN, Indios, v. 10, pt. 1, e. 113, fol. 60v.

99. AGN, Archivo Histórico de Hacienda, v. 1430, l. 52, fol. 733v.

100. AGN, Indios, v. 7 e. 21, fol. 9–9v.

101. AGN, Indios, v. 7, e. 465, fol. 222, which notes that León was a "satisfactory" choice. Other examples of the same procedure include the appointment of don Francisco Bautista Valeriano (r. 1616–20), AGN, Indios, v. 7, e. 21, fol. 9–9v, who replaced the ill don Juan Pérez de Monterrey.

102. Chimalpahin, *Annals,* 143; AGN, Indios, v. 7, e. 21, fol. 9–9v. Don Antonio Valeriano, though an important figure in Mexico Tenochtitlan who married into the royal line, was an Azcapotzalteca; more recently, don Juan Valeriano served, before his appointment in 1620, as the governor of Iztapalapa.

103. Gibson, *Aztecs,* 48–49, map 3, shows that these communities were tightly organized in close proximity to Tenochtitlan and Tlatelolco; see also Carrasco, *Tenochca Empire,* 102–103, in which he suggests that important children of tlatoque, especially in the early sixteenth century, ruled over regional towns. Cuitlahuac, tlatoani after the death of Moteucçoma Xocoyotzin, was Tlatoani of Iztapalapa. One of Itzcoatzin's sons, Teçoçomoctzin, was governor of Azcapotzalco as well; Hernán Cortés, "The Second Letter," in *Letters from Mexico,* 82–83, indicates that Cuitlahuac, the "brother of Mutezuma" was the ruler of Iztapalapa in 1519.

104. AGN, Archivo Histórico de Hacienda, v. 1430, l. 52, fols. 733–738. He became the governor of one of the parcialidades in Puebla; see AGN, Archivo Histórico de Hacienda, v. 1434, l. 18, fols. 213–245. His successor, don Martín González, took office in 1638; see AGN, Archivo Histórico de Hacienda, v. 1433, l. 1, fols. 1–4v; and AGN, Indios, v. 14, e. 7, fols. 6v–7. I update the spelling of "Acayacatzin" to "Axayacatzin," a traditional Nahua spelling that surely brought to mind the fifteenth-century precontact Mexica Tenochca tlatoani (r. 1469–83) of the same name; see Chimalpahin, *Annals,* 147.

105. In 1642 the contador worked out an arrangement with the ex-governor to pay back the 2,200 pesos in arrears owed from his brief stint as governor; see AGN, Archivo Histórico de Hacienda, v. 1436, l. 43, fols. 572–584.

106. The two major exceptions are don Francisco Jiménez, who came from Tecamachalco, in the orbit of Puebla, and served as a judge only; and don Juan Bautista, who came from Malinalco, a town that is also outside of the Basin of Mexico; see Chimalpahin, *Annals,* 145–147. For the location of Tecamachalco and Malinalco relative to Mexico Tenochtitlan and their position in the tributary structure of that altepetl, see Frances F. Berdan, Richard E. Blanton, Elizabeth Hill Boone, Mary G. Hodge, Michael E. Smith, and Emily Umberger, eds., *Aztec Imperial Strategies* (Washington, D.C.: Dumbarton Oaks Research Library), figs. A4-1, A4-4, A4-18.

107. AGN, Archivo Histórico de Hacienda, v. 1430, e. 1, fol. 733v.

108. Hoberman, "Bureaucracy and Disaster," 227.

109. AGN, Indios, v. 17, e. 56, fol. 78 (1654).

110. They use the term *matadero* in the document, but usually we find the term *carnecería*. It is unclear if this is a particular kind of slaughterhouse where they kill the livestock ("matar las reces y razgos" ["butcher the beef and remnants"]); see AGN, Indios, v. 14, e. 57, fol. 58.

111. AGN, Indios, v. 14, e. 57, fol. 58.

112. AGN, Indios, v. 14, e. 57, fol. 58v.

113. AGN, Indios, v. 17, e. 56, fol. 78; the document makes specific reference to the appointment of don Bartolomé Cortés y Mendoza to justify overturning the

election of don Juan de Velázquez. As with previous interim appointments, Viceroy Alburquerque resisted the advice of his advisors to appoint a governor of his own choosing and instead went with don Juan de Aguilar, the apparent community choice forwarded to the viceroy in a petition from the "caciques and principales."

CHAPTER 4

1. AGN, Indios, v. 23, e. 370, fols. 339–344v. Sánchez de Ocampo served as an oidor in Mexico City until his death on 10 February 1680; see Don Antonio de Robles, *Diario de sucesos notables*, t. 1, ed. Antonio Castro Leal (México: Editoral Porrúa, 1946), 276. He also must have been a prominent figure; he inspected obrajes and produced an important report chronicling their abuse, discussed in Javier Villa-Flores, "Voices from a Living Hell: Slavery, Death, and Salvation in a Mexican Obraje," in Martin Austin Nesvig, ed., *Local Religion in Colonial Mexico* (Albuquerque: University of New Mexico Press, 2006), 238, 254, n. 12.

2. AGN, Indios, v. 23, e. 370, fol. 340–340v. To establish don Lorenzo de Santiago's origin, the document relates that he was the son of don Josef de Santiago, "governor from the parcialidad of Santiago [Mexico] Tlatelolco." He claimed, however, to have been born in Santa María la Redonda Cuepopan, one of the four subdivisions of the altepetl of Mexico Tenochtitlan.

3. Challenges to election in indigenous communities have been a side discussion in numerous studies of different groups; see Terraciano, *Mixtecs*, 194–197, and Lockhart, *Nahuas after the Conquest*, 47–48, who touch briefly on the issue of elections within broader studies; for an in-depth treatment, see Haskett, *Indigenous Rulers*, chaps. 2–3.

4. Changes generally happened after the flood and the dismissal of the governor in 1635. See also the important challenge in 1649 in Mexico Tlatelolco, when the sitting governor (unnamed in the document) was disqualified for serving four successive terms against "the ordinances." This disqualification enabled don Diego de la Cruz Villanueva, who later served as governor in Mexico Tenochtitlan, to become governor; AGN, Indios, v. 15, e. 134, fols. 197–198.

5. Ruiz, *Crisis and Continuity*, 187–189. By the mid-seventeenth century the complexity of the indigenous cabildo seems to suggest that the indigenous government had outgrown exponentially the early model of government; see Lockhart, *Nahuas after the Conquest*, 36, 484 n. 81; and Terraciano, *Mixtecs*, 193.

6. Though it seemed open to all, the governorship was accessible only to those who could satisfy or had sufficient political savvy (or had knowledgeable handlers) to get around ordinances and also sufficient support among the community of electors. Social and political connections to wealthy backers further limited the choices, since suffrage was restricted to former officeholders and as the financial disclosures to the Spanish contador became increasingly elaborate. See the discussion in chapter 5.

7. See the discussion of the Moteucçomas in chapter 2 and the noted exception recounted there of don Diego Luis de Moteucçoma the younger, who served

as an alcalde for Mexico Tenochtitlan in 1607; Chimalpahin, *Annals*, 107. There are also some Moteucçomas who served as governor, but it is not apparent that they were or claimed to come from the royal lineage. Silva Prada, *La política*, 376–377, 404–407, assumes that the surnames may indicate a connection but provides nothing substantive to show how. Her argument on these connections is quite speculative, based largely on the amassing of circumstantial evidence (e.g., Tapia Moteucçoma, "who bore the surname of the old Tenochca nobility") but then concedes that "we may be mistaken [*nos equivocamos*] in our identification of these actors." Valeriano and Tapia y Barrera were important sixteenth-century names not associated with the lineage. Valeriano, the subject of chapter 2, was related by marriage to Huanitzin, the first judge-governor; Tapia was the Christian name adopted by the quauhtlatoani Motelchiuhtzin (r. 1525–30). I found no evidence to link Tapia y Barrera to Motelchiuhtzin. If the lineage had gone though his son don Hernando de Tapia, who apparently married a Spaniard and encouraged his daughters to do so as well, then governor Tapia y Barrera would have been a mestizo or a castizo (more Hispanicized); see chapter 2.

8. See AGN, Indios, v. 23, e. 74, fols. 64v–65v, for the "Zapotec" and "Mixtec" communities (*naciones* in the document), which had their own tribute collectors; see also Terraciano, *Mixtecs*, 334–335. This is part of a growing issue of matriculating groups into the tribute rolls and an increasing source of conflict whose contours have not been adequately defined in the scholarship. Matriculation should not be conflated with becoming a citizen; the process was more akin to becoming a taxpaying resident. Ethnicity derived from affiliation with a particular altepetl remained key to an individual's identity. Matriculation did not breed harmony; in fact, great discord sometimes characterized disputes. See AGN, Indios, v. 24, e. 231, fols. 147–148; and AGN, Indios, v. 24, e. 325, fol. 149–149v, for one manifestation in 1668 between the Mixtec and Zapotec communities in Mexico Tenochtitlan and Mexico Tlatelolco, which were protected by the Capilla de Nuestra Señora del Rosario against incursions by the governors and mandones of each parcialidad.

9. Annual elections are discussed below, but clear evidence that reelection was periodically a problem comes from Tlatelolco; see AGN, Indios, v. 15, e. 134, fols. 197–198 (1649). See also AGN, Indios, v. 14, e. 7, fols. 6v–7, in which the sitting governor in 1642 from Mexico Tenochtitlan, don Martín González, calls for the election of the cabildo and for the appointment of an election supervisor. He had been governor since 1638 and apparently did not face a reelection challenge, and he also appears as governor in AGN, Indios, v. 12, pt. 2, e. 68, fol. 199–199v (1640); and AGN, Criminal, v. 165, e. 10, fols. 235v–236 (1641). The inconsistencies in enforcement—and indeed, as I argue in this chapter, the nature of the viceregal government to allow local government leeway unless a complaint was filed— meant that even seemingly firm rules could be broken if no one complained. Perhaps this was a Habsburg accommodation to local custom and tradition.

10. Restricting suffrage to former officeholders likely reflects the diminished meaning of the term *principal* and other terms that once signified indigenous nobility. AGN, Civil, v. 740, e. 10, fols. 8v–16, lists all of the electors and gives their former office designation. Additional detail can be found in several disputes, but see AGN, Indios, v. 17, e. 207, fol. 202–202v, which states explicitly that in 1654 the cabildo elected the governor: "don Juan de Velasco . . . que fuisteis electo por el cabildo de los naturales de la parcialidad [Mexico Tenochtitlan]" ("don Juan de Velasco . . . who was elected by the indigenous cabildo of the parcialidad"). See also Lockhart, *Nahuas after the Conquest*, 130–138. Again, in the case of electors, it is unclear the extent to which such actions were enforced. In some documents, they "gather together the electors and principales" to elect a governor; see the 1657 case, AGN, Indios, v. 21, e. 146, fol. 136–136v.

11. AGN, Indios, v. 23, e. 370, fol. 342v.

12. Juan López worked quite hard to build up a support network beginning in 1654, as discussed in detail below; see, AGN, Indios, v. 17, e. 235; see also Gibson, *Aztecs*, 177. Intervention into the internal affairs of native government by the viceregal authorities seems also to have spilled over into Mexico Tlatelolco, where governor don Juan Toribio de Alcaraz (who had served more than twenty years) was removed "for just reasons" and replaced with don Joseph de Santiago in 1643 (who was never subject to an election); see AGN, Archivo Histórico de Hacienda, v. 1437, e. 78, fols. 962–963v. Another Tlatelolco example of such intervention brought to the governorship don Diego de la Cruz Villanueva, also discussed below.

13. AGN, Indios, v. 23, e. 370, fols. 339v–340; for Pedro Bernal's service in office, see AGN, Indios, v. 23, e. 227 (1658), and AGN, Indios, v. 21, e. 249 (1657); for his appointment in June 1657 to replace the ousted governor, see AGN, Indios, v. 21, e. 97, fols. 97–100.

14. The viceregal government's reluctance, particularly after the failure of don Bartolomé Cortés y Mendoza, who had been appointed without community input in 1636, to intervene directly on its own is apparent in the legal actions of 1659; see chapter 3.

15. Disputes over issues of birth were not uncommon, especially in the eighteenth century; see chapter 5; for Cuernavaca, see Haskett, *Indigenous Rulers*, 36–59. Juan López, however, is perhaps the strangest figure of those involved in the election of 1659. Mestizos born in the barrios of Mexico City might have cultural ties to the indigenous community indistinguishable from those of natives. Juan López, a Spanish functionary, likely had few such ties.

16. AGN, Indios, v. 23, e. 370. The law had been recently reissued and was clear; see Beleña, *Recopilación sumaria*, t. 2, ord. 49, p. 25, which is an ordinanza from 23 August 1642 restricting from office any who could not prove that their mother and father were natives. It also forced election supervisors to verify that elected officials were natives before certifying the results of an election.

17. AGN, Indios, v. 23, e. 370, fol. 341.

18. See Martínez, *Genealogical Fictions*, 44–54, for the important discussion of what she calls the "early modern concept of race" or "essentialized" concept of race that emerged in Spain in the sixteenth century. What she means and persuasively argues is that purity of blood (*limpieza de sangre*) functioned as an exclusionary force in much the same way that race did in and after the nineteenth century.

19. It would have been an extremely weak argument as well. Non-Tenocha governors had held the office as recently as 1653 (don Diego de la Cruz Villanueva), and a governor from the city of Puebla had ruled 1636–38; see AGN, Indios, v. 19, e. 45; and AGN, Archivo Histórico de Hacienda, v. 1434, l. 18.

Neither the current governor, Bernal, nor the other Tenochca candidate, Suárez, sought to disqualify Santiago, López, or Benítez on the basis of their ethnicity or lack of affiliation with the altepetl of Mexico Tenochtitlan. But that the viceregal courts did not find appeals to micro-patriotism relevant does not mean that such issues ceased to have meaning for Tenochca Nahua. Neither Governor Bernal nor don Pedro Suárez had any real support and must have recognized that their weak candidacies would make them poor prospects to challenge the election. They probably also lacked sufficient support to finance tribute as well, and indeed neither served as governor after 1658. Don Lorenzo de Santiago served as governor after Benítez; AGN, Tierras, v. 2776, e. 18, fols. 6v, 16; AGN, Indios, v. 24, e. 474, fols. 343v–344; AGN, Indios, v. 24, e. 127 fols. 79v–81v. Their inability to garner support likely indicated that the community of electors had no confidence in them and would not support them as leaders of government.

20. AGN, Indios, v. 23, e. 371, fol. 339–339v. This initial petition was the report of the supervising oidor, who approved the election of Benítez on Saturday, 4 January. It is standard, like the dozens of other such election confirmation documents in AGN, Ramo de Indios, and only different in that it includes the vote totals, which most do not.

21. AGN, Indios, v. 23, e. 370, fols. 240v–241. Lorenzo de Santiago stated that the legitimacy of office would suffer and that the title of office would be sickened (*enferma*).

22. AGN, Indios, v. 23, e. 370, fol. 339–339v. It is not surprising that Benítez was appointed without question, because it was not until the next day, Sunday, 5 January, that Santiago alleged that Benítez was a mestizo. It is interesting, considering that the electors must have known that Benítez was Andean, that the oidor made no comment about his ethnicity.

23. AGN, Indios, v. 23, e. 370, fol. 341v. The timing is important. Sánchez de Ocampo made this decision on 23 January 1659. The question of whether Benítez was indigenous or mestizo had yet to be resolved or even addressed by the court. Furthermore, Sánchez de Ocampo apparently wished to stifle the political will of the challenger by indicating that his motives were personal and that he should cease to harass Benítez.

24. AGN, Indios, v. 23, e. 370, fol. 342–342v. Apparently there were other Peruvians in Mexico Tenochtitlan; see AGN, Indios, v. 15, e. 4, fol. 3v, in which

Francisco Quintero de Guevara, a matriculated resident in the community, petitioned the viceroy to defend his right to work as a tailor. Apparently Spanish tailors had tried to bar him from working in 1648. According to Tatiana Seijas, Spanish artisans used the same kinds of exclusionary tactics against Asians; see "Asian Slaves and Freed People in Seventeenth-Century Mexico" (Ph.D. diss., Yale University, 2008), 142, 161.

25. It should be noted that, even though Benítez served consecutive terms in office, in 1672 he was disqualified from running because he was mestizo; see AGN, Indios, v. 24, e. 442, fol. 314–314v.

26. Richard Conway, who is studying the indigenous cabildo of Xochilmilco, has uncovered a reference to a don Francisco Benítez who was elected governor there in 1652. Based on the document, which Professor Conway was so generous to share with me, he is likely the very same person, although there is no reference in the biographical details in the Mexico Tenochtitlan document to his apparent service in Xochimilco; see AGN, Indios, v. 16, e. 137, fols. 129–130v. See also Conway, "Nahuas and Spaniards in the Socioeconomic History of Xochimilco" (Ph.D. diss., Tulane University, 2009).

27. AGN, Indios, v. 23, e. 370, fol. 344–344v; for Alburquerque and the cathedral, see Connell, "Morisco Assassin."

28. AGN, Indios, v. 23, e. 432, fol. 425.

29. AGN, Indios, v. 23, e. 370, fols. 339–344v; and AGN, Indios, v. 23, e. 432, f. 425. In the latter document (e. 432), Benítez was elected without challenge the following year, 1660.

30. The connection between community support and tribute deficits is discussed in chapter 3. I discuss the intervention of 1649 later in this chapter.

31. See the discussion in chapter 1 of the precontact political environment, and Lockhart, Nahuas after the Conquest, 32–33; López Austin, Human Body, 398; and Chimalpahin, Annals, 137, 136–137 n. 2.

32. Even though apparently only officeholders or former officeholders could vote, no such requirement barred those who had never held office from running even for the governorship. López had never held native office and apparently neither had Benítez. A system that restricted officeholding exclusively to former officeholders would eventually run out of candidates with no way of replenishing them.

33. See the discussion in chapter 2. It is also important to recognize that in the eighteenth century when these questions were revisited after another dismal period in tribute collection, Bourbon officials, according to Gibson, privatized the collections. As I discuss later in this chapter, it appears that López was attempting to contract out the service in a similar way a century earlier; see Gibson, Aztecs, 392–394.

34. Many jurisdictions technically tried to prohibit Spaniards from working in native communities. Admonitions against Spaniards and others interfering in the internal affairs of indigenous government also regularly appeared in public ordinances; see AGN, Ordenanzas, v. 4, e. 71, f. 68, (1591), which prohibited Spaniards from living in indigenous communities. Effectively, Velasco saw the

potential for abuse and exploitation if Spaniards lived in small pueblos, though it is unclear if this applied to the barrios of the city; see also AGI, Audiencia de México, l. 27, n. 52, fols. 4v–5 (1608), which prohibited mestizos and Afro-Mexicans from living in indigenous communities. On the nature of Spanish offices, both on the cabildo and beyond, see Altman, *Transatlantic Ties;* and Hoberman, *Mexico's Merchant Elite,* 147–167.

35. AGN, Indios, v. 17, e. 235, fols. 234–236. Even in Mexico Tenochtitlan non-Tenocha governors and mestizos had held the governorship. For the prevalence outside of Mexico Tenochtitlan, see Gibson, *Aztecs,* 177, 181–193. For the early mestizo governors, see Chimalpahin, *Las ocho relaciones,* t. 2, 179–269, esp. 229–233; for an example in Tlatelolco, see AGN, Archivo Histórico de Hacienda, v. 1420, e. 1, fols. 1–4v, which documents a case in 1622 in which the Marqués de Gelves replaced a native with a mestizo, arguing that the native, don Melchor de San Martín, was "prohibited" from holding the office.

36. AGN, Indios, v. 14, e. 117, is the first mention of López as an alguacil amparador (though the index improperly identifies him as simply the amparador de los naturales, a post López never held). The earliest instance I found of the position of amparador was in a 1574 lawsuit in which Pedro García de Avalos served as a liaison between the governor and the Spanish crown; AGN, Tierras, 56, e. 8. This is probably the office of amaparador de los naturales; the lieutenant or alguacil amparador came later.

37. See AGN, Indios, v. 15, e. 5, fol. 99–99v, for the appointment document from 1649. The term "go-between" was inspired by the work of Aida Metcalf and her discussion of native and Portuguese interactions in colonial Brazil, using particularly the idea of the representational go-betweens: see *Go-Betweens and the Colonization of Brazil* (Austin: University of Texas Press, 2005), 2–15.

38. The discussion of subtle politics is heavily informed by the theoretical work of others; see William Roseberry, "Hegemony and the Language of Contention," in Gilbert Joseph and Daniel Nugent, eds., *Everyday Forms of State Formation: Revolution and the Negotiation of Rule in Modern Mexico* (Durham: Duke University Press, 1994), 356–357, 358–360, especially his observation that "social situations with which we are familiar are infinitely more complex [than a bipolar model would suggest], which include multiple sites of domination or forms and elements of popular experience," and his conceptualization of hegemony as a "problematic, contested, political process of domination and struggle." See also Yannakakis, *Art,* 25–26.

39. Though the alguacil amparador was appointed officially by the amparador de los naturales, as in this case, the governor apparently could forward a recommendation; see AGN, Indios, v. 19, e. 37, fol. 18; and AGN, Indios, v. 19, e. 150, fol. 80. In 1653, Villanueva asked that Miguel de la Cruz (appointed in February) be replaced by don Felipe Valeriano (appointed in May). Neither don Felipe Valeriano or Miguel de la Cruz are identified in terms of race or ethnicity. They

may have been Spaniards or natives, and Valeriano seems to invoke the powerful native family descended from don Antonio Valeriano in the sixteenth century; without good corroborating evidence, there is no way to say for certain. With other alguaciles amparadores, however, the position was clearly given to Spaniards like Juan López.

40. AGN, Indios, v. 19, e. 37, fol. 18.

41. AGN, Indios, v. 15, e. 5. The amparador was charged to protect the naturales from their own government and also to protect Afro-Mexicans who worked specifically in obrajes and panaderías. The order does not mention other naciones like mestizos or Chinos (Asian migrants), both of whom would have been easily visible minorities in the parcialidades in the 1640s. For Chinos, see AGN, Indios, v. 13, e. 126; Seijas, "Asian Slaves and Freed People,"103–141; and Tatiana Seijas, "The Portuguese Slave Trade to Spanish Manilla." *Itinerario* 32, no. 1 (2008), 19–38.

42. Market regulation was an extremely complex enterprise in which many officials had a hand. Some were indigenous; apparently indigenous governors regulated some aspects of indigenous markets. Some were viceregal officials and others municipal officials tied to the Spanish cabildo of Mexico City. For an example of the complexity, see AGN, Indios, v. 15, e. 10, fol. 8, which discusses an appeal by an indigenous tailor in an indigenous market disputing Spanish guild (*gremios*) regulators who attempted to prohibit indigenous tailors from working. The Juzgado General appealed to the *veedores* (market inspectors) who were controlled by the Spanish cabildo to assist the indigenous tailors. For even more complexity within the guild system, see the dispute among cloth finishers (*tundidores*), cloth weavers (*tejedores de paños*), and clothing makers (*roperos*) over who had the right to sell where and at what moment in the process; AHCM, Real Audiencia, Panaderías, v. 3824, e. 2, fols. 6–62 (1690).

43. AGN, Indios, v. 15, e. 5.

44. There were exceptions. In 1653, don Felipe Valeriano was appointed alguacil amparador, see AGN, Indios, v. 19, e. 150, fol. 80.

45. For more on transatlantic patronage, see Arnold, *Bureaucracy and Bureaucrats;* and Rosenmüller, *Patrons, Partisans and Palace Intrigues.*

46. AGN, Indios, v. 20, e. 166; and AGN, Indios, v. 21, e. 97.

47. The post was minor enough also to escape mention in 1680 in the *Recopilación de leyes de los reynos de Indias.* Abel García Guízar, "El caos jurisdiccional Novohispano," *Vinculo Juridico* 6–7 (1991), www.uaz.edu.mx/vinculo/webrvj/rev6-7-5.htm (accessed 1/2010), briefly discusses the alguacil amparador as a commercial agent who helped to regulate the market at Tlatelolco. His purpose generally is to describe the institutions of the viceregal government designed to aid natives and protect them.

48. AGN, Indios, v. 13, e. 259. Native officials regularly mediated disputes in markets; see AGN, Indios, 13, e. 226, for a similar case from 1636.

49. Connell, "Emerging Ladino Spaces," 83–94, 127–134, esp. tab. 3.1, which shows the infrequency of denials to natives seeking amparo. On the notion of amparo, see Lira González, *El amparo colonial,* 17–34.

50. AGN, Indios, v. 13, e. 259. It should also be noted that indigenous cabildo members usually wore Spanish-style clothing as well. Indeed, principales generally asked for and received the right to wear such dress when they petitioned for the privilege to ride a horse and carry offensive weapons (usually swords). It is possible, as discussed in chapter 3, that native leaders used the ability to grant access to markets as a way to distribute patronage. This case at least demonstrates that they tried to exclude some, though there is no direct evidence here to suggest that it was to give privileged access to others (patronage). The probability is high, however, that this seemingly innocuous case is in reality the governor attempting to reward supporters. The Juzgado General and alguacil amparador seem to have found a way to disrupt and interfere in patronage networks.

51. For the corregidor and markets, see chapter 3, and AHCM, Rastros y Mercados, v. 3728, e. 5, fol. np.

52. Gibson, *Aztecs,* 206.

53. *Recopilación de leyes,* lib. 6, tit. 5, ley 8. The law comes from two decrees by Philip II, 18 May 1572 and 26 May 1573. See also Cope, *Limits,* 21, 176 n. 73, in which he argues that freed Afro-Mexicans with a skill were assessed a higher tribute rate in the late sixteenth century.

54. The existence of indios Chinos, who were Asians living in New Spain, raised some additional jurisdictional issues; see Seijas, "Asian Slaves and Freed People," 142–166. See also Ben Vinson III, "Race and Badge: Free-Colored Soldiers in the Colonial Mexican Militia," *The Americas* 56, no. 4 (2000), 471–496. Cope, *Limits,* 66–67, cites an early eighteenth-century example of an alcalde mayor of Tetzcoco collecting tribute from Afro-Mexicans.

55. According to Frank "Trey" Proctor III, "Gender and the Manumission of Slaves in New Spain," *Hispanic American Historical Review* 86, no. 2 (2006), 315, the slave population increased through what he calls "natural reproduction"— through the birth of slave children to slave mothers—after the slave trade to New Spain ended in 1640. For further discussion, see Proctor, "Afro-Mexican Slave Labor in the Obrajes de Paños of New Spain, Seventeenth and Eighteenth Centuries," *The Americas* 60, no. 1 (2003), 34–35, n. 10. See also Herman Bennett, *Africans in Colonial Mexico: Absolutism, Christianity, and Afro-Creole Consciousness, 1570–1640* (Indianapolis: Indiana University Press, 2003), 19–21, who notes that the free black population grew to surpass the enslaved population of Afro-Mexicans in the early to mid-seventeenth century.

56. The physical collection of tribute in the city from free Afro-Mexicans is understudied. Scattered appointment documents suggest that occasionally an official was in charge of this duty. I have not explored the extent to which such an officer was regularly appointed but have found only two references: AGN, Archivo Histórico de Hacienda, v. 1418, e. 2, fols. 168–170v (1620); and AGN,

Archivo Histórico de Hacienda, v. 1427, e. 15 (1619). In Puebla, the alcalde mayor seemed to have been responsible for Afro-Mexican tribute; see AGN, Archivo Histórico de Hacienda, v. 1440, l. 35. See also Cope, *Limits,* 21, 66, and Bennett, *Africans in Colonial Mexico,* 19–21. Bennett, unfortunately, does not provide a discussion of the mechanisms of tribute collection for this population. Cope, *Limits,* 74–85, observes that racial labels were fairly fluid and contributes the idea that the economic category he defines as the "plebeians" sometimes migrated into the Afro-Mexican categories.

57. Wood, *Transcending Conquest,* 42–46. Indigenous communities outside of the city often reported to the regional magistrate (corregidor or alcalde mayor), delivering tribute to this official; see Baskes, *Indians, Merchants, and Markets,* 20–24. Elections in communities outside Mexico City were supervised by the regional magistrate. In Mexico City's two parcialidades, the Audiencia sent an oidor to supervise elections and the contador general de reales tributos y azogues physically gathered tribute from the governor. I have argued that the governor acted in some ways like the corregidor and thus would have worked directly with the contador general. See Gibson, *Aztecs,* 84, 178–179. Horn, *Postconquest Coyoacan,* 70, notes the intermediary role played by the corregidor on the cabildo in Coyoacan.

58. AGN, Indios, v. 15, e. 5, fol. 99v.

59. The purposes of these inspections were multiple but included making sure that prisoners were being processed appropriately, to note the charges against them, and if they were being punished (in a workshop or bakery) to record the reason for their imprisonment. He also had to collect tribute if it was owed; see AGN, Indios, v. 15, e. 5, fol. 99–99v.

60. For the difficulties encountered by indigenous officials collecting tribute from natives living in the households of Spaniards, see AGN, Indios, v. 12, e. 215; and AGN, Indios, v. 15, e. 104. See Cope, *Limits,* 90–93, and Gibson, *Aztecs,* 391–392.

61. AGN, Indios, v. 19, e. 37, fol. 18. It appears that the alguacil amparador took over the duties of an office that already existed to aid the governor in collecting from Spaniards; see AGN, Indios, v. 7, e. 12, fol. 4–4v, in which Manuel de Salas was commissioned specifically to charge tribute from natives living in the service of Spaniards in 1616.

62. AGN, Indios, v. 16, e. 3bis, fol. 3. For the term *tequitlato* (*teguitlato* in the document), see Lockhart, *Nahuas after the Conquest,* 44 and 487, n. 116, about which he observes that Molina "glosses tequitlato as 'mandón or merino, or one in charge of assigning the tribute and duties to the macehuales.'"

63. AGN, Indios, v. 15, e. 104; AGN, Indios, v. 15, e. 5; see also the discussion of obraje labor in Proctor, "Afro-Mexican Slave Labor," 34–39, n. 24. Though Proctor is mostly interested in discussing the largely unrecognized importance of slaves in obrajes, his work suggests that before 1630 most workers in obrajes were free laborers, that after 1640 a gradual shift to slave labor occurred, and that slaves gradually dominated obraje labor because they could be confined. Convict

labor was not, according to Proctor, a sizable part of the labor force, and native labor declined in these institutions, though it clearly continued to exist. Proctor estimates that natives made up only 10 percent of the obraje workforce. See the 1670 census of obrajes and panaderías in AGN, Archivo del Tribunal Superior de Justicia del Distrito Federal, v. 5, e. 44; native workers, both free and incarcerated, dominated the panadería workforce. This seems to indicate that Proctor's evidence for the obrjes does not necessarily correlate with panaderías.

64. AGN, Indios, v. 15, e. 104. This case from 1651 is a solicitation by the indigenous governor and cabildo to enter and collect tribute from natives serving in obrajes and panaderías. They are granted full access, and those who impede them are liable to a large fine of twenty pesos.

65. AGN, Indios, v. 15, e. 7, fols. 100v–101 (1649). The complaint was issued by the amparador de los naturales, but presumably he offered the petition in response to a complaint he received from an alguacil amparador. The 200 pesos was more than double the salary of the governor of Mexico Tenochtitlan; see AGN, Indios, v. 23, e. 370, fol. 344, which lists the governor's salary at 100 pesos in 1659.

66. See the discussion below of native complaints against the alguacil amparador. For some particularly useful complaints, see AGN, Indios, v. 21, e. 97, fol. 97v.

67. AGN, Indios, 17, e. 235, fols. 234v–235v. See the larger discussion of this document below.

68. For the night patrols, see Scardaville, "Justice by Paperwork," 984–985; and Tamar Herzog, *La administración como un fenómeno social: La justicia penal de la ciudad de Quito (1650–1750)* (Madrid: Centro de Estudios Constitucionales, 1995), 89–91. The Rembrandt painting *The Nightwatch* is probably the best illustration of a seventeenth-century urban ronda, although the painting is set in Amsterdam and depicts a militia making rounds; see Egbert Haverkamp-Begemann, *Rembrandt: The Nightwatch* (Princeton: Princeton University Press, 1982), 6–8, 32–50. I thank Michael Scardaville for suggesting I look at the Rembrandt painting.

69. For a discussion of judicial procedure in Mexico City, see Haslip-Viera, *Crime and Punishment*; Teresa Lozano Armendares, *La criminalidad en la ciudad de México, 1800—1821* (México: Universidad Nacional Autónoma de México, 1987); Scardaville, "Crime and the Urban Poor"; and Herzog, *Administración*, 86–99. According to Gibson, *Aztecs*, 191, by the eighteenth century the tecpan was synonymous with jail, but in the period under discussion here it was principally the seat of native government.

70. AGN, Indios, v. 13, e. 394, fol. 323–323v.

71. AGN, Indios, v. 14, e. 96, fol. 99.

72. Gibson, *Aztecs*, 392. Native governors sometimes exceeded their authority by seeking to collect tribute in arrears once their terms had expired without special permission from the viceroy; see AGN, Indios, v. 19, e. 169; AGN, Indios, v. 15, e. 19; and AGN, Indios, v. 21, e. 26; in this last case the indigenous governor was barred from taking office because of his debts. By the eighteenth century

(see chapter 5), governors were regularly imprisoned for debt; see AGN, Indios, v. 36, e. 214; and AHCM, Obras Públicas en General, v. 1509a, e. 5.

73. See AGN, Indios, v. 17, e. 46 (1654), for one example in which the Real Hospital de Indios complained that it could not pay its staff for lack of funds, which came from tribute collection. For the flood, see chapter 3. On tribute shortages, see AGN, Indios, v. 10, e. 275; and AGN, Indios, v. 12, e. 215. During the period of floods beginning in 1629, because of the evacuation of the city the level of tribute was reduced, thus limiting its impact.

74. AGN, Indios, v. 15, e. 1, fol. 2; AGN, Indios, v. 15, e. 109, fol. 79–79v. I do not have data for his election, only that he served as governor during these two years. There is an inexplicable gap in AGN, Indios, from 1642 to 1648. The first document, v. 15, e. 1, is a call for the election of alcaldes and regidores made by the sitting governor, indicating that he had been in office the year previous.

75. AGN, Indios, v. 15, e. 109: In this case, the viceroy expressed with haste that an appointment must be made immediately and forwarded don Manuel de Tapia Moctezuma to serve as governor.

76. AGN, Indios, v. 15, e. 1, fol. 2, shows that in 1648 the alcaldes and regidores were already working to collect tribute under Cortés Pizarro; for the strategy under Tapia Moctezuma, see AGN, Indios, v. 15, e. 24, fols. 110v–111. Tapia Moctezuma's illustrious name has led some to suggest that he had come from the ancient royal lineage, though there is no good evidence to support such a conclusion or to assume that the viceroy attempted with his appointment to restore the ancient lineage; see note 7 in this chapter.

77. AGN, Indios, v. 15, e. 24, fol. 110v. This petition is dated 30 January 1649 but may be confusing because of its expediente number, which seems to indicate that it occurred before AGN, Indios, v. 15, e. 109, which appointed Tapia Moctezuma governor after the death of Cortés Pizarro in September 1648. This is simply one example of many nonsequential expedientes in Ramo de Indios.

78. AGN, Indios, v. 15, e. 24, fol. 111.

79. Gibson, *Aztecs*, 177; my ellipsis removed "another" from the quote to avoid confusion. Gibson is discussing seventeenth-century Spaniards who attempted to hold the governorship in many indigenous towns throughout the Basin, but López was the first to attempt this in Mexico Tenochtitlan. Even though, as Gibson argues, it was not unusual in central Mexico for Spaniards to run for indigenous office, it was unusual in Mexico Tenochtitlan and fought against by many native electors.

80. See AGN, Indios, v. 17, e. 56, fols. 77v–82v, for his unusual appointment; for his death in office, see AGN, Indios, v. 17, e. 235, fol. 234. It should also be noted that Francisco Benítez was similarly accused of currying favor in 1655; see AGN, Indios, v. 18, e. 220, fols. 161v–162v.

81. It should be noted, however, that soliciting votes had been part of elections since as early as1564 and probably derived from native tradition. Furthermore, in 1655 Francisco Benítez had also been accused of seeking votes, and a petition

from the cabildo had accused him of seeking to cheat or trick certain people by offering gifts of food and money. Though it is unclear to what extent the community was aware, there were rules against soliciting votes; see *Recopilación de leyes*, lib. 4, tit. 9, ley 10 (1613); and AGN, Indios, v. 18, e. 220, fols. 161v–162.

82. AGN, Indios, v. 17, e. 235, fol. 235. The ordinance is found in Beleña, *Recopilación sumaria*, t. 2, ord. 49, 25.

83. AGN, Indios, v. 17, e. 235, fols. 234v–235.

84. AGN, Indios, v. 21, e. 97, fols. 97–98v, includes two petitions from the contador and one from López. They are clearly working together; each reinforces the other.

85. AGN, Indios, v. 18, e. 58, fol. 49–49v (1655); don Martín de San Martín and Juan López acted together in this petition, which claimed that Villanueva did not have sufficient financial guarantors to cover the tribute owed. He was still governor in August 1656; see AGN, Indios, v. 20, e. 215, fol. 169v.

86. AGN, Indios, v. 21, e. 97, fol. 97–97v.

87. AGN, Indios, v. 18, e. 58, fol. 49–49v.

88. AGN, Indios, v. 21, e. 146, fols. 133–136v.

89. See AGN, Indios, v. 21, e. 97, fol. 97v, for López's complaint; and see AGN, Indios, v. 21, e. 146, fol. 133–133v, for the contador's opinion confirming López's complaint about fiadores. Both petitions were submitted on the same day, 24 March 1657.

90. AGN, Indios, v. 21, e. 97, fol. 97v, emphasis added.

91. AGN, Indios, v. 21, e. 97, fols. 97v–98.

92. AGN, Indios, v. 21, e. 97, fol. 98.

93. AGN, Indios, v. 21, e. 97, fols. 98v–99. The document uses the apparent false cognate *introducir*, which I translated as "to establish" (in the sense of creating) rather than "to introduce," as might be more common.

94. AGN, Indios, v. 21, e. 97, fol. 99–99v.

95. AGN, Indios, v. 21, e. 97, fol. 99–99v; the document uses the somewhat antiquated sounding *preponga perpetuo silencio*. The verb *preponer* ("to put before") is antiquated even in English usage, and the phrase would make better sense with a more modern verb like *imponer*, which is more in line with the meaning of this phrase, "to impose perpetual silence." For biographical details on Alburquerque, see Fernández Bulete, "La Desconocida," 684–685.

96. AGN, Indios, v. 21, e. 146, fol. 133–133v.

97 Quotation and evidence about the fiadores comes from AGN, Indios, v. 21, e. 146, fol. 133v.

98. AGN, Indios, v. 21, e. 146, fol. 134–134v. San Martín was probably not the most reliable source for this information, since he seemed intent on discrediting Cruz. Cruz, however, did not provide any additional fiadores. By calling him the governor-elect, San Martín is effectively questioning the validity of the election and the capacity of Cruz to serve, stating directly that a governor must have both the ability and resources to finance the tribute the community owed.

99. AGN, Indios, v. 21, e. 146, fol. 136v.

100. The appeal to order was not unique to this document; in fact, some later documents preserve the language "without any grievances or violence"; see AGN, Indios, v. 23, e. 227, fol. 206.

101. AGN, Indios, v. 21, e. 193, fols. 469–470 (1657), stipulates that his term was for one year only. He was prohibited from being elected again to the office of governor on 16 December 1658, when the oidor was appointed to supervise the coming election of 1659; see AGN, Indios, v. 23, e. 227, fol. 206 (1659). Though declared ineligible by the oidor, he ran anyway and received but one vote; see AGN, Indios, v. 23, e. 370, fol. 339v. Though it is tempting to argue that perhaps Bernal received so few votes because of his ineligibility, there is no indication of it in the documents.

102. AGN, Indios, v. 21, e. 249, fol. 223.

103. AGN, Indios, v. 21, e. 249, fol. 223v; he described them as "muy ociosos y mal pagadores," which I translate more figuratively than usual because "poor payers" does not make much sense and is vague in English.

104. Beyond the speculation implied by this statement, firm evidence makes his new role clear; see AGN, Indios, v. 23, e. 74, fols. 64v–65v, in which under Bernal in 1658 López had the title *cobrador de los reales tributos* and not *alguacil amparador*. He is required in this document to supervise the "alguaciles mayores" appointed for each ethnicity represented in Mexico Tenochtitlan, whose duties included gathering tribute from each of the ethnic communities within the barrios (e.g., Mixtecs and Zapotecs).

105. AGN, Indios, v. 18, e. 220.

106. AGN, Indios, v. 18, e. 220; this petition takes the exact form of surviving petitions from the Tlaxcala cabildo, suggesting beyond doubt that the indigenous cabildo of Mexico City authored the petition. For examples of such cabildo entries, see James Lockhart, Frances Berdan, and Arthur J. O. Anderson, eds., *The Tlaxcalan Actas: A Compendium of the Records of the Cabildo of Tlaxcala (1545–1627)* (Salt Lake City: University of Utah Press, 1986), 67–126.

107. AGN, Indios, v. 15, e. 25.

108. AGN, Indios, v. 18, e. 220; for a more detailed discussion, see Seijas, "Asian Slaves and Freed People," 133–137.

109. AGN, Indios, v. 18, e. 220, fol. 162; and AGN, Indios, v. 18, e. 58, fols. 49–49v. It is possible that this is just a strange detail absent in some documents and present in others. It appears that keeping a tribute log was not that unusual. Indeed, the Codex Valeriano is a 1574 log kept by the governor to record tribute collection. See Gibson, *Aztecs*, 391–393, and pl. 8; and Salvador Mateos, "Codice Valeriano," *El México Antiguo* 7 (1949), 315–321, the latter of which provides the text in Spanish glosses but none of the images and only some of the Nahuatl.

110. AGN, Indios, v. 18, e. 58, fols. 48v–49v. AGN, Indios, v. 17, e. 235; AGN, Indios, v. 20, e. 166; and AGN, Indios, v. 21, e. 97, provide further evidence of excessive tribute demands placed on those with the ability to pay. Some argue

they were charged multiple times. See AGN, Indios, v. 23, e. 370, fol. 344, which indicates that governors had to ensure as part of the contract they swore to uphold that no one was charged multiple times.

111. AGN, Indios, v. 20, e. 166, f. 117.

112. AGN, Indios, v. 15, e. 25. This order also forbade Spanish officials from entering pulquerías unless accompanied by a native alcalde or other officer from the cabildo; see also Connell, "Because I Was Drunk," 377–384.

113. Along with the above example, see AGN, Indios, v. 23, e. 370, fol. 344 (1659), which also occurred while Juan López was alguacil amparador.

114. AGN, Indios, v. 23, e. 74, fol. 65–65v.

115. This is an old issue, but one that was definitively settled in the sixteenth century; see AGN, Indios, v. 5, e. 265, fol. 140v, in which don Luis de Velasco the younger (r. 1590–95, 1607–1611) made it clear, based on the complaint of Juan de San Francisco, a native of Xochimilco who lived and owned property in Mexico Tenochtitlan, that he had to pay tribute or perform service only if he matriculated into the community. For Velasco, see Schwaller, "Early Life of Luis de Velasco."

116. AGN, Indios, v. 17, e. 235, fol. 234; also noted is the town of Tlamascalpa (Temascalpa?), which is in the north of the city in the region of Teotihuacan. See also Gibson, *Aztecs,* 391. *Chichimeca* is the Nahuatl term used pejoratively to describe certain people from the north, sometimes translated as "sons of dogs" because of the root word *chichi* (dog); see Lockhart, *Nahuas after the Conquest,* 15–16, 23. See also O'Hara, *Flock Divided,* 40–54.

117. AGN, Indios, v. 21, e. 60; and AGN, Indios, v. 23, e. 74.

118. By 1657, Juan López had reached the limit of his authority in Mexico Tenochtitlan. Several consecutive years of tribute shortfalls had created a crushing debt of back tribute amounting to more than 12,000 pesos. López fought to gain more control. In a petition filed on 17 February, he sought the authority to imprison natives or put them to work on public projects to pay their debts; AGN, Indios, v. 17, e. 211, and AGN, Indios, v. 21, e. 97.

119. AGN, Indios, v. 17, e. 235, fol. 234v. Recall that political maneuvering was a feature of sixteenth-century cabildo elections; see chapter 1.

120. AGN, Indios, v. 19, e. 510. A series of official pronouncements in the 1660s clarified the issue of Spaniards holding government offices and limited the amount Spaniards could interfere in the barrios.

121. See the discussion in Kellogg, *Law and the Transformation,* 214–215.

CHAPTER 5

1. AGN, Indios, v. 38, e. 228, fol. 305v; see Cañeque, *King's Living Image,* 55–58, on the nature of viceregal authority.

2. AGN, Indios, v. 38, e. 228, fol. 305v. See also AGN, Indios, v. 40, e. 1, fol. 1–1v, in which a similar group of petitioners argued that Ribera won the support of electors by passing out favors and gifts of alcohol.

3. Although it is difficult to speculate about the motives of those who petitioned, in at least one instance (from 1674) don Juan Montaño had been virtually barred from receiving votes; see the discussion of the election of 1674 in this chapter and AGN, Civil, v. 740, e. 10, fols. 20–21.

4. Yannakakis, *Art*, 56–63, identifies similar coalitions in her work on Oaxaca in the late seventeenth century. According to Yannakakis, in Oaxaca these coalitions were called *parcialidades* in the documentation. I have found no similar usage in Mexico Tenochtitlan, but she employs *parcialidad* in a way that fits better with the modern usage of the term.

5. AGN, Indios, v. 38, e. 228, fols. 305v–306; the group in question was led by former governors don Joseph de la Cruz and don Roque Eusebio de Lara and future governor don Felipe de Jesús.

6. AGN, Indios, v. 38, e. 228, fols. 305v–306; for the challenge in the election of 1716, see AGN, Indios, v. 40, e. 1, fol. 1–1v. Santa Veracruz is just north of the colonial park known as the Alameda.

7. Lockhart, *Nahuas after the Conquest*, 133–134, comments on native principales who worked in what Spaniards considered low-status occupations.

8. AGN, Indios, v. 40, e. 1, fol. 1v.

9. There is no further discussion of Ribera's eligibility. AGN, Indios, v. 41, e. 129, fols. 162v–163v, indicates that don Juan Marcelo Audelo won the election and served as governor in 1716. It is unclear how he came to occupy the office. Audelo won the election of 1717 but could not serve because the ordinances forbade reelection. Hence, Audelo was probably elected in 1716, though I have found no record of the 1716 election.

10. It is unclear who held the governorship in 1721, 1722, and 1723. For the other elections, see AGN, Indios, v. 44, e. 19, fol. 19–19v (1719, 1720); and AGN, Indios, v. 50, e. 17, fol. 25–25v (1724).

11. See AGN, Indios, v. 41, e. 105, fol. 139–139v, for Martínez; and AGN, v. 40, e. 1, fol. 1–1v. Some indications suggest that don Juan de Ribera and the governor who followed him in 1717, don Pedro Martínez, also represented similar interests and thus might be seen as a coalition that also sought to control the cabildo. Both Martínez and Ribera were accused of holding low-status occupations (Martínez allegedly a panadero and Ribera a barber) and of soliciting votes with gifts.

12. AGN, Indios, v. 44, e. 19, fol. 19–19v.

13. Precedent existed for interim rulers to continue to serve without election for the following year; see the 1657–58 example at AGN, Indios, v. 21, e. 193, fols. 169–170; and AGN, Indios, v. 23, e. 227, fol. 206.

14. AGN, Indios, v. 37, e. 110; AGN, Indios, v. 38, e. 228; and AGN, Indios, v. 44, e. 19.

15. AGN, Indios, v. 38, e. 7, fol. 5v; this 1712 document disputes the candidacy of Cruz with specific charges.

16. AGN, Indios, v. 38, e. 7; AGN, Indios, v. 44, e. 19.

17. AGN, Indios, v. 44, e. 19, fol. 19–19v.

18. Altman, *Transatlantic Ties*, 95–98, discussing the political culture in Puebla, argues that New World cabildos lacked a real connection to the medieval representative councils on which they were based. For the medieval institution, see chapter 1 of this volume, and Ruiz, *Crisis and Community*, chap. 6. See also Kenneth Andrien, "The Sale of Fiscal Offices and the Decline of Royal Authority in the Viceregalty of Peru, 1633–1700," *Hispanic American Historical Review* 62, no. 1, (1982), 49–71.

19. Likely mestizos include don Francisco Benítez de Inga, but the allegation surfaced repeatedly; see AGN, v. 23, e. 370; AGN, Indios, v. 23, e. 432; and AGN, Indios, v. 38, e. 228, fols. 305v–306.

20. For one example, see AGN, Indios, v. 44, e. 19, fol. 21–21v.

21. AGN, Indios, v. 38, e. 228, fols. 305v–306; AGN, Indios, v. 40, e. 1, fol. 1–1v.

22. On the uprising of 1696, see Juan de Ortega Montoñés, *Instrucción reservada que el Obispo-virrey Juan de Ortega Montañés dio a su sucesor en el mando el Conde de Moctezuma*, ed. Norman F. Martin (México: Editorial Jus, 1965), 25–29, 172; and Cope, *Limits*, 42–44.

23. Despite instances where governors served in both Mexico Tenochtitlan and Mexico Tlatelolco (e.g., don Diego de la Cruz Villanueva in Tlatelolco in 1649 and in Tenochtitlan in 1653 and 1655–56), Tlatelolco developed different traditions. Often in Tlatelolco, though, the governorship was much more like that of don Juan Toribio de Alcaraz, who served twenty years in office. See the discussion below of don Lucas de Santiago y Roja, who served in Tlatelolco many consecutive years. For the documentary evidence, see AGN, Indios, v. 39, e. 10, fols. 9v–11; and AGN, Indios, v. 39, e. 184, fol. 279–279v. The different political culture in Mexico Tlatelolco appeared to make it possible for Santiago y Rojas to pass the governorship on to his first alcalde, don Gregorio de San Buenaventura, in the 1720s, despite great opposition; see AGN, Indios, v. 50, e. 130, fols. 249–250v.

24. Timothy E. Anna, *The Fall of the Royal Government in Mexico City* (Lincoln: University of Nebraska Press, 1978), 26–30; John Lynch, "Intendants and Cabildos in the Viceregalty of La Plata, 1782–1810," *Hispanic American Historical Review* 35, no. 3, (1955), 340. See Gibson, *Aztecs*, 176–179; and Lockhart, *Nahuas after the Conquest*, 32–40, 131–134, on the idea of the gubernatorial lineage, along with chapter 3 of this volume.

25. Gibson, *Aztecs*, 391–397, chronicles the gradual loss of control over the collection of tribute, which in the eighteenth century was "farmed out" to "private Spanish bidders"; see also AGN, Tierras, v. 427, e. 3. J. Ignacio Rubio Mañé, ed., "Testamento del gobernador y cacique de Santiago [Mexico] Tlatelolco, don Lucas de Santiago y Rojas, 1724," *Boletín del Archivo General de la Nación* 25, no. 1 (1954), 63–74, provides a printed version of the will of native governor Santiago y Rojas from AGN, Tierras, v. 427; see also Connell, "Emerging Ladino Spaces," 333–335.

26. See Connell, "Because I Was Drunk," 377–378, 397–401; and Silva Prada, *La política*, for a discussion of the political ramifications of the uprising. Silva Prada's work is comprehensive and perhaps the first fresh look that departs significantly

from the thesis offered by don Carlos de Sigüenza y Góngora in his firsthand account. Her insight that the uprising was a conscious political act carried out by indigenous leaders bent on overthrowing the viceregal government is perhaps overstated, but it offers an important new perspective on the uprising.

27. For a 1695 example of the viceregal government attempting to exercise additional control over the collection of tribute and elections, see AGN, Indios, v. 33, e. 11, fol. 7–7v, in which the outgoing governor, don Bernabe de Santiago, in consort with twenty-six former and current officeholders, petitioned to limit the authority of the contador general, who was attempting to usurp some of the authority of the governor and cabildo to collect and deliver tribute. See also AGN, Indios, v. 31, e. 327, fol. 255v, and the discussion of governor don Felipe de Aguilar in this chapter.

28. AGN, Archivo Historico de Hacienda, v. 1430, l. 52; Chimalpahin, *Las ocho relaciones*, t. 2, 237. See chapters 1 and 3 of this volume as well for discussion of ways the viceregal government increased its oversight in 1564 and after 1636.

29. Numerous examples exist, including two alluded to above; see AGN, Indios, v. 33, e. 11, fol. 7–7v; and AGN, Indios, v. 40, e. 1, fol. 1–1v.

30. It is possible that the nomination process resembled that described by Womack in his work on Zapata, in which community members came to consensus on who should lead without any formal process at the time of the election; see his *Zapata and the Mexican Revolution* (New York: Vintage, 1968), 3–9.

31. AGN, Indios, v. 23, e. 370, fols. 339–344v.

32. AGN, Civil, v. 740, e. 10, fols. 16v–17.

33. AGN, Indios, v. 41, e. 129, fols. 162v–163v.

34. AGN, Indios, v. 44, e. 19, fols. 20v–21v.

35. AGN, Indios, v. 41,e . 105, f. 139.

36. AGN, Indios, v. 41, e. 105, fol. 139–139v. Royal law specifically prohibited the solicitation of votes; *Recopilación de leyes*, lib. 4, tit. 9, ley 10: "que ningún gobernador pueda pedir, ni solicitar votos, y al regularlos se hallan dos regidores."

37. AGN, Indios, v. 41, e. 105: "para lograr sus particulares intereses en perjuicio del publico."

38. AGN, Indios, v. 41, e. 105, f. 139v. Córdoba used the term *macehuales*, a Hispanicized variant of *macehualtin*.

39. See AGN, Indios, v. 41, e. 129, fol. 162–162v, for his election, 6 February 1717; and AGN, Indios, v. 41, e. 105, fol. 139–139v, for the oidor's response.

40. AGN, Indios, v. 38, e. 228, fols. 305v–306; AGN, Indios. v. 40, e. 1, fol. 1–1v.

41. Lockhart, *Nahuas after the Conquest*, 28–35; Schroeder, *Chimalpahin*, 118–139; Nader, *Liberty in Absolutist Spain*, 35–39.

42. There are hundreds of examples in Ramo de Indios, and most nominate an oidor and suggest that he is to supervise the election for that year. Sometimes they name the current governor; see the 1642 example at AGN, Indios, v. 14, e. 7, fols. 6v–7. Sometimes they contain extensive testimony that attempts to influence the election itself; see AGN, Indios, v. 40, e. 1, fol. 1–1v; and AGN, Indios, v. 23, e.

227, fol. 206. Most are fairly mundane; see, for example, AGN, Indios, v. 24, e. 433, fol. 304–304v; and AGN, Indios, v. 37, e. 221, fols. 233v–234.

43. See AGN, Indios, v. 38, e. 228, fol. 305v (1715); AGN, Indios, v. 41, e. 129, fol. 162–162v; and AGN, Indios, v. 41, e. 105, fol. 139–139v. Coalitions did not always hold together. In a complicated political environment it should not be expected that coalitions would remain monolithic. Such a revelation should only suggest the maturity of the political coalitions in Mexico Tenochtitlan.

44. AGN, Indios, v. 41, e. 129, fol. 162–162v; AGN, Indios, v. 41, e. 105, fol. 139–139v. The election was held and ratified on 6 February 1717, and the complaint against Martínez was issued months before on 2 November 1716, when the oidor was named to supervise the election.

45. On the new idea that "foreign" persons not be allowed to serve, see AGN, Indios, v. 41, e. 105, fol. 139–139v.

46. See AGN, Historia, v. 413, e. 1, fols. 61–74, and "Sobre los inconvenientes de vivir los indios en el centro de la ciudad," *Boletín del Archivo General de la Nación, México* 9 (1938), 1–34; and also Cope, *Limits*, 88–93.

47. AGN, Indios, v. 41, e. 129, fol. 163.

48. AGN, Indios, v. 41, e. 105, 139–139v.

49. AGN, Indios, v. 41, e. 129, fols. 162v–163v.

50. There is a useful discussion in Gibson, *Aztecs*, 175–176, though Gibson is mostly concerned with sixteenth-century elections; AGN, Indios, v. 41, e. 129; AGN, Indios, v. 46, e. 23. Remember as well that, as discussed in chapter 4, governors had been disqualified for various reasons in the seventeenth century.

51. See AHCM, Parcialidades, v. 3574, e. 4, fols. 18–20; AGN, Indios, v. 37, e. 110, fol. 106; and AGN, Indios, v. 38, e. 228, fols. 305–306v, for don Roque Eusebio de Lara; and AHCM, Obras Publicas en General, v. 1509a, e. 5, fols. 25–41; AHCM, Parcialidades, v. 3574, e. 1, fols. 1–8v, and e. 3, fols. 14–17; and AGN, Indios, v. 33, e. 176, fols. 122v–123v, for Cruz y Guerrero. See AGN, Indios, v. 35, e. 167, fol. 227v, a petition denouncing the constant reelection of the current governor (not identified by name). The unnamed governor had been in power for four years on 20 December 1703 when the petition was filed. See AHCM, Obras Publicas en General, v. 1509a, e. 5, fols. 25–32v, where don Bernardino Antonio de la Cruz y Guerrero established that he was governor in 1704. We can also deduce from this statement that he held the office of governor for 1702 and 1703 because the corregidor of the city was attempting to hold him in prison for failing to provide repartimiento labor for public works in those years. Furthermore, having occupied the office for several consecutive years suggests that he was likely reelected, despite the protests by former governors.

52. See the appendix for a complete list, but some noted examples are don Martín González (r. 1638–43) and don Cristóbal Pascual (r. 1630–36). These terms, however, were much shorter than those of earlier officeholders like don Antonio Valeriano (r. 1573–99), for reasons discussed in chapters 2 and 3. The viceregal

government and community of Mexico Tenochtitlan moved away from extended terms for governors in the mid-seventeenth century, probably to reduce abuse and limit the monopolization of authority that likely enabled abuses to take place.

53. On the uprising, see Connell, "Because I Was Drunk," 369–373, 395–396; and Silva Prada, *La política.*

54. AGN, Indios, v. 29, e. 101, fols. 92v–93v; AGN, Indios, v. 29, e. 138, fols. 120v–121. The act of making someone a cacique was exceptionally rare; I have not encountered another instance.

55. AGN, Indios, v. 29, e. 101, fols. 92v–93v (1685); AGN, Indios, v. 29, e. 138. A series of documents connect Cruz to don Felipe de Aguilar; see AGN, Indios, v. 28 e. 236, which indicates that Aguilar served as the cobrador de reales tributos under Cruz in 1686. For additional discussion of don Joseph de la Cruz, see also AHCM, Actas, 371-A, and the residencia of Viceroy Galve (AGI, Escribanía de Cámara, 230c), which are cited by Silva Prada, *La política,* 563, cuadro 4.

56. AGN, Indios, v. 32, e. 79, fols. 83v–84v.

57. AGN, Indios, v. 31, e. 175, fols. 133–134v. Rojas was allowed only to serve out the term and was not elected per se; he took over in lieu of holding a second election so late in the year. He served again in 1696 under similar circumstances but did not ever win an election outright; see AGN, Indios. v. 32, e. 336, fols. 296v–297.

58. For the San Buenaventura lineage, see AGN, Indios, v. 36, e. 221, fols. 198v–199 (1705); AGN, General de Parte, v. 22, (only one expediente) fols. 82–120: "pleito por los lideres de tierras entre los naturales de la parcialidad de Santiago [Mexico] Tlatelolco y Don Blas López de Aragon"; AGN, Indios, v. 36, e. 221; AGN, Indios, v. 50, e. 130; AGN, Indios, v. 51, e. 2; and AGN, Tierras, v. 440, e. 6. Don Lorenzo and don Gregorio were both governors and were father and son.

59. On occasion, don Lorenzo de San Buenaventura was an alcalde when don Lucas de Santiago y Rojas was governor; see AGN, General de Parte, v. 22, fol. 97; and AGN, Indios, v. 42, e. 13, fol. 29–29v. See AGN, Indios, v. 40, e. 116, fol. 174–174v, for San Buenaventura filing a petition on behalf of de Santiago y Rojas.

60. AGN, Indios, v. 42, e. 165, fols. 200v–201.

61. It is probably no coincidence that the pleas by the cabildo came immediately after the Audiencia's move to disqualify don Juan Marcelo Audelo from serving a second term after he had won reelection in 1717; see AGN, Indios, v. 41, e. 129, fols. 162v–163v.

62. AGN, Indios, v. 44, e. 7, fol. 10–10v.

63. AGN, Indios, v. 39, e. 10, fols. 9v–10. The petition indicates that some were regidores and others mandones, which meant that only some of the challengers could participate in the election.

64. AGN, Indios, v. 39, e. 10, fols. 9v–10.

65. AGN, Indios, v. 39, e. 10, fols. 10–11.

66. AGN, Tierras, v. 440, e. 6, fol. 8 (1723 and 1725), lists San Buenaventura as a fiscal in a will in Nahuatl, but that was a church office; on the office of native

fiscal, see Truitt, "Nahuas and Catholicism." San Buenaventura was governor in 1723; see AGN, Indios. v. 47, e. 107, fol. 199–199v, which makes it clear that he replaced don Pascual Ignacio, who had served in 1722.

67. AGN, Indios, v. 50, e. 130, fols. 249–250v.

68. AGN, Indios, v. 50, e. 130, fol. 249v.

69. AGN, Indios, v. 50, e. 130, fols. 249v–250v.

70. AGN, Indios, v. 46, e. 23, fols. 28v–29.

71. AGN, Indios, v. 46, e. 23, fol. 29, cites the law prohibiting reelection from the *Recopilación* incorrectly (lib. 6, tit. 3, ley 15). It should refer to *Recopilación*, lib. 4, tit. 9, ley 13.

72. The succession issues are complex, but it appears that don Juan and don Felipe de Aguilar alternated in the office of governor, probably from 1667 but certainly in the years 1672, 1673, 1674, and attempted to continue into 1675 until they met resistance. See AGN, Civil, v. 740, e. 10, fol. 8, which acknowledges the existence of the rotation in 1673: "current governor, don Felipe de Aguilar . . . whose brother don Juan de Aguilar was [elected] in the past and purports to become [*pretende de ser*] elected for the coming year (1674)." The brothers were accused of being mestizos and ineligible to serve as a result, hence the "purports to become." For their elections, see AGN, Indios, v. 24, e. 242, fol. 314–314v (1672); and AGN, Indios, v. 25, e. 9, fol. 7 (1674). For Felipe de Aguilar, see AGN, Indios, v. 24, e. 127, fols. 79v–81v (1667; it is unclear if he was governor from 1667 to 1671); and AGN, Indios, v. 24, e. 485, fol. 353 (1673). It is also likely that don Felipe and don Juan de Aguilar alternated in the office of governor from 1667 to 1673, but it is also possible that the rotation began earlier. See the petition in AGN, Civil, v. 740, e. 10, fol. 24, that states that don Juan and don Felipe de Aguilar alternated in office, "lo un año uno, y otro a otro" ("one year one and the next year the other").

73. AGN, Civil, v. 1688, e. 1, fol. 5.

74. AGN, Indios, v. 30, e. 7; AGN, Indios, v. 30, e. 191 (actual election confirmation); AGN, Tributos, v. 10, e. 6, fol. 139–139v; AHCM, Parcialidades, v. 3574, e. 1, fols. 1–8; AGN, Indios, v. 30, e. 115; AGN, Indios, v. 30, e. 191, fols. 180–183. See also the discussion in Silva Prada, *La política*, 406–407.

75. AHCM, Parcialidades, v. 3574, e. 1, fols. 1–8; and AGN, Indios, v. 28, e. 252. He is called a contador de tributos in the first document and a cobrador de reales tributos in the second; both are from 1684. He is essentially blamed by his brother-in-law and accused of stealing tribute for which don Bernardino was held accountable. He served as cobrador de tributes under don Joseph de la Cruz in 1686; see AGN, Indios, v. 28 e. 236, fols. 201v–202. In 1674, both Aguilar brothers were forbidden from participating in the collection of tribute; see AGN, Civil, v. 1688, e. 1, fols. 22v–23. Additional petitions in the 1690s include Aguilar and Cruz together, suggesting a political linkage; see AGN, Indios, v. 32, e. 139, fols. 162v–163 (1693); and AGN, Indios, v. 32, e. 328, fols. 291–292 (1696). For his service as an alcalde in 1692, see AGN, Indios, v. 32, e. 37, fol. 39v.

I suspect that the contador/cobrador de reales tributos is what became of the Spanish position discussed in chapter 4 once called the alguacil amparador, as López held the title in 1658; see AGN, Indios, v. 23, e. 74, fols. 64v–65v.

76. AGN, Civil, v. 740, e. 10, fol. 8.

77. AGN, Civil, v. 1688, e. 1.

78. AGN, Civil, v. 740, e. 10, fols. 20–21.

79. AGN, Civil, v. 740, e. 10, fol. 23v; the petition connects two ideas: that the brothers directed voters, and that they compelled the order by the oidor to the gathered electors that they not vote for Montaño.

80. AGN, Civil, v. 740, e. 10, fols. 23–23v.

81. AGN, Civil, v. 1688, e. 1, fol. 4–4v. Romero's subsequent recusal suggests that the Audiencia acted conservatively to preserve the integrity of the proceeding. I have no direct evidence to indicate whether the allegation against Romero was true or false. Romero was a scribe for the Audiencia but in its native division, the Juzgado General.

In addition, the don Joseph de la Cruz in 1675 is very likely not the same individual as the governor in 1686, 1692, and 1720. In terms of age, forty-four years separated him from the term as governor in 1720, meaning that he would have been very young in 1675, probably too young to take on such a leadership role in native government. Furthermore, we know that the governor don Joseph de la Cruz was elevated to the nobility in the 1680s, making him an unlikely candidate for governor in 1675. I can say with relative certainty that the governor in 1720 was the same Joseph de la Cruz as in 1686; see AGN, Indios, v. 38, e. 7, fol. 5v; and AGN, Indios, v. 44, e. 19, fol. 19–19v.

82. For the influence of the escribano, see Scardaville, "Justice by Paperwork," 981–985.

83. AGN, Civil, v. 740, e. 10, fols. 20, 27.

84. Charles Cutter, *The Legal Culture of Northern New Spain, 1700–1810* (Albuquerque: University of New Mexico Press, 1995), provides a useful discussion of the judicial apparatus of the viceregal government. Although he focuses his commentary on the north, his conclusions indicate a profound continuity in process and judicial philosophy with more densely populated central areas.

85. AGN, Civil, v. 740, e. 10, fol. 23v. The language of the appointment documents specified only those "of good character and reputation" (*de buena fama y costumbres*) could serve.

86. This may help to explain the hostility early eighteenth-century judges had for unfounded claims and the penchant for the Audiencia to silence those who filed such claims. See the discussion above, and AGN, Indios, v. 41, e. 105, fol. 139v, for an example from 1717.

87. AGN, Indios, v. 24, e. 442, fol. 314–314v. For the election of don Francisco Benítez, see chapter 4; AGN, Indios, v. 23, e. 370; and AGN, Indios, v. 23, e. 432.

88. AGN, Civil, v. 740, e. 10.

89. For his electoral victories, see AGN, Indios, v. 24, e. 442, fol. 314–314v; AGN, Civil, v. 740, e. 10; and AGN, Indios, v. 25, e. 9, fol. 7.

90. AGN, Civil, v. 1688, e. 1, fol. 6–6v (1675). See Caso, *Los barrios antiguos*, 12, for Tecuicaltitlan, part of Mexico Tenochtitlan.

91. AGN, Civil, v. 1688, e. 1, fol. 7–7v. Xihuitongo, a subdivision of Mexico Tenochtitlan, is spelled "Cibtongo" in the document; see Caso, *Los barrios antiguos*, 13–14.

92. AGN, Civil, v. 1688, e. 1, fols. 8v–9.

93. AGN, Civil, v. 1688, e. 1, fols. 12–15v, and there is also a nonpaginated section after 15v that is relevant.

94. AGN, Civil, v. 1688, e. 1, fols. 18–19; the court also found the charge difficult to sustain and ordered, without further inquiry, the release of Salvador almost immediately on hearing of his imprisonment (literally the same day, 28 February 1675).

95. AGN, Civil, v. 1688, e. 1, fol. 18–18v.

96. AGN, Civil, v. 1688, e. 1, fol. 18–18v.

97. AGN, Indios, v. 31, e. 327, fol. 255v.

98. AGN, Indios, v. 32, e. 37, fol. 39v.

99. Gibson, *Aztecs*, 175. Gibson is paraphrasing the commentary offered by Ramírez de Fuenleal, who argued in 1533 that natives should not serve on Spanish cabildos lest they be corrupted.

100. Altman, *Transatlantic Ties*, 91–97. Altman contends that on important matters in Brihuega, Spain, the *concejo abierto* (open council) afforded ordinary citizens the opportunity to voice concerns. The Spanish cabildo in Puebla that she also studied appears to have been far less open and more what she calls "elitist." On the abusive potential of Spanish cabildos in Mexico, see AGI, Escribanía de Cámara, l. 178a, e. 9.

101. For the relative cohesion of the political groups within the parcialidad, see AGN, Indios, v. 31, e. 146, fol. 108–108v. This document, executed on 2 August 1692, is a request from the native cofradía, which comprised the principales of Mexico Tenochtitlan, led by several former governors. They happen to be collected together in this document because they are asking en masse for the right to wear Spanish-styled clothing, a right taken from them after the uprising of 1692; see AGN, Historia, v. 413, e. 1, fols. 61–64. See also Schroeder, "Jesuits, Nahuas," 74–76.

102. AGN, Indios, v. 32, e. 79, fols. 83v–84v.

103. AGN, Indios, v. 32, e. 79, fol. 84v.

104. See AGN, Indios, v. 32, e. 207, fols. 187v–188, for the order that gives the contador control over recaudación.

105. AGN, Indios, v. 32, e. 207, fols. 186–188.

106. AGN, Indios, v. 32, e. 207, fols. 186v–187. One of the proposed solutions was to make native governors use Spanish fiadores exclusively, which would have had significant ramifications, giving Spaniards the ability to influence who could serve as governor. Of course, even when Spaniards served as fiadores, they sometimes did not pay; see AGN, Indios, v. 47, e. 107, fols. 198v–202v.

107. Silva Prada, *La política,* 79–82.

108. There are many allegations against Cruz y Guerrero. One petition suggests that he was accused of murder ("haber cometido una muerte") in 1687, for which he was later absolved; see AGN, Tributos, v. 10, e. 7, fol. 139–139v.

109. AGN, Indios, v. 32, e. 207, fol. 187; AHCM, Parcialidades, v. 3574, e. 1, fols. 1–8v; and AGN, Tributos, v. 10, e. 7, fol. 139–139v. Some have argued, mainly Chester L. Guthrie, that tribute collection rose after the uprising of 1692, from "8000 to 19,000 pesos" annually; see his "Riots in Seventeenth Century Mexico City: A Study in Social History with Emphasis on the Lower Classes" (Ph.D. diss., University of California at Berkeley, 1937). See also Cope, *Limits,* 92, who attributes this change to the return of natives to their barrios from the traza. The archival data provide additional insight into the upswing in tribute collection. It should also be noted that the tribute-paying population of the barrios changed significantly in the 1690s as a new drive to matriculate *indios forasteros* (foreign natives) into the tribute rolls was undertaken in 1696 by royal decree; see AHCM, Parcialidades, v. 3574, e. 2, fols. 9–13; and AGN, Indios, v. 33, e. 176, fols. 122v–123v.

110. AGN, Indios, v. 33, e. 176, fols. 122v–123v.

111. AGN, Indios, v. 35, e. 167, fol. 227v; and AHCM, Obras Publicas en General, v. 1509a, e. 5, fols. 25–32v.

112. AHCM, Obras Públicas en General, v. 1509a, e. 4; and AHCM, Parcialidades, v. 3574, e. 4 and 3. Part of the problem here is that the corregidor believed that the governors should use Spaniards as fiadores to guarantee their payment. Cruz y Guerrero had native fiadores who ultimately failed to cover the debt. Governor Montaño had been forced in 1675 to use Spaniards and mestizos and had only a small number of natives. Apparently, in subsequent years, native governors reclaimed their right to appoint fiadores freely; see AGN, Tributos, v. 10, e. 6; and the discussion in chapter 3, including table 2. It appears that, after the uprising of 1692, Spanish officials again clamored for Spanish fiadores, seeking to empower the contador general as they had the alguacil amparador in the mid-seventeenth century.

113. AGN, Indios, v. 36, e. 214; and AHCM, Obras Públicas en General, v. 1509a, e. 5.

114. Don Roque served from 1706 to 1709; see AHCM, Parcialidades, v. 3574, e. 4, fols. 18–20; and AGN, Indios, v. 37, e. 110, fol. 106. Although he did not directly petition, Eusebio de Lara was one of the principal allies of don Joseph de la Cruz, with whom this chapter began, and part of that emerging coalition. Remember too that don Joseph de la Cruz was also part of the group of ex-governors who tried to oust Cruz y Guerrero; AGN, Indios, v. 35, e. 167, fol. 227v.

CONCLUSION

Epigraph. Díaz made this remark to American journalist James Creelman in "President Díaz: Hero of the Americas," *Pearson's Magazine* 19, no. 3 (1908), 241.

284 NOTES TO PAGES 182–186

1. Lockhart, *Nahuas after the Conquest*, 47–48.

2. Gibson, *Aztecs*, 392–394. Gibson does not explicitly establish the connection made here that tribute arrears may have been a kind of passive resistance to Spanish collectors. Indeed, continuity exists with such moments in the mid-seventeenth century. The 100,000 pesos Gibson estimated for the total arrears for the eighteenth century may be testament, not to poverty, but to resistance to Bourbon interference, particularly the effort to farm out the collection of tribute to Spaniards.

3. An emerging literature, of which this book is a part, is beginning to provide numerous examples of how native peoples strove to create spaces of autonomy within a sometimes violent colonialism. For an excellent articulation, see Yannakakis, *Art*, especially this comment: "The fact and threat of violence, combined with the value that native peoples placed on local autonomy, positioned native intermediaries in a role complementary to that of the state makers" (13). See also Gibson, *Aztecs*, 392–94.

4. Lira González, *Comunidades Indígenas*, 161–191.

5. See Virginia Guedea, "De la fidelidad a la infidencia: Los gobernadores de la parcialidad de San Juan," in Jaime E. Rodríguez O., ed., *Patterns of Contention in Mexican History* (Wilmington: Scholarly Resources Press, 1992), 96–100. Guedea argues that independent native leaders passionately stood up to defend the city against the Hidalgo revolt in 1810 and even apparently fielded soldiers led by the native governors of the parcialidades. See also Guedea's argument (110–112) that the Constitution of 1812 effectively turned natives with special privileges into citizens and thus by implication empowered others in the communities of Mexico Tenochtitlan who had been excluded from holding native offices. At the same time, Guedea has also identified a native governor of Mexico Tenochtitlan who served on the Ayuntamiento of Mexico City. For more on this, see Jaime E. Rodríguez O., *The Independence of Spanish America* (New York: Cambridge University Press, 1998), 92–106; and Nettie Lee Benson, "The Contested Mexican Election of 1812," *Hispanic American Historical Review* 26, no. 3 (1946), 340–343.

6. See Chimalpahin, *Annals*, 137, 136–137, n. 2.

7. Lockhart, *Nahuas after the Conquest*, 33; see also Gibson, *Tlaxcala*, 104–108.

8. Haskett, *Indigenous Rulers*, 28, 225, n. 3; and Gibson, "Rotation of Alcaldes," 212–223.

9. Gibson, *Aztecs*, 171–178, 368–376; and Lockhart, *Nahuas after the Conquest*, 28–40.

10. Lockhart, *Nahuas after the Conquest*, 32–33; Gibson, "Rotation of Alcaldes," 212–223; and Haskett, *Indigenous Rulers*, chap. 2. For the speed with which indigenous groups assimilated Spanish legal ideas, see González-Hermosillo Adams, "Macehuales versus señores naturales," 128–129.

11. See Owensby, *Empire of Law*, 2–4, on the litigiousness of natives and their amazing capacity to learn litigation quickly and adapt it for their advantage.

APPENDIX

1. Chimalpahin, *Annals*, 133, 146–147.
2. Chimalpahin, *Annals*, 132–133. Ruled for only eighty days.
3. Chimalpahin, *Annals*, 133–135.
4. Hernán Cortés, *Letters from Mexico*, 321, 506, n. 51; Chimalpahin, *Annals*, 133; Chimalpahin, *Las ocho relaciones*, t. 2, 169.
5. Chimalpahin, *Las ocho relaciones* t. 2, 169; Chimalpahin, *Annals*, 135
6. Chimalpahin, *Las ocho relaciones*, t. 2, 187; Chimalpahin, *Annals*, 135–137; AGN, Tierras, v. 55, e. 2, fol. 166v, mentioned.
7. Chimalpahin, *Las ocho relaciones*, t. 2, 199, 201.
8. García Granados, *Diccionario Biográfico*, 204–205; Tezozomoc, *Crónica mexicayotl*, para. 277.
9. Chimalpahin, *Las ocho relaciones*, t. 2, 228, 211; AGN, Civil, v. 644, e. 1, fols. 190–191.
10. Chimalpahin, *Annals*, 137 and 138, n. 1.
11. AGN, Civil, v. 644, e. 1; AGN, Tierras, v. 22, e. 1; AGN, Tierras, v. 48, e. 4; AGN, Tierras, v. 55, e. 5.
12. Chimalpahin, *Annals*, 139, 141.
13. AGN, Tierras, v. 20, pt. 1, e. 2; Chimalpahin, *Annals*, 85, 141–143. Stepped aside in 1596 and retired in 1599.
14. Chimalpahin, *Annals*, 143, 147; AGN, Tierras, v. 55, e. 2, fol. 182v.
15. AGN, Tierras, v. 165, e. 4 (1600); AGN, Tierras, v. 866, e. 1 (1604); Chimalpahin, *Annals*, 145; Lockhart, *Nahuas after the Conquest*, 34.
16. Schroeder, *Chimalpahin*, 145–147. Juan Bautista appointed the judge-governor in Tenochtitlan. Lockhart, *Nahuas after the Conquest*, 34.
17. Lockhart, *Nahuas after the Conquest*, 34.
18. Lockhart, *Nahuas after the Conquest*, 34; AGN, Indios, v. 7 e. 21.
19. AGN, Indios, v. 7, e. 21, fol. 9–9v.
20. AGN, Indios, v. 7, e. 465, fol. 222.
21. AGN, Indios, v. 7, e. 465, fol. 222.
22. AGN, Indios, v. 9, e. 272, fol. 132; AGN, Archivo Historico de Hacienda, v. 1418, e. 28, fols. 400–403. In 1634; AGN, Tierras, v. 1720, e. 7, fol. 54.
23. AGN, Archivo Historico de Hacienda, v. 1423, e. 31.
24. AGN, Indios, v. 10, pt. 1, e. 113, fol. 60v; AGN, Indios, v. 10, pt. 1, e. 275, fol. 156.
25. AGN, Indios, v. 12, e. 116, fol. 77; AGN, Archivo Histórico de Hacienda, v. 1430, e. 52; AGN, Reales Cedulas Originales y Dubpicados, D11, e. 393, fol. 298v.
26. AGN, Archivo Histórico de Hacienda, v. 1430, l. 52, fols. 733–738; AGN, Archivo Historico de Hacienda, v. 1434, l. 18, fols. 213–245.
27. AGN, Archivo Historico de Hacienda, v. 1433, l. 1, fols. 1–4v.
28. AGN, Indios, v. 12, e. 68, fol. 199–199v. AGN, Indios, v. 14, e. 7, fols. 6v–7; AGN, Indios, v. 14, e. 117, fol. 113; AGN, Criminal, v. 165, e. 10, fols. 235v–236.

29. AGN, Indios, v. 15, e. 1; AGN, Indios, v. 15, e. 109, fols. 79–79v.

30. AGN, Indios, v. 15, e. 109, fol. 79–79v; AGN, Indios, v. 16, e. 3 bis, fol. 3. See also AGN, Archivo Histórico de Hacienda, v. 1433, l. 52, fols. 1–4v; AGN, Indios, v. 19, e. 169.

31. AGN, Indios, v. 15, e. 134, fols. 197–198 (Mexico Tlatelolco); AGN, Indios, v. 17, e. 21 bis, fol. 33v; AGN, Indios, v. 18, e. 58, fols. 48–49v; AGN, Indios, v. 19, e. 37, fol. 18; AGN, Indios, v. 19, e. 150, fol. 80. AGN, Indios, v. 20, e. 215, fol. 169v; Silva Prada, *La política*, 405.

32. AGN, Indios, v. 17, e. 56, fols. 77v–82v.

33. AGN, Indios, v. 17, e. 56, fol. 78.

34. AGN, Indios, v. 18, e. 58, fols. 48–49v; AGN, Indios, v. 20, e. 215, fol. 169v.

35. AGN, Indios, v. 21, e. 146, fols. 133–136v; AGN, Indios, v. 21, e. 97; AGN, Indios, v. 21, e. 149.

36. AGN, Indios, v. 21, e. 193, fols. 169–170; AGN, Indios, v. 21, e. 193 (served June 1657 until December 1658); AGN, Indios, v. 23, e. 227, fol. 206.

37. AGN, Indios, v. 23, e. 370, fols. 339–344v; AGN, Indios, v. 23, e. 432, fol. 425.

38. AGN, Tierras, v. 2776, e. 18, fols. 6v, 16 (1662, 1663, 1664); AGN, Indios, v. 24, e. 474, fols. 343v–344.

39. AGN, Indios, v. 24, e. 127, fols. 79v–81v.

40. AGN, Indios, v. 24, e. 442, fol. 314–314v.

41. AGN, Civil, v. 740, e. 10.

42. AGN, Indios, v. 25, e. 9, fol. 7; AGN, Civil, v. 740, e. 10, fol. 21.

43. AGN, Tributos, v. 10, e. 6.

44. AGN, Indios, v. 25, e. 113, fol. 91v.

45. AGN, Indios, v. 25, e. 226–231, fols. 171–173.

46. He was elected; AGN, Indios, v. 25, e. 442, fol. 306; AGN, Indios, v. 25, e. 440; Silva Prada, *La política*, cuadro 4; AGN, Indios, v. 32, e. 79.

47. AGN, Indios, v. 25, e. 440.

48. AHCM, Obras Publicas en General, v. 1509a, e. 1, fols. 1–5; AGN, Indios, v. 26, e. 11.

49. AGN, Indios, v. 26, e. 11, cuaderno 2.

50. AGN, Indios, v. 27, e. 223. Nullified.

51. AGN, Indios, v. 27, e. 223.

52. AGN, Indios, v. 26, e. 194; AGN, Indios, v. 27, e. 295; AGN, Indios, v. 27, e. 306; also mentioned in AGN, Indios, v. 32, e. 207, fol. 186.

53. AGN, Indios, v. 28, e. 26; AHCM, Parcialidades, v. 3574, e. 1, fols. 1–8.

54. AGN, Indios, v. 29, e. 101, fols. 92v–93v (1685); AGN, Indios, v. 29, e. 138; AGN, Indios, v. 28, e. 236; Silva Prada, *La política*, cuadro 4, where she cites document AHCM, Actas, 371-A.

55. AGN, Indios, v. 30, e. 7 (1687); AGN, Indios, v. 30, e. 191 (1688); AGN, Tributos, v. 10, e. 6, fol. 139–139v; AHCM, Parcialidades, v. 3574, e. 1, fols. 1–8.

56. AGN, Indios, v. 30, e. 115.

57. AGN, Indios, v. 32, e. 37; AGN, Indios, v. 32, e. 37, fols. 39v–41v.

58. AGN, Indios, v. 31, e. 175, fols. 133–134v.

59. AGN, Indios, v. 31, e. 175, fols. 133–134v; AGN, Tierras, v. 186, e. 9, fol. 33.

60. AGN, Indios, v. 32, e. 207, fols. 186–188. Elected in 1694.

61. AGN, Indios, v. 32, e. 207; AGN, Indios, v. 32, e. 79; AGN, Indios, v. 33, e. 7; AGN, Indios, v. 33, e. 11; AGN, Indios, v. 32, e. 328, fols. 291–292.

62. AGN, Indios, v. 32, e. 328; AHCM Parcialidades, v. 3574, e. 2. Died in office February 1696.

63. AHCM, Parcialidades, v. 3574, e. 2, fol. 12v; AGN, Indios, v. 32, e. 328; AGN, Indios. v. 32, e. 336, fols. 296v–297.

64. AGN, Indios, v. 33, e. 156; AGN, Indios, v. 35, e. 167; AGN, Indios, v. 40, e. 1.

65. AHCM, Parcialidades, v. 3574, e. 1, fols. 1–8v; AHCM, Parcialidades, v. 3574, e. 3, fols. 14–17; AGN, Indios, v. 33, e. 176, fols. 122v–123v; AGN, Indios, v. 35, e. 167, fol. 227v; AHCM, Obras Publicas en General, v. 1509a, e. 5, fols. 25–41.

66. AHCM, Parcialidades, v. 3574, e. 4, fols. 18–20; AGN, Indios, v. 37, e. 110, fol. 106; and AGN, Indios, v. 38, e. 228, fols. 305–306v. He was probably governor in 1707, though none of these documents make it absolutely clear.

67. AGN, Indios, v. 38, e. 7, f. 5v; AGN, Indios, v. 38, e. 72.

68. AGN, Indios, v. 38, e. 228, fols. 305v–306; AGN, Indios, v. 40, e. 1.

69. AGN, Indios, v. 41, e. 129, fols. 162v–163v.

70. AGN, Indios, v. 41, e. 129, fols. 162v–163v; AGN, Indios, v. 41, e. 105.

71. AGN, Indios, v. 44, e. 19, fol. 19–19v; AGN, Indios, v. 38, e. 7, fol. 5.

72. AGN, Indios, v. 44, e. 19, fol. 19–19v.

73. AGN, Indios, v. 50, e. 17, fol. 25–25v.

74. AHCM, Processiones, v. 3712, e. 2, fol. 7–9.

75. AGN, Indios, v. 54, e. 150.

BIBLIOGRAPHY

ARCHIVAL COLLECTIONS

Archivo General de la Nación, México, Mexico City

Archivo Historico de Hacienda, Archivo Judicial, Bienes Nacionales, Caminos y Calzadas, Civil, Criminal, General de Parte, Historia, Indios, Mercedes, Obras Públicas, Ordenanzas, Reales Cedulas, Reales Cedulas Duplicadas, Tierras, Tribunal Superior de Justicia del Distrito Federal, Tributos

Archivo Historico de la Ciudad de México, Mexico City

Actas; Aguas, Alcaicería; Calzadas y Caminos; Empedrados; Limpieza de Ciudad; Obras Públicas en General; Parcialidades; Paseos; Processiones; Puentes; Ríos y Acequias; Rastros y Mercados; Real Audiencia, Panaderías

Archivo de Indias, Sevilla

Audiencia de México, Escribanía de Cámara

Biblioteca Nacional de México, Mexico City

Fondo Reservado

Mapoteca de Orozco y Berra, Mexico City

Tulane University, Latin American Library

France V. Scholes Collection, Viceregal and Ecclesiastical Mexican Collection

PUBLISHED PRIMARY SOURCES

Bautista, Fray Juan. *Advertencias. Para los confessores de los naturales. Compuestas por el padre Ioan Baptista, de la orden del seraphico padre Sanct Fancisco, lector de Theologia, y guardian del convento de Sanctiago Tlatilulco: de la provincia de la Santo Evangelio.* México, 1600.

Bentura Beleña, don Eusebio. *Recopilación sumaria de todos los autos acordados de la Real Audiencia y Sala del Crimen de esta Nueva España, y providencias de su superior govierno; de varias reales cédulas y ordenes que después de publicada la Recopilación de Indias han podido recogerse así de las dirigidas á la misma audiencia ó gobierno, como de algunas otras que por sus notables decisiones convendrá no ignorar.* 2 vols. México: Zúñiga y Oniveros, 1787.

Berdan, Frances F., and Patricia Rieff Anawalt, eds. *The Codex Mendoza.* 4 vols. Berkeley: University of California Press, 1989.

Cervantes de Salazar, Francisco. *Life in the Imperial and Loyal City of Mexico in New Spain and the Royal and Pontifical University of Mexico as Described in the Dialogues for the Study of the Latin Language Prepared by Francisco Cervantes de Salazar for Use in His Classes and Printed in 1554.* Trans. Minnie Lee Barrett Shepard, ed. Carlos Eduardo Castañeda. Westport, Conn.: Greenwood Press, 1970 [1953].

———. *México en 1554: Tres diálogos latinos que Francisco Cervantes de Salazar escribió e imprimió en México en dicho año.* Ed. and trans. J. García Icazbalceta. México: Andrade y Morales, 1875.

Chimalpahin Quauhtlehuanitzin, don Domingo Francisco de San Antón Muñón. *Annals of His Time.* Ed. James Lockhart, Susan Schroeder, and Doris Namala. Stanford, Calif.: Stanford University Press, 2006.

———. *Codex Chimalpahin: Society and Politics in Mexico Tenochtitlan, Tlatelolco, Texcoco, Culhuacan, and Other Nahua Altepetl in Central Mexico: The Nahuatl and Spanish Annals and Accounts Collected and Recorded by don Domingo de San Antón Muñón Chimalpahin Quauhtlehuanitzin.* Vols. 1 and 2. Ed. Arthur J. O. Anderson and Susan Schroeder. Norman: University of Oklahoma Press, 1997.

———. *Las ocho relaciones y el memorial de Colhuacan.* 2 tomos. Ed. Rafael Tena. México: CONACULTA, 1998.

Cortés Hernán. *Letters from Mexico.* Ed. and trans. Anthony Pagden. New Haven, Conn.: Yale University Press, 1986.

Díaz del Castillo, Bernal. *The Conquest of New Spain.* Trans. J. M. Cohen. New York: Penguin, 1963.

———. *Historia de la conquista de Nueva España.* Ed. Joaquín Ramírez Cabañas. México: Editorial Porrúa, 1970.

Dibble, Charles E., ed. *Codice Aubin.* México: José Porrúa Turanza, 1963.

Gómez de Cervantes, Gonzalo. *La vida económica y social de Nueva España al finalizar del siglo XVI.* México: José Porrúa y Hijos, 1944 [1599].

Icazbalceta, Joaquín García, ed. *Nueva colección de documentos para la historia de México.* 5 tomos. Nendeln: Kraus Reprint, 1971 [1886].

Instrucciones que los virreyes de Nueva España dejaron a sus sucesores. Añadense algunos que los mismos trajeron de la corte y otros documentos semejantes a las instrucciones. México: Imprenta, 1867.

Las Casas, Bartolomé de. *Apologetica Historia Sumaria.* 2 vols. Ed. Edmundo O'Gorman. México: Universidad Autónoma de México, 1967.

Livre des comptes, des tributes, a payer par les indigenes de San Pablo Teocaltitlan á leur gourverneur D. Antonio Valeriano, 1574.

Lockhart, James, Frances Berdan, and Arthur J. O. Anderson, eds. *The Tlaxcalan Actas: A Compendium of the Records of the Cabildo of Tlaxcala (1545–1627).* Salt Lake City: University of Utah Press, 1986.

López, Gerónimo. "1545 Gerónimo López to the King on Native Policy." In *New Iberian World: A Documentary History of the Discovery and Settlement of Latin America to the Early Seventeenth Century*, ed. John H. Parry and Robert G. Keith, 447. New York: Times Books, 1984.

Molina, Fray Alonso de. *Vocabulario en lengua castellana y mexicana y mexicana y castellana*. Ed. Miguel León-Portilla. México, 1977 [1571].

Ortega Montoñés, Juan de. *Instrucción reservada que el Obispo-virrey Juan de Ortega Montañés dio a su sucesor en el mando el Conde de Moctezuma*. Ed. Norman F. Martin. México: Editorial Jus, 1965.

Parry, John H., and Robert G. Keith, eds. *New Iberian World: A Documentary History of the Discovery and Settlement of Latin America to the Early Seventeenth Century*. New York: Times Books, 1984.

Pintura del gobernador, alcaldes y regidores de Mexico. Ed. Vicenta Cortés Alonso. Madrid: Servicio de Publicaciones del Ministerio de Educación y Ciencia, 1973.

Quiñones Keber, Eloise, ed. *Codex Telleriano-Remensis: Ritual, Divination, and History in a Pictorial Aztec Manuscript*. Austin: University of Texas Press, 1995.

Real Academia Española, *Diccionario de la lengua Española*. Madrid: Real Academia Española, 1992.

Recopilación de leyes de los reynos de las indias, mandadas imprimir y publicar por la majestad Católica del rey don Carlos II, Nuestro Señor. 3 tomos. Madrid: Gráficas Ultra, 1943.

Robles, Don Antonio de. *Diario de sucesos notables*. 2 tomos. Ed. Antonio Castro Leal. México: Editoral Porrúa, 1946.

Rubio Mañé, J. Ignacio, ed. "Testamento del gobernador y cacique de Santiago [Mexico] Tlatelolco, don Lucas de Santiago y Rojas, 1724." *Boletín del Archivo General de la Nación* 25, no. 1 (1954): 63–74.

Sahagún, Fray Bernardino de. *Florentine Codex: General History of the Things of New Spain*. 12 vols. Ed. Arthur J. O. Anderson and Charles E. Dibble. Santa Fe, N.M., and Salt Lake City: School of American Research and University of Utah Press, 1950–.

———. *Historia general de las cosas de la Nueva España*. 5 tomos. Mexico: P. Robredo, 1938.

———. *Primeros Memoriales*. Ed. and trans. Thelma D. Sullivan. Norman: University of Oklahoma Press, 1997.

"Sobre los inconvenientes de vivir los indios en el centro de la ciudad." *Boletín del Archivo General de la Nación, México* 9 (1938): 1–34.

Tezozomoc, Hernando de Alvarado. *Crónica mexicayotl*. Ed. Adrián León. México: Universidad Nacional Autónma de Méxcio, 1998.

Torquemada, Fray Juan de. *Monarquía indiana*. facs. ed. 3 tomos. Ed. Andrés González de Barcía Caballido y Zúñiga. México: S. Chávez Hayhoe, 1943–1944 [1723].

Torres de Mendoza, don Luis, Joaquín Francisco Pacheco, and Francisco de Cardenas y Espejo, eds. *Colección de documentos inéditos relativos al descubrimiento, conquista y organización de las antiguas posesiones Españolas en América y Oceanía sacados de los archivos del reino y muy especialmente del de Indias.* 42 tomos. Madrid: Frías y Compañía, 1864–1884.

Zorita, Alonso de. *Historia de la Nueva España.* Madrid: Librería General de Victoriano Suárez, 1909.

———. *The Lords of New Spain: The Brief and Summary Relation of the Lords of New Spain.* Trans. Benjamin Keen. New Brunswick, N.J.: Rutgers University Press, 1963.

———. "On the Exploitation of the Indians." In *New Iberian World: A Documentary History of the Discovery and Settlement of Latin America to the Early Seventeenth Century,* ed. John H. Parry and Robert G. Keith, 438. New York: Times Books, 1984.

SECONDARY SOURCES

Acuna-Soto, Rodolofo, Leticia Calderón Romero, and James H. Maguire. "Large Epidemics of Hemorrhagic Fevers in Mexico, 1545–1815." *American Journal of Tropical Medicine and Hygiene* 62, no. 6 (2000): 734–735.

Alanis Boyso, José Luis. *Elecciones de república para los pueblos del corregimiento de Toluca, 1729–1811.* México: Biblioteca enciclopedica del estado de México, 1978.

Altman, Ida. *Transatlantic Ties in the Spanish Empire: Brihuega, Spain, and Puebla, Mexico, 1560–1620.* Stanford, Calif.: Stanford University Press, 2000.

Andrien, Kenneth. "The Sale of Fiscal Offices and the Decline of Royal Authority in the Viceregalty of Peru, 1633–1700." *Hispanic American Historical Review* 62, no. 1 (1982): 49–71.

Anna, Timothy E. *The Fall of the Royal Government in Mexico City.* Lincoln: University of Nebraska Press, 1978.

Aram, Bethany. *Juana the Mad: Sovereignty and Dynasty in Renaissance Europe.* Baltimore: Johns Hopkins University Press, 2005.

Arnold, Linda. *Bureaucracy and Bureaucrats in Mexico City, 1742–1835.* Tucson: University of Arizona Press, 1988.

Batres, Leopoldo. *Cartilla histórica de la Ciudad de México.* México: Gallegos Hnos. Libreros Editores, 1893.

Baudot, Georges. *Utopia and History in Mexico: The First Chronicles of Mexican Civilization, 1520–1569.* Trans. Bernard R. Ortiz de Montellano and Thelma Ortiz de Montellano. Boulder: University of Colorado Press, 1995.

Baskes, Jeremy. "Coerced or Voluntary? The *Repartimiento* and Market Participation of Peasants in Late Colonial Oaxaca." *Journal of Latin American Studies* 28, no. 1 (1996): 1–28.

———. *Indians, Merchants, and Markets: A Reinterpretation of the Repartimiento and Spanish-Indian Economic Relations in Colonial Oaxaca, 1750–1821.* Stanford, Calif.: Stanford University Press, 2000.

Bennett, Herman. *Africans in Colonial Mexico: Absolutism, Christianity, and Afro-Creole Consciousness, 1570–1640.* Indianapolis: Indiana University Press, 2003.

Benson, Nettie Lee. "The Contested Mexican Election of 1812." *Hispanic American Historical Review* 26, no. 3 (1946): 336–350.

Berdan, Frances. *The Aztecs of Central Mexico: An Imperial Society.* New York: Holt Rinehart and Winston, 1982.

Berdan, Frances F., Richard E. Blanton, Elizabeth Hill Boone, Mary G. Hodge, Michael E. Smith, and Emily Umberger, eds. *Aztec Imperial Strategies.* Washington, D.C.: Dumbarton Oaks Research Library and Collection, 1996.

Boone, Elizabeth Hill. *Stories in Red and Black: Pictorial Histories of the Aztecs and Mixtecs.* Austin: University of Texas Press, 2000.

Borah, Woodrow. *Justice by Insurance: The General Indian Court of Colonial Mexico and the Legal Aides of the Half-Real.* Berkeley: University of California Press, 1983.

———. *New Spain's Century of Depression.* Berkeley: University of California Press, 1951.

Boyer, Richard. "La Ciudad de México en 1628: La visión de Juan Gómez de Trasmonte." *Historia Mexicana* 29, no. 3 (1980): 447–471.

———. *La gran inundación: vida Vida y sociedad en la Ciudad de México (1629–1638).* México: Secretaria de Educación Pública, 1975.

Brading, D. A. *The First America: The Spanish Monarchy, Creole Patriots, and the Liberal State 1492–1867.* Cambridge: Cambridge University Press, 1991.

———. *Mexican Phoenix Our lady of Guadalupe: Image and Tradition across Five Centuries.* Cambridge: Cambridge University Press, 2001.

Broda, Johanna, Davíd Carrasco, and Eduardo Matos Moctezuma, eds. *The Great Temple of Tenochtitlan: Center and Periphery in the Aztec World.* Berkeley: University of California Press, 1987.

Burkhart, Louise. *The Slippery Earth: Nahua Christian Moral Dialogue in Sixteenth-Century Mexico.* Tucson: University of Arizona Press, 1989.

Burkholder, Mark. "Honor and Honors in Colonial Spanish America." In Lyman Johnson and Sonya Lipsett-Rivera, eds., *The Faces of Honor: Sex, Shame, and Violence in Colonial Latin America,* 18–44. Albuquerque: University of New Mexico Press, 1998.

Cahill, David. "Colour by Numbers: Racial and Ethnic Categories in the Viceroyalty of Peru, 1532–1824." *Journal of Latin American Studies* 26, no. 3 (1994): 325–346.

Cañeque, Alejandro. *The King's Living Image: The Culture and Politics of Viceregal Power in Colonial Mexico.* New York: Routledge, 2004.

Carr, David Charles Wright. *Los Franciscanos y su labor educativa en la Nueva España.* México: Instituto Nacional de Antropología e Historia, 1998.

Carrasco, Davíd. *City of Sacrifice: The Aztec Empire and the Role of Violence in Civilization.* Boston: Beacon Press, 1999.

Carrasco, Pedro. "Indian-Spanish Marriages in the First Century of the Colony." In Susan Schroeder, Stephanie Wood, and Robert Haskett, eds., *Indian Women of Early Mexico,* 87–104. Norman: University of Oklahoma Press, 1997.

———. *The Tenochca Empire of Ancient Mexico: The Triple Alliance of Tenochtitlan, Tetzcoco, and Tlacopan.* Norman: University of Oklahoma Press, 1999.

Caso, Alfonso. *Los barrios antiguos de Tenochtitlan y Tlatelolco.* México: Memorias de la Academia Mexicana de la Historia, 1956.

Cervantes, Fernando. *The Devil in the New World: The Impact of Diabolism in New Spain.* New Haven, Conn.: Yale University Press, 1994

Chávez Orozco, Luis. *Códice Osuna: Reproducción facsimilar de la obra del mismo título, editada en Madrid, 1878.* México: Ediciones del Instituto Indigenista Interamericano, 1947.

———. *Las instituciones democráticas de los indígenas Mexicanos en la época colonial.* México: Ediciones del Instituto Indigenista Interamericano, 1943.

Chipman, Donald E. *Moctezuma's Children: Aztec Royalty under Spanish Rule, 1520–1700.* Austin: University of Texas Press, 2005.

Chuchiak, John F. "In Servito Dei: Fray Diego de Landa, the Franciscan Order, and the Return of Extirpation of Idolatry in the Colonial Diocese of Yucatan, 1573–1579." *The Americas* 61, no. 4 (2005): 611–646.

———. "Secrets behind the Screen: *Solicitantes* in the Colonial Diocese of Yucatan and the Yucatec Maya, 1570–1785." In Susan Schroeder and Stafford Poole, eds., *Religion in New Spain,* 83–110. Albuquerque: University of New Mexico Press, 2007.

Clendinnen, Inga. *Ambivalent Conquests: Maya and Spaniard in Yucatan, 1517–1570.* New York: Cambridge University Press, 1987.

———. *Aztecs: An Interpretation.* New York: Cambridge University Press, 1991.

Cline, Howard F. "Hernando Cortés and the Aztec Indians in Spain." *Quarterly Journal of the Library of Congress* 26 (1969): 70–90.

Cline, S. L. *Colonial Culhuacan, 1580–1600: A Social History of an Aztec Town.* Albuquerque: University of New Mexico Press, 1986.

Collier, George A., Renato Rosaldo, and John D. Wirth, eds. *The Inca and Aztec States, 1400–1800: Anthropology and History.* New York: Academic Press, 1982.

Connell, William F. "'Because I was Drunk and the Devil Had Tricked me': Pulque, Pulquerías and Violence in the Mexico City Uprising of 1692." *Colonial Latin American Historical Review* 14, no. 4 (2005): 369–401.

———. "Emerging Ladino Spaces in the Parcialidades of Mexico City: Race, Identity and Indigenous Self-Government" Ph.D. diss., Tulane University, 2003.

———. "A 'Morisco Assassin' in the Cathedral of Mexico City: Due Process and Honor in the Seventeenth Century." *Journal of Colonialism and Colonial History* 11, no. 1 (2010).

Conway, Richard. "Nahuas and Spaniards in the Socioeconomic History of Xochimilco, New Spain, 1550–1725." Ph.D. diss., Tulane University, 2009.

Cook, Noble David. *Born to Die: Disease and New World Conquest, 1492–1650.* New York: Cambridge University Press, 1998.

Cook, Noble David, and Alexandra Parma Cook. *Good Faith and Truthful Ignorance: A Case of Transatlantic Bigamy.* Durham, N.C.: Duke University Press, 1991.

Cook, Noble David, and W. George Lovell, eds. *The Secret Judgments of God: Native Peoples and Old World Disease in Colonial Spanish America.* Norman: University of Oklahoma Press, 1992.

Cook, Sherburne F., and Woodrow Borah. *Essays in Population History: Mexico and the Caribbean.* 3 vols. Berkeley: University of California Press, 1970.

Cope, R. Douglas. *The Limits of Racial Domination: Plebeian Society in Colonial Mexico City, 1660–1720.* Madison: University of Wisconsin Press, 1994.

Cortés Alonso, Vicenta. "La imagen del otro: Indios, blancos y negros en el México del siglo XVI." *Revista de Indias* 51, no. 192 (1991): 259–292.

Creelman, James. "President Díaz: Hero of the Americas." *Pearson's Magazine* 19, no. 3 (1908): 231–277.

Curcio-Nagy, Linda. *The Great Festivals of Colonial Mexico City: Performing Power and Identity.* Albuquerque: University of New Mexico Press, 2004.

Cutter, Charles. *The Legal Culture of Northern New Spain, 1700–1810.* Albuquerque: University of New Mexico Press, 1995.

Dávalos, Marcela. *Basura e ilustración: La limpieza de la Ciudad de México a fines del siglo XVIII.* México: Instituto Nacional de Antropología e Historia, 1997.

Earle, Rebecca. "'If You Eat Their Food . . .': Diets and Bodies in Early Colonial Spanish America." *American Historical Review* 115, no. 3 (2010): 688–713.

Elson, Christina M., and R. Alan Covey, eds. *Intermediate Elites in Pre-Columbian States and Empires.* Tucson: University of Arizona Press, 2006.

Escalada, Javier, S. J. *Guadalupe arte y espelendor.* México: Enciclopedia Guadalupana, 2002.

Escalante, Pablo. "Un repertorio de actos rituales de los antiguos Nahuas." *Historia Mexicana* 35, no. 3 (1986): 373–388.

Estrada Díaz, Juan Antonio. *Identidad y reconocimiento del otro en una sociedad mestiza.* México: Universidad Iberoamericana, 1998

Feijoo, Rosa. "El tumulto de 1624." *Historia Mexicana* 14, no. 1 (1964): 42–70.

Fernández Bulete, Virgilio. "La desconocida relación de gobierno del Duque de Alburquerque, Virrey de Nueva España." *Anuario de Estudios Americanos* 55, no. 2 (1998): 677–702.

Figuero y Melgar (Duke of Tovar), Alfonso de. "Los Moctezuma en España y America." *Hidalguía* 20, no. 111 (1972): 203–230.

Florescano, Enrique. "Sahagún y el nacimiento de la crónica mestiza." *Relaciones: Estudios de Historia y Sociedad* 23, no. 91 (2002): 75–94.

García Granados, Rafael. *Diccionario biográfico de historia antigua de Méjico.* 3 tomos. México: Universidad Nacional Autónoma de México, 1995 [1952].

García Guízar, Abel. "El caos jurisdiccional Novohispano." *Vinculo Juridico* 6–7 (1991). http://www.uaz.edu.mx/vinculo/webrvj/rev6-7-5.htm.

Garraty, Christopher P. "Ceramic Indices of Aztec Eliteness." *Ancient Mesoamerica* 11, no. 2 (2000): 323–340.

Gibson, Charles. "The Aztec Aristocracy in Colonial Mexico." *Comparative Studies in Society and History* 2, no. 2 (1960): 169–196.

————. *The Aztecs under Spanish Rule: A History of the Indians of the Valley of Mexico, 1519–1810.* Stanford, Calif.: Stanford University Press, 1964.

————. "Rotation of Alcaldes in the Indian Cabildo of Mexico City." *Hispanic American Historical Review* 33, no. 2 (1953): 212–223.

————. *Tlaxcala in the Sixteenth Century.* Stanford, Calif.: Stanford University Press, 1967 [1952].

Gillespie, Susan. *The Aztec Kings: The Construction of Rulership in Mexica History.* Tucson: University of Arizona Press, 1989.

Gimeno Casalduero, Joaquín. *La Imagen del monarca en la Castilla del siglo XVI. Pedro el cruel, Enrique II y Juan I.* Madrid: Revista de Occidente, 1972.

Gonzalbo, Pilar. *Educación y colonización en la Nueva España, 1521–1821.* México: Universidad Pedagógica Nacional, 2001.

González González, Carlos Javier. "Ubicación e importancia del templo de Xipe Totec en la parcialidad Tenochca de Moyotlan." *Estudios de Cultura Nahuatl* 36 (2005): 47–65.

González-Hermosillo Adams, Francisco, ed. *Gobierno y economía en los pueblos indios del México Colonial.* México: Instituto Nacional de Antorpología e Historia, 2001.

Gruzinski, Serge. *La colonización de lo imaginario: Sociedades indígenas y occidentalización en el México español. Siglos XVI–XVIII.* México: Fondo de Cultura Económica, 1988.

————. "La red agujerada. Identidades tenicas y occidentalización en el México Colonial (Siglos XVI–XIX)." *Américan Indígena* 46, no. 3 (1986): 411–433.

Guedea, Virginia. "De la fidelidad a la infidencia: Los gobernadores de la Parcialidad de San Juan." In Jaime E. Rodríguez O., ed., *Patterns of Contention in Mexican History,* 95–123. Wilmington, Del.: Scholarly Resources Books, 1992.

Guthrie, Chester L. "Riots in Seventeenth Century Mexico City: A Study in Social History with Emphasis on the Lower Classes." Ph.D. diss., University of California at Berkeley, 1937.

Hamnett, Brian. "The Appropriation of Mexican Church Wealth by the Spanish Bourbon Government. The 'Consolidacion de Vales Reales,' 1805–1809." *Journal of Latin American Studies* 1, no. 2 (1969): 85–113.

————. *Politics and Trade in Southern Mexico: 1750–1821.* Cambridge: Cambridge University Press, 1971.

Hanke, Lewis. *The Spanish Struggles for Justice in the Conquest of America.* Boston: Little, Brown, 1965.

Haring, C. R. *The Spanish Empire in America.* New York: Oxford University Press, 1947.

Haskett, Robert. *Indigenous Rulers: An Ethnohistory of Town Government in Colonial Cuernavaca.* Albuquerque: University of New Mexico Press, 1991.

————. "'Our Suffering with the Taxco Tribute': Involuntary Mine Labor and Indigenous Society in Central New Spain." *Hispanic American Historical Review* 71, no. 3, (1992): 447–475.

Haslip-Viera, Gabriel. *Crime and Punishment in Late Colonial Mexico City, 1692–1810.* Albuquerque: University of New Mexico Press, 1999.

Hassig, Ross. *Aztec Warfare: Imperial Expansion and Political Control.* Norman: University of Oklahoma Press, 1988.

———. *Time, History, and Belief in Aztec and Colonial Mexico.* Austin: University of Texas Press, 2001.

Haverkamp-Begemann, Egbert. *Rembrandt: The Night Watch.* Princeton, N.J.: Princeton University Press, 1982.

Herrera Morena, Ethel. *500 planos de la ciudad de México, 1325–1933.* México: Secretaria de Asentamientos Humanos y Obras Publicas, 1982.

Herzog, Tamar. *La administración como un fenómeno social: La justicia penal de la ciudad de Quito (1650–1750).* Madrid: Centro de Estudios Constitucionales, 1995.

Hoberman, Louisa Schell. "Bureaucracy and Disaster: Mexico City and Flood of 1629." *Journal of Latin American Studies* 6, no. 2 (1974): 211–230.

———. "City Planning in Spanish Colonial Government: The Response of Mexico City to the Problem of Floods, 1607–1637." Ph.D. diss., Columbia University, 1972.

———. *Mexico's Merchant Elite, 1590–1660.* Durham, N.C.: Duke University Press, 1991.

Horn, Rebecca. *Postconquest Coyoacan: Nahua-Spanish Relations in Central Mexico, 1519–1650.* Stanford, Calif.: Stanford University Press, 1997.

Hulme, Peter. "Tales of Distinction: European Ethnography and the Caribbean." In Stewart B. Schwartz, *Implicit Understandings: Observing, Reporting and Reflecting on the Encounters between Europeans and Other Peoples in the Early Modern Era,* 158–170. New York: Cambridge University Press, 1991.

Israel, J. I. *Race, Class and Politics in Colonial Mexico, 1610–1670.* New York: Oxford University Press, 1975.

Johnson, Lyman. "Digging Up Cuauhtémoc." In Lyman Johnson, ed., *Body Politics: Death, Dismemberment, and Memory in Latin America,* 207–244. Albuquerque: University of New Mexico Press, 2004.

Johnson, Lyman, and Sonya Lipsett-Rivera, eds. *The Faces of Honor: Sex, Shame, and Violence in Colonial Latin America.* Albuquerque: University of New Mexico Press, 1998.

Kamen, Henry. *Spain, 1469–1714.* London: Longman, 1991.

Karttunen, Frances. *An Analytical Dictionary of Nahuatl.* Norman: University of Oklahoma Press, 1983.

———. "From Courtyard to the Seat of Government: The Career of Antonio Valeriano, Nahua Colleague of Bernardino de Sahagún." *Amerindia* 19/20 (1995): 113–120.

———. "Cuicapixqueh: Antonio Valeriano, Juan Bautista de Pomar, and Nahuatl Poetry." *Latin American Literatures Journal* 11, no. 1 (1995): 4–20.

Kellogg, Susan. *Law and the Transformation of Aztec Culture.* Norman: University of Oklahoma Press, 1995.

Lafaye, Jacques. *Quetzalcoatl and Guadalupe: The Formation of Mexican National Consciousness, 1531–1813*. Chicago: University of Chicago Press, 1976.

León-Portilla, Miguel. *Bernardino de Sahagún: Pionero de la antropología*. México: Universidad Nacional Autónoma de México, 1999.

León-Portilla, Miguel, and Carmen Agulera. *Mapa de Mexico Tenochtitlan y sus contornos hacia 1550*. México: Elanese Mexicana, 1986.

Leonard, Irving. *Baroque Times in Old Mexico: Seventeenth-Century Persons, Places, and Practices*. Ann Arbor: University of Michigan Press, 1959.

Lira González, Andrés. *El amparo colonial y el juicio de amparo México: Antecedentes novohispanos del juicio de amparo*. México: Fondo de Cultura Económica, 1971.

———. *Comunidades indígenas frente a la ciudad de México: Tenochtitlan y Tlatelolco, sus pueblos y barrios, 1812–1919*. México: El Colegio de México, 1983.

———. "Les divisions de Mexico aux XVIIIe et XIXe siècles: De la ville des deux Républiques à la ville républicaine." In Christian Topalov, ed., *Les divisions de la ville*, 101–122. Paris: Éditions de la Maison des science de l'homme, 2002.

Liss, Peggy. *Isabel the Queen: Life and Times*. Philadelphia: University of Pennsylvania Press, 2004.

Lockhart, James. *The Nahuas after the Conquest: A Social and Cultural History of the Indians of Central Mexico, Sixteenth through Eighteenth Centuries*. Stanford, Calif.: Stanford University Press, 1992.

———. *Nahuas and Spaniards: Postconquest Central Mexican History and Philology*. Stanford, Calif.: Stanford University Press, 1991.

———. *Nahuatl as Written: Lessons in Older Written Nahuatl, with Copious Examples and Texts*. Stanford, Calif.: Stanford University Press, 2001.

———. "Sightings: Initial Nahua Reactions to Spanish Culture." In Stewart B. Schwartz, *Implicit Understandings: Observing, Reporting and Reflecting on the Encounters between Europeans and Other Peoples in the Early Modern Era*, 218–248. New York: Cambridge University Press, 1991.

Lockhart, James, Lisa Sousa, and Stephanie Wood, eds. *Sources and Methods for the Study of Postconquest Mesoamerican Ethnohistory, Provisional Version*. Eugene: University of Oregon, Wired Humanities Project, 2007. http://whp .uoregon.edu/Lockhart/index.html.

Lomnitz, Claudio. *Deep Mexico, Silent Mexico: An Anthropology of Nationalism*. Minneapolis: University of Minnesota Press, 2001.

López Austin, Alfredo. *The Human Body and Ideology: Concepts of the Ancient Nahuas*. Trans. Thelma Ortiz de Montellano and Bernard Ortiz de Montellano. Salt Lake City: University of Utah Press, 1988.

Lozano Armendares, Teresa. *La criminalidad en la ciudad de México, 1800—1821*. México: Universidad Nacional Autónoma de México, 1987.

Lunenfeld, Marvin. *Keepers of the City: The Corregidores of Isabella I of Castile (1474–1504)*. Cambridge: Cambridge University Press, 1987.

Lynch, John. "Intendants and Cabildos in the Viceregalty of La Plata, 1782–1810." *Hispanic American Historical Review* 35, no. 3, (1955): 337–362.

————. *Spain under the Habsburgs*. 2nd ed. 2 vols. New York: Basil Blackwell, 1981.

MacLachlan, Colin M. *Criminal Justice in Eighteenth Century Mexico: A Study of the Real Tribunal de la Acordada*. Berkeley: University of California Press, 1974.

————. *Spain's Empire in the New World: The Role of Ideas in Institutional and Social Change*. Berkeley: University of California Press, 1988.

MacLachlan, Colin M., and Jaime E. Rodríguez O. *The Forging of the Cosmic Race: A Reinterpretation of Colonial Mexico*. Berkeley: University of California Press, 1980.

Martínez, María Elena. "The Black Blood of New Spain: 'Limpieza de Sangre,' Racial Violence, and Gendered Power in Early Colonial Mexico." *William and Mary Quarterly* 61, no. 3 (2004): 479–520.

————. *Genealogical Fictions: Limpieza de Sangre, Religion, and Gender in Colonial Mexico*. Stanford, Calif.: Stanford University Press, 2008.

Mateos, Salvador. "Codice Valeriano." *El México Antiguo* 7 (1949): 315–321.

Matos Moctezuma, Eduardo. *The Great Temple of the Aztecs: Treasures of Tenochtitlan*. Trans. Dorris Heyden. London: Thames and Hudson, 1988.

Matthew, Laura E., and Michel R. Oudijk, eds. *Indian Conquistadors: Indigenous Allies in the Conquest of Mesoamerica*. Norman: University of Oklahoma Press, 2007.

Maza, Francisco de la. *La Ciudad de México en el siglo XVII*. México: Fondo de Cultura Económica, 1968.

Metcalf, Aida. *Go-Betweens and the Colonization of Brazil*. Austin: University of Texas Press, 2005.

Miralles Osotos, Juan. *Hernán Cortés: Inventor de México*. Barcelona: Tusquets Editores, 2001.

Miranda, José. *El tributo indígena en la Nueva España durante el siglo xvi*. México: El Colegio de México, 1952.

Muriel, Josefina. *La sociedad novohispana y sus colegios de niñas*. México: Universidad Nacional Autónoma de México, 1995.

Nader, Helen. *Liberty in Absolutist Spain: The Habsburg Sale of Towns, 1516–1700*. Baltimore: Johns Hopkins University Press, 1990.

————. *The Mendoza Family in the Spanish Renaissance, 1350–1550*. New Brunswick, N.J.: Rutgers University Press, 1979.

Nesvig, Martin Austin. *Ideology and Inquisition: The World of the Censors in Early Mexico*. New Haven, Conn.: Yale University Press, 2009.

O'Hara, Matthew D. *A Flock Divided: Race, Religion, and Politics in Mexico, 1749–1857*. Durham, N.C.: Duke University Press, 2010.

————. "Stone, Mortar, and Memory: Church Construction and Communities in Late Colonial Mexico City." *Hispanic American Historical Review* 86, no. 4 (2006): 647–680.

Owensby, Brian. *Empire of Law and Indian Justice in Colonial Mexico*. Stanford, Calif.: Stanford University Press, 2008.

————. "How Juan and Leonor Won Their Freedom: Litigation and Liberty in Seventeenth-Century Mexico." *Hispanic American Historical Review* 85, no. 1 (2005): 39–79.

Parker, Geoffrey. *The Grand Strategy of Philip II.* New Haven, Conn.: Yale University Press, 1998.

Paz, Octavio. *The Labyrinth of Solitude.* Trans. Lysander Kemp, Yara Milos, and Rachel Phillips Belash. New York: Grove Weidenfeld, 1985.

Phelan, John Leddy. "Authority and Flexibility in the Spanish Imperial Bureaucracy." *Administrative Science Quarterly* 5, no. 1 (1960): 49–60.

————. *The People and the King: The Comunero Revolt of New Granada, 1791.* Madison: University of Wisconsin Press, 1978.

Poole, Stafford. *Our Lady of Guadalupe: The Origins and Sources of a Mexican National Symbol, 1531–1797.* Tucson: University of Arizona Press, 1995.

Poole, Stafford C. M., Lisa Sousa, and James Lockhart, eds. and trans. *The Story of Guadalupe: Luis Laso de la Vega's Huei tlamahuiçoltica of 1649.* Stanford, Calif.: Stanford University Press, 1998.

Prescott, William H. *History of the Conquest of Mexico with a Preliminary View of the Ancient Mexican Civilization, and the Life of the Conqueror Hernando Cortez.* 3 vols. Philadelphia: J. B. Lippincott, 1864.

Proctor III, Frank "Trey." "Afro-Mexican Slave Labor in the Obrajes de Paños of New Spain, Seventeenth and Eighteenth Centuries." *The Americas* 60, no. 1 (2003): 33–58.

————. "Gender and the Manumission of Slaves in New Spain." *Hispanic American Historical Review* 86, no. 2 (2006): 309–336.

Querol y Roso, Luis. "Negros y mulatos de la Nueva España: Historia de su alzamiento de 1612." *Anales de la Universidad de Valencia* 12, no. 90 (1931–1932): 121–162.

Ramírez, Susan. *Provincial Patriarchs: Land Tenure and the Economics of Power in Colonial Peru.* Albuquerque: University of New Mexico Press, 1986.

————. *The World Upside Down: Cross Cultural Contact and Conflict in Sixteenth-Century Peru.* Stanford, Calif.: Stanford University Press, 1996.

Ramos Medina, Manuel, ed. *Historia de la Ciudad de México en los fines del siglo (XV–XX).* México: Gropo Carso, 2001.

Restall, Matthew. *The Maya World: Yucatec Culture and Society, 1550–1850.* Stanford, Calif.: Stanford University Press, 1997.

————. *Seven Myths of the Spanish Conquest.* New York: Oxford University Press, 2003.

Ricard, Robert. *The Spiritual Conquest of Mexico: An Essay on the Apostolate and the Evangelizing Methods of the Mendicant Orders in New Spain, 1523–1572.* Trans. Leslie Byrd Simpson. Berkeley: University of California Press, 1966.

Rodríguez O., Jaime E. *The Independence of Spanish America.* New York: Cambridge University Press, 1998.

Rojas, José Luis de. *Mexico Tenochtitlan: Economía y sociedad en el siglo XVI*. México: Fondo de Cultura Económica y el Colegío de Michoacán, 1995.

Rojas Rabiela, Teresa. "La ogranización del trabajo para las obras públicas: El coatequitl y las cuadrillas de trabajadores." In Elsa Cecilia Frost, Michael C. Meyer, and Josefina Zoraída Vázquez, eds., *El trabajo y los trabajadores en la historia de México*, 53–60. México: El Colegio de México y University of Arizona Press, 1979.

Romero Galván, José Rubén. *Los privilegios perdidos: Hernando Alvarado Tezozomoc, su tiempo, su nobleza, y su crónica Mexicana*. México: Universidad Nacional Autónoma de México, 2003.

Romero de Terreros, Manuel. "El virrey duque de Alburquerque y las bellas artes."*Anales del Instituto de Investigaciones Estéticas* 19 (1951) 91–99.

Roseberry, William. "Hegemony and the Language of Contention." In Gilbert Joseph and Daniel Nugent, eds., *Everyday Forms of State Formation: Revolution and the Negotiation of Rule in Modern Mexico*, 355–366. Durham, N.C.: Duke University Press, 1994.

Rosenmüller, Chrisoph. *Patrons, Partisans and Palace Intrigues: The Court Society of Colonial Mexico, 1702–1710*. Calgary: University of Calgary Press, 2008.

Rounds, J. "Dynastic Succession and Centralization of Power in Tenochtitlan." In George A. Collier, Renato Rosaldo, and John D. Wirth, eds., *The Inca and Aztec States, 1400–1800: Anthropology and History*, 63–89. New York: Academic Press, 1982.

Ruiz, Teofilo F. *Crisis and Continuity: Land and Town in Late Medieval Castile*. Philadelphia: University of Pennsylvania Press, 1994.

Ruiz Medrano, Ethelia. *Reshaping New Spain: Government and Private Interests in the Colonial Bureaucracy, 1531–1550*. Trans. Julia Constantino and Pauline Marmasse. Boulder: University of Colorado Press, 2006.

Rumeu de Armas, Antonio. *Código del trabajo del indigena Americano*. Madrid: Ediciones Cultura Hispánica, 1953.

Sánchez de Tagle, Esteban. *Los dueños de la calle: Una historia de la vía pública en la época colonial*. México: Instituto Nacional de Antropología e Historia, 1997.

Sanders, William T., and Barbara J. Price. "The Native Aristocracy and the Evolution of the Latifundio in the Teotihuacan Valley, 1521–1917." *Ethnohistory* 50, no. 1 (2003): 69–88.

Scardaville, Michael. "Crime and the Urban Poor: Mexico City in the Late Colonial Period." Ph.D. diss., University of Florida, 1977.

———. "Justice by Paperwork: A Day in the Life of a Court Scribe in Bourbon Mexico City." *Journal of Social History* 36, no. 4, (2003): 979–1007.

Schmidt-Díaz de León, Ileana. "El colegio seminario de Indios de San Gregorio y el desarrollo de la indianidad en el valle de México, 1586–1856." Ph.D. diss., Tulane University, 2001.

Schroeder, Susan. "The Annals of Chimalpahin." In James Lockhart, Lisa Sousa, and Stephanie Wood, eds., *Sources and Methods for the Study of Postconquest*

Mesoamerican Ethnohistory, Provisional Version, 1–13. Eugene: University of Oregon, Wired Humanities Project, 2007.

———. *Chimalpahin and the Kingdoms of Chalco*. Tucson: University of Arizona Press, 1991.

———. "First American Valentine: Nahua Courtship and Other Aspects of Family Structuring in Mesoamerica." *Journal of Family History* 23, no. 4 (1998): 341–354.

———. "Jesuits, Nahuas, and the Good Death Society in Mexico City, 1710–1767." *Hispanic American Historical Review* 80, no. 1 (2001): 43–76.

———. "Writing Two Cultures: The Meaning of *"Amotli"* (Book) in Nahua New Spain." In David Cahill and Blanca Tovías, eds., *New World, First Nations: Native Peoples of Mesoamerica and the Andes under Colonial Rule*, 13–35. Brighton: Sussex University Press, 2006.

Schroeder, Susan, Stephanie Wood, and Robert Haskett, eds. *Indian Women of Early Mexico*. Norman: University of Oklahoma Press, 1997.

Schwaller, John F. "The Early Life of Luis de Velasco, the Younger: The Future Viceroy as a Boy and Young Man." *Estudios de Historia Novohispana* 29 (2003): 17–47.

Schwartz, Stewart B., ed. *Implicit Understandings: Observing, Reporting, and Reflecting on the Encounters between Europeans and Other Peoples in the Early Modern Era*. New York: Cambridge University Press, 1994.

Seed, Patricia. "Social Dimensions of Race: Mexico City, 1753." *Hispanic American Historical Review* 63, no. 4 (1992): 569–606.

Seijas, Tatiana. "Asian Slaves and Freed People in Seventeenth-Century Mexico." Ph.D. diss., Yale University, 2008.

———. "The Portuguese Slave Trade to Spanish Manilla." *Itinerario* 32, no. 1 (2008): 19–38.

Silva Prada, Natalia. *La política de una rebelión: Los indígenas frente al tumulto de 1692 en la Ciudad de México*. México: El Colegio de México, 2007.

———. "El uso de los baños temascales en la visión de dos médicos novo-hispanos: Estudio introductorio y transcripción documental de los informes de 1689." *Historia Mexicana* 52, no. 1 (2002): 5–56.

SilverMoon. "The Imperial College of Tlatelolco and the Emergence of a New Nahua Intellectual Elite in New Spain (1500–1760)." Ph.D. diss., Duke University, 2007.

Simpson, Lesley Byrd. *The Encomienda in New Spain: The Beginning of Spanish Mexico*. Reprint ed. Berkeley: University of California Press, 1966.

Spanoghe, Sander. "Los salarios dentro del systema del repartimiento forzado en el valle de México, 1549–1632." *Anuario de Esudios Americanos* 54, no. 1 (1997): 43–64.

Tanck de Estrada, Dorothy. *Atlas ilustrado de los pueblos de indios, Nueva España, 1800*. México: El Colegio de México, 2005.

Taylor, William. "Between Global Process and Local Knowledge: An Inquiry into Early Latin American Social History, 1500–1900." In Olivier Zunz, ed., *Reliving the Past: The Worlds of Social History*, 115–190. Chapel Hill: University of North Carolina Press, 1985.

———. *Drinking Homicide and Rebellion in Colonial Mexican Villages*. Stanford, Calif.: Stanford University Press, 1979.

———. *Magistrates of the Sacred: Priests and Parishioners in Eighteenth-Century Mexico*. Stanford, Calif.: Stanford University Press, 1997.

Terraciano, Kevin. *The Mixtecs of Colonial Oaxaca: Ñudzahui History, Sixteenth through Eighteenth Centuries*. Stanford, Calif.: Stanford University Press, 2001.

Townsend, Camilla. "Burying the White Gods: New Perspectives on the Conquest of Mexico." *American Historical Review* 108, no. 3 (2003): 659–687.

———. *Malintzin's Choices: An Indian Woman in the Conquest of Mexico*. Albuquerque: University of New Mexico Press, 2006.

———. "Sex, Servitude, and Politics among Pre-Conquest Nahuas." *The Americas* 62, no. 3 (2006): 347–389.

Tovar de Arechederra, Isabel, and Magdalena Mas, comps. *La muy noble y leal ciudad de México*. México: Universidad Iberoamericana, 1994.

Truitt, Jonathan. "Nahuas and Catholicism in Mexico Tenochtitlan: Religious Faith and Practice and La Capilla de San Josef de los Naturales, 1523–1700." Ph.D. diss., Tulane University, 2009.

Umberger, Emily. "Art and Imperial Strategy in Tenochtitlan." In Frances F. Berdan, Richard E. Blanton, Elizabeth Hill Boone, Mary G. Hodge, Michael E. Smith, and Emily Umberger, eds., *Aztec Imperial Strategies*, 85–106. Washington, D.C.: Dumbarton Oaks Research Library and Collection, 1996.

Valero de García Lascuraín, Ana Rita. *La ciudad de Mexico Tenochtitlan: Su primera traza, 1524–1534*. México: Editorial Jus, 1991.

Vargas Martínez, Ubaldo. *La ciudad de México, 1325–1960*. México: Departamento del Distrito Federal, 1960.

Vigil, Ralph H. *Alonso de Zorita: Royal Judge and Christian Humanist, 1512–1585*. Norman: University of Oklahoma Press, 1987.

Villa-Flores, Javier. "Voices from a Living Hell: Slavery, Death, and Salvation in a Mexican Obraje." In Martin Austin Nesvig, ed., *Local Religion in Colonial Mexico*, 235–258. Albuquerque: University of New Mexico Press, 2006.

Villasana Haggard, J. *Handbook for Translators of Spanish Historical Documents*. Austin: University of Texas Press, 1941.

Vinson III, Ben. "Race and Badge: Free-Colored Soldiers in the Colonial Mexican Militia." *The Americas* 56, no. 4 (2000): 471–496.

Womack, John. *Zapata and the Mexican Revolution*. New York: Vintage, 1968.

Wood, Stephanie. "Adopted Saints: Christian Images in Nahua Testaments of Late Colonial Toluca." *The Americas* 47, no. 3 (1991): 259–293.

———. *Transcending Conquest: Nahua Views of Spanish Colonial Mexico*. Norman: University of Oklahoma Press, 2003.

Yannakakis, Yanna. *The Art of Being In-Between: Native Intermediaries, Indian Identity, and Local Rule in Colonial Oaxaca*. Durham, N.C.: Duke University Press, 2008.

————. "Witnesses, Spatial Practices, and a Land Dispute in Colonial Oaxaca."
    The Americas 65, no. 2 (2008): 161–192.
Zantwijk, Rudolf A. M. *The Aztec Arrangement: The Social History of Pre-Spanish
    Mexico.* Norman: University of Oklahoma Press, 1985.
Zavala, Silvio. *La encomienda Indiana.* 2nd ed. México: Editorial Porrúa, 1973.
Zunz, Olivier, ed. *Reliving the Past: The Worlds of Social History.* Chapel Hill: Uni-
    versity of North Carolina Press, 1985.

INDEX

Acamapich, 230n37
Acequias, 18, 91, 92, 108, 116, 118, 216n61, 220n92, 249n18
Acuicacatl, Pedro, 47
Afro-Mexicans, 93, 130, 132, 145, 265n34, 267n41, 268 nn53–56
Aguero y Acedo, don Juan de, 169–170
Aguilar, don Felipe de, 106, 168–175, 190, 251n33, 255n67, 277n27, 279n55, 280n72, 280n75
Aguilar, don Felipe de Santiago y. *See* Santiago y Aguilar, don Felipe de
Aguilar, don Felix de, 190
Aguilar, don Juan de (the elder, el viejo), 102, 117, 130, 168, 190, 251n31, 255n67
Aguilar, don Juan de (the younger), 106, 168–175, 190, 255n67, 280n72, 280n75
Aguilar, don Juan Felix de, 191
Aguilar Lineage, 117, 135, 168–175, 255n67, 279n55, 280n72, 280n75
Alba, don Mateo de, 191
Alboroto. *See* Uprisings
Alburquerque, Duke of (the elder), 64, 117, 123, 124, 142–143, 219n77, 231n42, 260n113; Spanish, 40–41, 212n39; tribute collection, 271n76
Alburquerque, Duke of (the younger), 219n77, 231n42
Alcalde mayor, 132–133, 207n6, 253n54, 255n70, 258n87, 258n90; relationship

with native governors, 269n57; tribute collection, 268n54, 268n56. *See also* Corregidor
Alcalde: native, 3, 18, 22–28, 30, 37, 39, 41–43, 46–48, 50, 56, 59, 64, 78–80, 93, 111–113, 116, 133–134, 137–138, 140, 145, 151, 167, 169–171, 173–174, 194nn3–4, 204n73, 209n14, 211n28, 216n60, 217n74, 218n75, 219n80, 227n15, 231n44, 242n106, 246n147, 261n7, 274n112, 276n23, 279n59, 280n75; Pasados, 106, 173–176, 179, 183–185, 215n50, 231n44
Alcohol/Alcoholism. *See* Pulque
Alguacil, 41, 43, 78, 106, 194n4, 205n77, 217n71, 259n94
Alguacil amparador, 95, 128–149, 251n21, 266n36, 266n39, 267n41, 267n47, 268n50, 269n61, 270n65, 280n75. *See also* Contador; López, Juan
Altepetl, 3–4, 8–10, 12–13, 17–21, 41, 56, 65–66, 72–76, 97, 113, 118–119, 124–125, 184, 193n1, 195n6, 198n24, 216n58, 223n118, 228n25, 234n57, 251n35, 260n106; affiliated lands, 83; barrio, 203n65; calpolli, 223n117, 246n142; elections, 33–35, 44–45, 114, 218n76, 262n8, 264n1; rulership, 201nn45–46; Tlaxcala, 204n73; tlaxilacalli, 203n64, 207n3, 257n84
Alva Ixtlilxochitl, don Fernando de, 233n50

305

312